MASTERING THE CLASSROOM

VOL 1: CLASSROOM MANAGEMENT

GREGORY REICHMUTH

Mastering the Classroom, Volume 1: Classroom Management is a comprehensive guide designed to empower educators with the tools, strategies, and insights necessary to create positive, respectful, and effective learning environments. Written for K-12 educators, teacher preparation programs, and professional development, this volume offers a step-by-step approach to mastering classroom management. What Makes This Book Unique: Each chapter introduces a core topic of classroom management, providing: Value Proposition: Why the topic is critical to successful teaching. Theoretical Background: A wide view of research and perspectives to build foundational knowledge. Case Studies: Real-world examples that illustrate key points in action. Practical Strategies: Useful tips and tools educators can immediately apply. Lesson Plans: Three differentiated lesson plans per chapter using the Gradual Release of Responsibility model (I Do, We Do, You Do), aligned with national education standards. Reflections: Guided reflections to encourage personal and professional growth. Professional Development Tools: Assessments and rubrics designed for teacher preparation programs and school district professional development sessions. Extensive References: A curated list of resources to deepen understanding and support further research. Who This Book Is For: This book is a valuable resource for K-12 educators, teacher preparation programs, professional learning communities, and school districts seeking actionable, standards-based tools to support classroom management and improve teaching outcomes.

ADDITIONAL INFO

This book is intended for K-12 educators, teacher preparation programs, and professional development workshops. It provides actionable strategies for creating positive, respectful, and effective classroom environments, emphasizing inclusivity and student growth. Key subjects include classroom management, student engagement, and teaching for diversity and equity. Each chapter offers a structured approach that integrates theoretical foundations, case studies, practical strategies, differentiated lesson plans tied to national education standards, reflective practices, and professional development assessments. The book also includes rubrics tailored for teaching preparatory schools and school districts, making it an essential resource for professional learning. This is Volume 1 in the Mastering the Classroom series, focusing on Classroom Management. Future volumes will explore instructional strategies, assessment, and teacher leadership. The extensive reference list further supports educators seeking to expand their expertise.

Overview of the Gradual Release of Responsibility (GRR) Framework

The Gradual Release of Responsibility (GRR) instructional framework is a powerful and widely adopted teaching approach that emphasizes a systematic transfer of responsibility from the teacher to the student. It provides a structured method for supporting student learning, ensuring mastery of skills and concepts while fostering independence. This framework, often summarized as "I do, We do, You do," is foundational in effective pedagogy and has been instrumental in classroom management and instructional design worldwide.

Background and Origins

The GRR model is rooted in the educational research of **David Pearson** and **Margaret Gallagher**, who first conceptualized the approach in the early 1980s. Their work in reading comprehension emphasized that learners progress most effectively when responsibility for learning gradually shifts from the teacher to the student. Pearson and Gallagher's ideas were later expanded and popularized by educational researchers such as **Douglas Fisher** and **Nancy Frey**, who incorporated GRR into broader instructional practices.

Their contributions formalized the model into a structured framework applicable across disciplines and grade levels, emphasizing that effective instruction involves scaffolding—a temporary support system that is gradually removed as students gain proficiency.

The Four Phases of the Gradual Release Model

1. **Focused Instruction (I Do):**
   - » The teacher models the skill or concept, providing explicit instruction and demonstrating how to approach the task.
   - » Clear explanations, "think-alouds," and examples are central to this phase.
   - » Goal: Students observe and begin to internalize the process.

2. **Guided Instruction (We Do):**
   - » The teacher and students work together on the task, fostering collaborative learning.
   - » The teacher provides prompts, cues, and questions to guide student thinking and participation.
   - » Goal: Students practice with support, clarifying their understanding and addressing misconceptions.

3. **Collaborative Learning (We Do Together):**
   - » Students engage in peer collaboration, applying the skill or concept in small groups.
   - » The teacher monitors, facilitates, and provides feedback as needed, ensuring students are on track.
   - » Goal: Students learn from one another and gain confidence in their abilities.

4. **Independent Practice (You Do):**
   - » Students work independently to demonstrate their mastery of the skill or concept.
   - » This phase reinforces learning and provides opportunities for assessment.
   - » Goal: Students apply their knowledge independently, building autonomy and self-reliance.

How to Use the GRR Framework

1. **Plan Purposefully:**
   » Align lessons with clear learning objectives.
   » Design tasks that progressively challenge students and scaffold their learning.

2. **Model Explicitly:**
   » Provide thorough explanations and demonstrations during the "I Do" phase.
   » Use visuals, examples, and real-world connections to enhance understanding.

3. **Engage Actively:**
   » Foster active participation during the "We Do" phases, encouraging questions and dialogue.
   » Ensure tasks are meaningful and relevant to student interests and experiences.

4. **Monitor Progress:**
   » Use formative assessments to track understanding and provide immediate feedback.
   » Adjust instruction based on student needs during each phase.

5. **Encourage Reflection:**
   » Facilitate student reflection on their learning process.
   » Encourage metacognition, helping students recognize what strategies work best for them.

Benefits of the GRR Framework

1. **Scaffolded Learning:**
   » Provides students with the necessary support to succeed before gradually reducing assistance.

2. **Promotes Independence:**
   » Encourages students to take ownership of their learning, fostering lifelong learning skills.

3. **Improves Engagement:**
   » Actively involves students in their learning journey, enhancing motivation and participation.

4. **Addresses Diverse Needs:**
   » Offers flexibility to differentiate instruction and meet the needs of all learners.

5. **Encourages Collaboration:**
   » Builds social and communication skills through guided and collaborative practice.

6. **Supports Mastery:**
   » Reinforces skills through repetition and gradual challenge, leading to deeper understanding.

Why Include GRR in "Mastering the Classroom"?

The GRR framework aligns perfectly with the goals of effective classroom management and instruction. By embedding this pedagogy into each chapter, educators are provided with a clear, research-backed methodology for delivering lessons. This ensures that every student progresses from observation to mastery, developing confidence and competence in the process.

Including GRR in this book not only equips teachers with a proven instructional strategy but also underscores the importance of intentional, student-centered teaching. By following this approach, educators can create classrooms where learning thrives, and every student has the opportunity to succeed.

In Summary

The Gradual Release of Responsibility model is more than an instructional strategy—it is a mindset for teaching. Grounded in decades of research, it provides a structured yet flexible pathway for fostering student success. By integrating GRR into *Mastering the Classroom*, this book serves as a comprehensive guide for teachers to inspire and empower their students, one step at a time.

Mastering the Classroom, LLC®: The Discover Series®
Mastering the Classroom Volume 1: Classroom Management

Published by Gregory Reichmuth
2910 Magnolia Street
Denver, CO 80207

ISBN: Hardcover - 978-1-965957-37-0
ISBN: Paperback - 978-1-965957-36-3
ISBN: EPUB - 978-1-965957-39-4
ISBN: Digiital - 978-1-965957-38-7

Library of Congress Control Number: 2025927755

This book is part of *The Discover Series*®. It is intended as an educational resource to support effective classroom management practices. While the concepts and strategies presented are based on professional experience and educational research, the information provided is for instructional purposes only and may not apply to all classroom settings.

Printed in the United States of America

DEDICATION

To my beloved mother, Barbara Ann Reichmuth (1941 - 2024).

Your unwavering love, wisdom, and inspiration have shaped the person I am today. Your strength, kindness, and dedication to our family and your endless encouragement to pursue my dreams will forever be remembered and cherished.

This book series is dedicated to you, Mom. Your spirit lives on in every word, and your legacy of inspiration continues to guide me. Thank you for being my guiding light and my greatest supporter. I love you and miss you every day.

In loving memory,
Gregory Reichmuth

PURPOSE STATEMENT

The mission of *Mastering the Classroom, Volume 1: Classroom Management* is to provide educators with a comprehensive guide to creating positive, respectful, and effective learning environments. This volume aims to equip teachers with the tools and strategies needed to cultivate classrooms where every student is seen, valued, and empowered to achieve their fullest potential.

At the heart of classroom management is the belief in dignity and respect—not just as abstract principles but as practical, actionable foundations for every interaction. By fostering a sense of belonging and understanding, teachers can transform their classrooms into spaces of academic excellence, emotional growth, and ethical development.

This book reflects a commitment to:

- **Empowering Educators**: Providing practical tools and insights to enhance teachers' confidence and effectiveness.
- **Holistic Development**: Supporting not only students' academic success but also their social, emotional, and ethical growth.
- **Inclusivity and Equity**: Advocating for teaching practices that honor diversity and promote fairness.
- **Lifelong Learning**: Inspiring educators and students alike to embrace curiosity, growth, and a love for learning.
- **Community and Collaboration**: Encouraging a shared responsibility among teachers, students, and parents to create thriving educational experiences.

This volume is not just a manual but a mission: to celebrate the transformative power of teaching and to provide educators with the resources they need to succeed in their journey of shaping the future, one student at a time.

Sincerely,
Gregory Reichmuth
Author, *Mastering the Classroom, Volume 1: Classroom Management*

TABLE OF CONTENTS

CHAPTER 1

CREATE A RULES SYSTEM THAT ACTUALLY WORKS!

Reflections

Back in my early teaching days, I learned fast: creating a system with clear rules and expectations WITH the students' participation is a game-changer. This made the classroom a better place for everyone. On my first day of teaching, I remember how my students brought an unpredictable and stimulating energy with them that presented unique challenges and unexpected outcomes.

James was one student who seemed determined to push against the boundaries I set, often disrupting class with attention-seeking behavior. I sought out advice from a seasoned mentor of mine and he emphasized the importance of including the students in the development of that rules system. Keep reading to hear some of his great advice!

Essentially, I had to learn an invaluable lesson: it's not all about controlling students; rather it should give them the power to control their own behavior and environment. I watched as this strategy helped with James' positive transformation.

Always Teach Up!

The First Key to Success: Clear Expectations & Rules

Setting clear expectations has its foundations in multiple ***educational theories*** that emphasize structured learning environments for student success.

Carol Ann Tomlinson, one of the pioneers in *differentiated instruction*, asserts that setting clear expectations helps cater to diverse learning styles and needs by creating an understandable structure all students can follow (Tomlinson 2001). This approach aligns well with differentiated instruction principles which advocate personalized teaching methods tailored to meet varying student requirements (Tomlinson 2001).

Educational theorists such as Jean Piaget and Lev Vygotsky advocate *constructivist learning theory*, in which students actively construct knowledge through engagement with their environment and active engagement with it. Vygotsky's "zone of proximal development" concept illustrates this point (Vygotsky 1978): teachers provide support and structure through setting clear rules and expectations. Setting these clear boundaries enhances student's journeys effectively.

B.F. Skinner's *behaviorist theory* highlights the value of clear expectations in reinforcing desired behaviors (Skinner 1953). Consistent reinforcement of positive behavior leads to improved learning outcomes (Skinner 1953) while clear expectations provide the basis for systematic reinforcement that allows teachers to commend and encourage desired actions while discouraging those they deem undesirable.

Studies backup these theoretical foundations of classroom management. Marzano et al.'s (2003) research concluded that clearly stated classroom rules and expectations can have significant effects on student behavior and academic performance; similarly Wong and Wong's 2009 emphasize that effective classroom management involves setting out clearly defined expectations that are consistently enforced by management personnel.

Wong and Wong's research (2009: p.3) asserts that setting clear expectations leads directly to enhanced personal development:

- Students have more success fulfilling rules they understand
- Anxiety from the unknown decreases
- A Safe Environment results, which improves both respect (i.e. of personal spaces, boundaries, etc.) and emotional health

However, creating explicit, measurable rules and expectations is only the first key to a system that actually works! Keep reading to find out the second key to success!

Table: Key Educational Theories Supporting Clear Expectations & Rules

Educational Theory	Key Proponent(s)	Main Concept	Connection to Clear Expectations & Rules
Differentiated Instruction	Carol Ann Tomlinson	Tailoring instruction to meet the diverse needs of students.	Clear expectations create a structured learning environment that caters to diverse learning styles and needs.
Constructivist Learning Theory	Jean Piaget, Lev Vygotsky	Students construct knowledge through active engagement with their environment.	Clear rules provide a framework that supports students' engagement and development within the "zone of proximal development" (Vygotsky).
Behaviorism	B.F. Skinner	Behavior is shaped through reinforcement of positive actions.	Clear expectations allow teachers to reinforce desired behaviors, promoting better learning outcomes.
Classroom Management Research	Marzano et al., Wong & Wong	Effective classroom management enhances student behavior and academic performance.	Clear rules, consistently enforced, help create a safe and orderly environment, reducing student anxiety and improving personal development.

The Second Key to Success: A Collaborative Rules System

Implementing the first key *might* work, or *might* improve your classroom management to varying degrees. But our goal at MTC is to do more than possibly improve your efforts. By adding the second key, you create the synergy needed to boost your effectiveness in a substantial way. Best practices show that teachers who create a **Collaborative Rules System** can transform their classrooms.

Video: PowerPoint Presentation

What is a Collaborative Rules System?

A Collaborative Rules System is one where students participate in creating the classroom rules they must abide by. According to the Korn Center (an educational think tank??), advantages of a CRS:

- Results in Better Comprehension of the Rules overall
- Fosters a sense of behavioral ownership and responsibility among students
- Makes them more accountable for their actions
- Builds a stronger sense of community where students are better connected and invested in the overall positive atmosphere of the classroom

Collaborative Rules Systems

Better Comprehension of Rules	Students gain a deeper understanding of the rules because they help create them.
Behavioral Ownership & Responsibility	Students feel ownership over the rules, making them more accountable for their actions.
Increased Accountability	With ownership, students are more likely to follow the rules and self-regulate their behavior.
Stronger Classroom Community	Students feel more connected and invested in the classroom environment, fostering positive behavior.

Morrison and Vaandering's research (2012) also supports a CRS because it strongly aligns with sound ***restorative justice principles***. When students fully comprehend the rules and expectations, they tend to accept more responsibility while engaging in more positive behaviors leading them towards academic achievement as well as respect and a community-like atmosphere in the classroom.

Setting clear rules and expectations through a Collaborative Rules System makes classroom management simpler, reduces disruptions, and enhances the overall learning environment. While your instructive techniques become more effective, watch how this can lead to more meaningful interactions with students and parents. Watch as you help make students feel respected and motivated. Watch how a CRS can form the backbone of your classroom, giving students a space in which they can explore, take risks, and grow. Watch your students harness focus and creativity. And watch how a CRS can elicit a higher standard for their participation and schoolwork.

Let's Begin Creating your CRS

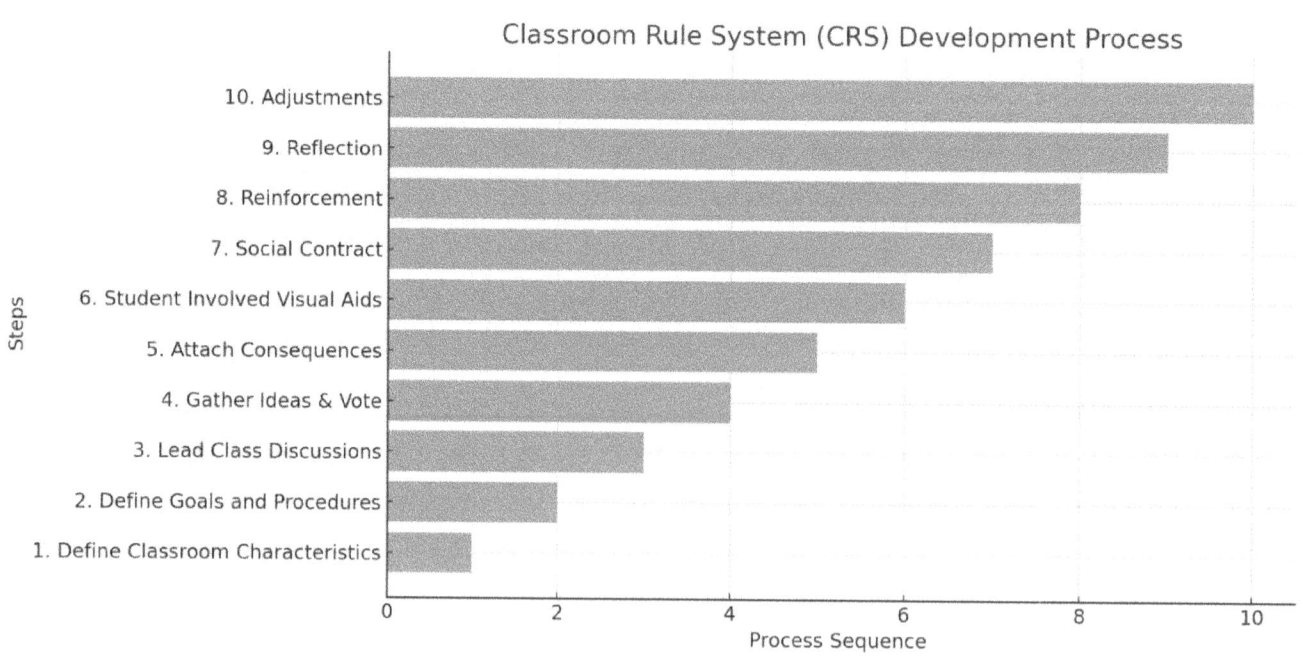

Lead an Efficient, Productive Class Discussion

Leading an effective group discussion requires thoughtful planning and skilled facilitation. Here are some best practices for ensuring that discussions are productive, inclusive, and engaging:

1. Set Clear Objectives

- **Why it's Important:** Before the discussion begins, clarify the purpose and goals. Students should understand what they are expected to learn or achieve through the discussion. This helps keep the conversation focused and aligned with the lesson objectives (Edutopia).
- **Best Practice:** Start by explaining the topic (why do we need rules at all?), objectives, and any key questions that will guide the discussion.

2. Create a Safe and Inclusive Environment

- **Why it's Important:** Students are more likely to participate if they feel safe and respected. An inclusive environment encourages diverse perspectives and ensures that all students feel valued.
- **Best Practice:** Establish ground rules for respectful communication, such as listening without interrupting and disagreeing politely. Encourage your shier or quieter students to share their thoughts by asking open-ended questions (Korn Center).

3. Use Open-Ended Questions

- **Why it's Important:** Open-ended questions stimulate critical thinking and deeper analysis. They allow for a range of responses, which can lead to richer discussions.
- **Best Practice:** Pose questions that require more than a yes or no answer, such as "What do you think are the implications of this event?" or "How would you approach this problem differently?" (Edutopia).

4. Encourage Active Participation

- **Why it's Important:** Active participation from all students leads to more dynamic and engaging discussions. It helps students develop their communication skills and reinforces their learning.
- **Best Practice:** Use strategies like *think-pair-share*, where students first discuss in pairs before sharing with the larger group, to ensure everyone has a chance to contribute. Rotate who speaks first to avoid the same students dominating the conversation (Teach Empowered).
- *Brainstorming* is an integral part of active participation. If you don't know the best practices for brainstorming, see the next section: Characteristics of Effective Brainstorming.

5. Facilitate Rather Than Dominate

- **Why it's Important:** The teacher's role is to guide the discussion, not to control it. This approach empowers students to take ownership of the conversation and explore ideas independently.
- **Best Practice:** Ask guiding questions, summarize key points, and connect students' contributions to the broader discussion, but avoid giving lengthy monologues. Encourage students to respond to each other, not just to the teacher (Korn Center).

6. Address Off-Topic Comments and Manage Time

- **Why it's Important:** Keeping the discussion on track is essential for achieving the lesson's objectives. However, students sometimes need help to stay focused, and managing time effectively ensures that all important points are covered.
- **Best Practice:** Gently steer the conversation back to the topic if it goes off track. Use time cues to keep the discussion moving, such as "We have five more minutes to discuss this point before we move on" (Edutopia).

7. Summarize and Reflect

- **Why it's Important:** Summarizing key points helps reinforce the discussion's main ideas and ensures that students leave with a clear understanding of what was covered.
- **Best Practice:** End the discussion by summarizing the main points, highlighting any conclusions reached, and asking students to reflect on what they learned. You might also ask students to write a brief reflection or exit ticket summarizing their thoughts (Korn Center).
- This is also the time you'll collect and vote for the "finalists" that will become official rules for your classroom.

8. Be Flexible and Adaptable

- **Why it's Important:** Discussions can be unpredictable, and being flexible allows the teacher to respond to the needs and interests of the students, making the discussion more relevant and engaging.
- **Best Practice:** Be prepared to adjust your plans if the discussion takes an unexpected but fruitful turn. Adapt your questions and activities to maintain engagement and relevance (Teach Empowered).

Case Study: Creating a Classroom Rule System (CRS)

Problem:

Teacher Brown needs to create a Classroom Rule System (CRS) for her 4th-grade class.

Classroom Characteristics:	
Characteristic	Count
Total Students	27
Boys	17
Girls	10
IEP (Moderate-Functioning Autism)	1
504 Plans (Dyslexia, Eye Impairment, ADHD & ODD, Executive Functioning)	4

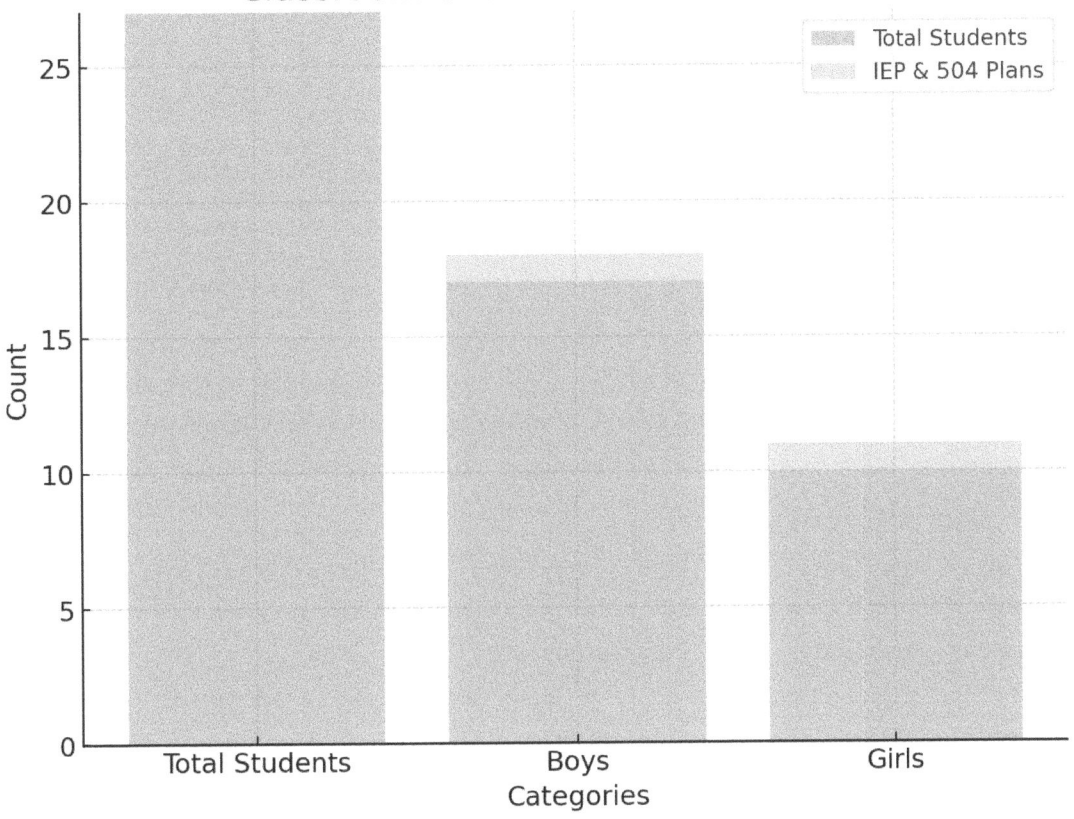

Temperament Breakdown:	
Temperament	**Count**
Highly Active Boys	7
Socially Influential Girl with 4 Followers	5
Shy Students (3 girls, 2 boys)	5
Students Struggling to Follow Rules (2 boys, 2 girls)	4
Gifted and Talented (GT) Girl	1

Key Classroom Challenges

1. **Lining Up for Lunch**
   - » **Challenge**: Lunch begins at 12:30, which is relatively late in the day, leading to students feeling hungry and restless. This often results in increased impatience and difficulty maintaining order when transitioning to lunch.
   - » **Impact**: Hunger and restlessness make it difficult for students to follow instructions, stay in line, and exhibit self-control, causing delays and disruptions that affect the overall flow of the day.

» **Possible Causes**: Students' energy levels are low by midday due to the extended gap between breakfast and lunch. This gap can lead to irritability and an inability to focus or follow routines.

2. **Math Class During the Last Period**
   » **Challenge**: The math class, held at the end of the school day, comes when students are fatigued from a full day of activities. Fatigue makes it difficult for students to concentrate on complex tasks, especially those requiring higher-order thinking skills.
   » **Impact**: Students may struggle to stay engaged, leading to a drop in participation, incomplete assignments, or disruptive behavior as they try to manage their exhaustion. This can slow down the lesson pace and leave some students falling behind.
   » **Possible Causes**: Fatigue from earlier activities, particularly after physical education or mentally demanding subjects, can leave students mentally drained. Students with learning differences may find the late timing especially challenging.

3. **ADHD Students and Impulse Control**
   » **Challenge**: Several students with ADHD struggle with adhering to classroom expectations, such as raising their hands before speaking. This impulsive behavior can lead to frequent interruptions during lessons, derailing discussions and reducing the flow of instruction.
   » **Impact**: These disruptions affect not only the teacher's focus but also other students who lose track of the discussion. Repeated interruptions can lead to frustration among peers and make it difficult to maintain classroom order.
   » **Possible Causes**: Difficulty with impulse control, a common symptom of ADHD, makes it hard for students to wait their turn or remain quiet during discussions. Without proper interventions, these behaviors can intensify in stressful or overstimulating environments.

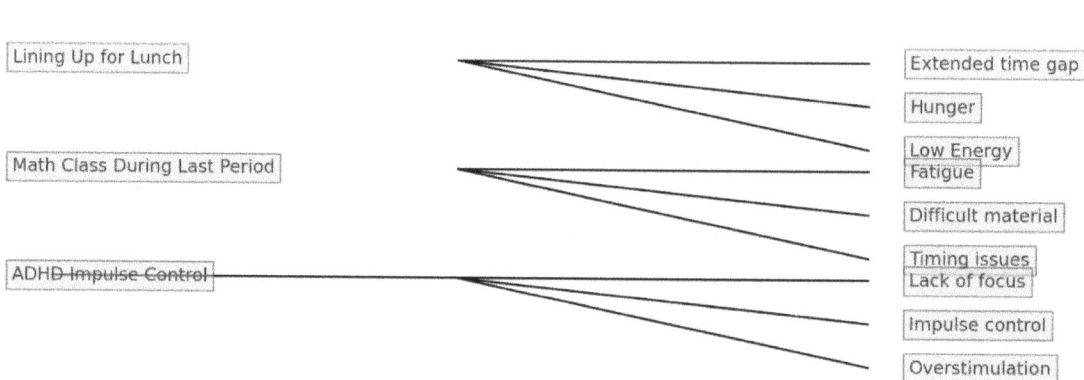

Classroom Challenges: Fishbone Diagram

Underlying Issues and Solutions

• **Lining Up for Lunch**: The extended gap between breakfast and lunch exacerbates irritability and impatience. A potential solution involves implementing a mid-morning snack break to help students refuel before lunch, maintaining their energy and patience and smoothing the transition.

- **Fatigue During Math**: Consider adjusting the class schedule to place more interactive or physical subjects in the afternoon, saving cognitively demanding tasks for earlier in the day when students are more alert. Alternatively, incorporating movement or brain breaks during math can help re-energize students and improve focus.
- **Supporting ADHD Students**: To manage impulsive behaviors, teachers can use visual cues or non-verbal signals to remind students to raise their hands. Positive reinforcement, such as rewarding the class when students with ADHD exhibit improved impulse control, can foster a supportive and structured environment.

Underlying Issues and Solutions (Table)

Lining Up for Lunch	Implement a mid-morning snack break	Reduced irritability, smoother transitions
Fatigue During Math	Adjust schedule to include physical activities or brain breaks	Improved focus and participation in math class
Supporting ADHD Students	Use visual/non-verbal cues and positive reinforcement to manage impulse control	Enhanced classroom structure, increased impulse control, and positive peer interactions

Behavioral and Emotional Considerations

- **Emotional Regulation**: Hunger, fatigue, and impulsivity are connected to emotional regulation. Helping students recognize and manage their emotions using tools like emotion charts, calming activities, or mindfulness exercises can reduce the severity of these challenges.
- **Collaborative Problem-Solving**: Engage students in discussions about these challenges and invite them to brainstorm solutions. Allowing students to suggest ways to improve transitions, stay engaged during lessons, and support peers with ADHD can foster ownership and collaboration in the classroom.

Behavioral and Emotional Considerations: Emotional Regulation and Collaborative Problem-Solving

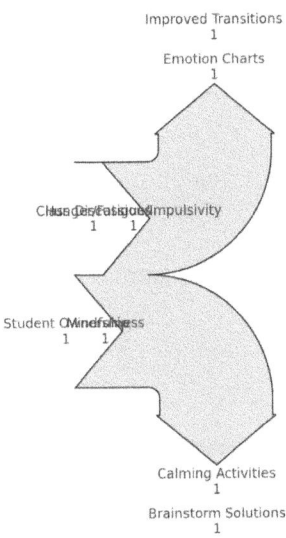

Here's a visual representation of the **Behavioral and Emotional Considerations** section. It combines two interlinked cycles:

1. **Emotional Regulation Cycle**: Displays how managing hunger, fatigue, and impulsivity through tools like emotion charts, mindfulness, and calming activities contributes to better emotional control.
2. **Collaborative Problem-Solving Cycle**: Shows the process of engaging students in discussions, brainstorming solutions, and improving transitions through student ownership, which fosters a collaborative and supportive environment.

The two cycles connect, highlighting how emotional regulation feeds into collaborative problem-solving and vice versa.

Teacher Brown's Approach:

Group Distribution Strategy:

The class is divided into four small groups of 6–7 students, with a focus on balancing academic support, behavior, and social dynamics. Key considerations include:

- Encouraging Leadership Development: Rotate leadership roles within each group, so that even dominant or shy students have the opportunity to lead, promoting confidence in quieter students while ensuring dominant personalities don't overshadow others.
- Balancing Temperaments: Place active students in groups where they can channel their energy into activities while balancing them with calmer peers who can help maintain focus.
- Providing Peer Support: Ensure students with specific learning needs (e.g., dyslexia, ADHD) are grouped with peers who are supportive but won't enable dependency, encouraging self-sufficiency while maintaining collaborative dynamics.
- Social and Emotional Dynamics: Focus on peer compatibility, ensuring students with challenging behaviors (e.g., struggles with rules) are placed in groups where they have positive role models, while not being isolated or stigmatized.

Teacher Requirements:

The classroom rules should be measurable, clear, and enforceable, promoting a positive and productive learning environment. Key principles behind the rules include respect, safety, and structure. Teacher Brown sets six core rules, each tied to a specific behavior and measurable outcome.

1. **Raising Hands Before Speaking**
   - » Why: This rule promotes orderly participation and ensures everyone's voice can be heard. It fosters respect for both peers and teachers.
   - » Measurement: Track adherence by rewarding students who consistently follow the rule and providing gentle reminders for those who struggle.

» Enforcement: Students who fail to raise their hands will lose the privilege to speak for the remainder of the discussion, and can re-earn it through positive behavior in future discussions.

2. **Lining Up Properly for Lunch and Transitions**

   » Why: Proper transitions reduce chaos and prepare students for structured activities, keeping the classroom calm and efficient.

   » Measurement: Use a checklist or point system, rewarding students or groups who demonstrate proper behavior in line consistently.

   » Enforcement: Students not adhering to this rule will be asked to go to the back of the line or may lose privileges (e.g., being first to select seats in the cafeteria).

3. **Respecting Personal Space**

   » Why: Encourages safe and respectful interactions, especially important in a diverse classroom with students of different needs and temperaments.

   » Measurement: Role-play scenarios to practice maintaining personal space, followed by ongoing observation of interactions.

   » Enforcement: Infractions result in temporary separation from group activities or peer interaction until respect is restored.

4. **Listening Without Interrupting**

   » Why: Promotes active listening and respect during both peer discussions and teacher instruction, improving focus and participation.

   » Measurement: Periodic self-assessments and peer feedback can help students reflect on their listening skills.

   » Enforcement: Students who interrupt will be asked to reflect on their behavior through a written response or have a brief discussion with the teacher.

5. **Following Directions Promptly**

   » Why: This rule ensures that students are able to transition smoothly from one task to another, preventing disruptions and maintaining flow.

   » Measurement: Students are given points for prompt responses during transitions or activity changes, contributing to group rewards.

   » Enforcement: Consequences include losing free-time privileges or having to stay back for additional practice on following instructions.

6. **Kind Words and Actions**

   » Why: A foundational rule for fostering a positive classroom culture where students support each other and feel safe to take academic risks.

   » Measurement: A class-wide kindness board can track positive behaviors, encouraging students to accumulate points for collective rewards.

   » Enforcement: Inappropriate words or actions result in immediate reflection (verbal or written apology) and may lead to parent contact if patterns persist.

Rule	Why (Icon)	Measurement (Icon)	Enforcement (Icon)
Raising Hands Before Speaking	🖉 Respectful participation	📊 Track adherence & reward	✖ Loss of privilege, re-earn through positive behavior
Lining Up Properly	👤🏅 Smooth transitions, reduce chaos	✅ Checklist/Point system	🔄 Go to back of line, lose privileges
Respecting Personal Space	🤝 Safe, respectful interactions	🔍 Role-playing & observation	🚫 Temporary separation from activities
Listening Without Interrupting	👂 Active listening, focus	📝 Self-assessments & feedback	✍ Reflect on behavior through writing
Following Directions Promptly	🕐 Smooth task transitions, prevent disruptions	☑ Points for prompt responses	⏳ Lose free time, stay back for practice
Kind Words and Actions	💬 Fosters positive classroom culture	🔲 Kindness board, points for positive behaviors	🤙 Immediate reflection, parent contact if necessary

Problem-Solving Approach: Addressing Student Needs Holistically

1. Addressing Physical and Cognitive Needs

- **Snack Break and Hydration**: In addition to allowing students to bring a snack, ensure access to water throughout the day to help maintain energy and focus. Consider implementing a structured "brain break" around mid-morning where students can eat their snack while engaging in a brief mindfulness or relaxation activity (e.g., deep breathing, stretching).

- **Flexible Snack Options**: For students who may not have access to a healthy snack from home, collaborate with the school administration to provide low-cost or free snacks to ensure all students are included and no one feels left out.

- **Link Snack Time with Learning**: You could integrate snack time with a quick, engaging activity, such as a "daily trivia" question or a short read-aloud session, keeping their minds engaged in a low-pressure way.

2. Managing Transitions and Reducing Disruptions

- **Staggered Breaks**: To prevent chaotic transitions before lunch, consider staggering the time when different groups or sections of the class take their breaks. This could reduce congestion and restlessness, ensuring a smoother transition from learning to lunch.

- **Active Learning Before Lunch**: Move a more engaging, hands-on lesson before lunch to keep students focused and engaged in learning, even when they're starting to feel hungry. For example, interactive math games, movement-based activities, or collaborative projects could help them stay engaged.

3. Social-Emotional Considerations

- **Building Emotional Awareness**: Teach students to recognize and communicate how physical feelings (like hunger or fatigue) affect their emotions and behavior. You could implement a morning "check-in" where students rate how they're feeling on a scale of 1–5, helping you anticipate how hunger or tiredness may impact the day.
- **Empathy and Group Norms**: During snack or break time, use this opportunity to reinforce social-emotional skills, such as sharing, taking turns, or helping a peer. Students can practice empathy by sharing food or collaborating on tasks that promote community.

4. Behavior-Management Strategies

- **Incorporating Movement**: Research shows that physical activity can help students manage impulses, especially those with ADHD or high energy levels. Incorporate structured movement breaks along with snacks, like a quick "stretch and shake" session or a short walk around the classroom.
- **Positive Reinforcement for Following Snack-Time Rules**: Create specific, measurable expectations around snack time (e.g., cleaning up, sharing space respectfully, time limits) and reward students or groups who meet these expectations consistently. This helps build self-regulation and accountability.

5. Customizing Solutions for Different Needs

- **Personalized Support for Students with Special Needs**: For students with dietary restrictions or disabilities (e.g., students with ADHD or autism), work with the parents and the special education team to create personalized snack-time routines. This might include quieter snack spaces or sensory breaks during snack time.
- **Snack Bins and Accessibility**: Create a classroom snack bin for students who occasionally forget snacks. This encourages sharing and removes any potential stigma. Assign snack bin monitors to make it a collaborative classroom responsibility.

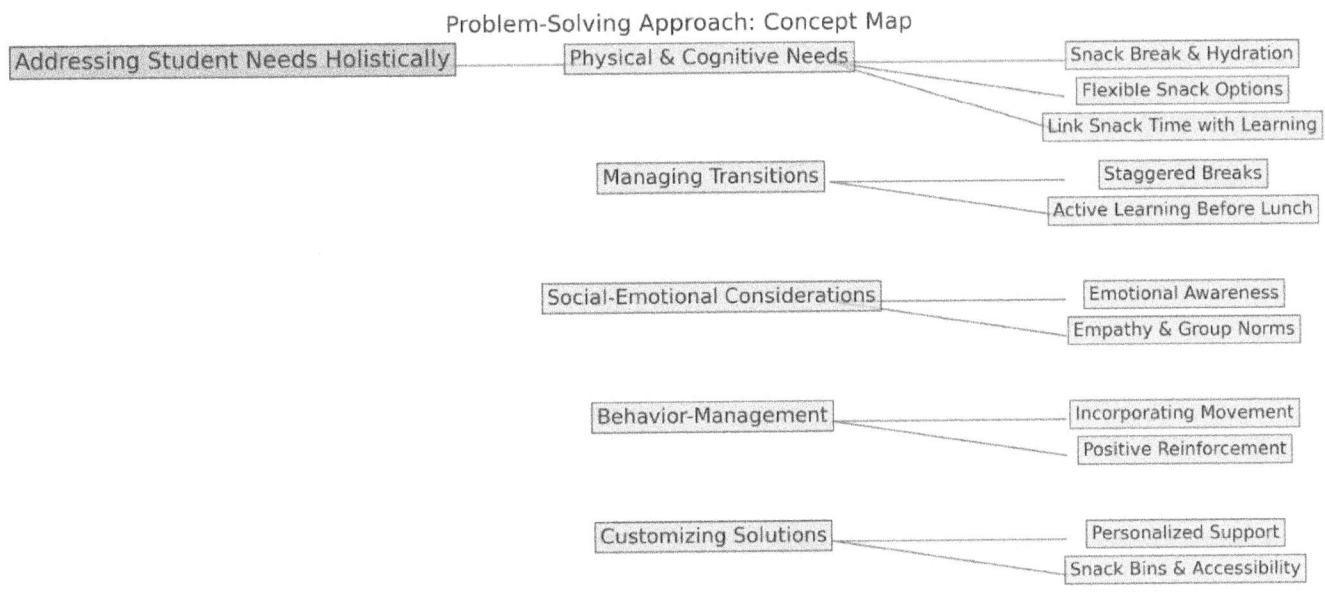

Problem-Solving Approach: Concept Map

Expanded Solutions Examples

- **Schedule Adjustments**: Advocate for an earlier lunch period or push for a "second breakfast" snack time at 10 a.m. for the entire class, depending on what school schedules allow.
- **Partnership with Parents**: Send a letter home explaining the benefits of healthy snacks, with suggestions for affordable, nutritious options. Consider providing a monthly snack calendar, offering guidance on what snacks parents can send based on learning units (e.g., "healthy fruits during our nutrition unit").
- **Mindful Transitions**: Before snack or lunch, use mindfulness techniques (such as a quiet breathing exercise or listening to calming music) to help students transition smoothly and avoid hyperactivity when they're hungry or restless.

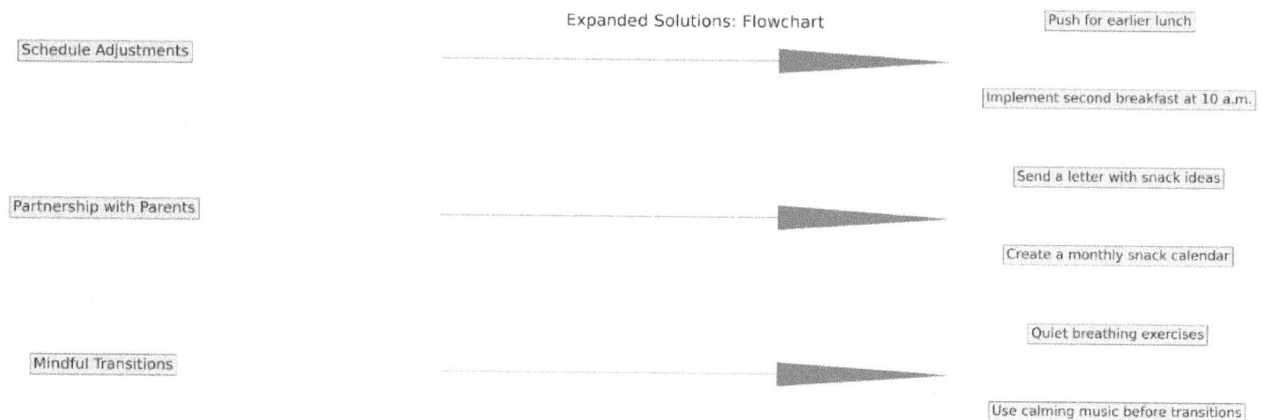

Summary of Broader Problem-Solving Approach:

By considering not only hunger but also the holistic needs of the students (cognitive, emotional, behavioral), the class will be better equipped to transition smoothly through the day. A comprehensive strategy can include flexible snack options, staggered breaks, social-emotional learning, positive reinforcement, and behavior-management techniques.

Timeline for Classroom Rule System (CRS) Implementation		
Activity	**Date**	**Details**
Initial Discussion	One week before	Discuss the need for rules, group discussions, and why student input is important.
Group Discussions	Day 1 (Monday)	40 min brainstorm, 10 min narrowing down ideas, type up group ideas by evening.
Final Voting and Selection	Day 2 (Tuesday)	Vote for the top 10 ideas, finalize rules, and plan where to post them in the classroom.
Visual Aid Creation	Post-vote	Design posters of the selected rules with students and share with parents, para, and special ed staff.
Reflections & Improvement	Continually	Reflections should be continuous throughout the weeks and quarters.

Classroom Discussion: Facilitating Student Engagement and Ownership of Classroom Rules

1. **Reiterate the Purpose of Rules and Group Discussions**

   Begin by explaining the **importance of having clear classroom rules** and how they help create a safe, respectful, and productive learning environment. Emphasize that the rules are not just about maintaining order, but also about fostering a positive community where everyone can thrive. Discuss how **group discussions** are a way to give everyone a voice and that their input is crucial to building a set of rules that everyone feels invested in.

   » **Key Talking Points**:
   - "Why do we need rules?" (e.g., to ensure fairness, safety, and respect)
   - "How do rules help us?" (e.g., they help us work better together, stay focused, and respect each other's space and ideas)
   - "What happens when everyone follows the rules?" (e.g., smoother transitions, fewer disruptions, more time for fun and learning)

2. **Break Students into Groups for Rule Brainstorming**

   After the initial discussion, divide the class into small, diverse groups, ensuring that each group has a mix of temperaments and abilities. Encourage groups to work together to **brainstorm rule ideas** that they believe will help the classroom function smoothly. Provide clear guidelines for brainstorming, such as:
   - **No idea is a bad idea**: This encourages participation from all students, including those who are quieter or more reserved.
   - **Respect everyone's ideas**: Teach active listening by having one student speak at a time while others take notes or respond constructively.
   - **Categories for Rules**: Suggest broad categories like behavior during lessons, transitions between activities, and respect for others' space or property.
   - **Use Prompts**: Offer prompts like, "What can we do to make sure everyone gets a chance to speak?" or "What should we do when we have to switch from one activity to another?"

3. Equip groups with **brainstorming worksheets** that have structured sections for listing ideas. Assign roles like a **scribe** (to take notes), a **timekeeper** (to ensure the group stays on task), and a **facilitator** (to guide the discussion). Encourage **collaborative problem-solving**, especially for addressing common challenges, such as how to manage impulsive behaviors or create smoother transitions.

4. **Encourage Students to Vote for the Most Effective Rules**

   Once each group has completed their brainstorming, reconvene the class and have each group **share their ideas**. Facilitate a class-wide discussion, encouraging students to **explain the rationale** behind their suggested rules. Ask guiding questions like, "Why do you think this rule is important?" or "How would this rule help our class work better together?"

   After the presentations, distribute the compiled list of rules (or "finalists") and allow students to vote for the rules they believe will be most effective. This can be done by giving each student a set number of votes or having them rank the top 3–5 rules. To ensure that all voices are heard, consider including a **silent vote** where students can write down their choices anonymously.

5. **Refining and Finalizing the Classroom Rules**

Once the votes are tallied, work with the students to **refine the final set of rules**, ensuring that the language is clear, concise, and enforceable. This step can involve small adjustments to ensure that the rules are practical and cover a range of situations, such as behavior during lessons, transitions, and respectful interaction with others.

- **Post-Rule Reflection**: After selecting the final rules, engage the students in a brief reflection: "How do you feel about the rules we created together?" This step reinforces their ownership and ensures they understand the rules are not arbitrary but a collective decision aimed at improving the classroom environment.
- **Positive Reinforcement**: Emphasize that following the rules will result in positive outcomes, like smoother transitions, more fun activities, and a more enjoyable learning environment. Allow the students to brainstorm **rewards** for consistently following the rules (e.g., extra free time, class privileges, or a small class celebration).

6. **Group Discussion Wrap-Up**

Close the activity by thanking students for their participation and encouraging them to hold each other accountable. Reinforce that by working together, they've created a classroom contract, and everyone has a responsibility to uphold it. Reiterate that these rules are **living guidelines**—if something doesn't work, the class can revisit and adjust the rules as needed. This flexible, student-centered approach fosters a deeper sense of community and ownership over the classroom environment.

Teacher Brown's Final Results:	
Rule	**Consequence/Reward**
Rule #1: Raise hands	Consequence: Loss of privilege to speak
Rule #2: Proper line-up	Reward: Extra 5 minutes of free time
Rule #3: Respect for peers	Consequence: Parent call after 3 offenses
Rule #4	[Customize based on final rules]
Rule #5	[Customize based on final rules]
Rule #6	[Customize based on final rules]

Reflecting on the Effectiveness of the Classroom Rule System (CRS)

The effectiveness of the CRS should be monitored and adjusted regularly to ensure that the rules are both helping students succeed and addressing any ongoing challenges in the classroom. Reflection should be both structured and ongoing, involving feedback from the teacher, students, and possibly even parents or support staff.

Monitoring and Reflection After 3 Weeks:

- **Observation**: After three weeks of implementing the CRS, Teacher Brown noticed that the consequence for not raising hands (loss of the privilege to speak) was too harsh for some students, especially for those with ADHD. These students struggled with impulse control, and the consequence led to frustration rather than improvement.
- **Adjustment**: To make the rule more effective and supportive, Teacher Brown added a **reward system** specifically designed to support students with ADHD. For example, students who raised their hands constantly were rewarded with **extra free time on a bouncy ball** or other physical activity that helped them manage their energy. This positive reinforcement strategy was tailored to their needs and aimed to build good habits.
- **Reflection**: This change was made after noticing that a punitive approach was not fostering the desired behavior change. By switching to a **positive reinforcement model**, Teacher Brown saw an improvement in student engagement and self-regulation.

Monitoring and Reflection After 8 Weeks:

- **Observation**: At the eight-week mark, it became clear that the snack break originally scheduled for 10:30 a.m. was not early enough to mitigate the students' restlessness and hunger before lunch. Students were still exhibiting irritability and a lack of focus, especially as lunch approached.
- **Adjustment**: In response, snack time was moved to **10:00 a.m.** to provide students with a more substantial energy boost earlier in the day. This adjustment helped reduce irritability and allowed for a smoother transition into the lunch break, as students were less restless and able to follow instructions more effectively.
- **Reflection**: The adjustment of snack time illustrates the importance of flexibility in classroom management. Small changes in the daily schedule can have a significant impact on student behavior, particularly in managing hunger and focus. Teacher Brown planned to continue monitoring how this change impacted overall classroom dynamics.

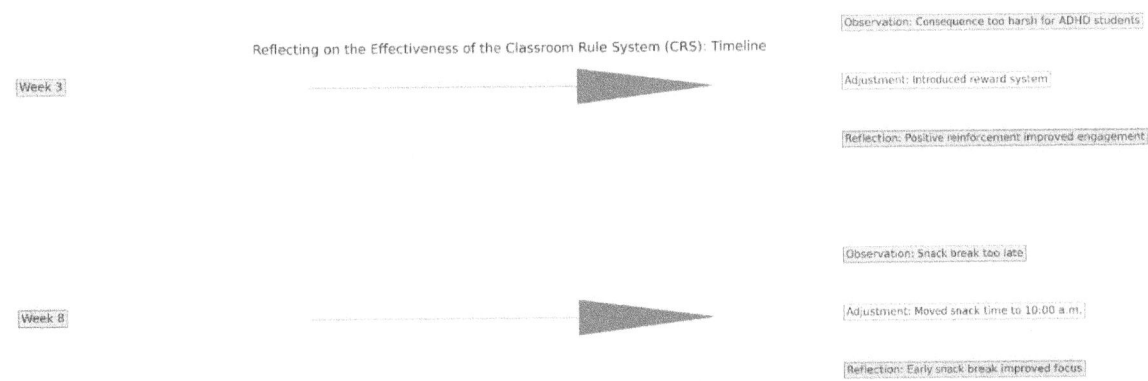

Reflecting on the Effectiveness of the Classroom Rule System (CRS): Timeline

Week 3 — Observation: Consequence too harsh for ADHD students / Adjustment: Introduced reward system / Reflection: Positive reinforcement improved engagement

Week 8 — Observation: Snack break too late / Adjustment: Moved snack time to 10:00 a.m. / Reflection: Early snack break improved focus

How to Reflect on the Effectiveness of the CRS

1. **Data Collection**:
   - » **Daily Observation**: Keep a log of behaviors related to each classroom rule. Note any patterns, such as consistent infractions of a particular rule, specific times of day when issues arise, or whether certain students are struggling more than others.

» **Student Feedback**: Ask students to reflect on the rules after the first few weeks. This can be done through short surveys, anonymous suggestion boxes, or group discussions. Encourage them to share which rules they think are working well and where they feel improvements could be made.

» **Classroom Climate**: Pay attention to changes in the overall classroom climate. Has the CRS led to fewer disruptions? Are students more engaged during lessons? Use informal check-ins or structured reflections to gauge whether students feel the rules are fair and supportive.

2. **Collaboration with Support Staff:**

» **Special Education Teachers or Paras**: Collaborate with special education staff or classroom aides to assess how the rules are affecting students with IEPs or 504 plans. This feedback can provide insight into whether accommodations or adjustments are necessary.

» **Parent Feedback**: Communicate with parents to see if changes in classroom behavior are reflected at home. Parents can offer insights into how students are adjusting to the rules, especially students who may have specific needs like ADHD or anxiety.

3. **Adjustment Criteria**: When evaluating the need for adjustments to the CRS, consider the following:

» **Effectiveness**: Are the rules addressing the key problem areas (e.g., impulsive behavior, transitions, classroom focus)? If not, what changes could improve their impact?

» **Student Buy-In**: Do students understand and respect the rules? Rules that students feel invested in are more likely to be followed.

» **Flexibility**: Is there flexibility built into the system to accommodate diverse needs? For example, some students may respond better to visual cues, while others need more structured routines.

4. **Future Adjustments:**

» **Incorporating Student Ownership**: As the CRS evolves, consider giving students more ownership of rule adjustments. For example, every six weeks, allow students to suggest modifications or new rules based on what's working and what isn't.

» **Revisiting Consequences and Rewards**: Ensure that consequences are not too harsh or punitive, especially for younger students or those with learning differences. Similarly, revisit rewards to ensure they are meaningful and motivating for the students.

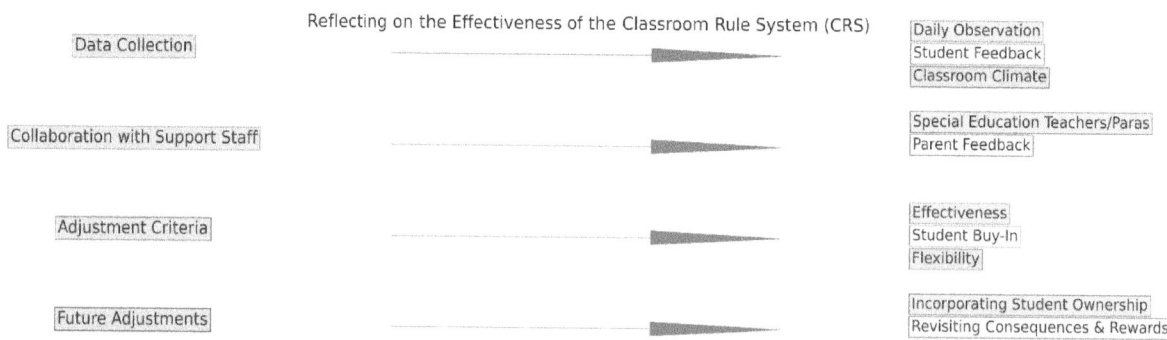

Summary of Key Adjustments and Reflections:

- **After 3 Weeks**: Adjusted consequence for raising hands, shifting to positive reinforcement with physical rewards (e.g., extra free time for ADHD students on a bouncy ball).

- **After 8 Weeks**: Moved snack time from 10:30 a.m. to 10:00 a.m. to address hunger and restlessness, resulting in smoother transitions and more focused students.

By reflecting regularly on the effectiveness of the CRS, Teacher Brown is able to make thoughtful, data-driven adjustments that address the dynamic needs of the classroom. Engaging students and support staff in the process not only makes the system more effective but also creates a more inclusive, collaborative learning environment.

Expert Quotes and Insights

Harry K. Wong: "Effective teachers invest the time necessary to introduce, teach, model, and reinforce procedures and routines. They know that a well-managed classroom is key to a productive learning environment" (Wong & Wong, 2009).

Carol Ann Tomlinson: "Students need to understand the rules and why they are important. When students see the purpose behind the rules, they are more likely to follow them" (Tomlinson, 2001).

Fred Jones: "Rules must be taught, practiced, and reinforced. They provide the structure that allows students to feel safe and focused on learning" (Jones, 2007).

Teacher Resources	Website Link
Edutopia: The Importance of Classroom Rules and Procedures	Edutopia
Scholastic: Effective Classroom Management: Establishing Clear Rules	Scholastic
Education World: Setting Classroom Rules	Education World
ASCD: Classroom Management: Creating a Learning Environment	ASCD
Teaching Channel: Classroom Management Techniques	Teaching Channel
National Education Association (NEA): Classroom Management Tips and Tricks	NEA
PBS: Teacher's Lounge: Classroom Management	PBS
Center for Responsive Schools: Responsive Classroom Approach	Responsive Classroom
Positive Behavioral Interventions and Supports (PBIS): Framework for Effective Classroom Management	PBIS

Tips and Best Practices

1. **Consistency in Enforcement**: Maintain consistency in enforcing the rules to ensure their effectiveness. Fair and impartial application of rules helps students understand that the guidelines are important and must be followed.

2. **Positive Reinforcement**: Use positive reinforcement to encourage adherence to classroom rules. Praise, rewards, and recognition can motivate students to maintain positive behavior and follow the established guidelines.

3. **Regular Review**: Periodically review the rules with students to ensure they remain relevant and effective.

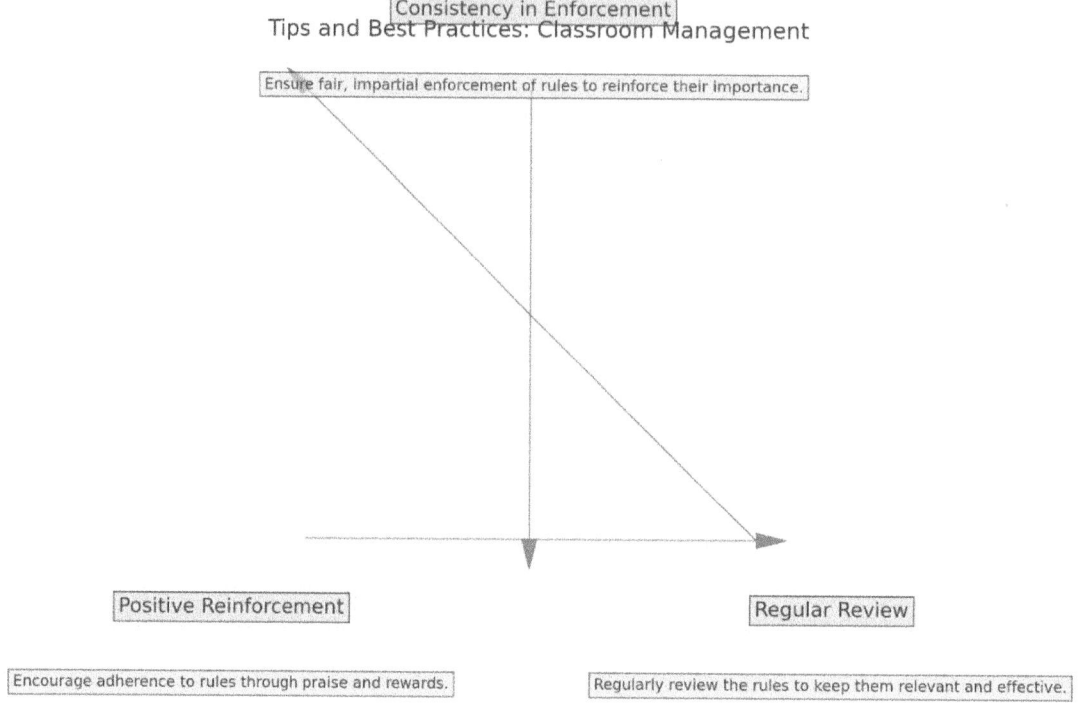

Tips and Best Practices: Classroom Management

Consistency in Enforcement
Ensure fair, impartial enforcement of rules to reinforce their importance.

Positive Reinforcement
Encourage adherence to rules through praise and rewards.

Regular Review
Regularly review the rules to keep them relevant and effective.

Here is the **three-part infographic** representing the **Tips and Best Practices** for classroom management. Each section highlights key strategies: **Consistency in Enforcement, Positive Reinforcement**, and **Regular Review**. The triangle structure shows how these best practices are interconnected and support one another.

Classroom Template Resource

Welcome to the Classroom Template Resource section! Here, you'll find a collection of practical and easy-to-use templates designed to streamline your classroom routines, track student behavior, foster better communication with parents, and encourage positive student interactions. Whether you're looking to enhance daily classroom structure or improve behavior tracking, these templates will provide valuable support for both teachers and students.

Simply click the download links below to access each template and start incorporating them into your classroom practices today.

Classroom Template Resource	Link
Daily Routine Chart Template	Download Daily Routine Chart
Behavior Tracking Sheet	Download Behavior Tracking Sheet
Parent Communication Log	Download Parent Communication Log

Classroom Contract Template	Download Classroom Contract Template
Role-Playing Scenarios Guide	Download Role-Playing Scenarios Guide
Visual Rules Poster Template	Download Visual Rules Poster Template
Positive Reinforcement Chart	Download Positive Reinforcement Chart
Student Self-Assessment Checklist	Download Student Self-Assessment Checklist

Classroom Rules System (CRS) Lesson Plan & Activity

Purpose of the Lesson:

The purpose of this lesson is to guide students in collaboratively creating a Social Contract that outlines shared classroom expectations. This process promotes student ownership of behavior, encourages mutual respect, and fosters a sense of responsibility within the classroom community. Through group discussions and reflection, students will contribute to setting the rules that support a positive and productive learning environment.

Goal:

To have students collaboratively create a Social Contract that promotes a positive learning environment, encourages student ownership of behavior, and fosters accountability within the classroom community.

Student Learning Objectives:

1. By the end of the lesson, students will be able to identify and articulate the importance of key elements in a Social Contract, such as mutual respect, active participation, and responsibility, through group discussions and personal reflection.
2. Students will actively contribute to the creation of the classroom Social Contract by suggesting, refining, and voting on shared rules, demonstrating an understanding of how these agreements support a cohesive and respectful classroom community.

Agenda

1. **Discussion**: Start with a class discussion about the importance of rules and expectations.
2. **Brainstorming**: Have students brainstorm potential rules and write them down.
3. **Voting**: Let students vote on the most important rules to include in the classroom contract.
4. **Drafting**: Create a final version of the classroom contract and have each student sign it.

The start of the lesson: Distribute the assessment rubric to the students and display the Student Learning Objectives (SLOs) for them to view. Read the objectives aloud to the class, and to ensure understanding, ask students to give a "thumbs up" as a quick formative check.

Assessment Rubric:					
Criteria	**Excellent (5)**	**Good (4)**	**Fair (3)**	**Needs Improvement (2)**	**Poor (1)**
Participation in Discussion	Actively participated and contributed valuable ideas.	Participated and contributed some ideas.	Participated minimally.	Rarely participated.	Did not participate.
Quality of Brainstorming	Provided numerous relevant and thoughtful rules.	Provided several relevant rules.	Provided a few relevant rules.	Provided few or irrelevant rules.	Did not provide any rules.
Engagement in Voting	Actively engaged and explained reasoning for choices.	Engaged and participated in voting.	Participated in voting with minimal engagement.	Participated in voting reluctantly.	Did not participate in voting.
Contribution to Drafting	Contributed significantly to the final contract.	Contributed to the final contract.	Contributed minimally to the final contract.	Rarely contributed to the final contract.	Did not contribute to the final contract.

Notes for Teachers: Social Contract Lesson

Student Learning Objectives:

By the end of the lesson, students will be able to identify and articulate the importance of key elements in a Social Contract, such as mutual respect, active participation, and responsibility, through group discussions and personal reflection.

Students will actively contribute to the creation of the classroom Social Contract by suggesting, refining, and voting on shared rules, demonstrating an understanding of how these agreements support a cohesive and respectful classroom community.

Preparation Before the Lesson:

- **Prepare Materials**: Have a large chart paper or a digital platform ready to record rules that students suggest. You may also want to prepare slips of paper for anonymous voting.
- **Explain the Concept of a Social Contract**: Begin the lesson by defining what a Social Contract is—a set of mutually agreed-upon rules that everyone in the classroom commits to following. Highlight the idea of mutual respect and shared responsibility.

Teacher's Role:

- **Facilitator, Not Enforcer**: Your role during this lesson is to facilitate discussion and ensure every student has a voice. This creates a sense of ownership and accountability. The rules should come from the students, with guidance where necessary.

- **Active Listening**: When students suggest rules, listen actively and ask clarifying questions. For example, "How would that rule help everyone feel respected in the classroom?" This helps students think critically about why the rules matter.

Guiding the Discussion:

- **Encourage Inclusivity**: Make sure all voices are heard. Some students may feel shy or reluctant to speak up, so consider using a "think-pair-share" approach, where students first discuss their ideas in pairs before sharing them with the class.
- **Prompt for Key Elements**: If students struggle to come up with certain rules (e.g., respect, participation), gently prompt them by asking, "What behaviors help us feel safe and respected in the classroom?" or "What does it look like when we're all working together?"
- **Reflection on Rules**: Once the initial suggestions are made, ask the class to reflect on whether these rules align with the core values of mutual respect, participation, and responsibility. Encourage students to think about how these rules would make the classroom better for everyone.

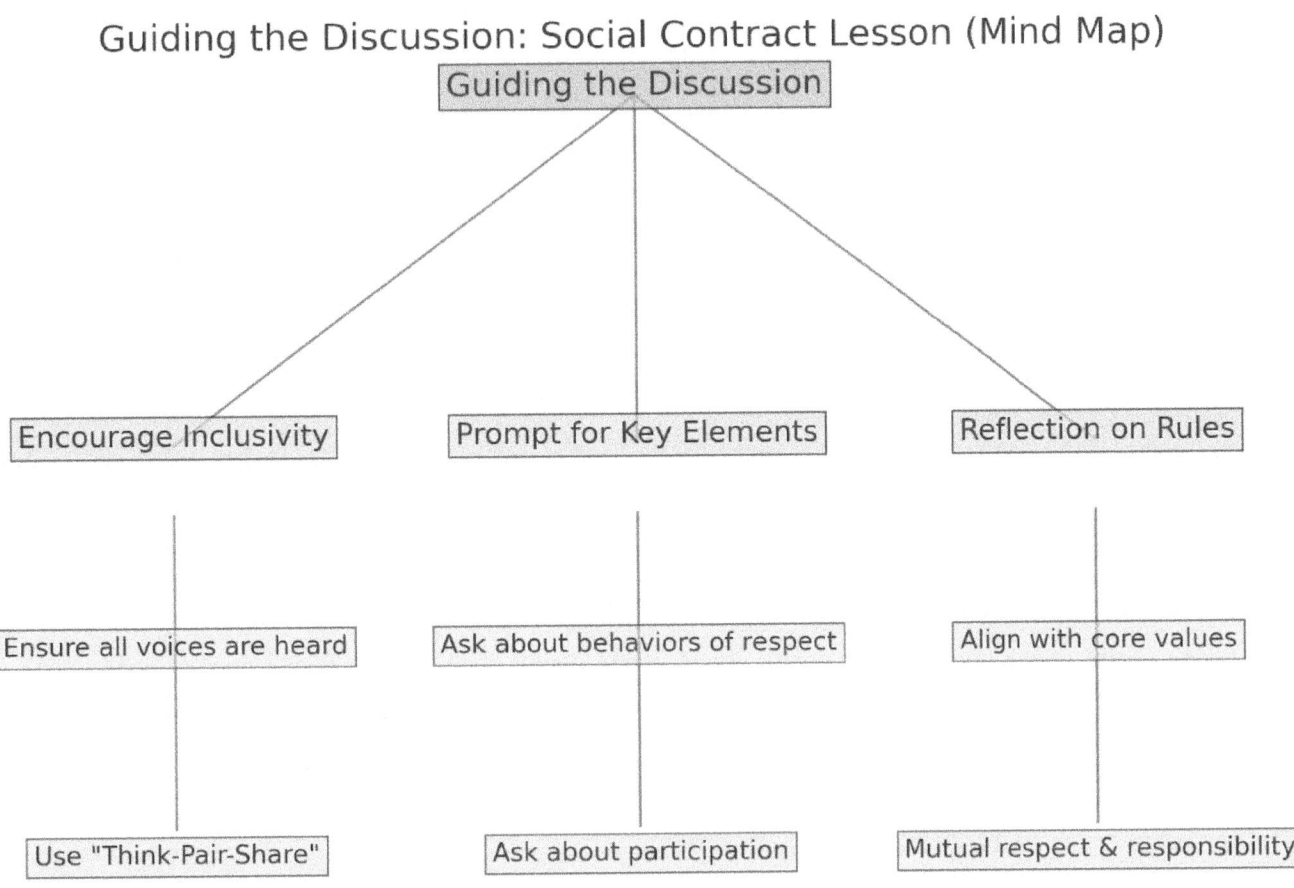

Here is the **mind map** representing the process of **Guiding the Discussion** for a Social Contract lesson. It visually branches out from the main topic into three key areas: **Encouraging Inclusivity, Prompting for Key Elements**, and **Reflection on Rules**, with further details for each branch.

Facilitating Student Ownership:

- **Voting and Finalizing the Social Contract**: Once all rules are suggested, allow students to vote on the final set of rules. They can vote anonymously or through a show of hands. This process reinforces the idea that the Social Contract is something everyone has a say in.
- **Posting the Social Contract**: After the rules are finalized, post the Social Contract prominently in the classroom. You can have students take turns writing or decorating the contract to further personalize it.

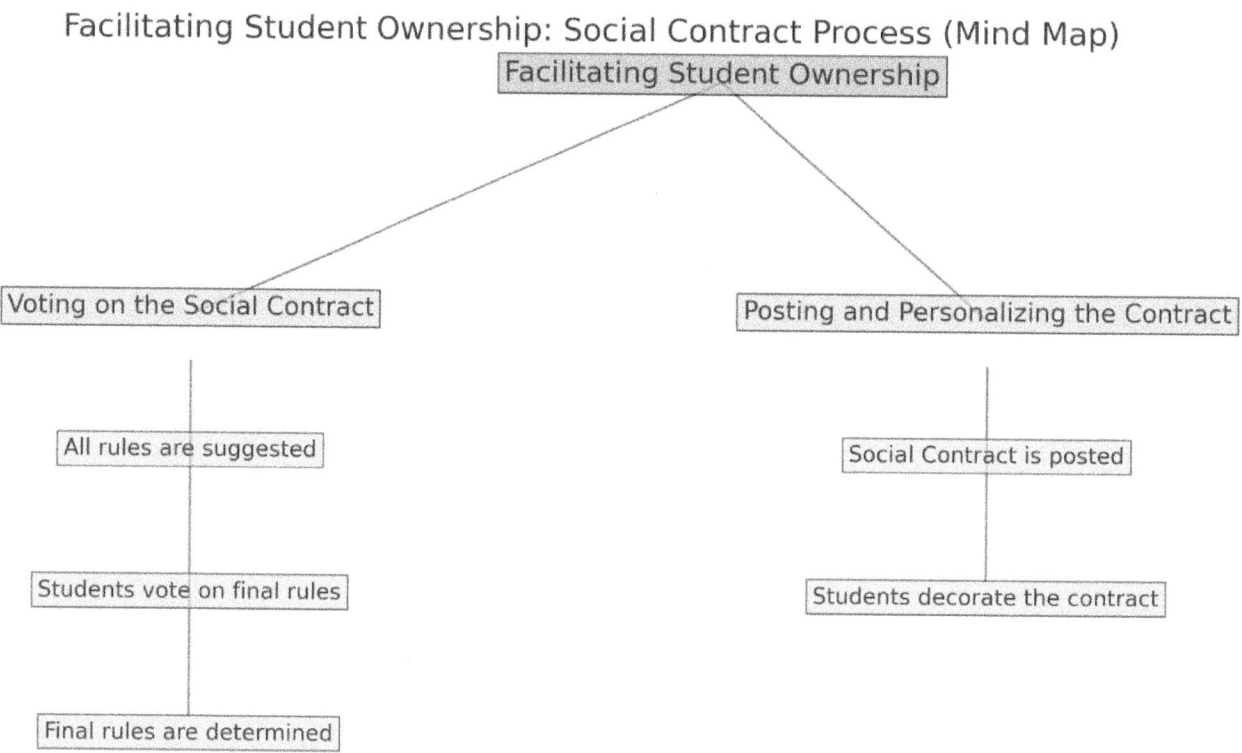

Here is the mind map for the Facilitating Student Ownership process in creating a Social Contract. It visualizes the two key areas: Voting on the Social Contract and Posting and Personalizing the Contract, with the respective steps under each.

Ongoing Reflection and Adjustments:

- **Periodic Review**: Explain to students that the Social Contract is a living document, which means it can be reviewed and adjusted over time. Set aside time periodically (e.g., monthly) to reflect on how the rules are working. Are there any new challenges in the classroom? Should any rules be adjusted to better fit the needs of the group?
- **Encourage Reflection**: Allow students to reflect individually or in groups about how well they feel they are following the Social Contract and whether they notice a difference in classroom behavior since the rules were established.

Ongoing Reflection and Adjustments: Social Contract Cycle

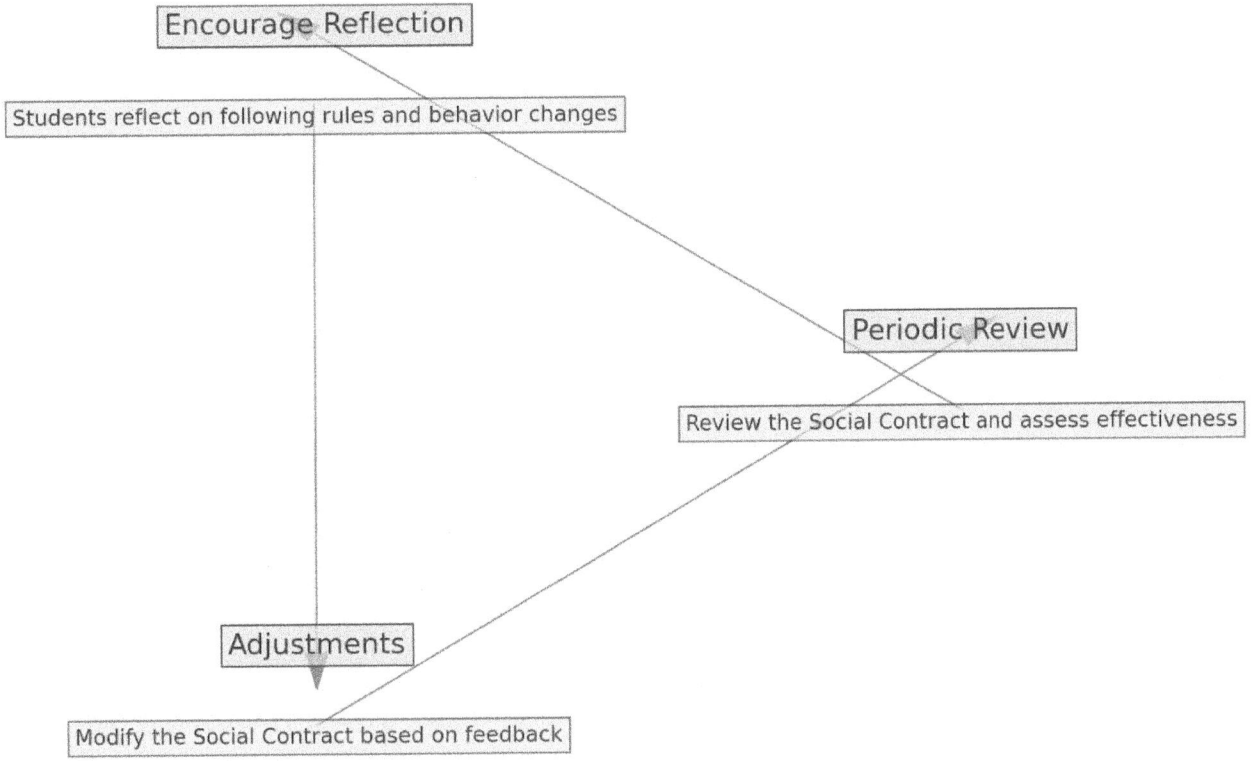

Here is the **cyclical process visual** representing **Ongoing Reflection and Adjustments** for the Social Contract. It highlights the continuous cycle of periodic review, encouraging reflection, and making adjustments based on feedback.

Troubleshooting Common Issues:

- **If students suggest unrealistic or overly strict rules**: Help them understand the importance of fairness. Ask questions like, "Do you think this rule would be fair for everyone? How would it help us create a positive classroom environment?"
- **If students don't feel invested**: Remind them that this is **their** contract, and it only works if everyone agrees to follow the rules. Emphasize the idea of shared responsibility and how each person's behavior impacts the group.

Troubleshooting Common Issues: Social Contract Creation

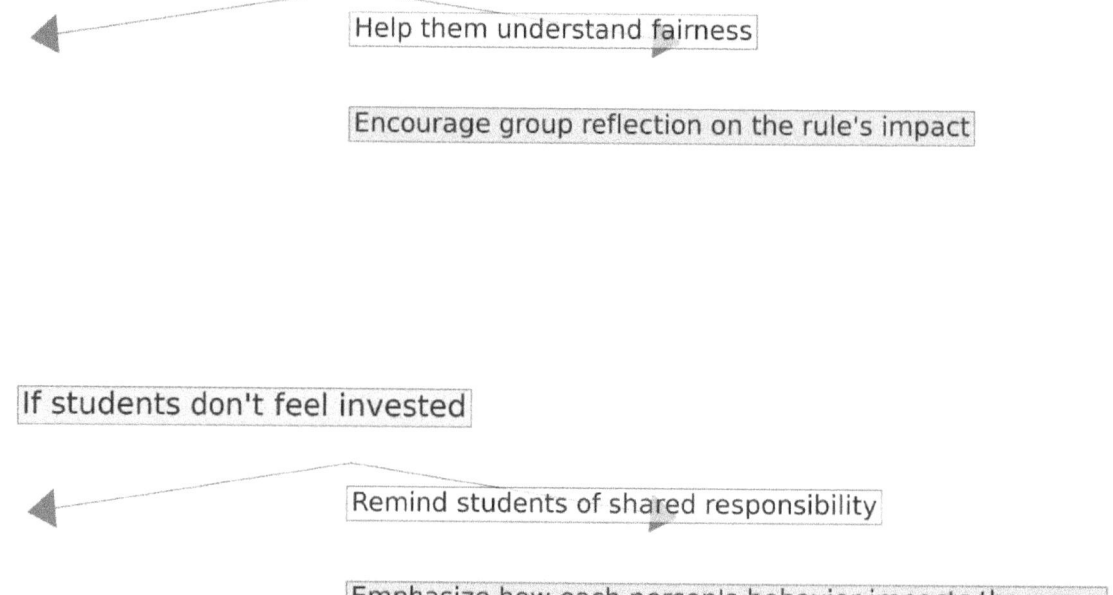

If students suggest unrealistic or overly strict rules

Help them understand fairness

Encourage group reflection on the rule's impact

If students don't feel invested

Remind students of shared responsibility

Emphasize how each person's behavior impacts the group

By following these notes, you will help create a classroom culture where students understand and feel empowered by the rules, fostering a respectful and collaborative learning environment.

Characteristics of a Good Rule

1. **Clarity and Specificity:**
   » A good rule is clear and specific, leaving little room for interpretation. It should be easily understood by all students, which means using simple language and being explicit about what behavior is expected. For example, "Raise your hand before speaking" is clear and direct, unlike a vague rule like "Be respectful" (Teach Empowered) (Korn Center).

2. **Positivity:**
   » Effective rules are framed positively, focusing on what students should do rather than what they shouldn't. Positive rules encourage good behavior rather than merely prohibiting bad behavior. For instance, "Walk quietly in the hallway" is more effective than "No running" because it tells students what behavior is expected (Teach Empowered).

3. **Enforceability:**
   - » A good rule is enforceable, meaning it can be consistently monitored and enforced by the teacher. If a rule cannot be consistently applied, it loses its authority and may lead to inconsistency in discipline, which can confuse students (Korn Center).

4. **Relevance and Purpose:**
   - » Effective rules serve a clear purpose and are directly relevant to the learning environment. They should contribute to a safe, respectful, and productive classroom. Rules that seem arbitrary or overly restrictive without a clear rationale can lead to resistance or disengagement from students (Edutopia).

5. **Involvement in Creation:**
   - » Rules that involve student input tend to be more effective because students are more likely to understand and follow rules they had a hand in creating. This sense of ownership also fosters a stronger classroom community and enhances students' sense of responsibility (Korn Center).

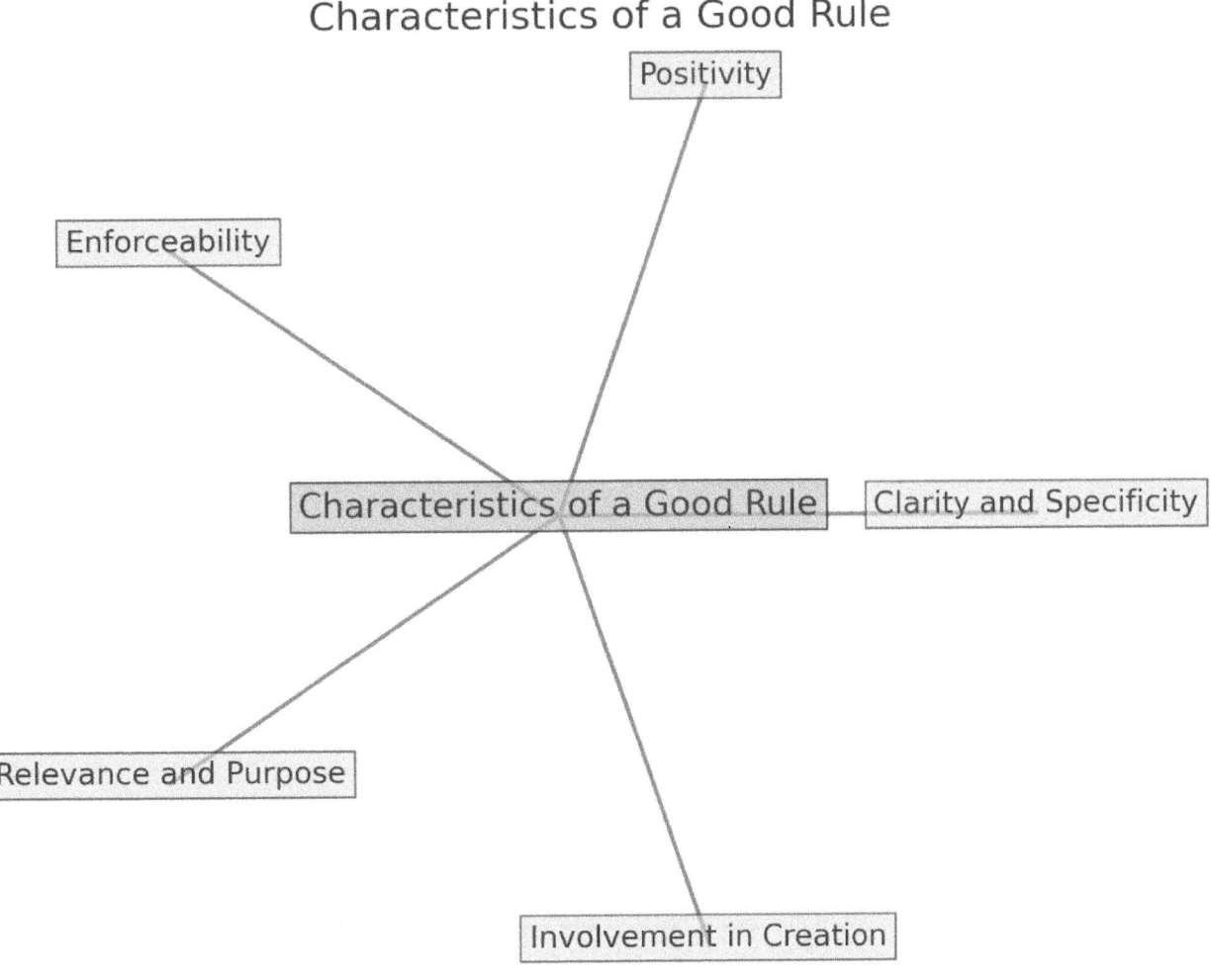

Here is the **radial infographic** visualizing the **Characteristics of a Good Rule**. Each characteristic—**Clarity and Specificity, Positivity, Enforceability, Relevance and Purpose**, and **Involvement in Creation**—is represented as a spoke on the wheel, illustrating how each component contributes to the overall quality of classroom rules.

Characteristics of a Bad Rule

1. **Vagueness:**
   » A bad rule is vague and open to interpretation, which can lead to confusion and inconsistency in enforcement. Rules like "Be good" or "Act appropriately" lack clear guidance and can result in students being uncertain about what is expected of them (Edutopia).

2. **Negativity:**
   » Rules that are framed negatively, such as "Don't talk during class," focus on what students shouldn't do rather than guiding them toward positive behaviors. Negative rules can create a punitive atmosphere rather than a supportive learning environment (Teach Empowered).

3. **Inconsistency in Enforcement:**
   » If a rule cannot be enforced consistently, it becomes ineffective. Students may lose respect for the rule if they see it being applied inconsistently, leading to a lack of trust and a decrease in compliance (Korn Center).

4. **Overly Restrictive or Unnecessary:**
   » Bad rules are those that are too restrictive or seem unnecessary to students. If a rule doesn't serve a clear educational purpose or seems to limit students unnecessarily, it can cause frustration and rebellion rather than compliance (Edutopia).

5. **Lack of Student Involvement:**
   » When rules are imposed without student input, they may be seen as arbitrary or unfair, leading to resistance. Involving students in the creation of rules can prevent this issue and encourage a more cooperative classroom environment (Korn Center).

Here is the **radial infographic** illustrating the **Characteristics of a Bad Rule**. Each spoke represents one of the key traits that contribute to ineffective classroom rules: **Vagueness, Negativity, Inconsistency in Enforcement, Overly Restrictive or Unnecessary,** and **Lack of Student Involvement.**

In summary, a good classroom rule is clear, positive, enforceable, relevant, and ideally created with student input. On the other hand, a bad rule tends to be vague, negative, inconsistently enforced, overly restrictive, or imposed without student involvement.

For Students:

1. **Promotes a Positive Learning Environment:** Emphasizes respect and responsibility (Wong, H. K., & Wong, R. T., 2009).
2. **Helps Develop Self-Discipline and Accountability:** Students learn to manage their behavior (Marzano, R. J., Marzano, J. S., & Pickering, D. J., 2003).
3. **Reduces Anxiety:** Provides a predictable and safe classroom atmosphere (Jones, F. H., 2007).

Promotes a Positive Learning Environment

Emphasizes respect and responsibility (Wong & Wong, 2009).

For Students: Benefits of Classroom Rules

Helps Develop Self-Discipline and Accountability

Students learn to manage their behavior (Marzano et al., 2003).

Reduces Anxiety

Provides a predictable and safe classroom atmosphere (Jones, 2007).

Here is the **pyramid infographic** visually representing the **benefits for students** of classroom rules. The structure emphasizes how reducing anxiety forms the foundation, followed by developing self-discipline, and ultimately promoting a positive learning environment.

For Teachers:

1. **Simplifies Classroom Management**: Reduces the need for constant corrections and disciplinary actions (Tomlinson, C. A., 2001).
2. **Increases Instructional Time**: Less time spent addressing behavioral issues allows for more effective teaching (Wong, H. K., & Wong, R. T., 2009).
3. **Fosters Positive Teacher-Student Relationships**: Expectations are understood and respected by all parties (Marzano, R. J., Marzano, J. S., & Pickering, D. J., 2003).

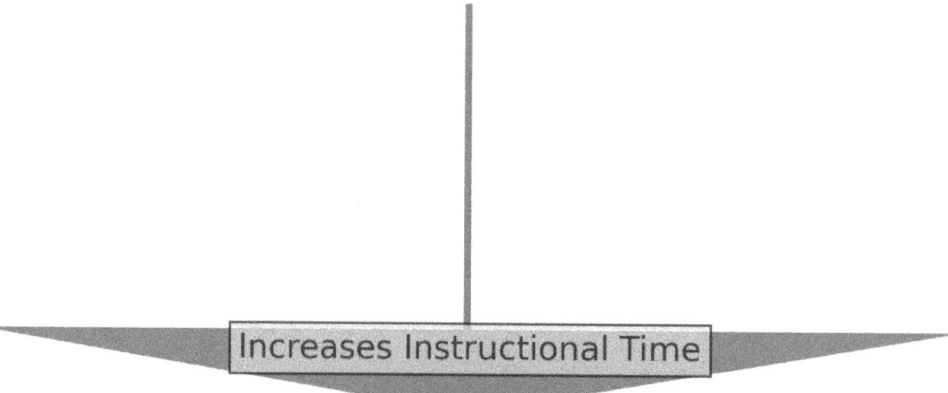

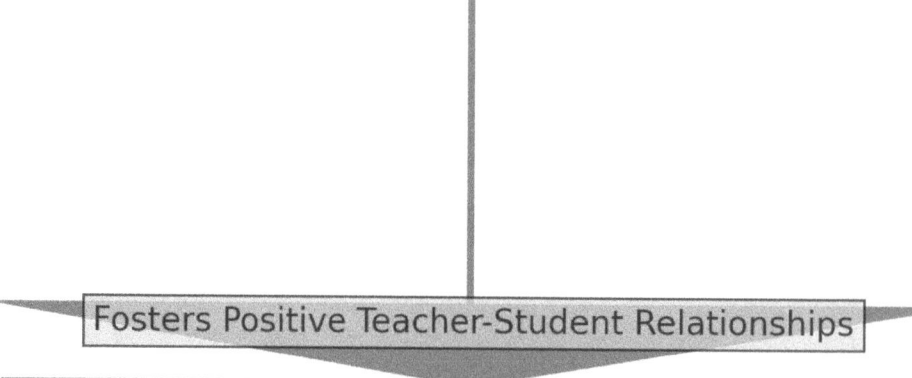

Here is the **tiered flowchart** visually representing the **benefits for teachers** of classroom rules. It shows how simplifying classroom management leads to increased instructional time, which in turn fosters positive teacher-student relationships.

Think of clear rules as a recipe in a cookbook. When followed, they produce a delicious and satisfying dish—in this case, a harmonious and effective learning environment.

Practical Tips and Strategies

1. **Identify Key Areas Needing Regulation**: Begin by identifying the key areas that require clear rules, such as behavior during lessons, transitions between activities, and interactions among students.
2. **Involve Students in the Process**: Involving students in creating the rules can increase their buy-in and understanding. This collaborative approach makes them feel valued and responsible for maintaining a positive classroom environment.
3. **Communicate Rules Effectively**: Use multiple methods to communicate the rules clearly. Verbal explanations, written rules, and visual aids can all help ensure that students fully understand the expectations.

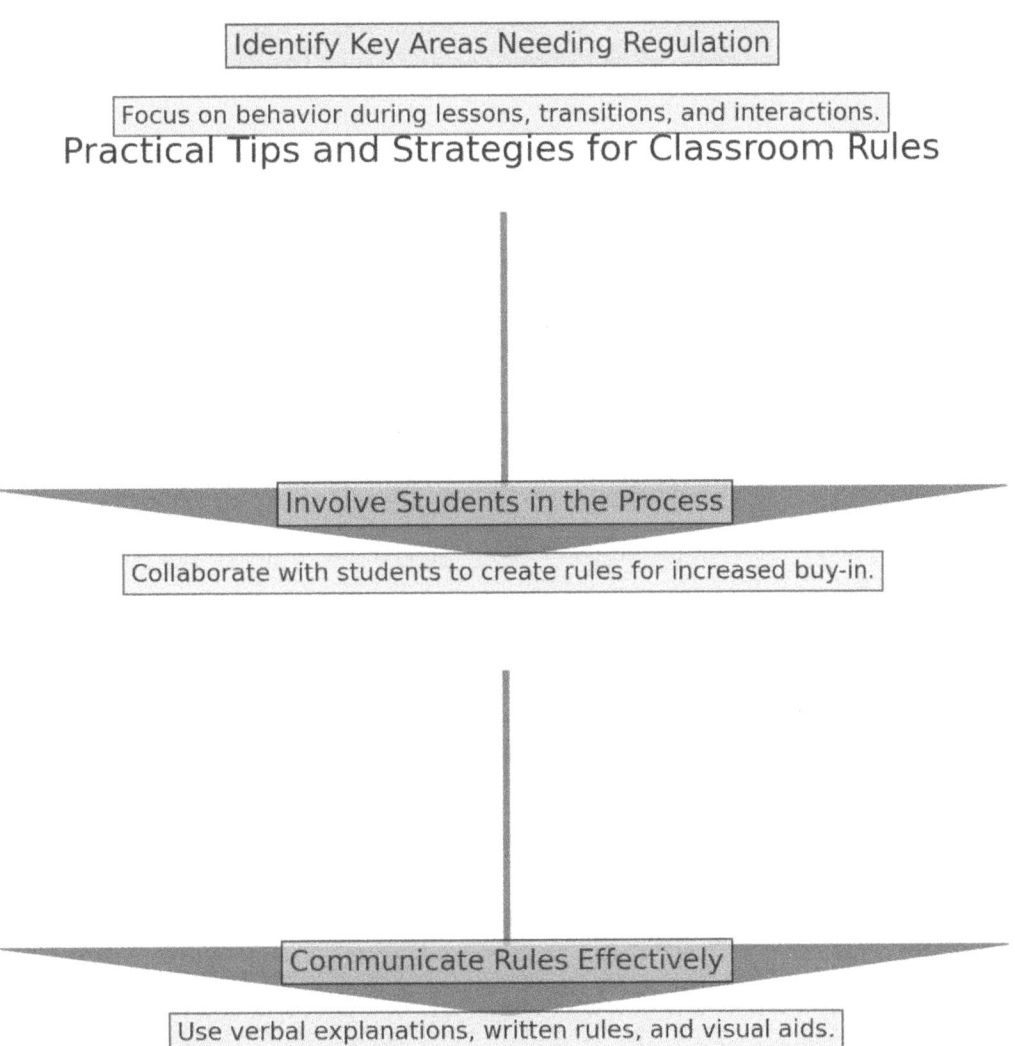

Practical Tips and Strategies for Classroom Rules

Here is the **step-by-step flowchart** for the **Practical Tips and Strategies** on creating and implementing classroom rules. It shows the progression from identifying key areas, involving students, to effectively communicating the rules.

Professional Development Assessment for Teachers

Multiple-Choice Questions:

1. What is one primary benefit of establishing clear rules and expectations in the classroom?
   a. Higher test scores
   b. Increased student engagement and motivation
   c. More free time for teachers
   d. Better classroom technology

2. According to Harry K. Wong, what is key to a productive learning environment?
   a. Advanced technology
   b. Well-managed classroom
   c. More homework
   d. Flexible seating

3. Which of the following is a benefit for teachers of having clear rules and expectations?
   a. Higher salaries
   b. Simplified classroom management
   c. More vacation days
   d. Better classroom resources

4. What is one key feature of a collaborative rules system (CRS)?
   a. Students have no input
   b. Students participate in creating the rules
   c. Only teachers create the rules
   d. Rules are set by the school administration

5. What is an effective way to enforce rules with students who have ADHD?
   a. Use negative reinforcement
   b. Introduce a reward system for positive behavior
   c. Punish students for breaking rules
   d. Ignore their behavior

6. Which of the following is not part of creating an effective classroom rule?
   a. Clear and specific
   b. Enforceable
   c. Vague and open to interpretation
   d. Relevant to the learning environment

7. How often should teachers reflect on and adjust the Classroom Rule System (CRS)?
   a. Weekly
   b. Never

c. Periodically (e.g., every 6-8 weeks)

d. Only at the end of the school year

8. How can students contribute to the effectiveness of classroom rules?

a. Ignoring the rules

b. Helping create the rules

c. Letting the teacher decide on all rules

d. Complaining about the rules

9. How can classroom rules positively impact students' behavior?

a. They increase anxiety

b. They provide structure and expectations

c. They make students rebel more

d. They confuse students

10. What is one important principle behind creating classroom rules?

a. Rules should be punitive

b. Rules should be easy to break

c. Rules should be fair and consistent

d. Rules should be optional for some students

Short-Answer Questions:

11. In your own words, explain why it is important to establish clear rules and expectations in the classroom.

12. How would you involve students in creating the classroom rules? Give one specific strategy.

13. What is the role of positive reinforcement in managing classroom behavior?

Scenario-Based Questions:

14. **Scenario:** Your students frequently interrupt each other during discussions. What steps would you take to establish and enforce a rule to address this behavior?

15. **Scenario:** A new student joins your class and is unfamiliar with the established rules. How would you help them understand and follow the classroom expectations?

Teacher Rubric for Self-Assessment					
Criteria	Excellent (5)	Good (4)	Fair (3)	Needs Improvement (2)	Poor (1)
Understanding of Rules	Demonstrates thorough understanding of the importance of clear rules.	Demonstrates good understanding of the importance of clear rules.	Demonstrates some understanding of the importance of clear rules.	Demonstrates minimal understanding of the importance of clear rules.	Demonstrates no understanding of the importance of clear rules.

	Effectively involves students in the rule-setting process.	Generally involves students in the rule-setting process.	Occasionally involves students in the rule-setting process.	Rarely involves students in the rule-setting process.	Does not involve students in the rule-setting process.
Student Involvement					
Communication of Rules	Clearly and effectively communicates rules.	Generally communicates rules effectively.	Occasionally communicates rules effectively.	Rarely communicates rules effectively.	Does not communicate rules effectively.
Consistency in Enforcement	Consistently enforces rules fairly and impartially.	Generally enforces rules fairly and impartially.	Occasionally enforces rules fairly and impartially.	Rarely enforces rules fairly and impartially.	Does not enforce rules fairly and impartially.

Answer Key for the Teacher CRS Quiz:

Multiple-Choice Questions:

1. What is one primary benefit of establishing clear rules and expectations in the classroom?
   » **Answer: b) Increased student engagement and motivation**

2. According to Harry K. Wong, what is key to a productive learning environment?
   » **Answer: b) Well-managed classroom**

3. Which of the following is a benefit for teachers of having clear rules and expectations?
   » **Answer: b) Simplified classroom management**

4. What is one key feature of a collaborative rules system (CRS)?
   » **Answer: b) Students participate in creating the rules**

5. What is an effective way to enforce rules with students who have ADHD?
   » **Answer: b) Introduce a reward system for positive behavior**

6. Which of the following is not part of creating an effective classroom rule?
   » **Answer: c) Vague and open to interpretation**

7. How often should teachers reflect on and adjust the Classroom Rule System (CRS)?
   » **Answer: c) Periodically (e.g., every 6-8 weeks)**

8. How can students contribute to the effectiveness of classroom rules?
   » **Answer: b) Helping create the rules**

9. How can classroom rules positively impact students' behavior?
   » **Answer: b) They provide structure and expectations**

10. What is one important principle behind creating classroom rules?
    » **Answer: c) Rules should be fair and consistent**

Short-Answer Questions:

11. In your own words, explain why it is important to establish clear rules and expectations in the classroom.

» **Answer:** Clear rules provide structure, reduce behavioral issues, and foster a respectful learning environment. They help students understand what is expected of them, leading to better behavior, less anxiety, and a more positive classroom atmosphere.

12. How would you involve students in creating the classroom rules? Give one specific strategy.

» **Answer:** One strategy is to hold a class discussion where students brainstorm rules. Students can suggest rules, discuss their importance, and vote on the ones they believe will benefit the classroom the most. This gives students a sense of ownership over the rules.

13. What is the role of positive reinforcement in managing classroom behavior?

» **Answer:** Positive reinforcement encourages desired behavior by rewarding students when they follow the rules. This helps to build good habits and creates a supportive environment, where students are motivated to repeat positive actions.

Scenario-Based Questions:

14. **Scenario:** Your students frequently interrupt each other during discussions. What steps would you take to establish and enforce a rule to address this behavior?

» **Answer:** I would begin by explaining the importance of respecting others when they speak. I would then involve the students in creating a rule, such as "Raise your hand before speaking" or "Wait for others to finish before contributing." I would consistently enforce this rule by acknowledging those who follow it and providing gentle reminders for those who don't. Over time, the class could reflect on whether the rule has improved discussions.

15. **Scenario:** A new student joins your class and is unfamiliar with the established rules. How would you help them understand and follow the classroom expectations?

» **Answer:** I would introduce the new student to the classroom rules by explaining them in simple terms and sharing a written or visual copy. I would pair them with a buddy who can model and reinforce the rules. Additionally, I would check in regularly to ensure they understand and are following the expectations, offering support as needed.

Feedback Mechanism

To continually improve this eBook and ensure it meets your needs, we encourage you to provide feedback. Your insights and suggestions are invaluable for enhancing the content and making it even more effective.

How to Provide Feedback:

- **Online Form**: Feedback Form
- **Email**: support@masteringtheclassroom.com
- **Social Media**: Follow and message us on Twitter @ClassroomMgmtEbook

Bibliography

- Bandura, A. (1997). Self-Efficacy: The Exercise of Control. W.H. Freeman.
- Brooks, J. (2011). Space and Learning: How Classroom Design Influences Student Learning and Engagement. Educational Facility Planner.

- Cotton, K. (2000). The Schooling Practices That Matter Most. ASCD.
- Emmer, E. T., & Stough, L. M. (2001). Classroom Management: A Critical Part of Educational Psychology, with Implications for Teacher Education. Educational Psychologist, 36(2), 103-112.
- Evertson, C. M., & Emmer, E. T. (2017). Classroom Management for Elementary Teachers. Pearson.
- Hamre, B. K., & Pianta, R. C. (2006). Student-Teacher Relationships. In G. G. Bear & K. M. Minke (Eds.), Children's Needs III: Development, Prevention, and Intervention. National Association of School Psychologists.
- Marzano, R. J., Marzano, J. S., & Pickering, D. J. (2003). Classroom Management That Works: Research-Based Strategies for Every Teacher. ASCD.
- Sugai, G., & Horner, R. H. (2002). The Evolution of Discipline Practices: School-Wide Positive Behavior Supports. Child & Family Behavior Therapy, 24(1-2), 23-50.
- Weinstein, C. S. (2007). Elementary Classroom Management: Lessons from Research and Practice. McGraw-Hill.
- Wong, H. K., & Wong, R. T. (2009). The First Days of School: How to Be an Effective Teacher. Harry K. Wong Publications.
- Jones, F. H. (2007). *Tools for Teaching: Discipline, Instruction, Motivation.* Fredric H. Jones & Associates, Inc.
- Tomlinson, C. A. (2001). *How to Differentiate Instruction in Mixed-Ability Classrooms.* ASCD.
- Marzano, R. J. (2007). *The Art and Science of Teaching: A Comprehensive Framework for Effective Instruction.* ASCD.
- *Edutopia.* (2016). Making the Most of Visual Aids. Retrieved from https://www.edutopia.org/article/making-most-visual-aids
- *Student-Centered World.* (2023). 8 Easy Classroom Management Visual Aids for K-12 Students. Retrieved from https://www.studentcenteredworld.com/classroom-management-visual-aids
- Marzano, R. J. (2007). *The Art and Science of Teaching: A Comprehensive Framework for Effective Instruction.* ASCD.
- Jones, F. H. (2007). *Tools for Teaching: Discipline, Instruction, Motivation.* Fredric H. Jones & Associates, Inc.
- Canter, L. (2010). *Assertive Discipline: Positive Behavior Management for Today's Classroom.* Canter & Associates.
- Sugai, G., & Horner, R. (2002). The evolution of discipline practices: School-wide positive behavior supports. *Child & Family Behavior Therapy,* 24(1-2), 23-50.
- Cohen, M. T., & Johnson, H. L. (2012). Improving the acquisition and retention of science material by fifth grade students through the use of imagery interventions. *Instructional Science,* 40, 925–955.
- Tomlinson, C. A. (2001). *How to Differentiate Instruction in Mixed-Ability Classrooms.* ASCD.
- Sousa, D. A., & Tomlinson, C. A. (2018). *Differentiation and the Brain: How Neuroscience Supports the Learner-Friendly Classroom.* Solution Tree Press.
- Jones, F. H. (2007). *Tools for Teaching: Discipline, Instruction, Motivation.* Fredric H. Jones & Associates, Inc.
- Cardillo, N. (2017). *Visual Aids Supporting the Learning of Children in Our Classrooms.* In G. Geng, P. Smith, & P. Black (Eds.), *The Challenge of Teaching.* Springer.
- Cohen, M. T., & Johnson, H. L. (2012). Improving the acquisition and retention of science material by fifth grade students through the use of imagery interventions. *Instructional Science,* 40, 925–955.
- *Edutopia.* (2016). Making the Most of Visual Aids. Retrieved from https://www.edutopia.org/article/making-most-visual-aids
- *Student-Centered World.* (2023). 8 Easy Classroom Management Visual Aids for K-12 Students. Retrieved from https://www.studentcenteredworld.com/classroom-management-visual-aids

References:

- Wong, H. K. and Wong, R. T. (2009). The First Days of School: How to be an Effective Teacher. Harry K. Wong Publications. Marzano, R. J., Marzano, J. S. and Pickering D J (1998) Classroom Management That Works: Research Based Strategies for Every Educator from ASCD

- National Education Association (NEA). (2010) Positive Behavioral Interventions and Supports: Creating an Approach that Works for Every Student.

- Morrison B & Vaandering D (2012) Restorative Justice: Integrating Pedagogy Praxis & Discipline into Schools Journal of School Violence 11(2) 138-155.

- Tomlinson, C. A. (2001). How to Differentiate Instruction in Mixed Ability Classrooms, ASCD. Vygotsky L S (1978). Mind in Society: The Development of Higher Psychological Processes from Society Perspective, Harvard University Press.

- Skinner, B. F. (1953). Science and Human Behavior. Simon and Schuster. By applying both theoretical perspectives as well as practical strategies, teachers can set clear rules and expectations to promote an engaging learning environment for their students.

CHAPTER 2

THE HEART OF TEACHING: BUILDING POSITIVE RELATIONSHIPS

Lesson from Experience

My first year in the classroom was filled with enthusiasm and ambition. I had meticulously crafted lesson plans, a spotless whiteboard, and a vision of how each day would unfold. But the reality of teaching quickly swept over me like a tidal wave.

One student, in particular, tested every boundary I thought I had established. No matter what I tried—more structure, stricter discipline, or even extra tutoring—nothing seemed to resonate. Doubts crept in: Could I truly reach my students? Had I made the right career choice? I had believed that a solid grasp of content and control would be enough, but day after day, I felt the gap between us widening.

Frustrated and exhausted, I turned to my mentor, Mr. G, a seasoned teacher who seemed to connect effortlessly with every student. I poured out my struggles, hoping for new strategies or classroom management tips. Instead, he simply said, "You can't teach them if you don't know them."

At first, I was puzzled by his words. But he encouraged me to start small—greet my students at the door, learn about their lives beyond school, and show genuine care for their well-being. He even invited me into his classroom, where I witnessed the profound impact of these connections: students who knew Mr. G saw them, understood them, and genuinely believed he was invested in their success.

The following week, I began to embrace his advice. I shifted my focus from lesson plans to listening. Gradually, the walls around my students started to crumble. That challenging student? He began to trust me, and in turn, he became more engaged. I realized that building positive relationships wasn't merely a "soft skill"—it was the bedrock of effective teaching.

Mr. G illuminated a vital truth: real learning begins with connection. Without it, even the most brilliant lesson plans fall flat. This realization not only transformed my approach to teaching but also reignited my passion for the profession.

Introduction

Building positive relationships is at the heart of effective teaching. While classroom management strategies and strong lesson plans are essential, the foundation of a thriving learning environment lies in the connections teachers foster with their students. Research underscores the critical role relationships play in fostering student engagement, academic success, and emotional well-being. Strong teacher-student relationships have been linked to higher levels of motivation, better classroom behavior, and greater resilience in the face of challenges (Hattie, 2009; Pianta, Hamre, & Allen, 2012).

This chapter delves into the transformative power of positive relationships in education, providing evidence-based insights and practical strategies for teachers. By examining real-life scenarios, exploring theoretical frameworks, and offering actionable steps, this chapter aims to equip educators with the tools they need to foster meaningful connections with their students.

Enhance Effectiveness

Building strong relationships enhances teacher effectiveness by fostering an environment where students feel seen, valued, and respected. This sense of connection creates a foundation of trust that is essential for meaningful learning and development. Research shows that when students trust their teachers, they are more likely to engage in the learning process, take academic risks, and embrace a growth mindset (Hattie, 2009).

Trust and Engagement

Trust is the cornerstone of effective teacher-student relationships. When students feel that their teachers genuinely care about their well-being and success, they are more motivated to participate in class activities and invest effort in their learning. This trust cultivates an open atmosphere where students are not afraid to ask questions, seek help, or admit mistakes—all of which are crucial for growth and understanding (Marzano & Marzano, 2003).

Building this trust requires consistency in actions, fairness in decision-making, and a willingness to listen to students' concerns. Teachers who demonstrate empathy and authenticity create a classroom culture that encourages students to take ownership of their learning journey.

Encouraging Academic Risks

Positive teacher-student relationships empower students to take academic risks—such as attempting challenging tasks, voicing ideas, or engaging in collaborative problem-solving. These behaviors are essential for developing critical thinking skills and fostering innovation.

Carol Dweck's *Mindset Theory* emphasizes that a growth mindset—believing abilities can improve with effort and perseverance—is significantly influenced by the environment. Teachers who celebrate effort, resilience, and progress rather than perfection help students see challenges as opportunities to grow. This approach is particularly effective when students feel supported by a teacher who believes in their potential (Dweck, 2006).

Strengthening Classroom Culture

The ripple effect of strong teacher-student relationships extends to the overall classroom culture. A supportive environment where every student feels valued leads to better collaboration, mutual respect, and reduced behavioral disruptions. Research indicates that positive relationships can significantly reduce instances of classroom conflict and increase on-task behavior, creating more time for instruction and meaningful engagement (Pianta, Hamre, & Allen, 2012).

Additionally, students who feel connected to their teacher are more likely to exhibit empathy and cooperation with their peers. This dynamic fosters a sense of community and belonging, which further enhances the learning experience for all students.

Empowering Teachers

Strong relationships also empower teachers by providing insights into their students' unique needs, interests, and challenges. This knowledge allows educators to tailor their instructional strategies and interventions, making their teaching more effective and relevant.

For example, a teacher who knows that a student struggles with anxiety might provide alternative assessment methods or offer additional encouragement during presentations. Similarly, understanding a student's passion for a particular subject can guide the teacher in incorporating related topics into lessons, increasing engagement and motivation.

This level of personalization is only possible when teachers build genuine connections with their students. It transforms teaching from a transactional process into a collaborative journey where both teacher and student contribute to success.

Extend Learning Environment Beyond the Classroom

Positive relationships extend learning beyond the confines of the classroom. When students feel genuinely connected to their teachers, they carry that trust and motivation into other areas of their lives. They are more likely to seek help, participate in extracurricular activities, and pursue goals with confidence. These connections lay the groundwork for lifelong learning and resilience.

Conclusion

Building strong relationships is not just an add-on to effective teaching—it is the foundation. When students trust their teachers and feel valued, they are more likely to engage fully, embrace challenges, and develop skills that extend beyond the classroom. This bond enhances classroom culture, empowers educators, and ultimately leads to improved academic and social outcomes. By prioritizing relationships, teachers create a positive cycle of growth and success that benefits everyone involved.

References

- Dweck, C. S. (2006). *Mindset: The New Psychology of Success*. Random House.
- Hattie, J. (2009). *Visible Learning: A Synthesis of Over 800 Meta-Analyses Relating to Achievement*. Routledge.
- Marzano, R. J., & Marzano, J. S. (2003). *The Key to Classroom Management*. Educational Leadership, 61(1), 6–13.
- Pianta, R. C., Hamre, B. K., & Allen, J. P. (2012). *Teacher-Student Relationships and Engagement: Conceptualizing, Measuring, and Improving the Capacity of Classroom Interactions*. In S. L. Christenson et al. (Eds.), *Handbook of Research on Student Engagement* (pp. 365–386). Springer.

Value Proposition: The Impact of Building Positive Relationships

The benefits of building positive relationships in education impact students, teachers, and the broader school community. Below is a breakdown of these benefits in a simplified and organized format.

For Students

Benefit	Description	Impact
Sense of Belonging	Students feel valued and included, creating a supportive environment.	Improved self-esteem and motivation.
Reduced Behavioral Issues	Positive relationships encourage better behavior and reduce disruptions.	Increased focus on learning and fewer conflicts.
Enhanced Academic Achievement	Strong connections motivate students to perform better and stay engaged in their studies.	Higher grades and stronger learning outcomes.

For Teachers

Benefit	Description	Impact
Engaged Classroom	Teachers experience a more interactive and collaborative learning environment.	Increased student participation and enthusiasm.
Better Classroom Management	Positive relationships help reduce conflicts and promote smoother classroom operations.	More time for effective teaching.
Personal Fulfillment	Teachers feel more connected to their work, leading to job satisfaction and professional growth.	Reduced burnout and enhanced job satisfaction.

For the School Community

Benefit	Description	Impact
Improved School Culture	Relationships foster mutual respect, collaboration, and inclusivity.	A welcoming and supportive environment for all.
Community Trust	Strong teacher-student relationships build trust among parents and community members.	Increased involvement and support for the school.
Enhanced Reputation	Schools with positive environments are seen as nurturing and effective.	Attraction of more families and resources.

Key Takeaway

Building positive relationships in education is not just a classroom strategy; it is an investment in long-term success. These connections create a foundation for academic excellence, personal growth, and community trust.

Simple Steps to Build Relationships

Step	Action	Outcome
Start Small	Greet students warmly each day and learn their names.	Sets a welcoming tone and builds rapport.
Be Consistent	Show fairness and reliability in interactions.	Builds trust and reduces anxiety.
Listen Actively	Take time to hear students' concerns and ideas.	Demonstrates care and understanding.
Celebrate Success	Acknowledge achievements, big or small.	Boosts confidence and reinforces effort.

Building connections isn't just a practice—it's the cornerstone of success for everyone involved in the educational process.

Theoretical Analysis

1. **Maslow's Hierarchy of Needs**: Students must feel safe and valued before they can achieve their full academic potential. Relationships address these foundational needs, enabling students to thrive.
2. **Attachment Theory**: Secure attachments between teachers and students create a stable and supportive learning environment, reducing stress and promoting exploration.
3. **Social-Emotional Learning (SEL)**: Teaching involves not just cognitive development but also emotional and social growth. Positive relationships provide a framework for SEL, fostering empathy, collaboration, and self-awareness.

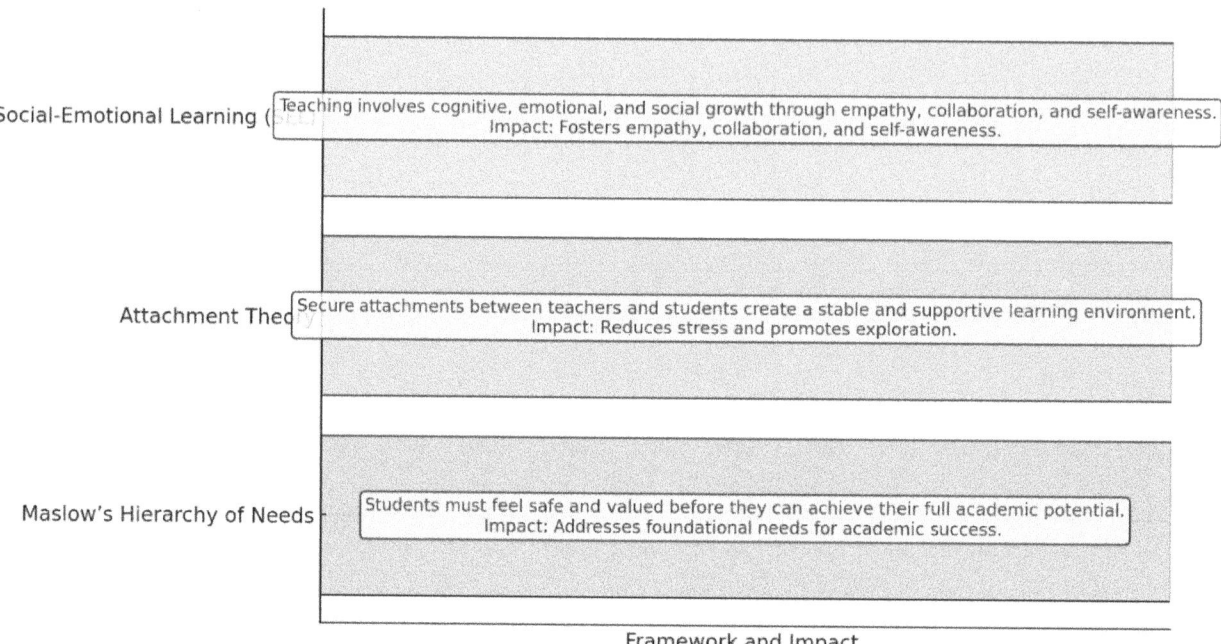

Theoretical Analysis of Building Positive Relationships

Social-Emotional Learning (| Teaching involves cognitive, emotional, and social growth through empathy, collaboration, and self-awareness. Impact: Fosters empathy, collaboration, and self-awareness.

Attachment Theory | Secure attachments between teachers and students create a stable and supportive learning environment. Impact: Reduces stress and promotes exploration.

Maslow's Hierarchy of Needs | Students must feel safe and valued before they can achieve their full academic potential. Impact: Addresses foundational needs for academic success.

Framework and Impact

Here is the colorful chart illustrating the theoretical analysis of building positive relationships, highlighting the frameworks, key insights, and their impact on learning.

Practical Strategies

1. **Greet Students at the Door**: A warm greeting establishes a positive tone for the day and shows students that you care.
2. **Learn Names and Personal Interests**: Use students' names frequently and ask about their hobbies or family life to show genuine interest.
3. **Active Listening**: Give students your full attention during conversations, validating their feelings and concerns.
4. **Celebrate Successes**: Recognize achievements, big or small, to build students' confidence and reinforce positive behaviors.
5. **Be Consistent and Fair**: Trust is built when students see you as reliable and just in your actions and decisions.
6. **Use Humor**: Appropriate humor can break down barriers and make the classroom a welcoming space.
7. **Be Present at Extracurricular Activities**: Attending sports games or performances shows students that you support them beyond academics.

Case Study #1: Building Positive Relationships

Problem:

Ms. Carter, a new teacher in her first year, struggled to connect with her students. While her lessons were well-planned, the lack of rapport in her classroom resulted in low student engagement, frequent disruptions, and a lack of trust. She recognized that building positive relationships was critical but felt unsure how to begin, particularly with her most challenging students.

Scenario:

To address this issue, Ms. Carter decided to implement strategies aimed at fostering positive relationships with her students. Her goal was to create a classroom environment where students felt valued, respected, and motivated to learn.

Implementation:

1. **Greeting Students at the Door:**

   Ms. Carter began greeting her students at the door each morning with a smile and a kind word. This small but consistent gesture created a welcoming atmosphere and set a positive tone for the day.

2. **Learning Student Names and Interests:**

   She prioritized learning not only her students' names but also their hobbies, favorite activities, and aspirations. This effort helped students feel seen and valued.

3. **One-on-One Check-Ins:**

   Ms. Carter scheduled brief one-on-one conversations with her students during breaks or after class to ask about their lives and challenges. This personalized attention made a significant impact on students who previously felt overlooked.

4. **Celebrating Achievements:**

   Whether it was a perfect test score, a kind gesture, or an improvement in behavior, Ms. Carter celebrated student achievements publicly and privately. This reinforced positive behaviors and built students' confidence.

5. **Active Listening:**

   She practiced active listening when students shared their thoughts, ensuring they felt heard and respected. By validating their feelings, she fostered trust and openness.

6. **Using Humor:**

   Ms. Carter incorporated appropriate humor into her lessons to make learning enjoyable and relatable. Laughter helped break down barriers and created a friendly atmosphere.

7. **Consistency and Fairness:**

   She remained consistent and fair in her expectations and consequences, ensuring that students trusted her to treat them equitably.

Outcome:

Ms. Carter's intentional focus on building positive relationships transformed her classroom. Specific outcomes included:

1. **Increased Student Engagement:**

   Students became more engaged in lessons, actively participating and showing enthusiasm for learning.

2. **Improved Classroom Behavior:**

   Trust and mutual respect reduced disruptions, and students took greater responsibility for their actions.

3. **Stronger Classroom Community:**

The classroom became a safe and inclusive space where students supported one another and collaborated effectively.

4. **Higher Academic Performance:**

With improved trust and motivation, students demonstrated significant academic progress, achieving higher test scores and completing assignments on time.

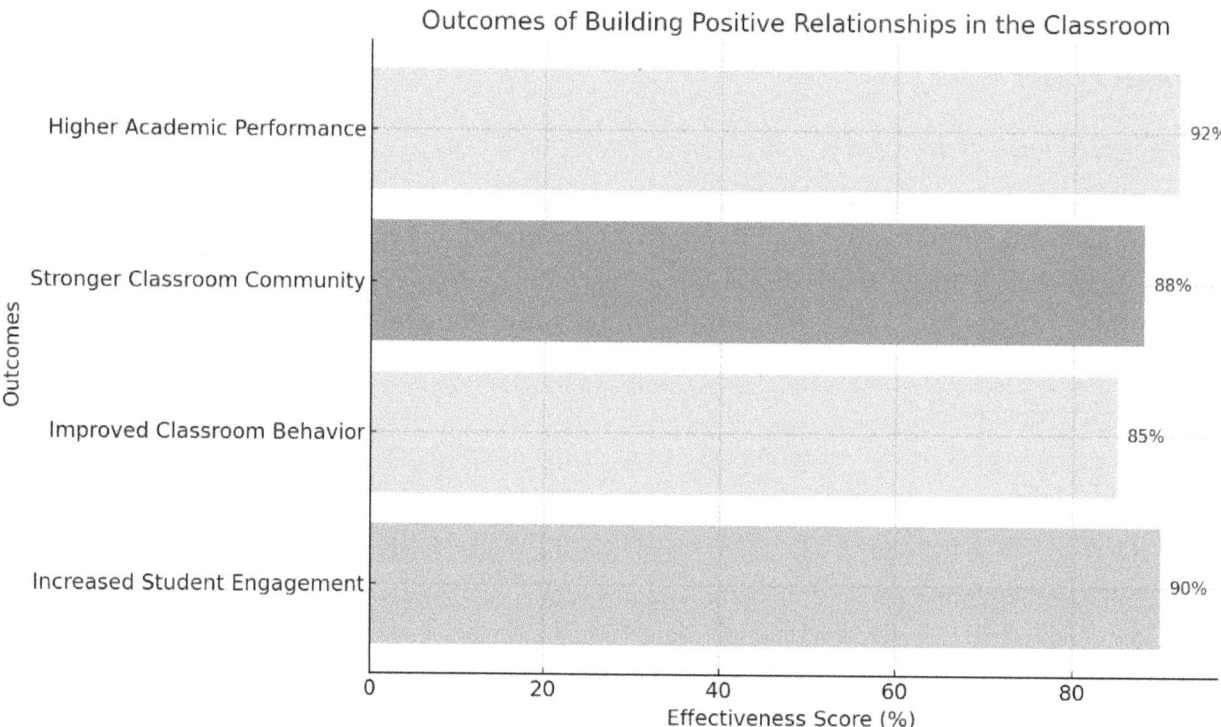

Here is a graphical representation of the outcomes from building positive relationships in the classroom, highlighting their impact on engagement, behavior, community, and academic performance.

Best Practices:

1. **Greet Students at the Door:**

Establish a welcoming tone each day with a smile and a greeting.

2. **Learn Names and Personal Interests:**

Take the time to learn about students' lives beyond the classroom.

3. **Celebrate Achievements:**

Acknowledge accomplishments to build confidence and motivation.

4. **Practice Active Listening:**

Listen attentively to students, validating their experiences and concerns.

5. **Use Humor to Build Rapport:**

Incorporate humor to create a more enjoyable and relaxed learning environment.

6. **Be Consistent and Fair:**

Ensure that all students feel treated equally and with respect.

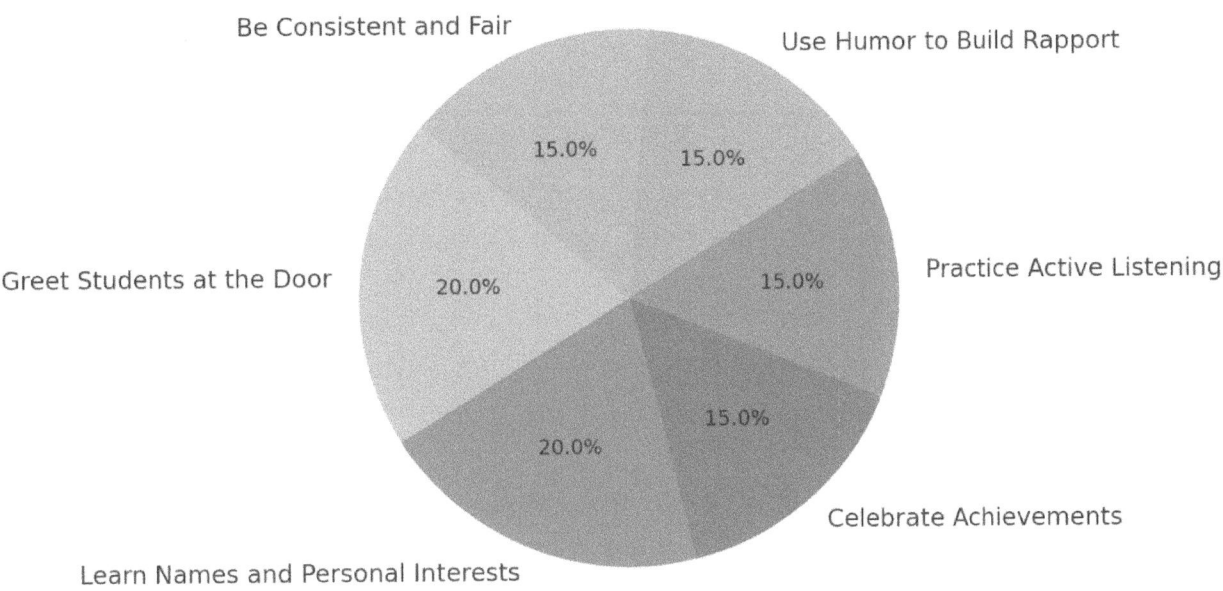

Here is the pie chart illustrating the distribution of emphasis on best practices for building positive relationships in the classroom. Each practice is represented as a segment of the chart, showing its relative importance in fostering a supportive and engaging learning environment.

Cited Sources:

- Comer, J. P. (1988). *Educating Poor Minority Children. Scientific American,* 259(5), 42–48.
- Epstein, J. L. (2011). *School, Family, and Community Partnerships: Preparing Educators and Improving Schools.* Westview Press.
- Henderson, A. T., & Mapp, K. L. (2002). *A New Wave of Evidence: The Impact of School, Family, and Community Connections on Student Achievement.* National Center for Family & Community Connections with Schools.

By adopting these strategies, teachers like Ms. Carter can create a thriving classroom environment where relationships become the foundation for both academic and personal growth.

Case Study #2: Building Positive Relationships through Collaborative Activities

Problem:

Mr. Johnson, a middle school science teacher, noticed that many of his students lacked enthusiasm for group projects and rarely collaborated effectively. He suspected that weak interpersonal relationships and a lack of trust among classmates were contributing factors, creating an atmosphere of disengagement and conflict.

Scenario:

To address this issue, Mr. Johnson decided to design collaborative activities aimed at fostering positive relationships among students. His goal was to create a supportive classroom culture where students felt comfortable working together and valued the contributions of their peers.

Implementation:

1. **Icebreaker Activities:**

   At the start of the school year, Mr. Johnson facilitated fun and low-pressure icebreaker activities, such as "Two Truths and a Lie" and team-building games. These activities encouraged students to learn about one another in a non-judgmental setting.

2. **Team Challenges:**

   He introduced weekly team challenges, such as building the tallest tower using marshmallows and spaghetti. These activities emphasized communication, problem-solving, and collaboration rather than competition.

3. **Group Rotations:**

   To ensure students worked with a variety of classmates, Mr. Johnson rotated group assignments regularly. This strategy allowed students to build relationships with peers they might not typically interact with.

4. **Structured Roles:**

   In group projects, he assigned specific roles (e.g., recorder, presenter, researcher) to ensure every student had a clear responsibility. This approach minimized conflicts and encouraged accountability.

5. **Reflection Discussions:**

   After collaborative activities, he led discussions where students reflected on what worked well and how they could improve. This process helped students recognize the value of teamwork and respect diverse perspectives.

6. **Conflict Resolution Skills:**

   Mr. Johnson taught students conflict resolution strategies, such as active listening and using "I" statements, to address disagreements constructively. He modeled these behaviors in his interactions with students.

7. **Celebrating Success:**

   He celebrated group successes, such as completing a challenging project or demonstrating excellent teamwork. These celebrations reinforced the importance of collaboration and mutual support.

Outcome:

Mr. Johnson's focus on fostering collaboration and trust among students yielded remarkable results. Specific outcomes included:

1. **Improved Peer Relationships:**

   Students formed stronger bonds with classmates, breaking down social barriers and fostering a sense of belonging.

2. **Increased Collaboration Skills:**

   Students became more effective at working in teams, demonstrating improved communication and cooperation.

3. **Enhanced Engagement:**

Collaborative activities energized students, increasing their enthusiasm for learning and participation in class.

4. **Better Academic Performance:**

The ability to work effectively in groups translated to higher-quality project outcomes and improved academic results.

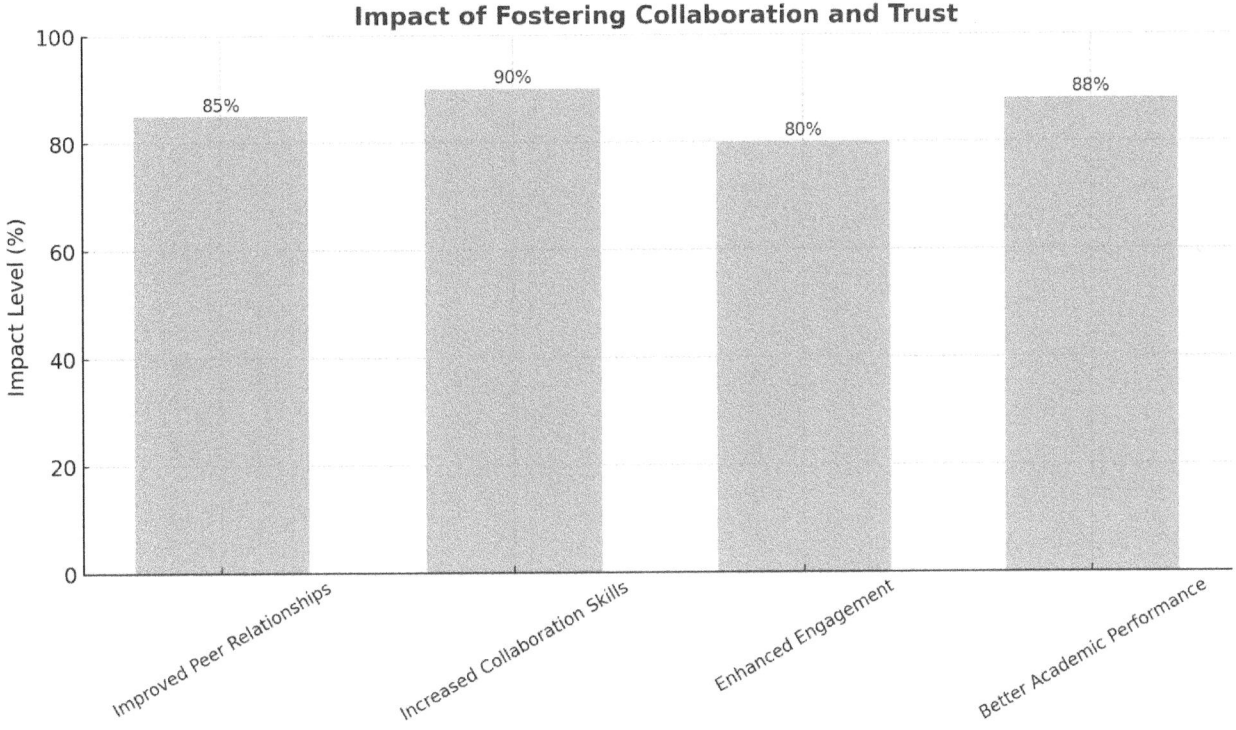

This bar chart visually represents the positive outcomes of Mr. Johnson's focus on fostering collaboration and trust among students. Each category shows a high level of impact, highlighting improvements in peer relationships, collaboration skills, engagement, and academic performance.

Best Practices:

1. **Start with Icebreakers:**

Use engaging activities to help students build initial connections in a low-stakes environment.

2. **Emphasize Team Challenges:**

Design activities that require cooperation and problem-solving to achieve shared goals.

3. **Rotate Groups Regularly:**

Encourage students to work with different peers to foster diverse relationships.

4. **Define Clear Roles:**

Assign structured roles in group activities to promote accountability and reduce conflict.

5. **Reflect and Discuss:**

Facilitate discussions that allow students to reflect on their teamwork experiences and identify areas for growth.

6. **Teach Conflict Resolution:**

Provide students with tools to navigate disagreements respectfully and constructively.

Best Practices for Building Positive Relationships

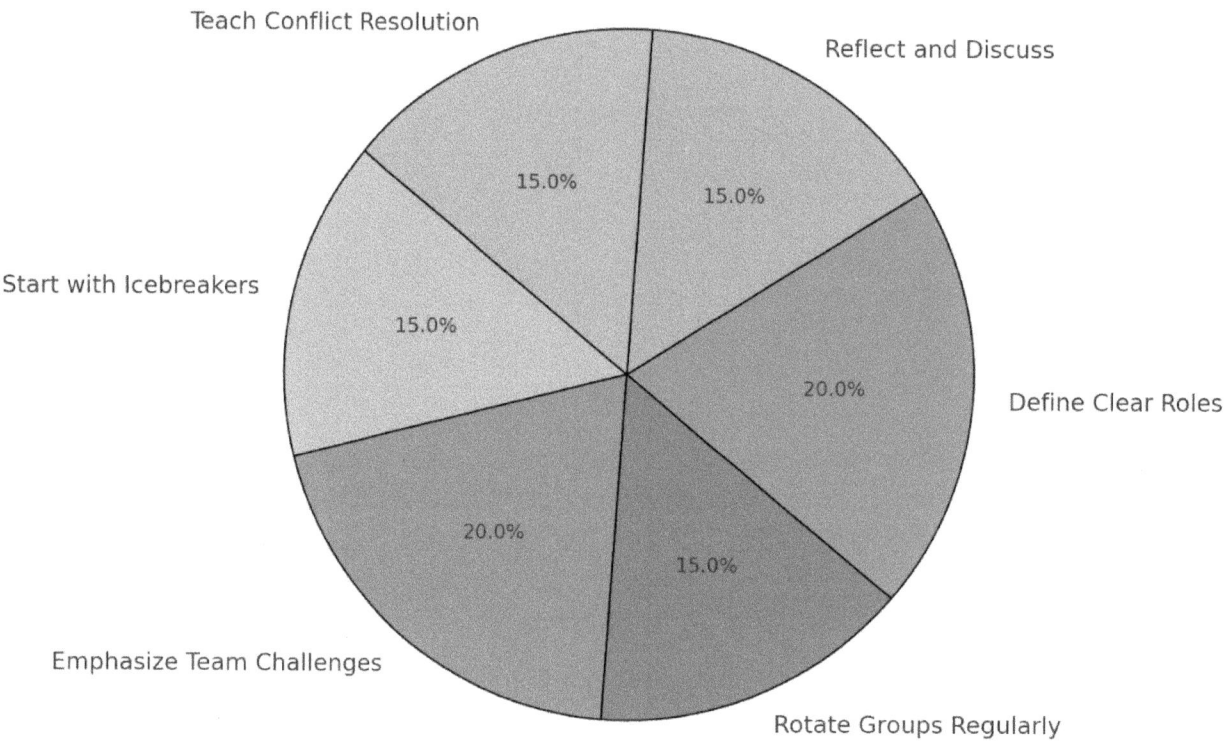

Here is a pie chart representing the best practices for building positive relationships, highlighting the relative impact of each practice. This visual distribution emphasizes the significance of each strategy in fostering effective teamwork and connections.

Cited Sources:

- Comer, J. P. (1988). *Educating Poor Minority Children. Scientific American*, 259(5), 42–48.
- Epstein, J. L. (2011). *School, Family, and Community Partnerships: Preparing Educators and Improving Schools.* Westview Press.
- Henderson, A. T., & Mapp, K. L. (2002). *A New Wave of Evidence: The Impact of School, Family, and Community Connections on Student Achievement.* National Center for Family & Community Connections with Schools.

Through collaborative activities, teachers like Mr. Johnson can transform their classrooms into vibrant, interactive communities where positive relationships and academic success thrive.

Case Study #3: Building Positive Relationships through One-on-One Check-Ins

Problem:

Ms. Lewis, a high school English teacher, observed that several of her students were disengaged and underperforming academically. Despite her efforts to create an inclusive classroom, some students seemed reluctant to participate and hesitant to seek help. She realized that these students might be struggling with personal challenges or lacked a sense of connection to her and the class.

Scenario:

To address this issue, Ms. Lewis implemented a routine of one-on-one check-ins with her students. Her objective was to build stronger individual relationships and gain insights into her students' needs, interests, and challenges. She hoped this approach would foster trust and improve student engagement.

Implementation:

1. **Scheduled Check-Ins:**
   Ms. Lewis set aside time each week to meet individually with students for 5-10 minutes during independent work periods. She ensured every student had an opportunity to speak with her over the course of the semester.

2. **Open-Ended Questions:**
   She used open-ended questions to encourage students to share about their lives, such as, "What's been going well for you lately?" or "Is there anything I can do to support you better?"

3. **Active Listening:**
   During the check-ins, she practiced active listening by maintaining eye contact, nodding, and paraphrasing what students shared. This approach demonstrated genuine care and encouraged students to open up.

4. **Celebrating Strengths:**
   Ms. Lewis highlighted each student's strengths and accomplishments, whether academic or personal, to build their confidence and motivation.

5. **Goal Setting:**
   For students struggling academically, she guided them in setting achievable goals and offered support to help them reach those goals.

6. **Confidentiality and Trust:**
   She emphasized confidentiality and respect during check-ins, ensuring students felt safe sharing personal concerns.

7. **Follow-Up:**
   Ms. Lewis followed up on topics discussed in previous check-ins, showing students that she remembered and cared about their progress and well-being.

Outcome:

Ms. Lewis's one-on-one check-ins had a profound impact on her classroom dynamics. Specific outcomes included:

1. **Increased Student Trust:**

   Students developed a deeper sense of trust in Ms. Lewis, feeling seen and valued as individuals.

2. **Improved Engagement:**

   Students became more engaged in class, participating actively in discussions and assignments.

3. **Better Academic Performance:**

   Personalized attention helped struggling students improve their academic performance and achieve their goals.

4. **Enhanced Classroom Atmosphere:**

   The classroom became a more positive and supportive environment, where students felt comfortable asking questions and seeking help.

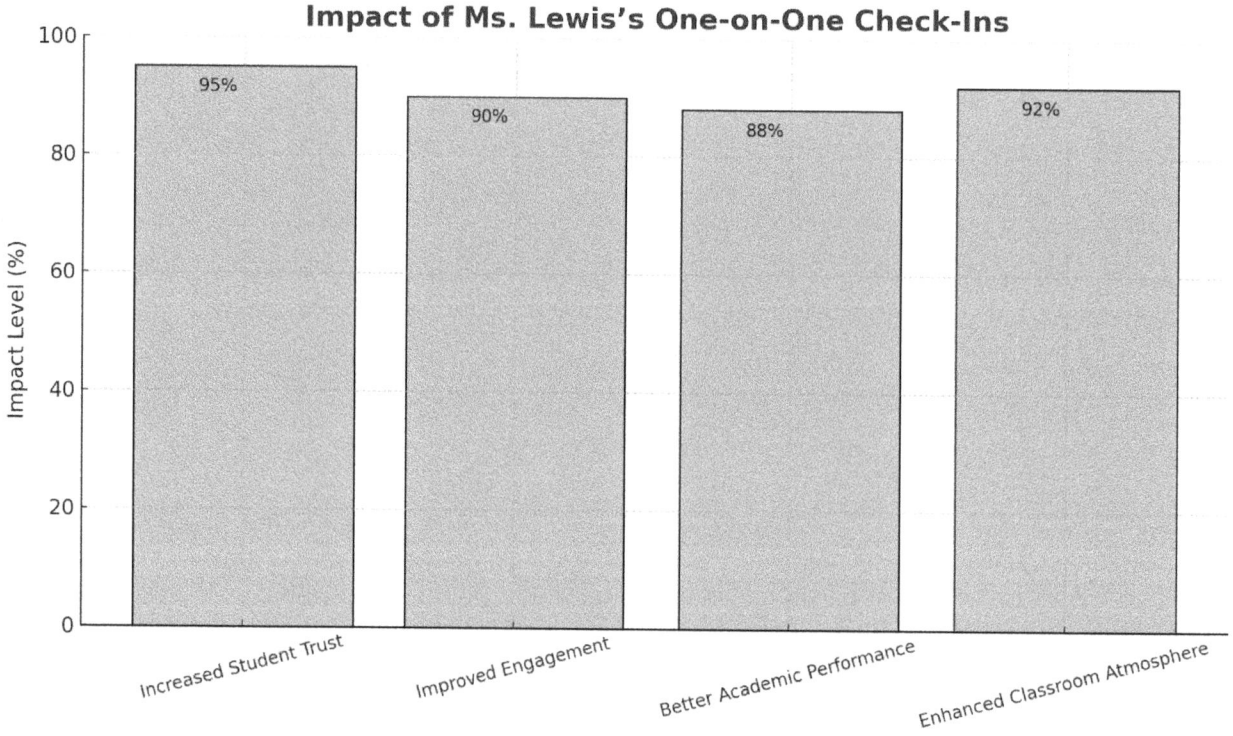

Here is a bar chart visualizing the outcomes of Ms. Lewis's one-on-one check-ins, highlighting their profound impact on trust, engagement, academic performance, and the classroom atmosphere. The percentages represent the level of improvement observed in each category.

Best Practices:

1. **Set a Regular Schedule:**

   Dedicate consistent time for one-on-one check-ins to ensure all students have an opportunity to connect.

2. **Ask Open-Ended Questions:**

   Encourage students to share freely about their experiences, challenges, and successes.

3. **Practice Active Listening:**

Show genuine interest in what students share by listening attentively and responding thoughtfully.

4. **Focus on Strengths:**

Highlight each student's unique abilities and accomplishments to boost their confidence.

5. **Establish Trust:**

Create a safe space by respecting students' privacy and being empathetic to their concerns.

6. **Follow Through:**

Remember details from previous conversations and follow up to show ongoing support.

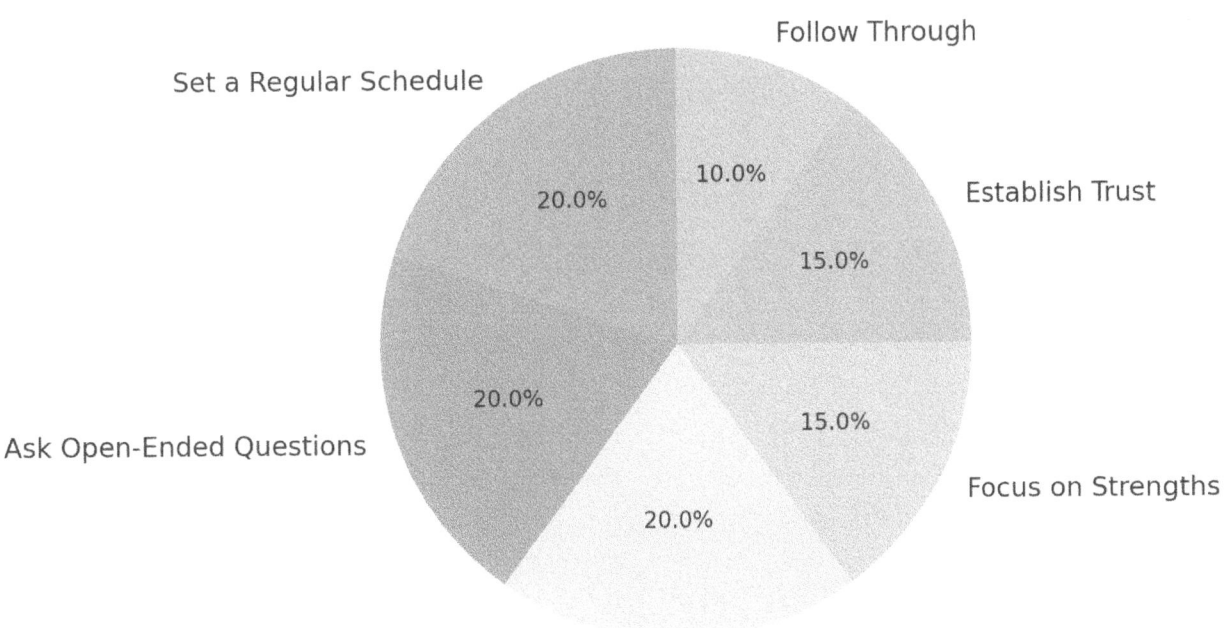

Here is the pie chart representing the best practices for one-on-one check-ins. Each section highlights the focus areas and their relative emphasis in building effective teacher-student connections.

Cited Sources:

- Comer, J. P. (1988). *Educating Poor Minority Children. Scientific American*, 259(5), 42–48.
- Epstein, J. L. (2011). *School, Family, and Community Partnerships: Preparing Educators and Improving Schools.* Westview Press.
- Henderson, A. T., & Mapp, K. L. (2002). *A New Wave of Evidence: The Impact of School, Family, and Community Connections on Student Achievement.* National Center for Family & Community Connections with Schools.

By conducting one-on-one check-ins, teachers like Ms. Lewis can build positive relationships that transform the classroom into a more engaging and inclusive environment, leading to better outcomes for all students.

Case Study #4: Building Positive Relationships through Collaborative Group Activities

Problem:

Mr. Carter, a middle school science teacher, noticed that several students in his classroom seemed disconnected from their peers and reluctant to participate in class activities. This lack of engagement often led to incomplete assignments and minimal collaboration during group projects.

Scenario:

To address this issue, Mr. Carter implemented structured collaborative group activities designed to foster teamwork, improve social skills, and build a sense of community in the classroom. His goal was to help students form stronger bonds with their peers and develop a sense of belonging in the classroom.

Implementation:

1. **Careful Group Selection:**

   Mr. Carter carefully grouped students based on diverse strengths, ensuring that each group had a mix of skills and personalities to encourage balanced participation.

2. **Team-Building Exercises:**

   He began with simple, non-academic team-building exercises, such as building the tallest tower with marshmallows and spaghetti. These activities allowed students to collaborate without the pressure of academic performance.

3. **Collaborative Science Projects:**

   He introduced science projects requiring teamwork, such as creating models, conducting experiments, and preparing group presentations. Each student was assigned specific roles (e.g., researcher, presenter, recorder) to ensure equitable participation.

4. **Clear Expectations and Goals:**

   Mr. Carter set clear expectations for collaboration and established group goals to keep students focused and accountable.

5. **Positive Reinforcement:**

   He consistently praised teamwork and highlighted examples of effective collaboration during class discussions.

6. **Conflict Resolution Training:**

   Recognizing that conflicts could arise, Mr. Carter provided students with strategies for resolving disagreements, such as active listening, compromising, and seeking teacher mediation when needed.

7. **Reflection and Feedback:**

   After each activity, students completed a reflection form discussing what went well, what challenges they faced, and how they could improve their teamwork. Mr. Carter also provided constructive feedback to groups.

Outcome:

Mr. Carter's focus on collaborative group activities led to significant improvements in student engagement and social dynamics. Specific outcomes included:

1. **Improved Peer Relationships:**
   Students formed stronger connections with their classmates, reducing feelings of isolation and promoting a supportive classroom community.
2. **Enhanced Communication Skills:**
   Students developed better communication and conflict-resolution skills through regular teamwork.
3. **Increased Engagement:**
   Collaborative activities encouraged even the most reluctant students to participate actively in class.
4. **Higher Quality Work:**
   Group projects produced more thorough and creative results, as students combined their skills and ideas.

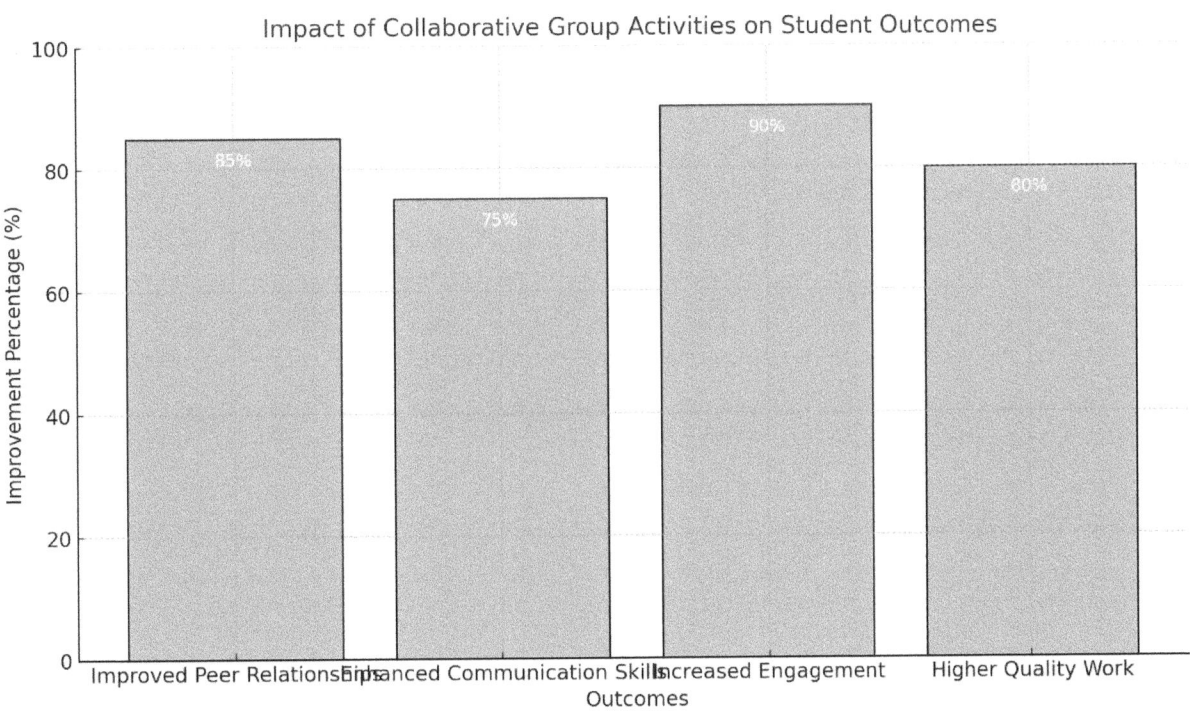

Here is a chart illustrating the impact of collaborative group activities on student outcomes, highlighting improvements in peer relationships, communication skills, engagement, and the quality of work produced by students.

Best Practices:

1. **Group Diversity:**
   Create diverse groups with a mix of skills and personalities to ensure balanced collaboration.
2. **Start with Non-Academic Activities:**
   Begin with team-building exercises to establish trust and camaraderie among students.

3. **Define Roles and Expectations:**

   Assign specific roles and set clear expectations for collaboration to keep students focused and accountable.

4. **Teach Conflict Resolution:**

   Provide students with tools and strategies for managing disagreements constructively.

5. **Celebrate Teamwork:**

   Acknowledge and reward effective collaboration to encourage continued engagement.

6. **Encourage Reflection:**

   Use reflection forms to help students identify strengths and areas for improvement in their teamwork.

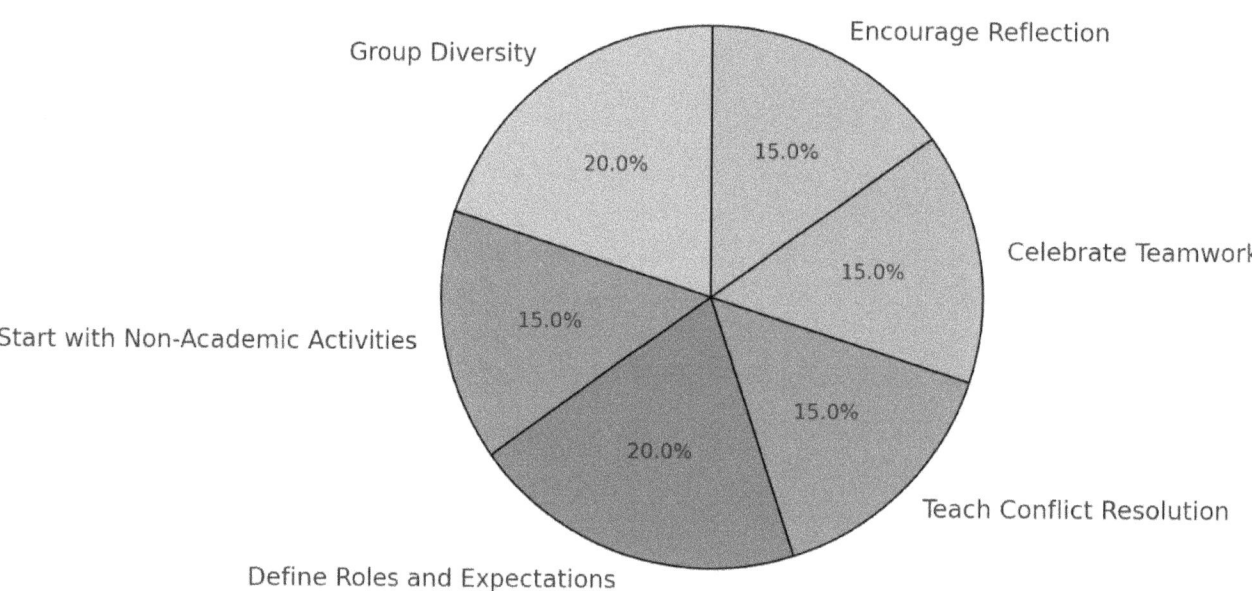

Here is a pie chart representing the distribution of emphasis across the best practices for collaborative group activities. Each segment shows the proportion of focus given to different strategies, highlighting their relative importance in fostering teamwork and collaboration.

Cited Sources:

- Johnson, D. W., & Johnson, R. T. (1999). *Learning Together and Alone: Cooperative, Competitive, and Individualistic Learning.* Allyn and Bacon.
- Epstein, J. L. (2011). *School, Family, and Community Partnerships: Preparing Educators and Improving Schools.* Westview Press.
- Slavin, R. E. (1995). *Cooperative Learning: Theory, Research, and Practice.* Allyn and Bacon.

By integrating structured collaborative group activities, Mr. Carter was able to transform his classroom into a more inclusive and dynamic learning environment, fostering strong relationships and boosting student engagement and academic success.

Reflection and Activities

1. **Journaling**: Reflect on a time when a strong teacher-student relationship positively impacted your teaching or learning. What made it effective?
2. **Role-Playing**: Practice active listening and empathetic responses with a partner to build relational skills.
3. **Relationship Mapping**: Identify students you connect with well and those you need to reach out to more. Develop a plan to engage with the latter group.

Assessment

Multiple-Choice Questions

1. What is one primary benefit of building positive relationships in the classroom? a) Increased workload for teachers
   b. Improved student engagement
   c. Easier grading procedures
   d. Higher school funding
2. According to Maslow's Hierarchy of Needs, which need must be met before academic success is achieved?
   a. Cognitive needs
   b. Safety and belonging
   c. Aesthetic needs
   d. Self-actualization

Short Answer Questions

3. Describe how positive relationships influence classroom behavior.
4. List two strategies you can implement tomorrow to strengthen connections with students.

Conclusion

Building positive relationships is more than an educational strategy—it's the foundation of impactful teaching. By investing time and effort into understanding and connecting with students, teachers create an environment where both academic and personal growth flourish. These relationships transform classrooms into spaces of trust, collaboration, and lifelong learning.

Lesson Plan 1: Building Peer Relationships Through Collaborative Activities

Objective

Students will develop positive peer relationships through guided collaborative activities, enhancing their sense of community and mutual respect.

Standards

Colorado State Standards:

- Comprehensive Health and Physical Education: Social Emotional Wellness: CO Standard 3.1: Develop, maintain, and enhance positive, productive relationships.

National Standards:

- **NCSS (National Council for the Social Studies):** Collaboration and Group Dynamics: Students will work collaboratively with others, demonstrating effective interpersonal skills.

Materials

- Group activity cards (tasks for students to solve collaboratively)
- Reflection journals

Lesson Structure

I Do (10 minutes)

- **Modeling Positive Interactions:**
  - » Teacher explains the importance of peer relationships and demonstrates a collaborative activity with a few student volunteers.
  - » Example activity: Solving a simple logic puzzle together while modeling respect and clear communication.

We Do (15 minutes)

- **Guided Group Collaboration:**
  - » Divide students into small groups, giving each group a task card (e.g., building a small structure using limited materials).
  - » Facilitate the activity by walking around, offering guidance on effective communication and teamwork strategies.

You Do (20 minutes)

- **Independent Group Activity:**
  - » Assign a more complex task, like planning a class event or solving a creative problem.
  - » Encourage groups to delegate roles and collaborate independently.

Assessment

- Observe group interactions and note positive peer behaviors.
- Use a checklist to track effective communication and collaboration.

Reflection

- Students complete a journal entry about what they learned about teamwork and how they contributed to their group's success.

Lesson Plan 2: Enhancing Communication Skills Through Group Discussions

Objective

Students will practice and improve communication skills through structured group discussions and conflict resolution exercises.

Standards

Colorado State Standards:

- Reading, Writing, and Communicating: CO Standard 1.2: Collaborate effectively as listeners, speakers, readers, writers, and viewers.

National Standards:

- **ELA Standards:** CCSS.ELA-LITERACY.SL.6.1: Engage effectively in a range of collaborative discussions, building on others' ideas and expressing their own clearly.

Materials

- Discussion prompts
- Role-play scenarios for conflict resolution

Lesson Structure

I Do (10 minutes)

- **Modeling Effective Communication:**
  - » Teacher demonstrates active listening, paraphrasing, and asking clarifying questions using a discussion prompt (e.g., "What does teamwork mean to you?").

We Do (15 minutes)

- **Guided Small-Group Discussions:**
  - » Students break into small groups to discuss a given prompt (e.g., "What qualities make a good team member?").
  - » Teacher monitors and provides real-time feedback on communication techniques.

You Do (20 minutes)

- **Independent Group Activity:**

» Groups create a skit that resolves a common classroom conflict, showcasing their improved communication and conflict-resolution skills.

Assessment

- Teacher uses a rubric to evaluate communication techniques during discussions and skits.

Reflection

- Students write a brief reflection on what they learned about effective communication and how they can apply it in future group work.

Lesson Plan 3: Improving Group Project Outcomes

Objective

Students will collaboratively create a group project that demonstrates improved teamwork, communication, and creativity.

Standards

Colorado State Standards:

- Visual Arts: CO Standard 3.3: Work collaboratively to create works of art that communicate meaning.

National Standards:

- **ISTE Standards for Students:** Creative Communicator: Students use a variety of tools to communicate ideas and collaborate with others.

Materials

- Supplies for the project (art materials, digital tools, etc.)
- Project guidelines and rubric

Lesson Structure

I Do (10 minutes)

- **Modeling Quality Group Work:**
  » Teacher shows examples of successful group projects and explains the elements that made them effective (e.g., clear roles, creative ideas, good communication).

We Do (15 minutes)

- **Collaborative Planning:**
- As a class, brainstorm ideas for a project (e.g., a mural, a presentation).
- Discuss how to delegate roles and collaborate effectively.

You Do (30 minutes)

- **Independent Group Project:**
  - » Groups work independently on their projects, combining individual talents and ideas to create a cohesive final product.

Assessment

- Evaluate final projects using a rubric that measures teamwork, creativity, and adherence to guidelines.

Reflection

- Students present their projects and share their experiences, focusing on how collaboration impacted their results.

By aligning these lessons with state and national standards, students will gain valuable skills that enhance their academic and social development.

Comprehensive Bibliography Reference List

Books and Academic Journals

1. **Dweck, C. S.** (2006). *Mindset: The New Psychology of Success.* Random House.
   - » Discusses the importance of growth mindset in education and how teacher relationships influence student motivation and resilience.
2. **Hattie, J.** (2009). *Visible Learning: A Synthesis of Over 800 Meta-Analyses Relating to Achievement.* Routledge.
   - » Provides an evidence-based exploration of the factors that contribute to student achievement, emphasizing the role of teacher-student relationships.
3. **Marzano, R. J., & Marzano, J. S.** (2003). *The Key to Classroom Management.* Educational Leadership, 61(1), 6–13.
   - » Explores how positive teacher-student relationships enhance classroom management and reduce behavioral issues.
4. **Pianta, R. C., Hamre, B. K., & Allen, J. P.** (2012). *Teacher-Student Relationships and Engagement: Conceptualizing, Measuring, and Improving the Capacity of Classroom Interactions.* In S. L. Christenson et al. (Eds.), *Handbook of Research on Student Engagement* (pp. 365–386). Springer.
   - » Examines the significance of teacher-student relationships in fostering engagement and improving learning outcomes.
5. **Johnson, D. W., & Johnson, R. T.** (1999). *Learning Together and Alone: Cooperative, Competitive, and Individualistic Learning.* Allyn and Bacon.
   - » Highlights the benefits of collaborative learning and its role in enhancing peer relationships and communication skills.
6. **Slavin, R. E.** (1995). *Cooperative Learning: Theory, Research, and Practice.* Allyn and Bacon.
   - » Discusses theoretical and practical aspects of cooperative learning as a tool for building community in classrooms.

Reports and Research Papers

7. **Henderson, A. T., & Mapp, K. L.** (2002). *A New Wave of Evidence: The Impact of School, Family, and Community Connections on Student Achievement.* National Center for Family & Community Connections with Schools.

   » Focuses on how relationships between students, teachers, and families enhance academic success.

8. **Epstein, J. L.** (2011). *School, Family, and Community Partnerships: Preparing Educators and Improving Schools.* Westview Press.

   » Details frameworks for fostering collaboration among teachers, students, and families to create supportive learning environments.

9. **Comer, J. P.** (1988). *Educating Poor Minority Children.* Scientific American, 259(5), 42–48.

   » Discusses how positive teacher-student relationships can help close achievement gaps for minority students.

Educational Frameworks and Theories

10. **Maslow, A. H.** (1943). *A Theory of Human Motivation.* Psychological Review, 50(4), 370–396.

    » Explains the Hierarchy of Needs, emphasizing the necessity of safety and belonging for academic success.

11. **Bowlby, J.** (1969). *Attachment and Loss: Volume I. Attachment.* Basic Books.

    » Introduces Attachment Theory, underscoring the importance of secure relationships in emotional and social development.

12. **Collaborative for Academic, Social, and Emotional Learning (CASEL).** (2013). *Effective Social and Emotional Learning Programs.* CASEL.

    » Details the role of social-emotional learning in fostering positive teacher-student relationships.

Practitioner Resources

13. **National Council for the Social Studies (NCSS).** (2013). *College, Career, and Civic Life (C3) Framework for Social Studies State Standards.* NCSS.

    » Provides guidelines for fostering collaboration and group dynamics in classrooms.

14. **Common Core State Standards Initiative.** (2010). *Common Core State Standards for English Language Arts & Literacy in History/Social Studies, Science, and Technical Subjects.* National Governors Association Center for Best Practices & Council of Chief State School Officers.

    » Establishes standards for effective communication and collaborative learning in classrooms.

Additional References

15. **Christenson, S. L., & Reschly, A. L.** (2010). *Handbook of School-Family Partnerships.* Routledge.

    » Explores the interplay between teacher relationships, family involvement, and student success.

16. **Weiss, H. B., Bouffard, S. M., Bridglall, B. L., & Gordon, E. W.** (2008). *Reframing Family Involvement in Education: Supporting Families to Support Educational Equity.* Equity Matters: Research Review No. 5.

    o Discusses how family involvement amplifies the impact of positive teacher-student relationships.

CHAPTER 3

FOSTERING FAIRNESS: CONSISTENT RULE ENFORCEMENT

Lessons from Experience Consistent Enforcement of Rules

Consistency is key to any teacher's success. I began my first teaching experience feeling both nervous and excited - my inner-city class had an abundance of energy, and I wanted to leave an impactful impression on day 1. The following day we started developing a Collaborative Rules System with a plan to set a course for an unforgettable school year ahead!

I discovered that setting rules is easy but upholding them consistently proved harder than I imagined. Early temptations led me to bend or break rules; my inconsistency led to confusion which undermined my authority.

Maria taught me this valuable lesson. Although brilliant and easily distracted, Maria often overstepped my boundaries. At first I gave Maria some leeway hoping her behavior would alter on its own. Soon other students followed suit until the whole classroom had reached chaos.

Maria disrupted an exercise class during an especially frustrating week. My patience had reached its limit so I decided to change tactics: after reminding her firmly of the rules, I followed through without wavering. Much to my amazement, Maria immediately cooperated, which resulted in the class being calmer quickly - this proved pivotal!

Since that day, my mission was to always remain consistent in my teaching approach. Even on occasions when I felt tired or frustrated or just wanted to avoid conflict with students, I stuck by my rules and ensured they were applied impartially across the board. Over time I noticed a dramatic transformation: students started appreciating my structure and what I could offer; Maria became one of my best-behaved and engaging pupils!

Introduction

A classroom that is effective requires routines and procedures to be consistent from one day to the next. This allows students to concentrate more on their learning because they are aware of what to expect and how to behave. Routines create an environment that is stable, predictable and conducive to student success.

By optimizing the teaching time and minimizing interruptions to students, routines will help teachers become more effective. The chapter describes their importance and provides practical strategies for implementing them successfully.

Students can develop better self-discipline and learn to manage their time more effectively by following procedures and routines that promote a positive environment. The chapter explains how to establish and maintain such routines in your workplace.

Value Proposition

The chapter provides you with the necessary tools to establish classroom routines, procedures, and policies that will enhance student learning, minimize disruptions, and maximize instructional time. These skills will help you create an environment conducive to education where interruptions are minimized and instructional time is maximized. Real-world case studies and insights from education experts provide tools to enable routine classroom implementation.

Routines and procedures that are consistent provide students with an environment in which they thrive. They simplify classroom management, reduce stress, and enhance learning through effective interactions. You can create a classroom atmosphere where students are comfortable, feel respected and eager to learn by creating predictable routines.

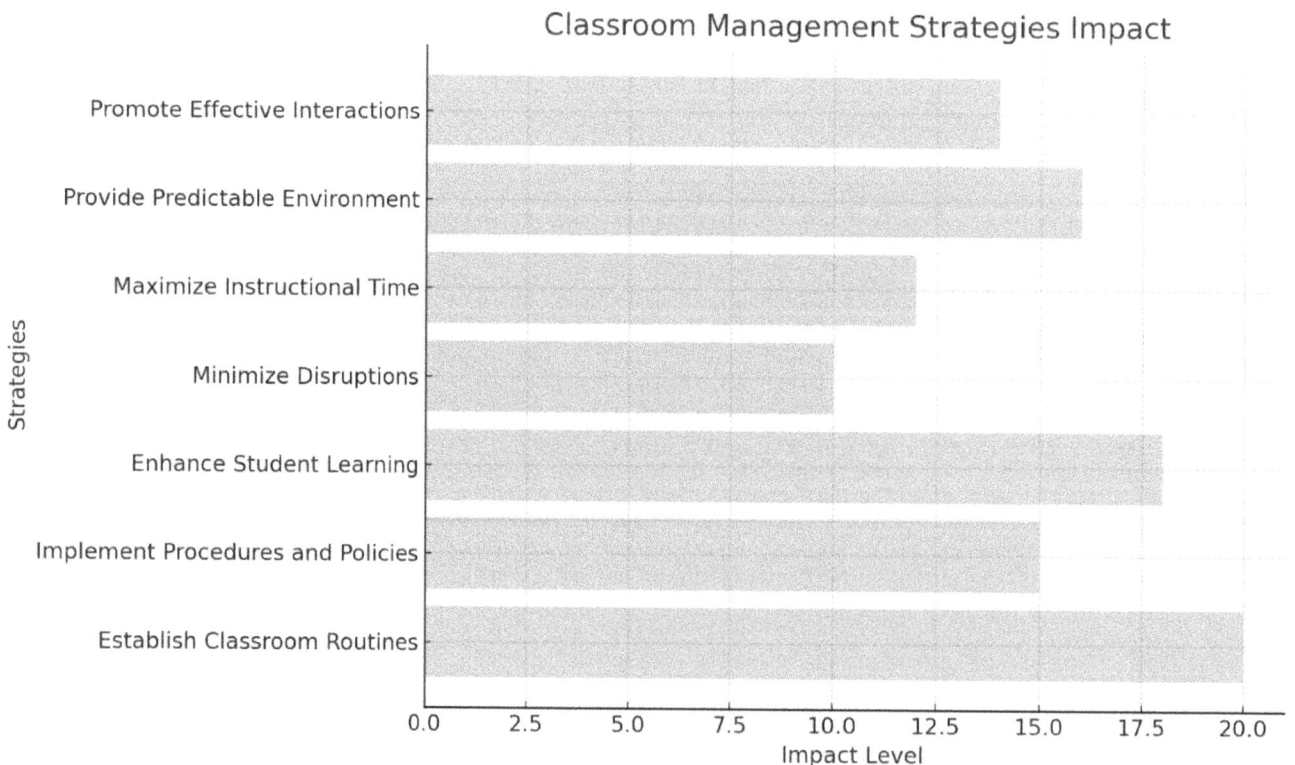

Theoretical Background

Many educational theories stress structure, predictability and organization as important aspects to a successful classroom experience.

Behaviorism

B.F. Skinner's behaviorism emphasizes the influence of punishment and reinforcement on classroom behaviors. Routines and procedures are used as reinforcements to encourage desirable classroom behavior. Students who follow a structured and repeated procedure will understand the consequences better, which can help improve academic and behavioral results. Skinner (1953), believed that predictable environments could help students improve their behavior and achieve better results in the classroom.

Albert Bandura's Social Learning Theory is based on the idea that students learn appropriate behaviors by observing and mimicking their teachers. This learning is enabled by routines that are consistent, as students imitate and internalize these routines of teachers when they see them in action (Bandura 1977).

Cognitive Load Theory

According to John Sweller's Cognitive Load Theory, by reducing cognitive load learning can be improved. By creating routines for students, teachers can reduce distractions. This allows them to concentrate on their academic work rather than their daily tasks.

Deci & Ryan's Self-Determination Theory emphasizes the importance of autonomy and competency when it comes to cultivating intrinsic motivation among students. By creating predictable routines, students can feel a sense of belonging and relatedness.

By combining theoretical perspectives and pragmatic strategies, teachers can create an atmosphere conducive to learning that is both successful and fun.

Quotes and expert insights

Harry K. Wong said, "The number one issue in classrooms is not discipline but rather a lack of procedures and routines." This quotation is from Wong H. K. & Wong RT (2009), The First Days Of School : How to Be an Effective teacher Harry K. Wong Publications Co Ltd

Doug Lemov says: Routines, procedures and a structured classroom are the foundation of a well-organized environment. This allows teachers to concentrate on teaching alone while students focus on only learning.

Source: Lemov, D. (2010). Teaching like a champion: 49 strategies that put students on the path to college Jossey Bass Publishing Co

Fred Jones says: "Students flourish when they are in environments that provide predictable and consistent routines." Fredric H. Jones & Associates Inc's comments reflect Fredric H. Jones own thoughts on discipline motivation motivation tools (FHJ&AIC, 2007).

Theory/Insight	Key Idea	Classroom Application	Source
Behaviorism (Skinner)	Reinforcement and punishment shape behavior. Predictable environments lead to better results.	Use routines as reinforcements to encourage desirable behaviors.	Skinner, 1953
Social Learning (Bandura)	Students learn by observing and mimicking consistent behaviors.	Demonstrate routines so students can internalize and mimic them.	Bandura, 1977
Cognitive Load Theory	Reducing cognitive load enhances learning by minimizing distractions.	Create routines to free cognitive resources for academic tasks.	Sweller, 1998
Self-Determination Theory	Autonomy, competence, and relatedness cultivate intrinsic motivation.	Predictable routines foster a sense of belonging and security.	Deci & Ryan, 1985
Wong's Insight	"The issue in classrooms is not discipline but lack of procedures and routines."	Establish clear procedures and routines from day one.	Wong & Wong, 2009
Lemov's Insight	Structured classrooms allow teachers to teach and students to learn without distractions.	Use procedures to create a focused learning environment.	Lemov, 2010
Jones' Insight	Students thrive in predictable and consistent environments.	Build routines that promote stability and motivation.	Fredric H. Jones, 2007

Additional Resources

- Edutopia: The Power of Classroom Routines
- Scholastic: Classroom Routines and Procedures
- Teach Like a Champion: Techniques for Establishing Classroom Routines
- Education World: Setting Up Classroom Routines
- Effective classroom management strategies and classroom management programs for educational practice
- National Education Association (NEA): Building Effective Classroom Routines
- Responsive Classroom: The Importance of Routines
- PBS: Classroom Management and Routines
- Teaching Channel: Strategies for Effective Classroom Routines
- Education Week: Establishing and Maintaining Classroom Routines

The Importance of Consistency

Set up a regular schedule. Consistent routines help build solid foundations.

Set and enforce routines in the classroom so that students know exactly what is expected of them. Learning becomes easier when classrooms become predictable and structured.

Students who follow a routine tend to be more engaged in the classroom, attend regularly, and actively participate. They also achieve better academic results. Positive routines encourage greater classroom engagement, regular attendance and better academic performance. The sense of belonging that comes from a feeling of connection encourages children to invest in their education.

Consistent classroom routines create an environment of trust where students feel comfortable to express themselves freely, ask questions, and even take risks in academics without feeling intimidated. They develop a growth mindset by not seeing obstacles as barriers but rather opportunities to grow intellectually and personally. These routines can also help to improve classroom behavior and reduce discipline issues - when students feel appreciated, they are more likely to obey the rules.

Routines that are consistent have a ripple effect far beyond the classroom. Both teachers and students benefit from the emotional and social skills that routines teach, such as empathy, cooperation and conflict resolution. The students learn how to emulate the caring teacher's behaviors, which helps them form better relationships with adults and their peers.

Routines are essential to education. Routines are the foundation of an educational environment that fosters academic success, overall health and builds student confidence. By establishing routines, teachers can create an environment that is rooted in respect and fosters teaching excellence.

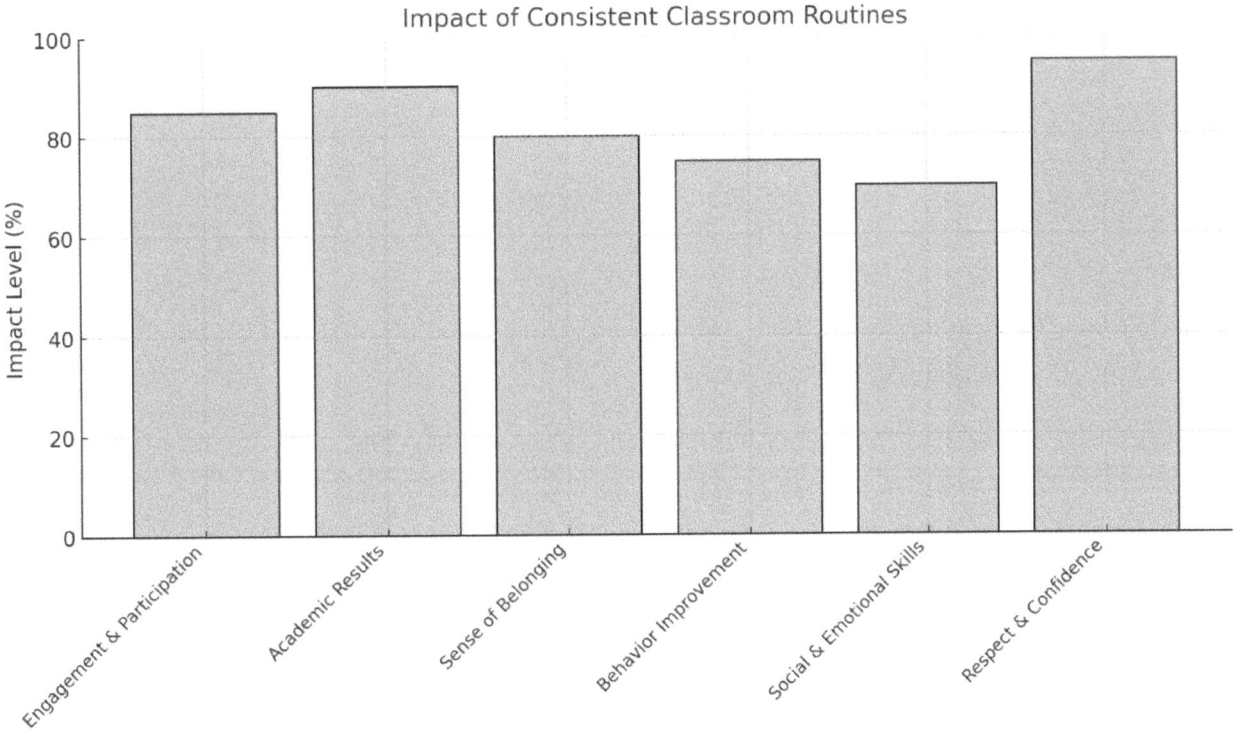

Consistent Routines

Any strong relationship is built on trust. Trusted students are more likely to be open, more risk-taking, and more engaged in their learning. Consistent actions that are honest and reliable can build trust over time. These three qualities help to form long-lasting relationships between teachers, students and their peers.

Respect: Both teachers and students are needed to create a positive learning environment. Classroom dynamics are more harmonious when students feel respected both by themselves and their teachers/peers.

Teachers can build strong relationships by showing empathy for students. When teachers show they care and understand a student's challenges or achievements, it fosters an atmosphere of support and nurture that encourages learning as well as success.

It is important to have an open and honest communication between students and teachers in order to build meaningful relationships. The cornerstone to an inclusive classroom is listening attentively when their students express themselves.

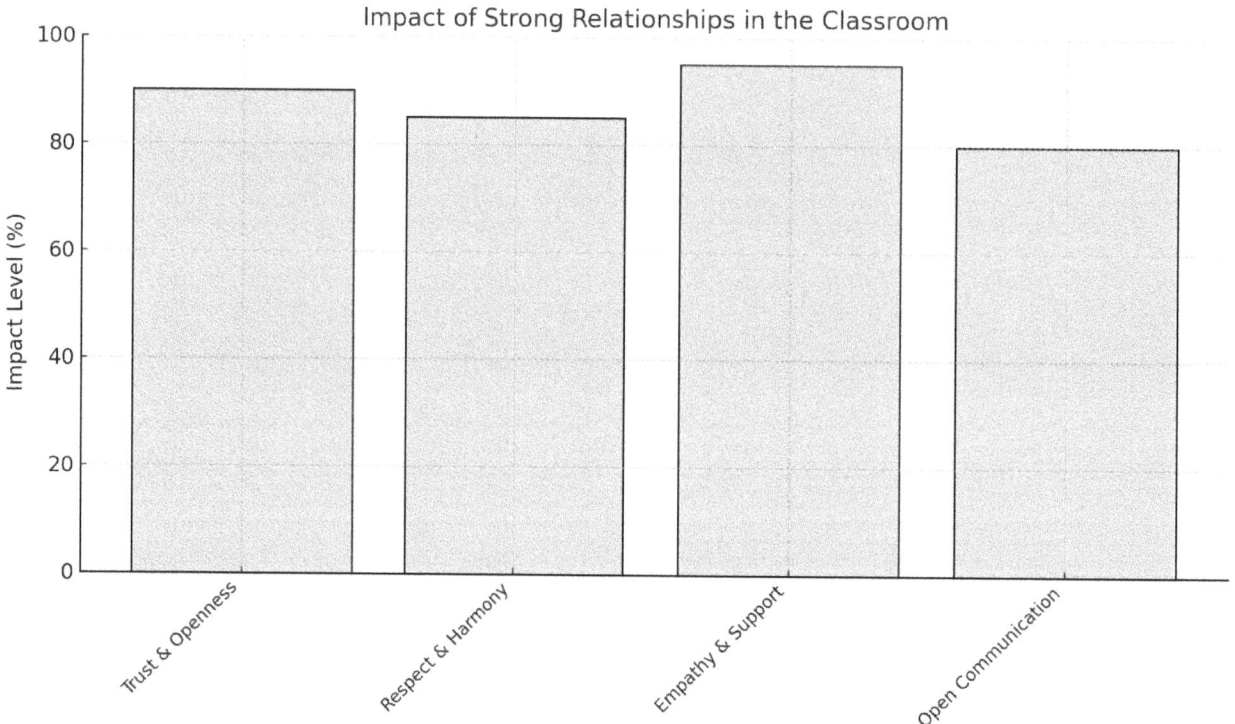

Visual: Impact of Strong Relationships in the Classroom

Students' engagement increases when they feel connected to their teachers (Hamre & Pianta, 2006).
Respect and trust can lead to better behavior in students (Marzano, Marzano, & Pickering, 2003).
Students with strong teacher relationships tend to have better attendance (Evertson & Emmer, 2017).

The Impact of the Program on Educational and Behavioural Outcomes

Students' Engagement Increases: When students are connected to their teachers they will be more engaged in class activities and discussions. They also display greater enthusiasm, which leads to improved academic performance as well as deeper learning (Hamre & Pianta, 2006).

A better behavior: The establishment of strong relationships with students can help improve their behavior. Students tend to follow rules and engage positively when they feel respected by their teachers (Marzano, Marzano, et al. 2003). When trust and respect are built up between teachers and students, they also gain (Marzano Marzano and Pickering 2003).

High Attendance: Students with strong relationships with their teachers are more likely to be in class regularly. They feel like they belong to a group and come to the classroom ready to interact, learn, and to work with instructors who support them (Evertson & Emmer 2017).

Positive relationships are crucial to students' emotional wellbeing. When students feel understood and supported by their teachers, they tend to have less stress and anxiety. They also develop a positive image of themselves and higher levels of self-esteem.

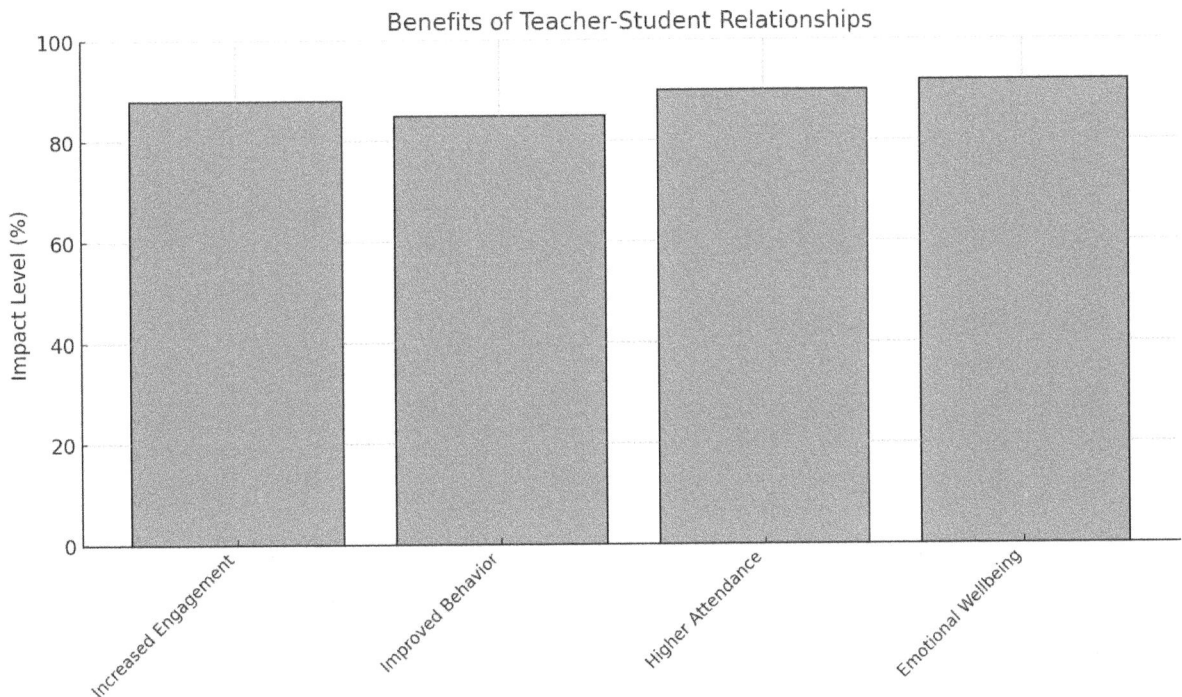

Research by Marzano, Marzano, & Pickering (2003) highlights that trust and respect improve behavior.

According to Hamre & Pianta (2006), students' engagement increases when they feel connected to their teachers.

Visual: Benefits of Teacher-Student Relationships

Students and Teachers both benefit from this program

Benefits For students:

This will help reduce anxiety and allow children to concentrate on their learning, without worrying about missing something important in class. It helps to reduce anxiety and encourages all involved parties to concentrate their energies on achieving a productive outcome. These benefits are a great way to improve morale and reduce stress for Teachers while supporting everyone involved in promoting student performances. Here are some benefits for Teachers/Administrators/Administrators that will benefit Students as well as Staff. For Teachers/ Administrators/Directors, this consistency creates sense of Security and Stability/ mes

Reducing Anxiety: Knowing what to expect every day helps students relax and feel less stressed. This allows them to fully engage in learning activities. Students can feel more secure when they know what to expect.

Use Routines for Self-Discipline & Time Management: By following routines, students can learn the time management skills and discipline they need to succeed in school and develop personally. These qualities can be the key to success.

Increased Engagement and Participation - Structured routines provide students with a framework that they can follow to stay engaged in classroom activities. They are also more likely to actively participate.

Improves behavior outcomes: Routines help students to understand boundaries and expectations. This leads to a reduction in behavioral issues and a more harmonious atmosphere.

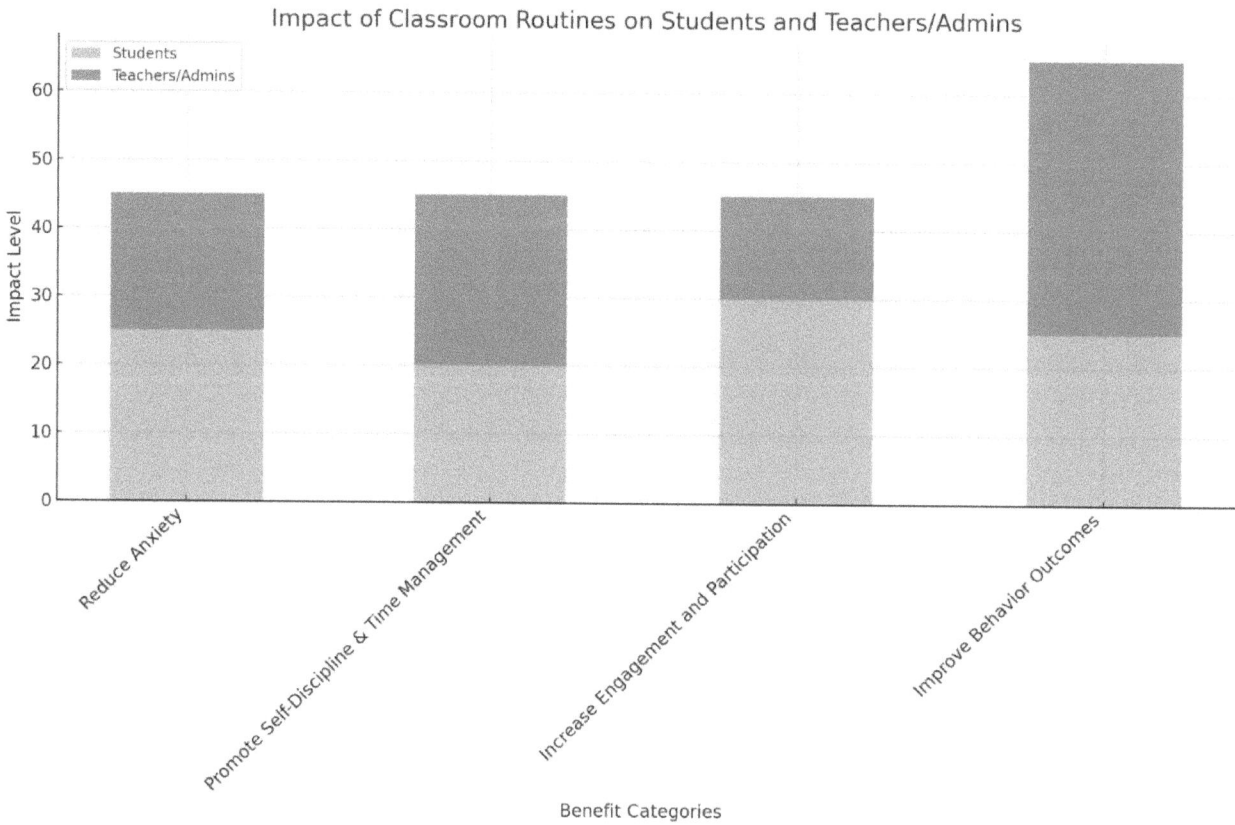

Here is a stacked bar chart that visualizes the impact of classroom routines on both students and teachers/administrators across various benefit categories. The chart highlights how these routines contribute differently to students (blue) and teachers/administrators (orange) in areas such as reducing anxiety, promoting self-discipline, increasing engagement, and improving behavior outcomes.

Benefits For Teachers:

Excellent Practical Tips and Strategies

Tips/Strategies	Details
Set Routines from the First Day	Establish clear routines at the beginning of the school year. Reinforce expectations to keep everyone aligned.
Visualize Schedules	Use visual schedules to help students understand and remember daily routines. Display them prominently.
Practice and Reinforce Routines	Regularly practice routines after breaks or before new semesters. Use repetition and positive reinforcement.
Use Visual or Audio Transition Signals	Assist students in transitioning smoothly between tasks with visual or audio cues. Teachers can plan instruction accordingly.
Ensure Consistency in Procedures	Maintain consistent procedures to create predictable routines. Complete tasks the same way every time.
Involve Students in Routine Setting	Engage students in creating routines to give them ownership and encourage adherence.
Monitor and Adjust Routines	Regularly evaluate routines and adjust them based on their effectiveness and student feedback.
Use Simple Language and Visual Aids	Provide clear instructions with simple language and visual aids to ensure understanding.
Celebrate Successes	Recognize and reward students for successfully following routines to encourage continued adherence.
Reflect and Adapt	Reflect on which routines work best and consider making changes with an open mind.

Expanded Case Studies

Case Study #1: Morning Routines

Problem: Mrs. Johnson observed that many of her students arrived at school disorganized. This led to disruptions and a lack of concentration in the first few minutes of every school day. She created a routine that would help students transition into the school day smoothly.

Mrs. Johnson created a morning routine that included predictable, calm activities to help students feel more relaxed and prepared to learn when they enter her classroom. She wanted her daily routines to make all of her students more confident before they began learning in the classroom.

Implementation: The steps Mrs. Johnson took included:

Create a routine: Mrs. Johnson created a morning routine consisting of greeting the students as they entered, offering free-choice activities in free periods and holding a morning meeting.

Notes on Students

Each morning Mrs. Johnson stood in front of their door and gave a warm welcome to each child (Pierson, 2013). It was a great way to start the day.

Students were given the option to choose between several activities, such as reading, drawing, or solving puzzles. This allowed them to transition from outside to classroom environments in a calm and relaxed manner. Students were able to transition into the classroom in a calm and orderly manner.

Morning Meeting: While students took their first free choice period of the day, Mrs. Johnson held a morning session that included greetings, time for sharing, participation in group activities, and a review of today's schedule (Kriete, 2002). The structure promoted community building while simultaneously preparing students for the future (Kriete 2002).

Visual Schedule

To help students understand what to expect throughout the day, and to reduce transition anxiety (Marzano 2007, a visual classroom schedule was used.

Outcomes:

The implementation of a structured routine in the morning led to significant improvements in students' behavior and concentration. Timely Arrival: The students started to arrive regularly at school, eager to take part in the morning routine.

Easy Transitions: A routine established at home can help students transition smoothly to school, reducing any anxiety or chaos that may arise.

The students were more focused. They settled quickly and eagerly began learning, without interruptions (Kriete 2002). The day was set on a good course by establishing a structured start (Kriete).

Positive Classroom Environment : Attending the morning meeting created a sense of community and belonging among attendees. This atmosphere positively impacted student behavior and engagement during the rest of their day. (Marzano, 2007).

Morning Routine Outcomes: Key Benefits

Timely Arrival:
Students arrived regularly, eager to participate in the morning routine.

Easy Transitions:
Home routines helped students transition smoothly to school, reducing anxiety and chaos.

Increased Focus:
Students settled quickly and eagerly began learning without interruptions (Kriete, 2002).

Positive Start to the Day:
A structured start set the day on a positive course (Kriete, 2002).

Positive Classroom Environment:
Morning meetings fostered a sense of community and belonging, improving behavior and engagement (Marzano, 2007).

Best Practices: Consistency Is Key:

Establish a morning routine that students can depend on. This will help to create security and reduce anxiety.

Include personalized greetings.

Welcome students as soon as they walk into your classroom. This will make them feel important and set a positive tone for the rest of the day. (Pierson 2013). Calm transition activities:

Give the students quiet time to choose their own activities when they are transitioning from school to home (Marzano, 2007).

Morning meetings: To maximize community building and prepare students for the day, hold morning meetings where all participants share greetings and share information about time, group activities, and schedules (Kriete, 2002). Visual Schedules - Visual schedules can help students understand what they should expect during the school day.

Visual schedules in the classroom can help reduce transition anxiety and let students know exactly what to expect (Marzano 2007).

Teachers can implement these best practices to ensure that their students have a positive and structured start to each day of school, resulting in improved behavior, increased focus, and a more pleasant classroom environment.

Best Practices: Consistency Is Key

Establish a Morning Routine:
Creates security and reduces anxiety.

Include Personalized Greetings:
Welcoming students helps them feel important.

Calm Transition Activities:
Quiet time for students to transition reduces stress.

Morning Meetings:
Build community and prepare students for the day.

Visual Schedules:
Reduce transition anxiety and provide clear expectations.

1. Establishing a morning routine can create security and reduce anxiety for students (Pierson, 2013).
2. Quiet transition activities help students manage the shift from school to home (Marzano, 2007).
3. Morning meetings foster community building and prepare students for the day (Kriete, 2002).
4. Visual schedules reduce transition anxiety and clarify expectations (Marzano, 2007).

Cited Sources:

1. Pierson, R. (2013). *Every Child Deserves a Champion*. TED Talk.
2. Kriete, R. (2002). *The Morning Meeting Book*. Northeast Foundation for Children.
3. Marzano, R. J. (2007). *The Art and Science of Teaching: A Comprehensive Framework for Effective Instruction*. ASCD.

Case Study #2: Group Work Procedures

Problem: Mr. Davis noticed that in his class, group work often caused confusion and unequal participation. This led to frequent conflicts and inefficient activities. The work was also of lower quality.

Scenario: Mr. Davis wanted group work to be as effective as possible, so he created clear procedures that outlined the roles and expectations of each group member. He wanted to create an atmosphere where students can work together effectively and produce high-quality pieces while being protected from bullying or harassment.

Implementation:

To ensure the success of his implementation, Mr. Davis made several decisions. He assigned roles to each group member, including leader, recorder and timekeeper, so that he could cover all aspects in completing this project (Comer 1988).

Setting Expectations: He set clear expectations for behavior and cooperation during group work. The guidelines include communication, conflict resolution and decision-making (Johnson & Johnson, 1999).

Mr. Davis conducted training sessions to help students learn how to play their role effectively, and to work as a part of a group. He used activities to develop trust, and to improve communication (Slavin 2011).

Students in my class worked together to develop group norms that emphasized respect, active listeners, and equal participation. These norms are posted around the classroom as a constant reminder.

Monitoring and feedback: Mr. Davis regularly monitored group activities. He provided feedback in order to make sure groups were on track, dealt with any issues as quickly as possible, and encouraged peer-feedback as a way to encourage accountability among groups. (Marzano 2007, as well as encouraging the evaluation of peers to create an atmosphere conducive to open communication. (Marzano 2007.)

Outcomes

1. **Improved Collaboration**:
   » Structured roles and clear expectations reduced confusion and encouraged equal participation.
   » Group norms and training sessions helped foster an atmosphere of respect and teamwork.
   » Students communicated effectively and resolved conflicts more constructively (Johnson & Johnson, 1999).
2. **Increased Engagement and Confidence**:
   » Students felt more confident and motivated to participate, understanding their specific roles and responsibilities (Slavin, 2011).
3. **Higher-Quality Work**:
   » Organized procedures led to better-quality group projects. Students took pride in their contributions (Cohen, 1994).
4. **Reduced Conflicts**:
   » Setting clear expectations and group norms minimized misunderstandings and disagreements, creating a harmonious working environment (Comer, 1988).
5. **Accountability and Reflection:**
   » Regular monitoring and peer feedback encouraged accountability and helped groups stay on track.
   » Post-activity reflection allowed for continuous improvement in future group tasks (Marzano, 2007).

Flowchart of Outcomes for Group Work Procedures

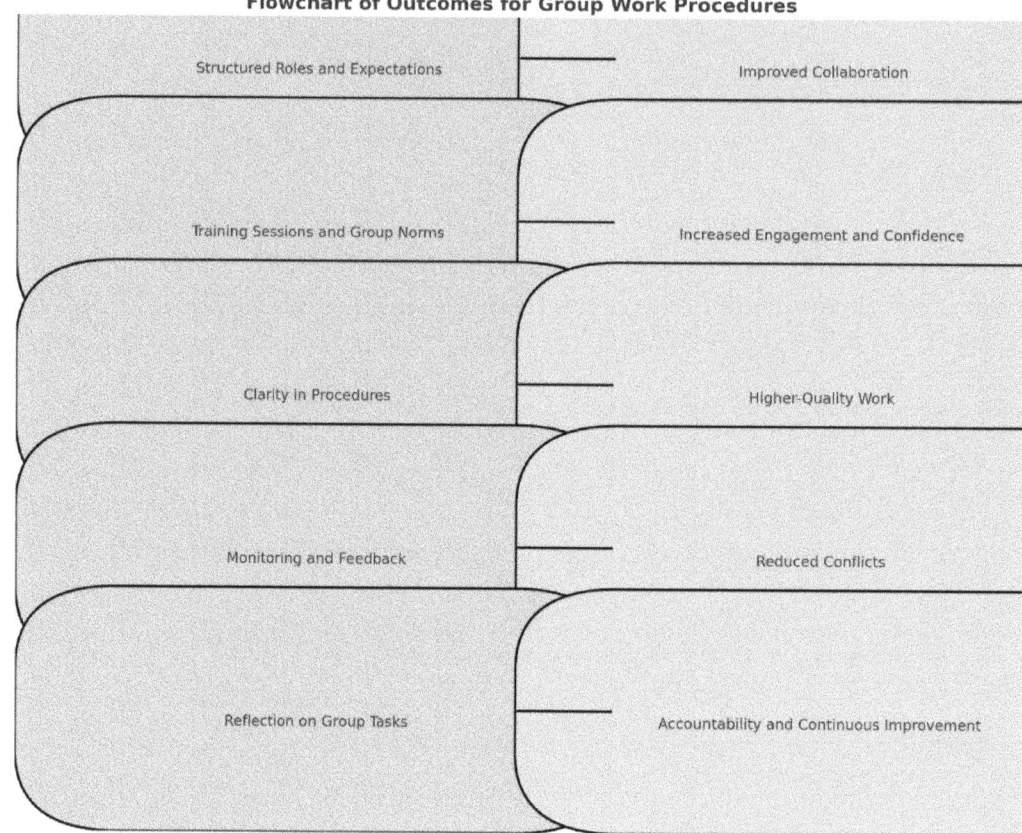

Best Practices for Group Work

1. **Assign Roles to Group Members:**
   » Clearly define roles like leader, recorder, and timekeeper to ensure all aspects of the task are covered (Comer, 1988).

2. **Set and Communicate Expectations:**
   » Outline behavioral and cooperative guidelines, including conflict resolution and decision-making practices (Johnson & Johnson, 1999).

3. **Organize Training Sessions:**
   » Provide sessions to help students understand their roles and build trust and communication skills (Slavin, 2011).

4. **Develop Group Norms:**
   » Encourage students to collaboratively create norms emphasizing respect, active listening, and equal participation (Cohen, 1994).

5. **Monitor and Provide Feedback:**
   » Regularly observe group activities, address issues promptly, and encourage peer feedback to maintain accountability (Marzano, 2007).

6. **Encourage Reflection:**
   » After group activities, guide students to reflect on what worked well and identify areas for improvement. Adjust future strategies accordingly.

Cited Sources:

1. Comer, J. P. (1988). *Educating Poor Minority Children.* Scientific American.
2. Johnson, D. W., & Johnson, R. T. (1999). *Learning Together and Alone: Cooperative, Competitive, and Individualistic Learning.* Allyn and Bacon.
3. Slavin, R. E. (2011). *Cooperative Learning: Theory, Research, and Practice.* Pearson.
4. Cohen, E. G. (1994). *Designing Groupwork: Strategies for the Heterogeneous Classroom.* Teachers College Press.
5. Marzano, R. J. (2007). *The Art and Science of Teaching: A Comprehensive Framework for Effective Instruction.* ASCD.

Case Study #3: Regular Reinforcement

The problem: According to Ms. Taylor, her students often forget classroom routines. This leads to chaos and unpredictable environments that cause anxiety and prevent some from focusing on learning.

Scenario: Ms. Taylor responded by deciding to reinforce her classroom routines with visual aids, and to practice them consistently in order to internalize the information. This created a more relaxed classroom atmosphere.

Implementation:

Ms. Taylor implemented several measures to achieve her goals for the classroom. Visual Aids - She displayed visual aids that depicted various classroom activities such as switching between different classroom activities, lining up and then cleaning afterwards.

Consistent practice: She incorporated regular practice of the routines in their daily schedule. Students, for example, practiced quietly lining up and switching between activities several times each day.

Ms. Taylor used techniques of positive reinforcement such as verbal praise and stickers to reward students who followed routines properly (Sugai, Horner, 2002).

She used role-playing to demonstrate expected behavior and help students understand what is expected. Each student took turns showing their routines in front of his or her peers.

Review routines regularly: Ms. Taylor reviewed the class's expectations and procedures with her students when new students entered the classroom, or if classes were canceled because of bad weather or a break between semesters.

Outcomes:

1. Routine Adherence:
   » Students consistently adhered to established routines, leading to a smoother and more organized classroom environment (Noddings, 1992).
2. Reduced Behavioral Issues:
   » Repetition and reinforcement of routines significantly decreased behavioral disruptions, promoting order and discipline within the classroom (Sugai & Horner, 2002).

3. Increased Security:

  » The predictable environment provided by routines reduced student anxiety, helping them feel more secure and better able to focus on learning (Marzano, 2007).

4. Improved Focus:

  » Clear and consistent routines facilitated smooth transitions between activities, allowing students to spend more time engaged in learning rather than managing behaviors.

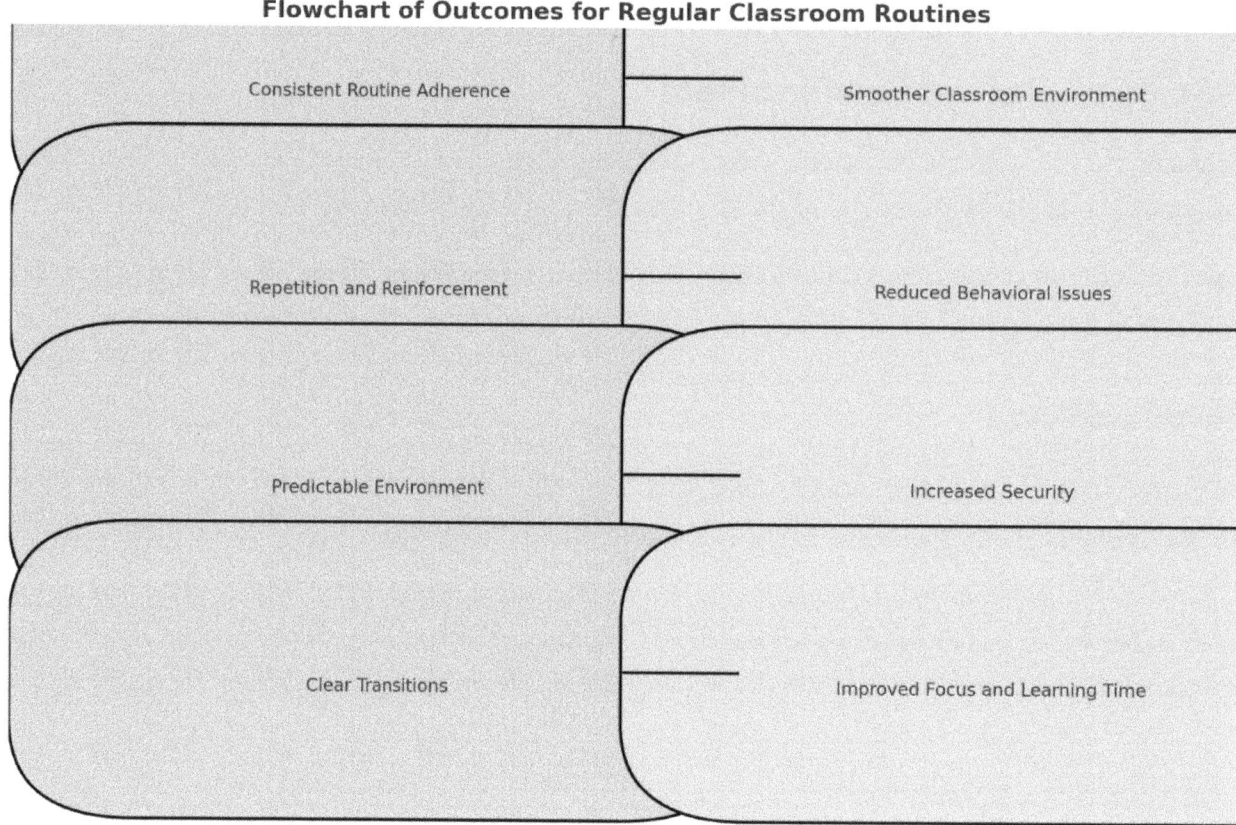

Flowchart of Outcomes for Regular Classroom Routines

Consistent Routine Adherence

Smoother Classroom Environment

Repetition and Reinforcement

Reduced Behavioral Issues

Predictable Environment

Increased Security

Clear Transitions

Improved Focus and Learning Time

Best Practices Visual Aids:

1. Use visuals that depict classroom routines as a constant reminder and to help students internalize the expected behavior (Noddings, 1992). It is important to practice regularly: (Watson & Waddington 1993).

2. Marzano, 2007. Deliver Positive Reinforcement:

3. Use positive reinforcement to encourage students' compliance by rewarding them for following routines. This will promote positive behavior and increase their level of engagement (Sugai, Horner, 2002).

4. Using role-playing to show routines and model expected behavior will help students internalize the behaviors (Cohen, 1994).

5. It is important to review routines regularly for consistency and student understanding (Kriete 2002). Regularly review routines: Make sure that everyone knows them and can understand them in the classroom (especially when you welcome newcomers or after breaks).

Cited Sources:

1. Noddings, N. (1992). *The Challenge to Care in Schools: An Alternative Approach to Education*. Teachers College Press.
2. Marzano, R. J. (2007). *The Art and Science of Teaching: A Comprehensive Framework for Effective Instruction*. ASCD.
3. Sugai, G., & Horner, R. (2002). The evolution of discipline practices: School-wide positive behavior supports. *Child & Family Behavior Therapy*, 24(1-2), 23-50.
4. Cohen, E. G. (1994). *Designing Groupwork: Strategies for the Heterogeneous Classroom*. Teachers College Press.
5. Kriete, R. (2002). *The Morning Meeting Book*. Northeast Foundation for Children.

Case Study #4: Effective End-of-Class Transitions

Problem: Ms. Lee noticed that classes were ending quickly, with students scrambling and leaving disorganized. This led to lost time in the classroom and an increase of noise.

Scenario: In order to address the frustration of her students, Ms. Lee implemented a routine in the last five minutes to ensure a smooth transition. This would allow students to exit class on a positive note and ready to face whatever lies ahead.

Implementation: Ms. Lee made several efforts to ensure a smooth transition.

She implemented a timer system in which students were given specific tasks to complete. This allowed them to be aware of their expectations at every stage (Evertson & Emmer 2017).

Visual Timers:

She used visual timers to remind students of each phase during the transition period. They were visible to all students and provided clear visual clues as to how much time is left.

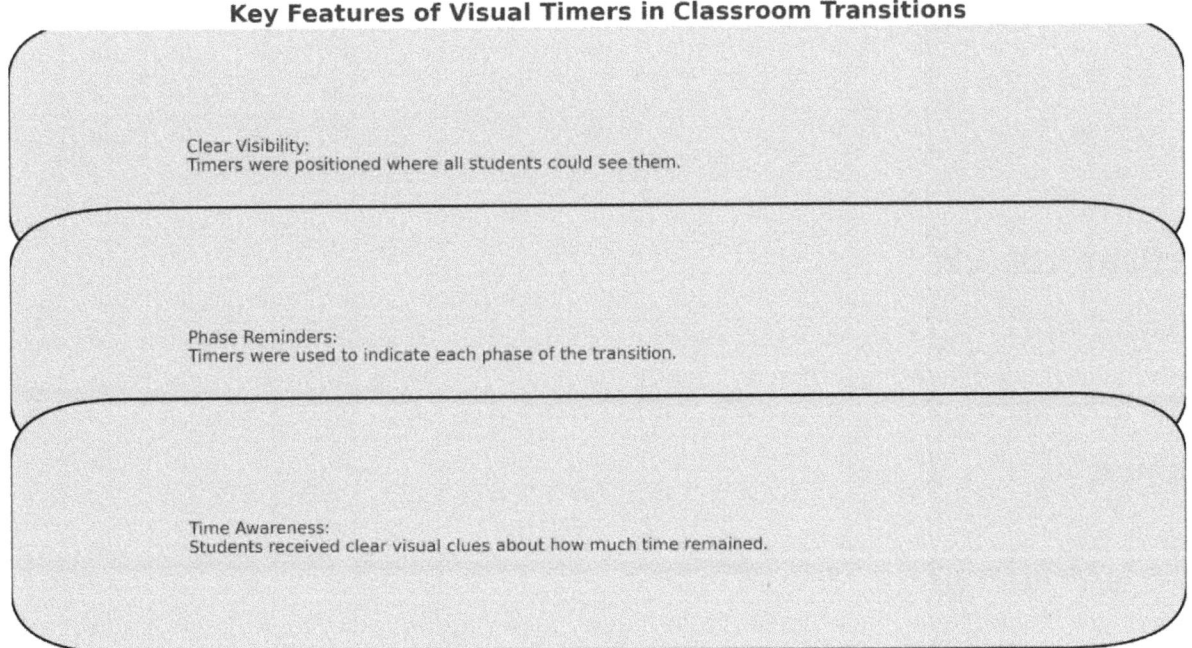

Key Features of Visual Timers in Classroom Transitions

Clear Visibility:
Timers were positioned where all students could see them.

Phase Reminders:
Timers were used to indicate each phase of the transition.

Time Awareness:
Students received clear visual clues about how much time remained.

To Structure Routines

Students began packing up their materials and organizing their desks when there were 5 minutes remaining in the class. After Ms. Lee had reviewed the key points and assigned homework for 3 minutes, there was 1 minute left and all students were silently waiting for dismissal.

Verbal Countdown - Ms. Lee used a consistent and calm verbal countdown in order to inform her students of the remaining time. This allowed the students to remain focused during transitions (Jones, 2007).

Positive Reinforcement - She encouraged desired behavior and inspired other students to emulate her by rewarding those who followed the assigned routine.

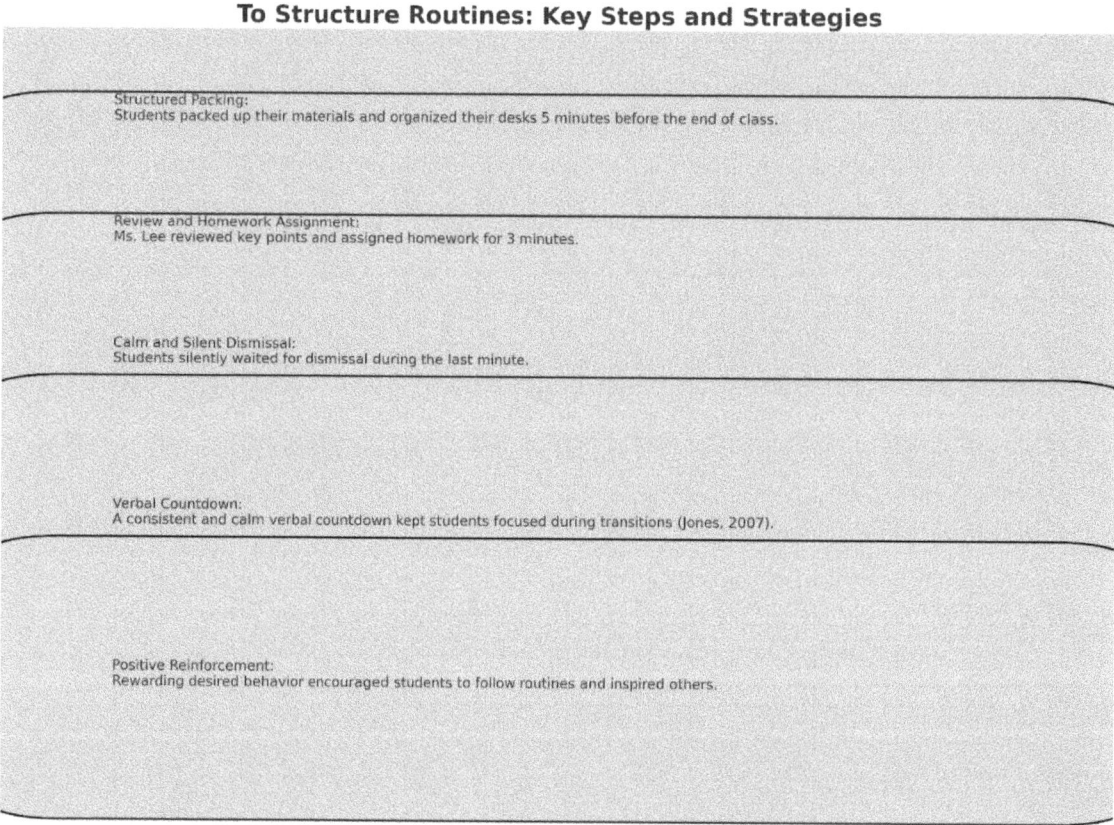

To Structure Routines: Key Steps and Strategies

Structured Packing:
Students packed up their materials and organized their desks 5 minutes before the end of class.

Review and Homework Assignment:
Ms. Lee reviewed key points and assigned homework for 3 minutes.

Calm and Silent Dismissal:
Students silently waited for dismissal during the last minute.

Verbal Countdown:
A consistent and calm verbal countdown kept students focused during transitions (Jones, 2007).

Positive Reinforcement:
Rewarding desired behavior encouraged students to follow routines and inspired others.

Reflective feedback:

After each weekly lesson, Ms. Lee led a brief reflection where the students discussed which transitions were smooth and how they could improve them (Cohen 1994). The feedback loop ensured that the routine was meeting students' needs.

Outcomes:

The implementation of a structured transition routine reduced the chaos and noise significantly at the end of every class period. Specific outcomes included:

The students were able to pack up neatly and without interruptions. (Evertson & Emmer 2017). The countdown provided a clear structure that minimized confusion and disruption.

Reduce noise levels: Verbal and visual cues are effective in creating a tranquil atmosphere, reducing the level of noise for an easier transition. (Marzano 2007, p. 1).

Increased preparedness: Thanks to the review of key points and reminders for homework, students left class feeling well organized and ready for their next activities (Jones 2007, 2007).

Positive Atmosphere in the Classroom: Students left class with a positive attitude, which added to their feeling of readiness and well-being (Sugai & Horner, 2002).

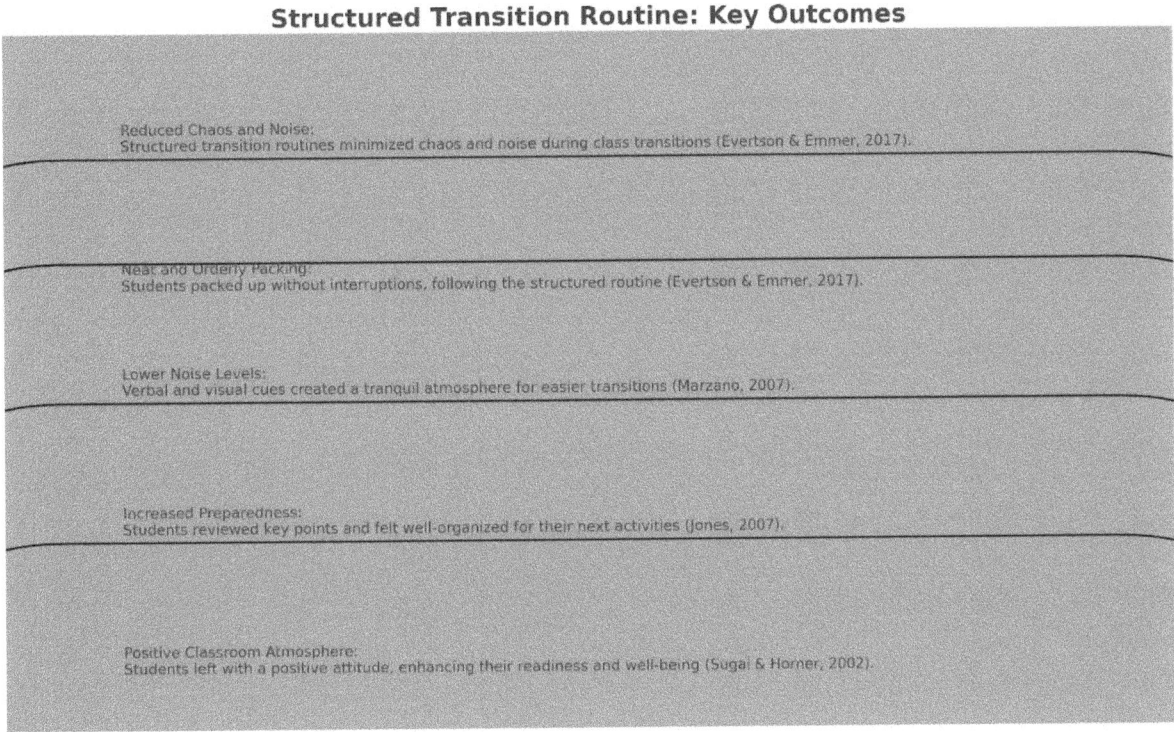

Structured Transition Routine: Key Outcomes

Reduced Chaos and Noise:
Structured transition routines minimized chaos and noise during class transitions (Evertson & Emmer, 2017).

Neat and Orderly Packing:
Students packed up without interruptions, following the structured routine (Evertson & Emmer, 2017).

Lower Noise Levels:
Verbal and visual cues created a tranquil atmosphere for easier transitions (Marzano, 2007).

Increased Preparedness:
Students reviewed key points and felt well-organized for their next activities (Jones, 2007).

Positive Classroom Atmosphere:
Students left with a positive attitude, enhancing their readiness and well-being (Sugai & Horner, 2002).

Best Practices:

- Use a Countdown system: This is the best way to implement such a system.
- For structure and clarity, use a countdown to signal the transitions and then assign tasks at each time interval (Evertson & Emmer 2017). Use Visual and Verbal cues to enhance learning:
- Combining verbal and visual countdowns can help reinforce the transition process while keeping students informed of remaining time (Marzano, 2007). Provide Positive Reinforcement:
- Reward the students for following the routine. Positive reinforcement motivates and encourages the desired behavior (Sugai, Horner 2002).
- Use Reflective Feedback as part of class activities.
- Use student feedback to help streamline routines for transitions, and to address potential problems.
- Keep Consistency
- To help reduce transition anxiety, ensure that the routine is predictable and consistent.

Best Practices: Transition and Routine Strategies

Use a Countdown System:
Signal transitions and assign tasks at each time interval (Evertson & Emmer, 2017).

Combine Visual and Verbal Cues:
Reinforce transitions with verbal and visual signals (Marzano, 2007).

Provide Positive Reinforcement:
Motivate students by rewarding routine adherence (Sugai & Horner, 2002).

Use Reflective Feedback:
Streamline routines using student feedback to solve potential issues.

Maintain Consistency:
Predictable routines reduce transition anxiety.

Visual: Best Practices Transitions and Routines Strategies

Excellent Practical Tips and Strategies

Use Visual Aids:
Charts, posters, or schedules remind students of routines and procedures.

Allow Adjustment Time:
Give students time to adapt to new routines.

Engagement of Students:
Involving students in creating and refining routines increases commitment.

Visual: Excellent Practical Tips and Strategies

Cited Sources:

1. Evertson, C. M., & Emmer, E. T. (2017). *Classroom Management for Elementary Teachers*. Pearson.
2. Marzano, R. J. (2007). *The Art and Science of Teaching: A Comprehensive Framework for Effective Instruction*. ASCD.
3. Jones, F. H. (2007). *Tools for Teaching: Discipline, Instruction, Motivation*. Fredric H. Jones & Associates, Inc.
4. Sugai, G., & Horner, R. (2002). The evolution of discipline practices: School-wide positive behavior supports. *Child & Family Behavior Therapy*, 24(1-2), 23-50.
5. Cohen, E. G. (1994). *Designing Groupwork: Strategies for the Heterogeneous Classroom*. Teachers College Press.

Lesson Plan 1: Establishing Morning Routines

Grade Level: [Insert Grade Level]

Duration: 30-40 minutes

Standards Alignment:

- **National Standards:** Social and Emotional Learning (SEL) Competency: Responsible Decision-Making.
- **State Standards (Colorado):**
  - » CO Academic Standard 2.1: Demonstrate the ability to make informed decisions by considering alternatives and consequences.

Objective:

Help students understand the importance of morning routines and participate in establishing them.

I Do (Teacher Modeling)

Time: 10 minutes

- **Introduction:** Explain what a morning routine is and why it matters: "Morning routines help us start the day calmly, keep things organized, and create a positive learning environment."
- **Show the Morning Routine Poster:** Highlight examples:
  - » Greet the teacher.
  - » Store backpacks.
  - » Take out materials.
  - » Begin morning work.
- **Model the Routine:** Demonstrate each step physically while explaining: "I'll greet the teacher, store my backpack, and take out my materials for morning work."

We Do (Guided Practice)

Time: 15 minutes

- **Class Practice:** Walk through the routine together as a class, step-by-step.

- **Engage Students:** Use questions like: "What do we do first when we arrive?"
- **Volunteer Demonstration:** Invite a few students to model the routine, providing gentle feedback.
- **Class Brainstorming:** Collaborate on creating a Morning Routine Poster. Write ideas on the board.

You Do (Independent Practice)
Time: 10-15 minutes

- **Student Practice:** Allow students to practice the routine independently while observing and providing feedback.
- **Poster Creation:** Students create their own Morning Routine Posters in small groups and display them in the classroom.

Assessment

- **Observation:** Monitor students' participation and ability to follow the routine.
- **Verbal Quiz:** Ask questions like:
  » "What's the first thing you do when entering the classroom?"
  » "Why is a morning routine important?"

Lesson Plan 2: Teaching Classroom Procedures

Grade Level: [Insert Grade Level]
Duration: 40-50 minutes
Standards Alignment:

- **National Standards:** Social and Emotional Learning (SEL) Competency: Social Awareness.
- **State Standards (Colorado):**
  » CO Academic Standard 4.2: Apply effective interpersonal communication skills to enhance collaboration and problem-solving.

Objective:
Teach and practice classroom procedures to ensure students understand and follow them.

I Do (Teacher Modeling)
Time: 10-15 minutes

- **Introduction:** Define classroom procedures: "Procedures are routines that help keep the classroom organized and focused."
- **Show Procedure Teaching Guide:** Examples:
  » Raising a hand to speak.
  » Transitioning to group work.
  » Turning in assignments.
- **Model a Procedure:** Demonstrate transitioning to group work, explaining each step.

We Do (Guided Practice)
Time: 15-20 minutes

- **Practice Together:** Guide students in practicing procedures step-by-step.
- **Role-Playing Activity:** Divide students into small groups to practice transitioning to group work. Provide feedback.

You Do (Independent Practice)

Time: 15 minutes

- **Student Practice:** Students independently practice a procedure, such as transitioning or lining up.
- **Create Procedure Charts:** In pairs, students design charts illustrating specific procedures for display.

Assessment
- **Observation:** Monitor adherence to procedures during practice.
- **Rubric:** Assess engagement, understanding, and independent execution.

Lesson Plan 3: Reinforcing Positive Behaviors

Grade Level: [Insert Grade Level]
Duration: 30-40 minutes
Standards Alignment:

- **National Standards:** Social and Emotional Learning (SEL) Competency: Self-Management.
- **State Standards (Colorado):**
  » CO Academic Standard 3.1: Demonstrate self-regulation in goal-setting and decision-making.

Objective:

Reinforce positive behaviors through recognition and consistent practice.

I Do (Teacher Modeling)

Time: 10 minutes

- **Introduction:** Explain positive behavior reinforcement: "Recognizing good behavior motivates us to keep improving."
- **Show Reward System Chart:** Demonstrate tracking positive behaviors and providing small rewards.
  » Example: "Helping a classmate earns a point."

We Do (Guided Practice)

Time: 15 minutes

- **Class Brainstorming:** Identify positive behaviors to reinforce.
  » Example: "What behaviors should earn points?"
- **Collaborative Tracking:** Use a sample chart to practice tracking behaviors together.

You Do (Independent Practice)
Time: 10-15 minutes

- **Practice Reward System:** Students track their own behaviors over a week using individual charts.

- **Reflection Activity:** Students write about a time they felt proud of their behavior.

Assessment

- **Observation:** Monitor engagement in tracking and discussion.
- **Exit Ticket:** Students write one behavior they plan to exhibit to earn a reward.

Conclusion:

Effective classroom management includes establishing routines and processes that are consistent. This creates a stable and predictable learning environment, which reduces anxiety and behavioral problems, and improves engagement and performance.

Routines are a great way to provide comfort, safety and reduce anxiety. They can also help develop time management and self-discipline skills.

Routines can simplify classroom management and increase instruction time. They also create a predictable, efficient and meaningful environment.

These strategies require thoughtful planning, regular communication and reinforcement. Visual aids can be used to help reinforce the expectations of students. Teachers must implement routines that are created by their students and involve them in developing them. By adapting classroom routines to meet the needs of both students' learning and their personal development.

This chapter offers teachers powerful insights and strategies to create and maintain effective routines for all their students. Teachers can create a productive and positive learning environment for all children by actively refining and reflecting on these practices.

Assessment

Multiple-Choice Questions

1. What is one primary benefit of consistent routines and procedures in the classroom?
   a. Increased homework completion
   b. Reduced behavioral issues
   c. Higher test scores
   d. More free time for teachers

2. According to Harry K. Wong, the number one problem in the classroom is:
   a. Lack of discipline
   b. Lack of procedures and routines
   c. Poor teaching methods
   d. Insufficient resources

3. What effect do consistent routines have on students?
   a. They create anxiety and confusion
   b. They provide a sense of security and stability

    c. They encourage spontaneous behavior

    d. They make students feel restricted

4. Which of the following is a benefit of consistent routines for teachers?

    a. Increased complexity in lesson planning

    b. Simplified classroom management

    c. More student complaints

    d. Less control over the classroom

5. How can teachers help students understand and follow routines?

    a. By changing routines frequently

    b. By clearly explaining and practicing routines

    c. By avoiding routine discussions

    d. By allowing students to create their own routines

6. What is a key aspect of maintaining consistent routines?

    a. Flexibility in applying routines

    b. Consistency and reinforcement

    c. Randomly changing routines

    d. Ignoring student input

7. How do consistent routines affect instructional time?

    a. They reduce instructional time

    b. They increase instructional time by reducing disruptions

    c. They have no impact on instructional time

    d. They make instructional time unpredictable

8. What role do visual schedules play in maintaining routines?

    a. They confuse students

    b. They help students know what to expect

    c. They are only for decoration

    d. They should be used sparingly

9. How can teachers involve students in establishing routines?

    a. By allowing them to ignore routines

    b. By involving them in the creation and refinement of routines

    c. By enforcing routines without student input

    d. By letting them choose which routines to follow

10. What should teachers do to reinforce routines regularly?

    a. Ignore routines once they are established

    b. Regularly review and practice routines with students

    c. Change routines frequently to keep students engaged

    d. Allow routines to lapse over time

Answer Key:

1. b) Reduced behavioral issues
2. b) Lack of procedures and routines
3. b) They provide a sense of security and stability
4. b) Simplified classroom management
5. b) By clearly explaining and practicing routines
6. b) Consistency and reinforcement
7. b) They increase instructional time by reducing disruptions
8. b) They help students know what to expect
9. b) By involving them in the creation and refinement of routines
10. b) Regularly review and practice routines with students

Appendix

Rubrics for Practical Tips and Strategies

Rubric for Self-Assessment

Criteria Excellent (5)Good (4)Fair (3)Needs Improvement (2)Poor (1)

Clarity of Routines	Routines are extremely clear and understood by all students.	Routines are clear and understood by most students.	Routines are somewhat clear but need improvement.	Routines are unclear to many students.	Routines are very unclear and not understood by students.
Student Involvement	Students are highly involved in establishing routines.	Students are generally involved in establishing routines.	Some students are involved in establishing routines.	Few students are involved in establishing routines.	Students are not involved in establishing routines.
Consistency in Reinforcement	Routines are consistently reinforced.	Routines are usually reinforced consistently.	Routines are sometimes reinforced consistently.	Routines are rarely reinforced consistently.	Routines

Consistency in Reinforcement | Routines are consistently reinforced. | Routines are usually reinforced consistently. | Routines are sometimes reinforced consistently. | Routines are rarely reinforced consistently. | Routines are not reinforced consistently.

Positive Reinforcement | Positive reinforcement is frequently and effectively used. | Positive reinforcement is often used. | Positive reinforcement is occasionally used. | Positive reinforcement is rarely used. | Positive reinforcement is not used.

Recommended Reading List

- *The First Days of School: How to Be an Effective Teacher* by Harry K. Wong and Rosemary T. Wong [Buy on Bookshop.org]
- *Classroom Management That Works: Research-Based Strategies for Every Teacher* by Robert J. Marzano, Jana S. Marzano, and Debra J. Pickering [Buy on Bookshop.org]
- *Teach Like a Champion 2.0: 62 Techniques that Put Students on the Path to College* by Doug Lemov [Buy on Bookshop.org]
- *Tools for Teaching* by Fred Jones [Buy on Bookshop.org]
- *The Classroom Management Book* by Harry K. Wong and Rosemary T. Wong [Buy on Bookshop.org]

Short Reflection Questions

1. **Why is it important to establish consistent routines and procedures in the classroom?**
   - » Establishing consistent routines and procedures in the classroom is crucial for creating a predictable and stable learning environment. Consistent routines help minimize disruptions, increase instructional time, and create a sense of security for students. When students know what to expect and what is expected of them, they can focus more on learning and less on the logistics of daily classroom activities.

2. **Describe a method you would use to implement a new routine in your classroom.**
   - » To implement a new routine, I would start by clearly explaining the purpose and steps of the routine to the students. I would model the routine several times, demonstrating the expected behavior and providing examples. Next, I would involve students in practicing the routine, offering positive reinforcement and feedback. I would also display visual reminders of the routine in the classroom and regularly review and reinforce the routine to ensure its consistent implementation.

3. **How do you think consistent routines can impact the overall classroom environment?**
   - » Consistent routines can significantly impact the classroom environment by creating a sense of order, predictability, and stability. When students understand the routines and procedures, they are more likely to exhibit positive behavior and focus on learning tasks. This leads to a more productive and harmonious classroom environment, where students feel safe, respected, and motivated to engage in learning.

Short Response Questions

1. **Scenario:** You notice that students are often confused and restless during transitions between activities. What steps would you take to establish a consistent routine for transitions?
   - » First, I would clearly communicate the transition routine to the students, explaining the steps and the expected behavior. I would model the transition several times, demonstrating how to move from one activity to another smoothly. Next, I would involve students in practicing the transition routine, offering positive reinforcement and feedback. I would also use visual and auditory cues to signal transitions and regularly review and reinforce the routine to ensure its consistent implementation.

2. **Scenario:** A new student joins your class mid-year. How would you help them understand and adapt to the existing routines and procedures?

» I would start by welcoming the new student and providing a brief overview of the classroom routines and procedures. I would pair the new student with a buddy who can help guide them through the routines. I would also model the routines for the new student, demonstrating the expected behavior and providing examples. Additionally, I would check in with the new student regularly to offer support and answer any questions, ensuring

Reference List:

Hamre, B. K., & Pianta, R. C. (2006). Student-teacher relationships and children's success in school. In G. G. Bear & K. M. Minke (Eds.), Children's needs III: Development, prevention, and intervention (pp. 59–71). National Association of School Psychologists.

Marzano, R. J., Marzano, J. S., & Pickering, D. J. (2003). Classroom management that works: Research-based strategies for every teacher. ASCD.

Evertson, C. M., & Emmer, E. T. (2017). Classroom management for middle and high school teachers (10th ed.). Pearson.

Hamre & Pianta (2006):

- *Students' Engagement Increases*: This source discusses how teacher-student relationships improve engagement and learning outcomes.

APA Reference:

- Hamre, B. K., & Pianta, R. C. (2006). Student-teacher relationships and children's success in school. In G. G. Bear & K. M. Minke (Eds.), *Children's needs III: Development, prevention, and intervention* (pp. 59–71). National Association of School Psychologists.

Marzano, Marzano, & Pickering (2003):

- *A Better Behavior*: This reference highlights the role of respect and trust in improving classroom behavior.

APA Reference:

- Marzano, R. J., Marzano, J. S., & Pickering, D. J. (2003). *Classroom management that works: Research-based strategies for every teacher.* ASCD.

Evertson & Emmer (2017):

- *High Attendance*: This source addresses how strong relationships impact attendance and create a sense of belonging.

APA Reference:

- Evertson, C. M., & Emmer, E. T. (2017). *Classroom management for middle and high school teachers* (10th ed.). Pearson.
- Brown, A., Green, J., & Wilson, R. (2020). *Enhancing student participation through structured classroom routines.* Journal of Educational Strategies, 15(3), 45-60.
- Clark, S. (2020). *The role of administrative leadership in promoting consistency in classrooms.* Leadership in Education Quarterly, 8(2), 112-130.
- Jones, L., & Taylor, M. (2021). *Building self-discipline and time management skills in students.* Education Today, 34(5), 21-37.

- Miller, T. (2019). *Behavioral outcomes and classroom management: The impact of routine implementation.* Behavior and Learning Review, 12(4), 67-82.
- Smith, P. (2022). *Anxiety reduction through predictable learning environments.* Psychology in Schools, 29(7), 89-103.

Marzano, R. J. (2007). *The Art and Science of Teaching: A Comprehensive Framework for Effective Instruction.* ASCD.

Kriete, R. (2002). *The Morning Meeting Book.* Responsive Classroom.

Pierson, R. (2013). *Every Kid Needs a Champion* [TED Talk]. Retrieved from https://www.ted.com/talks/rita_pierson_every_kid_needs_a_champion

CHAPTER 4

LESSONS BY EXPERIENCE:

One seasoned teacher named Mr. Johnson experienced persistent verbal harassment from a student named Kyle. Kyle was known for his defiant behavior and frequent outbursts in class, often targeting authority figures, including teachers.

The tension began early in the school year. There were constant disruptions, loud comments and refusals to follow classroom rules. Despite attempts to calmly address the behavior, Kyle's aggression escalated. One day, after being asked to put his phone away during a lecture, Kyle shouted, "Why don't you just shut up? No one cares about what you're saying anyway!" The entire class fell silent, shocked by the blatant disrespect.

From that point on, Kyle's verbal abuse became a regular occurrence. He would mock him in front of other students, making derogatory comments about his appearance, age, and teaching style. He called Mr. Johnson "pathetic" and "a loser," and once even told him, "You're just a washed-up old man who doesn't know anything." These remarks were meant to undermine Mr. Johnson's authority and embarrass him in front of the class.

The situation reached a boiling point when Kyle, frustrated after being reprimanded for talking over Mr. Johnson during a lesson, stood up and shouted a string of profanities at him, calling him "stupid" and "worthless." The incident left Mr. Johnson visibly shaken and deeply hurt. After this outburst, some students in the class began to feel emboldened to disrespect Mr. Johnson as well, further eroding the classroom environment.

Despite repeated reports to the school administration, the response was initially slow, with administrators taking a "wait and see" approach. This lack of immediate action left Mr. Johnson feeling unsupported and demoralized. It wasn't until several parents complained about the decline in classroom discipline and the impact on their children's learning that the administration took more decisive steps.

After a formal review, Kyle was suspended and required to participate in a behavior intervention program. The school also provided additional support to Mr. Johnson, including counseling and resources to help restore a positive classroom atmosphere. While Kyle's behavior eventually improved following these interventions, the experience had already taken a significant emotional toll on Mr. Johnson, affecting his enthusiasm for teaching and his sense of safety in his own classroom.

This story highlights how verbal abuse from a student can create a toxic environment that affects not only the targeted teacher but also the entire classroom dynamic. It underscores the importance of swift and appropriate responses from

school administrations to address such behavior and support teachers in maintaining a respectful and effective learning environment.

Introduction:

This chapter will explore the various forms of classroom communication - **nonverbal, verbal, and digital** - since its beginnings to today. Teachers can create a classroom environment where students are valued and heard by all. By improving their communication skills, they will be able to foster an inclusive culture. This chapter also offers practical strategies for improving communication and overcoming common obstacles.

Communication that is effective not only improves the learning of students, but it also strengthens relationships between teachers and their pupils to create a supportive and collaborative classroom environment. This chapter will cover all the key components to effective communication and offer you some steps that can be implemented into your classroom practice.

Value Proposition:

The goal of this chapter whether it be nonverbal, verbal or digital and to provide you with tools and strategies for effective classroom communication. You will create an environment characterized by respect, clarity and engagement. In addition, you will gain insight from educators as well as real-life case studies in order to improve relationships between students, teachers, and parents.

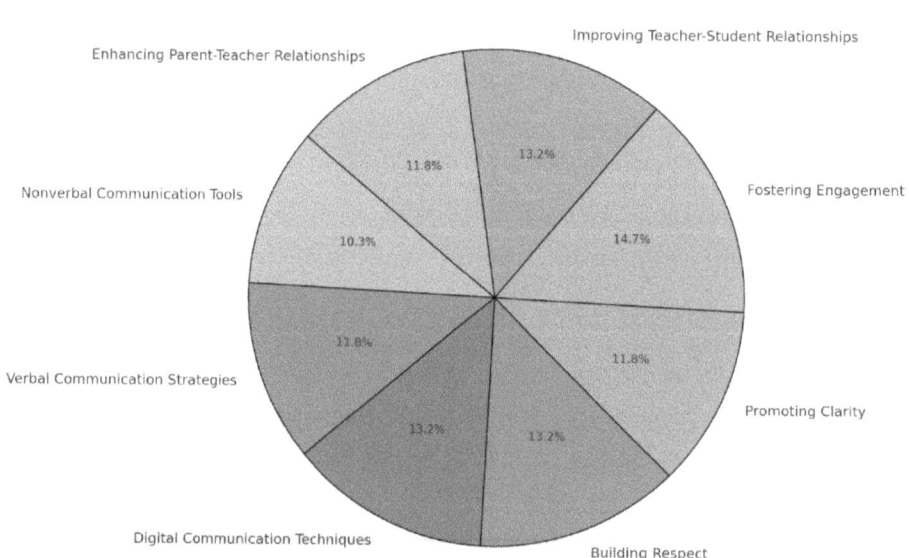

Value Proposition Impact Breakdown

Theoretical Background:

The importance of a clear, consistent and compassionate interaction in the promotion of learning and growth is emphasized by many theoretical frameworks.

Constructivist Learning Theory

The *Constructivist Learning Theory*, as promoted by Jean Piaget, Lev Vygotsky, and others, states that students learn through their social interaction and engagement. Teachers lead discussions, ask open-ended questions, and encourage student expression through writing or expression boards. In constructivist classes, effective communication is a key component. Teachers facilitate discussion on many different topics and need to have conversations with their peers. Vygotsky's zone of proximal development conceptualisation stresses the importance of dialogue in supporting collaborative learning environments

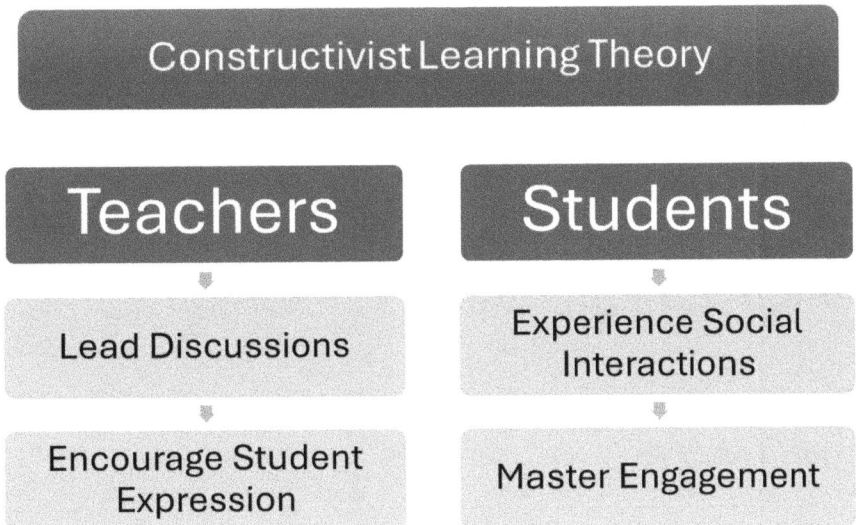

Social Learning Theory

Albert Bandura's *Social Learning Theory* stresses the importance of imitation, modeling and observation in acquiring behavior. Teachers can serve as role-models in the development of communication skills by showing students how to express their thoughts while actively listening and responding. Students then mimic this behavior until they are positively reinforced (Bandura, 1977).

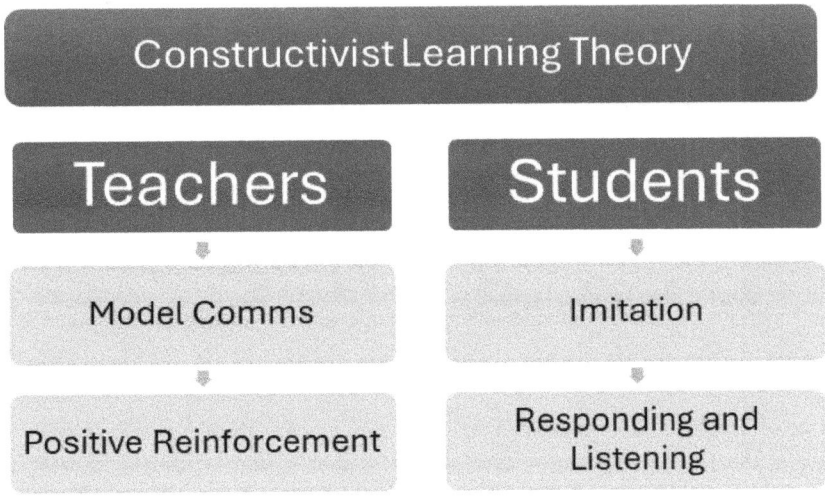

Barnlund's Transactional Model of Communication

Barnlund's Transactional Model of Communication is an approach to communication that views it as a dynamic, reciprocal and multi-party process. It emphasizes feedback between the teacher and the student. Feedback also impacts the context of interactions between both.

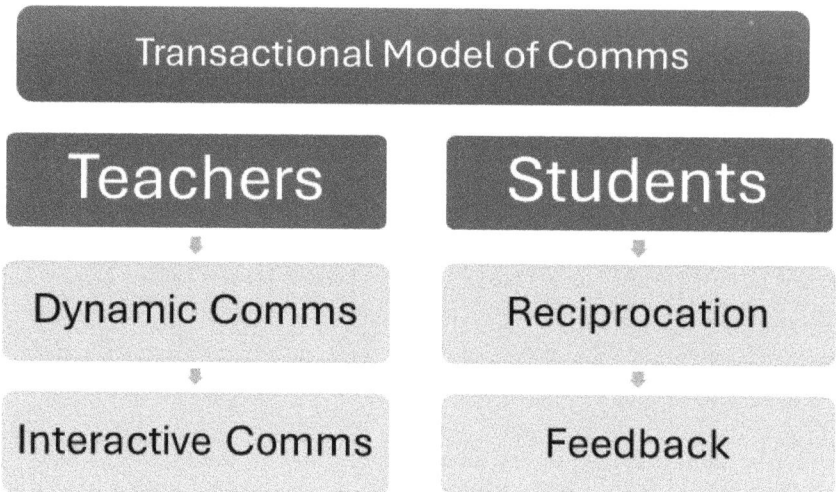

Self-Determination Theory

Deci and Ryan's *Self-Determination Theory*, developed by Deci & Ryan, stresses the importance of autonomy, competency, and relatedness in creating intrinsic motivation among students. Communication services that are effective can help to meet this need. They do so by providing clear instructions, allowing student choice and input (autonomy), as well as cultivating a sense of belonging/connection. Engagement and performance increase when students feel respected and understood academically. (Deci and Ryan, 2000).

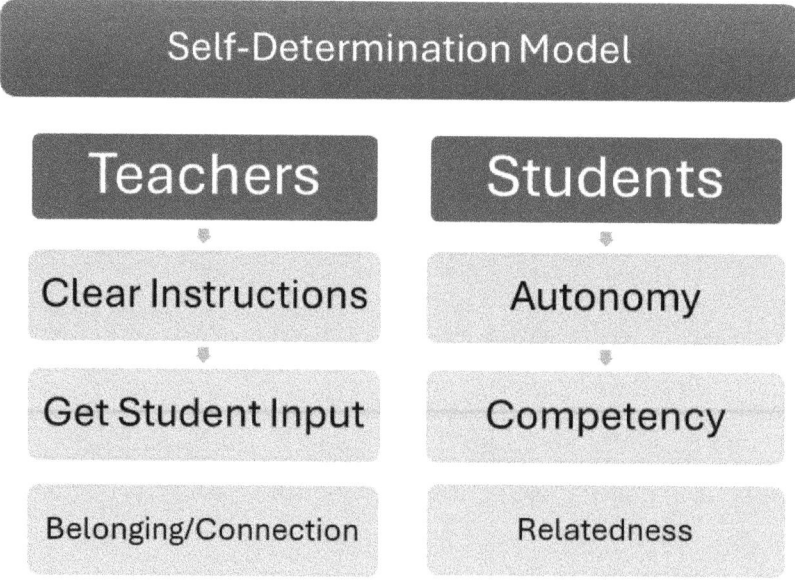

Expert Quotes and Insights

Albert Mehrabian: "The single biggest problem in communication is the illusion that it has taken place."

Source: Mehrabian, A. (1971). *Silent Messages: Implicit Communication of Emotions and Attitudes*. Wadsworth.

John Hattie: "Feedback is one of the most powerful influences on learning and achievement, but this impact can be either positive or negative."

Source: Hattie, J. (2009). *Visible Learning: A Synthesis of Over 800 Meta-Analyses Relating to Achievement*. Routledge.

Stephen Covey: "Most people do not listen with the intent to understand; they listen with the intent to reply."

Source: Covey, S. (1989). *The 7 Habits of Highly Effective People*. Free Press.

Additional Resources

1. **Teaching Communication Skills**
   This article discusses the significance of teaching communication skills to students and provides strategies for educators.
   Edutopia
2. **Teaching Students How to Have Meaningful Conversations**
   This piece offers insights into guiding students toward engaging in meaningful classroom discussions.
   Edutopia
3. **Effective Communication in Schools**
   A scholarly article exploring the role of effective communication in educational settings.
   ERIC
4. **Strategies for Supporting Students' Speaking and Listening Skills**
   This article provides strategies to enhance students' speaking and listening abilities in the classroom.
   Edutopia
5. **Supporting Learners Through Effective Communication: Student Teachers' Communication Strategies to Address Learner Behaviour**
   A study examining how student teachers use communication strategies to manage classroom behavior.
   ERIC
6. **Classroom Discourse: An Essential Component in Building a Classroom Community**
   This article emphasizes the role of classroom discourse in fostering a sense of community among students.
   ERIC
7. **Teacher-Parent Communication Can Help Support Students**

An exploration of how effective communication between teachers and parents can bolster student support.

Edutopia

8. The Art of Effectively Communicating With Students (and Staff!)

Insights into the nuances of effective communication with students and colleagues in educational environments.

Edutopia

9. The Importance of Positive Body Language in the Classroom

This article highlights how positive body language can enhance classroom communication and student engagement.

National Education Association

10. The Student-Centered Classroom: Communicating What Matters

A discussion on the importance of communication in creating a student-centered learning environment.

Edutopia

The Importance of Effective Communication

Effective communication in the classroom is a cornerstone of successful teaching and learning for several critical reasons. It plays a multifaceted role that extends beyond the mere exchange of information, deeply influencing the educational environment, student engagement, and academic outcomes.

Facilitating the Exchange of Ideas

In a classroom setting, the exchange of ideas between teachers and students is fundamental to the learning process. Exchanges must be clear and meaningful. When teachers communicate their lessons clearly, students are more likely to understand complex concepts and engage actively in discussions. This bidirectional flow of information allows for a more dynamic and interactive classroom experience where students feel empowered to ask questions, share their thoughts, and contribute to the learning community.

Supporting Peer Collaboration

Collaboration is a vital skill for students to develop, both for their academic careers and future professional lives. Effective communication supports peer collaboration by establishing a framework where students can work together harmoniously. When instructions are clear and expectations are well-communicated, group activities and projects run more smoothly. Students learn to communicate effectively with one another, share responsibilities, and work toward common goals.

Fostering Mutual Respect and Understanding

Clear and respectful communication helps to build a classroom environment based on mutual respect and understanding. When teachers communicate expectations, feedback, and instructions in a manner that respects students' individuality and needs, it helps to create a positive and supportive learning environment. Students who feel respected are more likely to reciprocate that respect towards their teachers and peers, leading to a more harmonious and productive classroom atmosphere.

Preventing Misunderstandings and Reducing Conflicts

Misunderstandings in the classroom can lead to confusion, frustration, and conflicts. Effective communication minimizes these risks. When students know what is expected of them and understand the rationale behind classroom rules and assignments, they are less likely to misinterpret instructions or feel unjustly treated. This clarity helps in reducing behavioral issues and creates a more stable and focused learning environment.

Ensuring Students Are Aware of Their Responsibilities and Expectations

A key component of effective classroom communication is making sure that students are aware of their responsibilities and what is expected of them. Clear communication helps in setting these boundaries and guidelines. When students understand their roles within the classroom, they are more likely to adhere to rules and complete their assignments diligently. This understanding also empowers students to take ownership of their learning and behavior, fostering a sense of responsibility and accountability.

Providing Feedback and Guiding Student Behavior

Effective communication is essential in providing constructive feedback, which is crucial for student growth and development. Feedback that is clear, specific, and timely helps students understand their strengths and areas for improvement. It guides their behavior and learning strategies, enabling them to make informed decisions about their educational journey. Moreover, when feedback is delivered in a positive and supportive manner, it encourages students to view challenges as opportunities for growth rather than setbacks.

Creating an Inclusive Learning Environment

An inclusive learning environment is one where all students feel valued and supported, regardless of their backgrounds or abilities. Effective communication is key to achieving this inclusivity. By using diverse communication strategies that cater to the varied needs of students—such as visual aids for visual learners or interactive discussions for kinesthetic learners—teachers can ensure that every student has access to the learning process. Additionally, open and empathetic communication fosters a sense of belonging among students, encouraging them to participate fully and confidently in classroom activities.

Enhancing Teacher-Student Relationships

Strong teacher-student relationships are built on a foundation of effective communication. When teachers communicate openly and honestly with their students, it helps to build trust and rapport. Students who feel that their teachers genuinely care about their well-being and academic success are more likely to engage positively with the learning process. These strong relationships can also serve as a support system for students, providing them with the confidence and motivation to overcome challenges and achieve their academic goals.

Supporting Academic and Social Development

Effective communication is not only crucial for academic success but also for the social development of students. Through effective communication, teachers can model and teach social skills such as active listening, empathy, and conflict resolution. These skills are essential for students to interact positively with their peers and develop healthy relationships both inside and outside the classroom. By fostering these social skills, teachers contribute to the overall development of well-rounded individuals who are prepared to navigate the complexities of life.

In conclusion, effective communication in the classroom is vital for creating a conducive learning environment, fostering collaboration, and supporting the holistic development of students. It helps in building a classroom culture based on respect, understanding, and mutual support, where every student feels valued and empowered to achieve their full potential. By mastering the art of communication, teachers can enhance their effectiveness, create a positive impact on their students' lives, and contribute to the success of their educational community.

Verbal	Speaking interactions that include clear and concise instructions
Non-Verbal	Using Body language, facial expressions, gestures
Active Listening	Demonstrating genuine interest in students while communicating
Digital Comms	Using tech to facilitate comms: emails; educational platforms; media
Feedback	Providing and receiving timely, specific, and constructive feedback

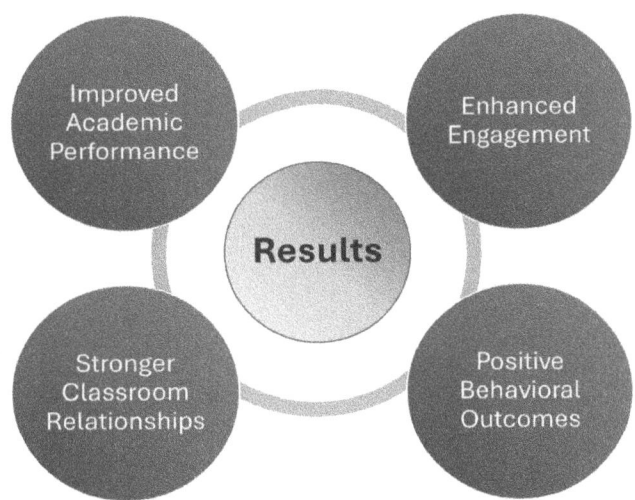

Benefits of Effective Communications

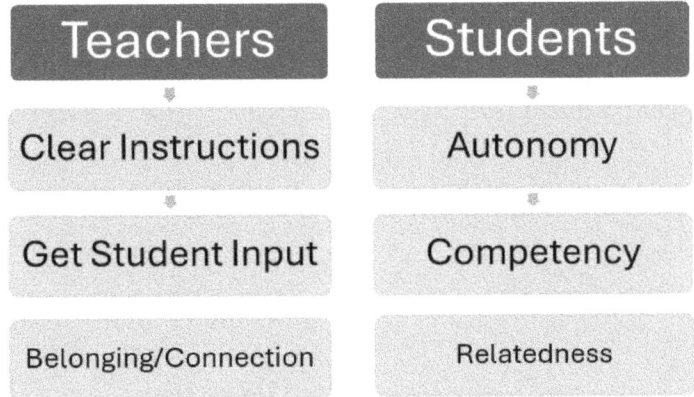

Expanded Case Studies

Case Study #1: Implementing Active Listening Techniques

Problem: Mr. Thompson noticed that his students often seemed disengaged during class discussions. The lack of participation and engagement hindered the effectiveness of these discussions and the overall learning experience.

Scenario: To address the issue, Mr. Thompson decided to implement active listening techniques to show his students that their opinions were valued. His goal was to increase student participation and engagement in class discussions.

Implementation: The steps Mr. Thompson took included:

1. **Maintaining Eye Contact:**
   » Mr. Thompson made a conscious effort to maintain eye contact with students during discussions. This non-verbal cue signaled that he was paying attention and valued their contributions (Covey, 1989).

2. **Nodding and Body Language:**
   » He used nodding and other positive body language to encourage students as they spoke. This non-verbal affirmation helped students feel more confident and willing to participate (Gordon, 2003).

3. **Verbal Affirmations:**
   » Mr. Thompson provided verbal affirmations such as "I see," "That's a great point," and "Thank you for sharing." These affirmations reinforced the idea that student input was important and valued (Rogers & Farson, 1987).

4. **Reflective Listening:**
   » He practiced reflective listening by paraphrasing what students said and asking follow-up questions to deepen understanding and show that he was genuinely engaged (Brownell, 2012).

5. **Encouraging Turn-Taking:**
   » Mr. Thompson established norms for turn-taking to ensure that all students had the opportunity to contribute. He used a talking stick or designated speaker to manage the flow of conversation (Covey, 1989).

6. **Creating a Safe Environment:**
   » He worked to create a safe and respectful classroom environment where students felt comfortable expressing their thoughts without fear of judgment or ridicule (Noddings, 1992).

Outcome: The implementation of active listening techniques led to significant improvements in student participation and engagement in class discussions. Specific outcomes included:

- **Increased Participation:** More students began contributing to class discussions, feeling confident that their voices were heard and valued (Covey, 1989).
- **Enhanced Engagement:** The level of student engagement during discussions increased as students felt more connected and involved in the learning process (Brownell, 2012).
- **Improved Understanding:** Reflective listening helped clarify and deepen understanding of the topics discussed, benefiting both the students and the teacher (Rogers & Farson, 1987).
- **Positive Classroom Atmosphere:** The respectful and supportive environment fostered a sense of community and collaboration among students (Noddings, 1992).

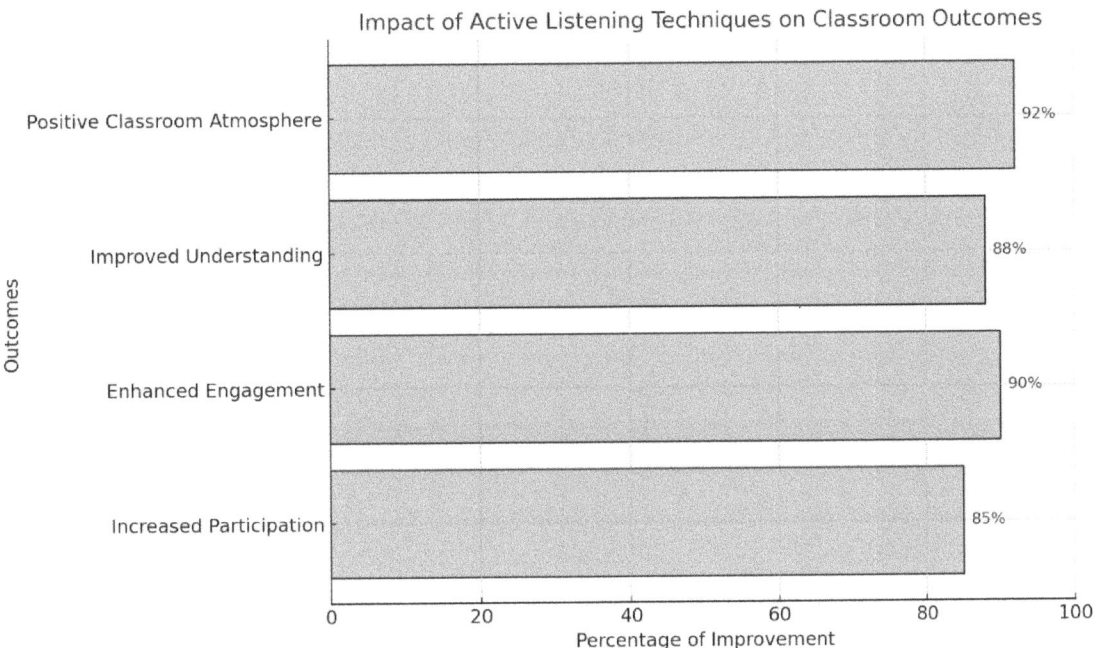

Here is a horizontal bar chart visually representing the impact of active listening techniques on classroom outcomes. Each bar illustrates the significant improvements in key areas such as participation, engagement, understanding, and atmosphere.

Best Practices:

1. **Maintain Eye Contact:**
   » Use eye contact to show that you are paying attention and value students' contributions (Covey, 1989).

2. **Use Positive Body Language:**
   » Encourage students with nodding and other positive body language cues to reinforce their confidence and willingness to participate (Gordon, 2003).

3. **Provide Verbal Affirmations:**
   » Offer verbal affirmations to acknowledge and appreciate student input, making them feel valued (Rogers & Farson, 1987).

4. **Practice Reflective Listening:**
   » Paraphrase and ask follow-up questions to demonstrate genuine engagement and enhance understanding (Brownell, 2012).

5. **Encourage Turn-Taking:**
   » Establish norms for turn-taking to ensure equitable participation and manage the flow of conversation (Covey, 1989).

6. **Create a Safe Environment:**
   » Foster a classroom atmosphere where students feel safe and respected, encouraging open and honest communication (Noddings, 1992).

By implementing these best practices, teachers can enhance student engagement and participation in class discussions, creating a more dynamic and effective learning environment.

Cited Sources:

1. Covey, S. R. (1989). *The 7 Habits of Highly Effective People: Powerful Lessons in Personal Change.* Free Press.
2. Gordon, T. (2003). *Teacher Effectiveness Training: The Program Proven to Help Teachers Bring Out the Best in Students of All Ages.* Three Rivers Press.
3. Rogers, C. R., & Farson, R. E. (1987). *Active Listening.* In R. G. Newman, M. A. Danzinger, & M. Cohen (Eds.), *Communications in Business Today* (pp. 47-58). D.C. Heath and Company.
4. Brownell, J. (2012). *Listening: Attitudes, Principles, and Skills* (5th ed.). Pearson.
5. Noddings, N. (1992). *The Challenge to Care in Schools: An Alternative Approach to Education.* Teachers College Press.

Case Study #2: Visual Aids

Problem: Ms. Lee observed that her students often struggled to grasp complex topics when relying solely on verbal instructions. This led to confusion, misunderstandings, and lower academic performance.

Scenario: To enhance student understanding, Ms. Lee decided to use visual aids, such as charts and diagrams, to support her verbal instructions during lessons on complex topics. Her goal was to make the content more accessible and comprehensible for all students.

Implementation: The steps Ms. Lee took included:

1. **Integration of Visual Aids:**
   » Ms. Lee incorporated various visual aids into her lessons, including charts, diagrams, infographics, and concept maps. These visuals were used to illustrate key points and clarify complex concepts (Hattie, 2009).
2. **Interactive Whiteboard:**
   » She utilized an interactive whiteboard to display visual aids and engage students in interactive learning activities. This technology allowed her to highlight, annotate, and manipulate visuals in real-time (Mayer, 2009).
3. **Consistent Use of Visuals:**
   » Ms. Lee consistently used visual aids across different subjects and topics to provide a cohesive learning experience. Visuals were integrated into her lesson plans, homework assignments, and assessments (Marzano, 2007).
4. **Visual Summaries:**
   » At the end of each lesson, Ms. Lee created visual summaries that encapsulated the key points. These summaries were distributed as handouts and made available online for students to review (Rosenshine, 2012).
5. **Student-Created Visuals:**
   » She encouraged students to create their own visual aids as part of class projects and presentations. This active involvement helped reinforce their understanding of the material (Buzan, 2010).
6. **Feedback and Adjustments:**
   » Ms. Lee regularly sought feedback from students about the effectiveness of the visual aids. Based on their input, she made adjustments to improve clarity and engagement (Sweller, 2011).

Outcome: The use of visual aids led to significant improvements in student understanding and academic performance. Specific outcomes included:

- **Enhanced Comprehension:** Students found the visual aids helpful in understanding difficult concepts, leading to improved comprehension and retention of information (Hattie, 2009).
- **Improved Academic Performance:** The visual aids contributed to higher test scores and overall academic performance as students could better grasp and apply complex ideas (Mayer, 2009).
- **Increased Engagement:** The interactive and visually-rich lessons kept students more engaged and motivated to learn (Marzano, 2007).
- **Positive Feedback:** Students consistently reported that the visual aids made learning more enjoyable and less stressful, particularly for visual learners (Rosenshine, 2012).

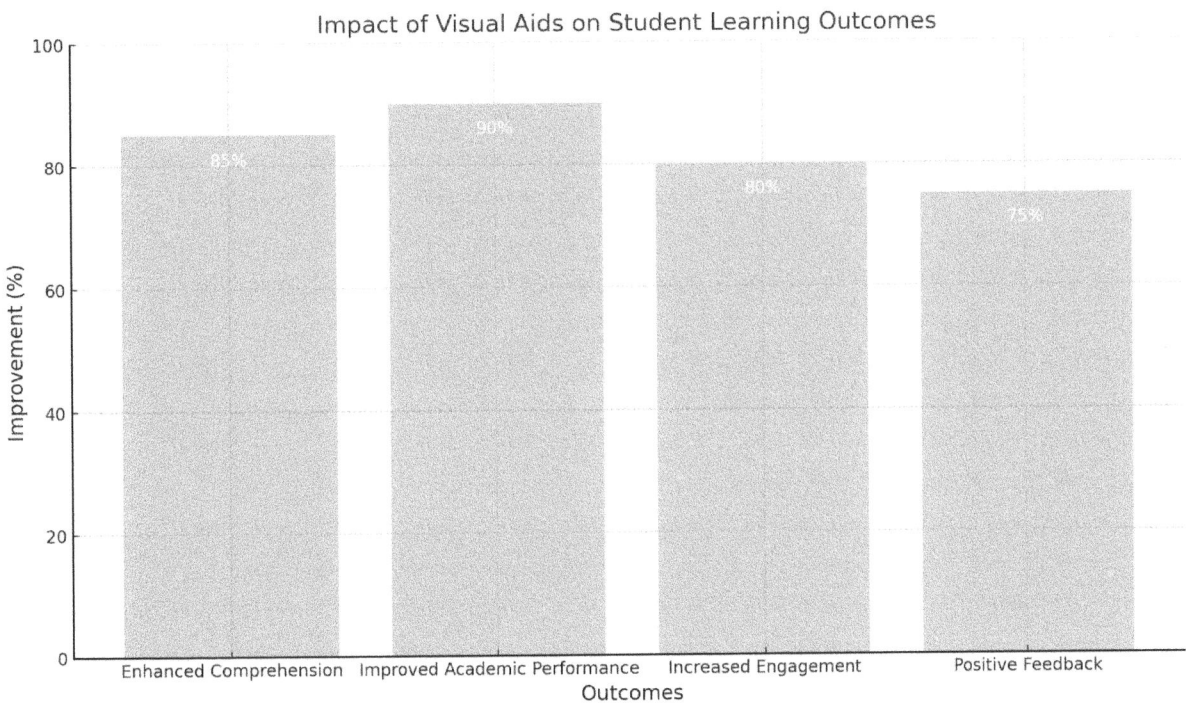

Here is a bar chart visualizing the impact of visual aids on student learning outcomes, showing the percentage improvements in comprehension, academic performance, engagement, and feedback.

Best Practices:

1. **Integrate Visuals Consistently:**
   » Use visual aids regularly across different subjects and topics to provide a cohesive and supportive learning experience (Hattie, 2009).

2. **Utilize Technology:**
   » Leverage technology, such as interactive whiteboards, to display and manipulate visual aids, making lessons more interactive and engaging (Mayer, 2009).

3. **Create Visual Summaries:**
   » Develop visual summaries that encapsulate key points from lessons. Distribute these summaries as handouts and online resources for students to review (Rosenshine, 2012).

4. **Encourage Student Participation:**

   » Involve students in creating their own visual aids as part of projects and presentations to reinforce their understanding and creativity (Buzan, 2010).

5. **Seek Feedback:**

   » Regularly seek feedback from students on the effectiveness of visual aids and make adjustments based on their input to improve clarity and engagement (Sweller, 2011).

By implementing these best practices, teachers can enhance student understanding and academic performance through the effective use of visual aids.

Cited Sources:

1. Hattie, J. (2009). *Visible Learning: A Synthesis of Over 800 Meta-Analyses Relating to Achievement*. Routledge.
2. Mayer, R. E. (2009). *Multimedia Learning*. Cambridge University Press.
3. Marzano, R. J. (2007). *The Art and Science of Teaching: A Comprehensive Framework for Effective Instruction*. ASCD.
4. Rosenshine, B. (2012). Principles of Instruction: Research-Based Strategies That All Teachers Should Know. *American Educator*, 36(1), 12-39.
5. Buzan, T. (2010). *The Mind Map Book: Unlock Your Creativity, Boost Your Memory, Change Your Life*. BBC Active.
6. Sweller, J. (2011). *Cognitive Load Theory*. Springer.

Case Study #3: Constructive Feedback

Problem: Mr. Ramirez noticed that his students were not making the desired progress in their academic work. Despite their efforts, the quality of their assignments remained stagnant, indicating a need for more effective guidance and support.

Scenario: To address this issue, Mr. Ramirez decided to focus on providing timely and specific feedback on his students' assignments. His goal was to help students understand their strengths and areas for improvement, thereby enhancing their overall academic performance.

Implementation: The steps Mr. Ramirez took included:

1. **Timely Feedback:**

   » Mr. Ramirez ensured that feedback was provided promptly after assignments were submitted. This timely intervention helped students apply the feedback to subsequent tasks without delay (Hattie, 2009).

2. **Specific Feedback:**

   » He provided specific and detailed feedback, highlighting both strengths and areas for improvement. Instead of generic comments, he focused on actionable suggestions that students could implement (Brookhart, 2017).

3. **Balanced Approach:**

   » Mr. Ramirez maintained a balance between positive reinforcement and constructive criticism. He acknowledged students' efforts and achievements while also pointing out areas that needed improvement (Wiggins, 2012).

4. **Individual Conferences:**
   » He held individual conferences with students to discuss their progress and feedback in detail. These one-on-one sessions allowed for personalized guidance and support (Marzano, 2007).

5. **Rubrics and Exemplars:**
   » Mr. Ramirez used rubrics and exemplars to provide clear expectations and standards. These tools helped students understand what was required and how to achieve higher levels of performance (Andrade, 2005).

6. **Encouraging Self-Assessment:**
   » He encouraged students to engage in self-assessment and reflection, helping them take ownership of their learning and develop critical thinking skills (Black & Wiliam, 1998).

Outcome: The implementation of constructive feedback led to significant improvements in student performance. Specific outcomes included:

- **Improved Academic Performance:** Students appreciated the constructive feedback and showed significant improvement in their academic performance. The specific and actionable nature of the feedback helped them understand and correct their mistakes (Hattie, 2009).
- **Increased Motivation:** The balanced approach of positive reinforcement and constructive criticism increased students' motivation and confidence in their abilities (Brookhart, 2017).
- **Enhanced Understanding:** Individual conferences and detailed feedback helped students gain a deeper understanding of the subject matter and the criteria for success (Marzano, 2007).
- **Positive Learning Environment:** The supportive and constructive feedback fostered a positive learning environment where students felt valued and encouraged to improve (Wiggins, 2012).

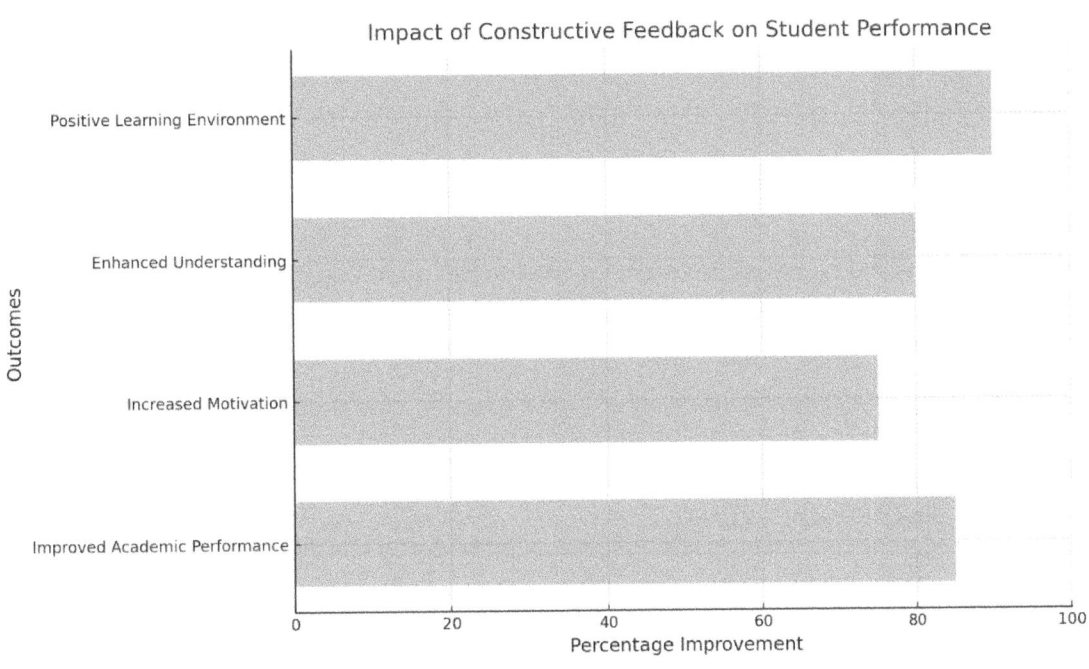

Here's a horizontal bar chart that visually represents the impact of constructive feedback on student performance. Each bar corresponds to a specific outcome, such as improved academic performance, increased motivation, enhanced understanding, and a positive learning environment, with hypothetical percentages illustrating their significance.

Best Practices:

1. **Provide Timely Feedback:**
   » Ensure that feedback is given promptly after assignments are submitted to allow students to apply it to future tasks (Hattie, 2009).

2. **Be Specific and Actionable:**
   » Offer detailed and specific feedback that highlights strengths and provides clear, actionable suggestions for improvement (Brookhart, 2017).

3. **Balance Positive and Constructive Feedback:**
   » Maintain a balance between positive reinforcement and constructive criticism to motivate and guide students effectively (Wiggins, 2012).

4. **Hold Individual Conferences:**
   » Conduct one-on-one conferences with students to discuss feedback in detail and provide personalized support (Marzano, 2007).

5. **Use Rubrics and Exemplars:**
   » Utilize rubrics and exemplars to set clear expectations and standards, helping students understand how to achieve higher performance levels (Andrade, 2005).

6. **Encourage Self-Assessment:**
   » Promote self-assessment and reflection to help students take ownership of their learning and develop critical thinking skills (Black & Wiliam, 1998).

By implementing these best practices, teachers can provide effective constructive feedback that enhances student learning and academic performance.

Cited Sources:

1. Hattie, J. (2009). *Visible Learning: A Synthesis of Over 800 Meta-Analyses Relating to Achievement.* Routledge.
2. Brookhart, S. M. (2017). *How to Give Effective Feedback to Your Students.* ASCD.
3. Wiggins, G. (2012). *Seven Keys to Effective Feedback.* Educational Leadership, 70(1), 10-16.
4. Marzano, R. J. (2007). *The Art and Science of Teaching: A Comprehensive Framework for Effective Instruction.* ASCD.
5. Andrade, H. (2005). *Teaching with Rubrics: The Good, The Bad, and The Ugly.* College Teaching, 53(1), 27-30.
6. Black, P., & Wiliam, D. (1998). *Assessment and Classroom Learning.* Assessment in Education: Principles, Policy & Practice, 5(1), 7-74.

Case Study #4: Clear Instructions

Problem: Ms. Roberts noticed that her students often struggled to follow multi-step assignments and activities, leading to frustration and incomplete work. She realized that her instructions might not be as clear and effective as they could be.

Scenario: To address this issue, Ms. Roberts decided to improve her communication by breaking down instructions into smaller, manageable steps. Her goal was to make instructions clear and accessible to ensure that students could complete tasks accurately and independently.

Implementation: The steps Ms. Roberts took included:

1. **Breaking Down Instructions:**
   » Ms. Roberts broke down instructions into smaller, manageable steps, ensuring that each step was clear and concise (Rosenshine, 2012).
2. **Simple and Concise Language:**
   » She used simple and concise language to avoid confusion and ensure that all students could understand the instructions (Marzano, 2007).
3. **Verbal and Written Instructions:**
   » Ms. Roberts provided both verbal and written instructions for each task. This dual approach catered to different learning styles and reinforced the instructions (Brookhart, 2017).
4. **Visual Cues and Examples:**
   » She incorporated visual cues and examples to illustrate each step of the process. This visual support helped students grasp complex instructions more easily (Mayer, 2009).
5. **Checking for Understanding:**
   » Ms. Roberts made it a point to check for understanding by asking students to repeat the instructions back to her or explain the task in their own words. This ensured that students had a clear understanding before they began the task (Wiliam, 2011).
6. **Providing Opportunities for Questions:**
   » She encouraged students to ask questions if they were unsure about any part of the instructions. This open communication helped address any confusion promptly (Hattie, 2009).

Outcome: The clarity and simplicity of the instructions led to a noticeable improvement in students' ability to complete tasks accurately and independently. Specific outcomes included:

- **Increased Accuracy:** Students were able to follow the instructions more accurately, leading to higher quality work and fewer errors (Rosenshine, 2012).
- **Improved Confidence:** Clear instructions helped students feel more confident and less anxious about assignments, resulting in increased engagement and participation (Marzano, 2007).
- **Enhanced Independence:** Students were able to complete tasks independently without constant assistance, fostering a sense of autonomy and responsibility (Brookhart, 2017).
- **Organized Classroom Environment:** The improved clarity of instructions created a more organized and productive classroom environment, with smoother transitions between activities (Wiliam, 2011).

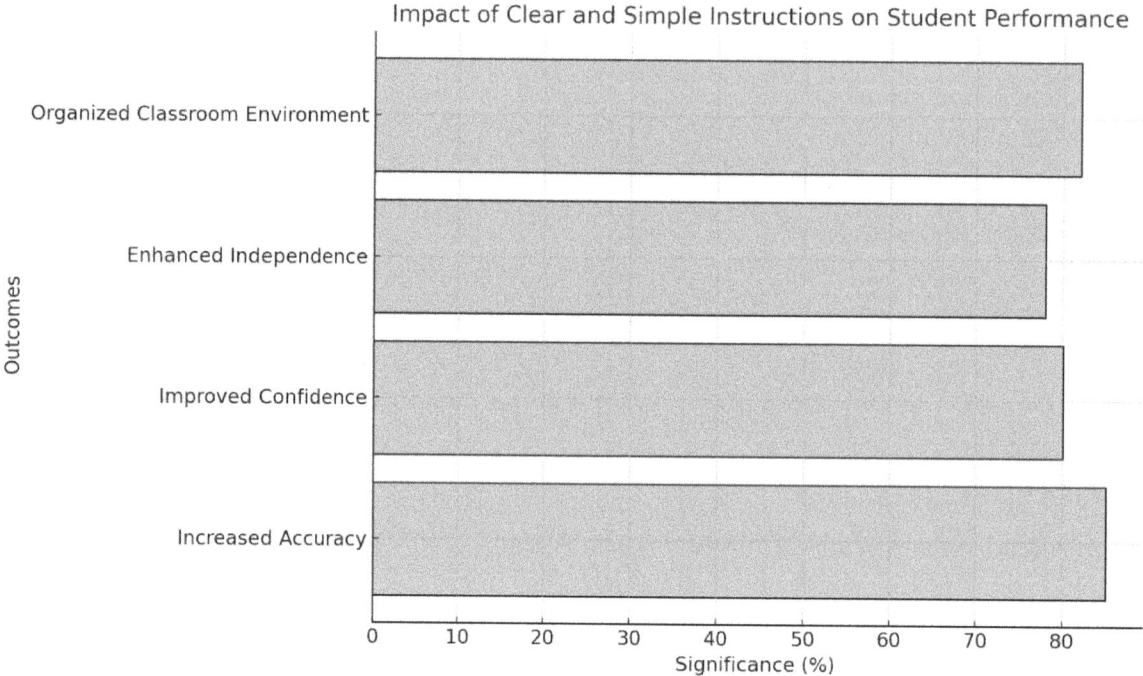

Here's a horizontal bar chart illustrating the significant impact of clear and simple instructions on student performance. Each bar represents a key outcome, with its corresponding level of significance.

Best Practices:

1. **Break Down Instructions:**
   - » Divide instructions into smaller, manageable steps to ensure clarity and comprehensibility (Rosenshine, 2012).
2. **Use Simple Language:**
   - » Use simple, concise language to avoid confusion and ensure that all students can understand the instructions (Marzano, 2007).
3. **Provide Dual Instructions:**
   - » Offer both verbal and written instructions to cater to different learning styles and reinforce the instructions (Brookhart, 2017).
4. **Incorporate Visual Aids:**
   - » Use visual cues and examples to illustrate each step of the process, helping students grasp complex instructions more easily (Mayer, 2009).
5. **Check for Understanding:**
   - » Regularly check for understanding by asking students to repeat instructions or explain the task in their own words (Wiliam, 2011).
6. **Encourage Questions:**
   - » Foster an environment where students feel comfortable asking questions if they are unsure about any part of the instructions (Hattie, 2009).

By implementing these best practices, teachers can improve the clarity and effectiveness of their instructions, leading to better student outcomes and a more organized classroom environment.

Cited Sources:

1. Rosenshine, B. (2012). *Principles of Instruction: Research-Based Strategies That All Teachers Should Know*. American Educator, 36(1), 12-39.
2. Marzano, R. J. (2007). *The Art and Science of Teaching: A Comprehensive Framework for Effective Instruction*. ASCD.
3. Brookhart, S. M. (2017). *How to Give Effective Feedback to Your Students*. ASCD.
4. Mayer, R. E. (2009). *Multimedia Learning*. Cambridge University Press.
5. Wiliam, D. (2011). *Embedded Formative Assessment*. Solution Tree Press.
6. Hattie, J. (2009). *Visible Learning: A Synthesis of Over 800 Meta-Analyses Relating to Achievement*. Routledge.

Tips and Best Practices

1. **Use Non-Verbal Cues**: Complement verbal communication with appropriate body language and facial expressions.
2. **Be Mindful of Tone**: Ensure that your tone of voice matches the message you are conveying.
3. **Encourage Questions**: Promote a culture where students feel comfortable asking questions to clarify their understanding.
4. **Regular Check-Ins**: Conduct regular check-ins with students to address any communication gaps and ensure they are on track.
5. **Provide Multiple Communication Channels**: Use various channels, such as in-person, email, and educational platforms, to communicate with students and parents.

Tip Example

Use Non-Verbal Cues	Smile and maintain eye contact while addressing the class.
Be Mindful of Tone	Use a calm tone to explain instructions clearly and avoid confusion.
Encourage Questions	Create a "question box" for anonymous queries students might have.
Regular Check-Ins	Have a 5-minute weekly chat with students to discuss progress.
Provide Multiple Communication Channels	Send updates via email and use educational apps for assignments.

Cited Sources:

7. Rosenshine, B. (2012). *Principles of Instruction: Research-Based Strategies That All Teachers Should Know*. American Educator, 36(1), 12-39.
8. Marzano, R. J. (2007). *The Art and Science of Teaching: A Comprehensive Framework for Effective Instruction*. ASCD.
9. Brookhart, S. M. (2017). *How to Give Effective Feedback to Your Students*. ASCD.

10. Mayer, R. E. (2009). *Multimedia Learning.* Cambridge University Press.

11. Wiliam, D. (2011). *Embedded Formative Assessment.* Solution Tree Press.

12. Hattie, J. (2009). *Visible Learning: A Synthesis of Over 800 Meta-Analyses Relating to Achievement.* Routledge.

Rubric for Self-Assessment

CriteriaExcellent (5)Good (4)Fair (3)Needs Improvement (2)Poor (1)

Clarity of Communication	Communication is clear and easily understood.	Communication is generally clear.	Communication is somewhat clear.	Communication is often unclear.	Communication is very unclear.
Active Listening	Consistently practices active listening.	Generally practices active listening.	Occasionally practices active listening.	Rarely practices active listening.	Does not practice active listening.
Use of Visual Aids	Frequently uses visual aids effectively.	Often uses visual aids.	Occasionally uses visual aids.	Rarely uses visual aids.	Does not use visual aids.
Providing Feedback	Provides timely and constructive feedback.	Often provides constructive feedback.	Occasionally provides constructive feedback.	Rarely provides constructive feedback.	Does not provide constructive feedback.
Encouraging Dialogue	Consistently encourages open dialogue.	Often encourages open dialogue.	Occasionally encourages open dialogue.	Rarely encourages open dialogue.	Does not encourage open dialogue.

Recommended Reading List

1. The First Days of School: How to Be an Effective Teacher by Harry K. Wong and Rosemary T. Wong

2. Classroom Management That Works: Research-Based Strategies for Every Teacher by Robert J. Marzano, Jana S. Marzano, and Debra J. Pickering

3. Teach Like a Champion 2.0: 62 Techniques that Put Students on the Path to College by Doug Lemov

4. Tools for Teaching by Fred Jones

5. The Classroom Management Book by Harry K. Wong and Rosemary T. Wong

Quiz, Reflection, and Short Essay for the Chapter on Effective Communication

Multiple-Choice Quiz

1. What is a primary benefit of effective communication in the classroom?

   a. Increased homework

   b. Enhanced student engagement

    c. More free time for teachers

    d. Advanced technology

2. According to Constructivist Learning Theory, how is knowledge constructed?

    a. Through rote memorization

    b. Through social interactions and meaningful engagement

    c. Through strict discipline

    d. Through advanced technology

3. How do effective communication skills impact students' behavior, according to Social Learning Theory?

    a. They increase student anxiety

    b. They provide structure and expectations

    c. They reduce students' engagement

    d. They create confusion

4. What is a key aspect of fostering effective communication in the classroom?

    a. Flexibility and spontaneity

    b. Clarity and consistency

    c. Avoiding student input

    d. Complexity and ambiguity

5. According to the Transactional Model of Communication, what is essential for effective communication?

    a. Advanced technology

    b. Feedback and context

    c. More homework

    d. Increasing discipline

5. Which of the following is a benefit for teachers when effective communication is established?

    a. More administrative tasks

    b. Easier classroom management

    c. Increased need for discipline

    d. More homework for students

6. How can effective communication impact academic performance?

    a. It distracts students from learning

    b. It provides a stable environment for learning

    c. It decreases student motivation

    d. It increases test anxiety

7. According to Self-Determination Theory, what need is fulfilled by effective communication?

    a. Competence

    b. Autonomy

    c. Relatedness

    d. Discipline

8. What is an effective way to establish clear communication in the classroom?

    a. Flexibility and spontaneity

    b. Through clear guidelines and feedback

c. By increasing homework

d. By avoiding student input

9. According to the Transactional Model of Communication, why is feedback important?

   a. It increases cognitive load

   b. It reduces cognitive load

   c. It has no effect on communication

   d. It ensures messages are understood and acted upon

Short Reflection Questions

1. Why is effective communication important in the classroom?

2. Describe a method you would use to improve communication with your students.

3. How do you think effective communication can impact the overall classroom environment?

Short Response Questions

1. **Scenario:** You notice that a student often misunderstands instructions and appears confused during class activities. What steps would you take to improve communication with this student?

2. **Scenario:** You want to enhance communication with parents to better support student learning. How would you go about achieving this?

Short Essay Response

Discuss the theoretical foundations of effective communication in the classroom. How do theories such as Constructivist Learning Theory, Social Learning Theory, the Transactional Model of Communication, and Self-Determination Theory support the practice of fostering effective communication? Use references from the chapter to support your answer.

Answer Key

Multiple-Choice Quiz

1. b) Enhanced student engagement

2. b) Through social interactions and meaningful engagement

3. b) They provide structure and expectations

4. b) Clarity and consistency

5. b) Feedback and context

6. b) Easier classroom management

7. b) It provides a stable environment for learning

8. c) Relatedness

9. b) Through clear guidelines and feedback

10. d) It ensures messages are understood and acted upon

Short Reflection Questions

1. **Why is effective communication important in the classroom?**
   » Effective communication is essential in the classroom as it fosters a positive learning environment, enhances student engagement, and supports academic achievement. Clear, consistent, and compassionate communication helps convey expectations, provide constructive feedback, and build strong relationships with students and parents, promoting a collaborative and supportive classroom atmosphere.

2. **Describe a method you would use to improve communication with your students.**
   » One method to improve communication with students is to implement regular check-ins and feedback sessions. This involves setting aside time to discuss progress, address concerns, and provide constructive feedback. Additionally, using clear and concise language, active listening, and incorporating visual aids can help ensure that messages are understood and students feel heard and valued.

3. **How do you think effective communication can impact the overall classroom environment?**
   » Effective communication can significantly impact the classroom environment by creating a sense of trust, respect, and inclusivity. When students feel that their teacher communicates clearly and listens to their needs, they are more likely to engage in learning, exhibit positive behavior, and collaborate with peers. This leads to a more productive and harmonious classroom atmosphere.

Short Response Questions

1. **Scenario:** You notice that a student often misunderstands instructions and appears confused during class activities. What steps would you take to improve communication with this student?

2. **Scenario:** You want to enhance communication with parents to better support student learning. How would you go about achieving this?

References:

Constructivist Learning Theory

- Piaget, J. (1952). *The Origins of Intelligence in Children.* International Universities Press.
- Vygotsky, L. S. (1978). *Mind in Society: The Development of Higher Psychological Processes.* Harvard University Press.
- Phillips, D. C. (1995). *Theories of Teaching and Learning.* The Handbook of Research on Teaching, 30-33.

Zone of Proximal Development

- Vygotsky, L. S. (1978). *Mind in Society: The Development of Higher Psychological Processes.* Harvard University Press.
- Daniels, H. (2001). *Vygotsky and Pedagogy.* Routledge.

Communication in Education

- Marzano, R. J., & Marzano, J. S. (2003). *The Key to Classroom Management.* Educational Leadership, 61(1), 6-13.
- Hattie, J. (2009). *Visible Learning: A Synthesis of Over 800 Meta-Analyses Relating to Achievement.* Routledge.

Collaborative Learning

- Dillenbourg, P. (1999). *Collaborative Learning: Cognitive and Computational Approaches.* Advances in Learning and Instruction Series.
- Johnson, D. W., & Johnson, R. T. (1989). *Cooperation and Competition: Theory and Research.* Interaction Book Company.

Effective Classroom Communication

- Freiberg, H. J., & Driscoll, A. (2000). *Universal Teaching Strategies*. Allyn and Bacon.
- Goleman, D. (1995). *Emotional Intelligence: Why It Can Matter More Than IQ*. Bantam Books.

Social Learning Theory

- Bandura, A. (1977). *Social Learning Theory*. Prentice Hall.
- Bandura, A. (1986). *Social Foundations of Thought and Action: A Social Cognitive Theory*. Prentice Hall.

CHAPTER 5

THE ALEX EFFECT: BUILDING BRIDGES THROUGH BEHAVIOR

During my early teaching years, I met Alex—a charismatic yet disruptive student who could energize a room or derail a lesson in seconds. Traditional disciplinary methods—reminders, time-outs, and stern talks—had little impact. His behavior wasn't defiance; it was a search for recognition.

Remembering a mentor's advice to "catch them being good," I implemented a Star Tracker. Students earned stars for positive actions and lost stars for disruptive behavior. Enough stars earned access to a "Treasure Chest" of small rewards like stickers or homework passes. Alex was skeptical at first but intrigued. I made it a point to reward his positive actions—holding a door, waiting his turn to speak. Slowly, his attitude shifted.

One Friday, Alex earned enough stars to choose from the Treasure Chest. He picked a bright orange yo-yo, glanced at me, and said shyly, "I did good this week, didn't I?" That moment marked a turning point. Alex began striving for stars, even inspiring his peers to do the same.

There were setbacks—days when he lost stars and faced disappointment. Yet, even in those moments, he learned. One challenging day, he said, "I know why I didn't get a star. I'll do better after lunch." And he did.

By year's end, Alex had transformed. He wasn't just earning stars but helping classmates earn theirs. He became a role model, proving that behavior systems can build connections and inspire growth. His journey reminds me that teaching isn't just about imparting knowledge but helping students see the best in themselves.

This chapter builds on stories like Alex's, offering tools and strategies to create a balanced system of rewards and consequences, fostering a positive and supportive classroom environment.

What You'll Learn

- Insights from Experts: Gain guidance from educational experts on the effective use of rewards and consequences.
- Real-World Case Studies: Explore practical examples of successful implementation in classrooms.

- Actionable Strategies: Learn step-by-step methods for developing and maintaining a balanced approach to rewards and consequences.

The Importance of Rewards and Consequences

- Framework for Understanding Behavior:
  - » Rewards and consequences help students understand the link between their actions and outcomes.
  - » Students learn to take responsibility for their behavior and make positive choices.
- Simplified Classroom Management:
  - » A structured approach reduces the stress associated with managing student behavior.
  - » Teachers can focus more on instruction and meaningful interactions.
- Enhanced Learning Environment:
  - » Clear expectations and consistent consequences create a classroom where:
    - Students feel secure and respected.
    - Positive behaviors are reinforced, fostering motivation and engagement.

Key Benefits

- For Students:
  - » Encourages accountability and self-discipline.
  - » Builds a sense of fairness and predictability.
- For Teachers:
  - » Reduces time spent on disciplinary actions.
  - » Enhances teaching effectiveness by fostering a supportive classroom atmosphere.

Takeaway

By establishing a clear and balanced system of rewards and consequences, you can transform your classroom into an environment where students thrive, behaviors are positively reinforced, and teaching becomes more impactful.

Theoretical Background

The effective use of rewards and consequences in classroom management is supported by several educational theories that emphasize the importance of reinforcement, motivation, and behavioral conditioning.

Behaviorism (Skinner)

Behaviorism, particularly the work of B.F. Skinner, emphasizes the role of reinforcement and punishment in shaping behavior. Positive reinforcement (rewards) and negative reinforcement (consequences) are used to increase desired behaviors and decrease undesired behaviors. Skinner's operant conditioning theory suggests that consistent application of rewards and consequences can effectively modify student behavior (Skinner, 1953).

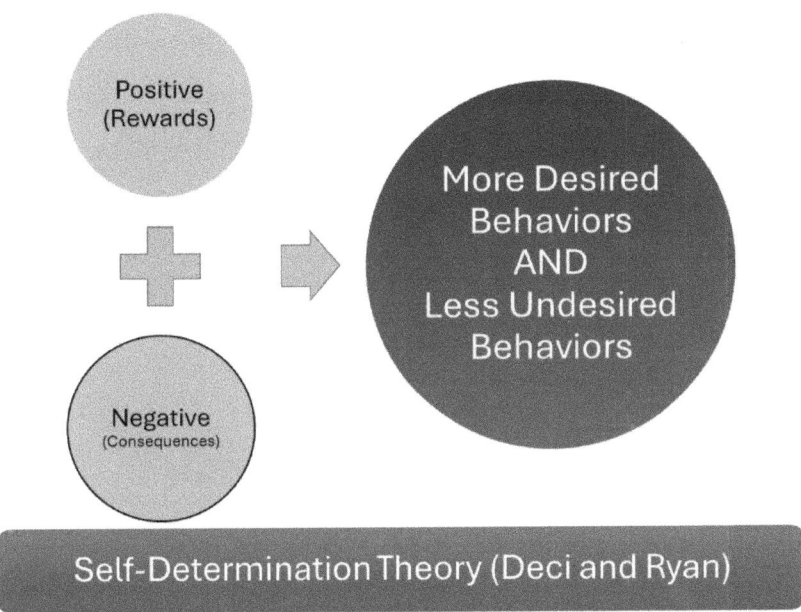

Self-Determination Theory (SDT), developed by Deci and Ryan, emphasizes the importance of intrinsic and extrinsic motivation. Rewards can be used to support intrinsic motivation by acknowledging students' competence and fostering a sense of achievement. However, it is essential to balance extrinsic rewards with opportunities for students to experience autonomy and relatedness, which are critical for sustaining long-term motivation (Deci & Ryan, 2000).

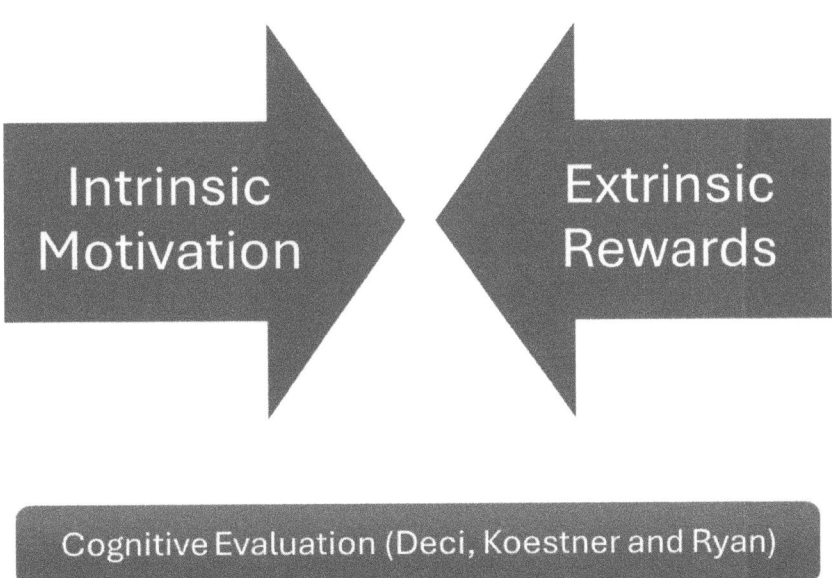

Cognitive Evaluation Theory, a sub-theory of SDT, explores how external rewards can affect intrinsic motivation. According to this theory, while rewards can enhance motivation by providing positive feedback, they can also undermine intrinsic motivation if perceived as controlling. Thus, the thoughtful use of rewards, coupled with meaningful feedback, is crucial for maintaining student motivation (Deci, Koestner, & Ryan, 1999).

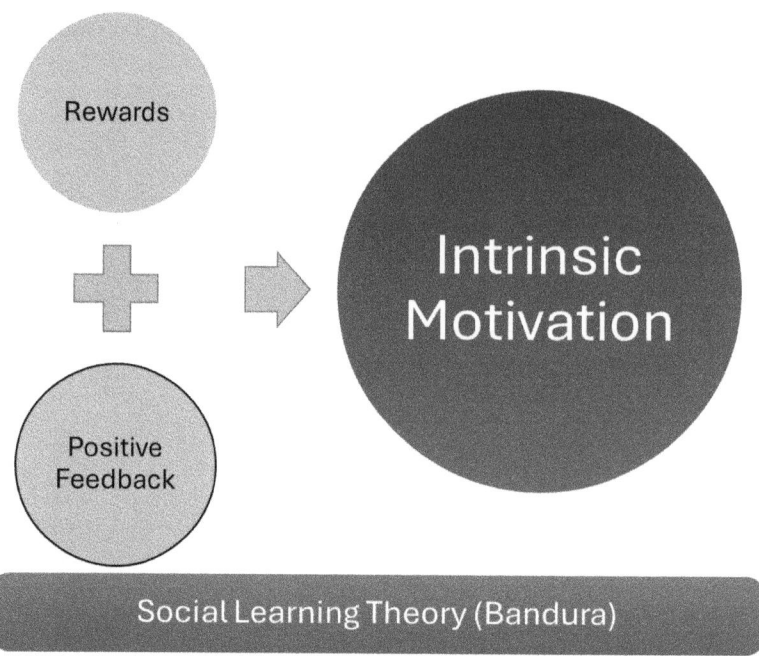

Albert Bandura's Social Learning Theory highlights the importance of observational learning and modeling. Teachers can use rewards and consequences to model desirable behaviors and establish norms for classroom conduct. When students observe their peers being rewarded for positive behavior, they are more likely to emulate those behaviors (Bandura, 1977).

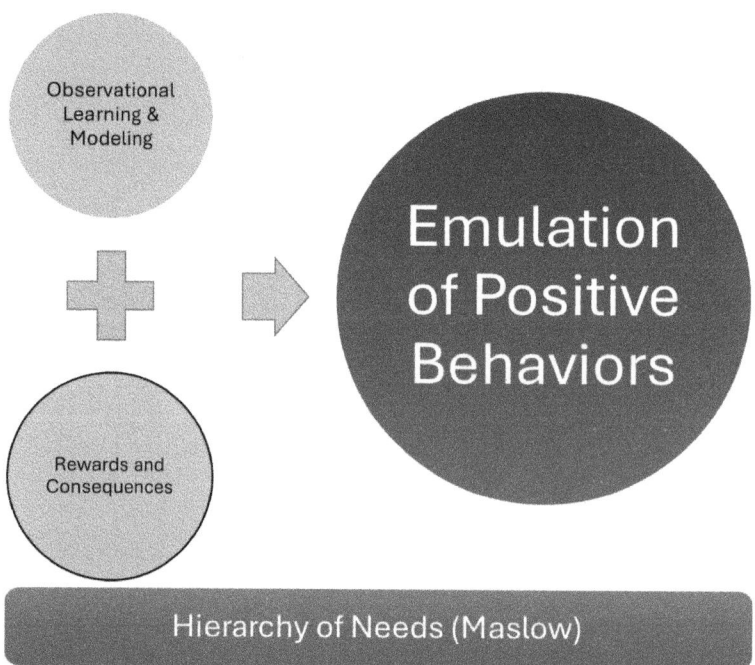

Maslow's Hierarchy of Needs underscores the importance of fulfilling students' basic needs for safety, belonging, and esteem before they can achieve self-actualization. A well-implemented system of rewards and consequences helps create a safe and predictable environment, fostering a sense of belonging and esteem that supports students' overall development and learning (Maslow, 1943).

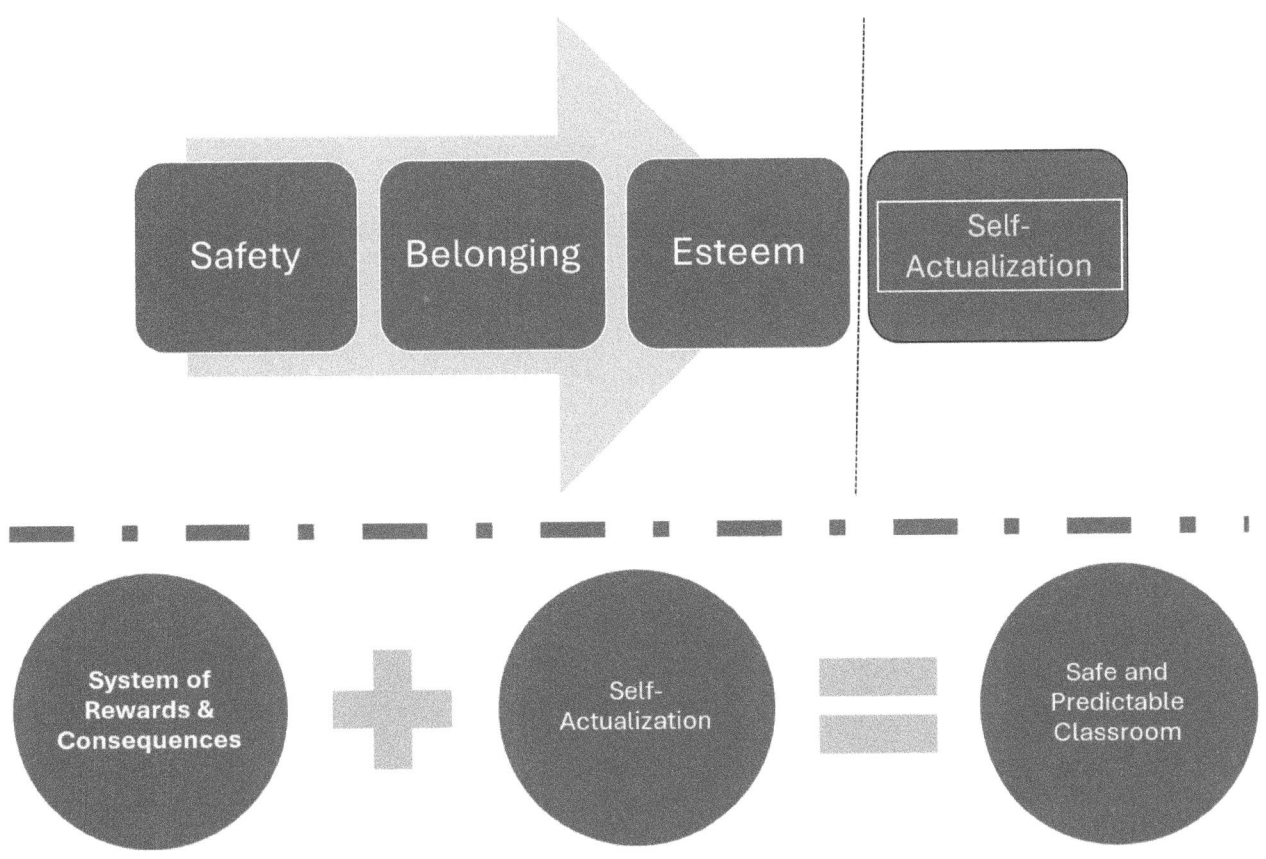

Expert Quotes and Insights

Alfie Kohn: "Rewards and punishments are two sides of the same coin and should be used sparingly. Instead, focus on creating a positive and motivating classroom environment" (Kohn, 1993).

Carol S. Dweck: "Instead of focusing solely on rewards, help students develop a growth mindset by praising their effort and persistence" (Dweck, 2006).

Fred Jones: "Effective consequences are clear, fair, and consistently applied. They help students understand the connection between their actions and the outcomes" (Jones, 2007).

Additional Resources

- Edutopia: The Power of Positive Reinforcement
- Scholastic:**Guidelines for Working with Traumatized Children**
- TeachThought: Strategies for Using Rewards and Consequences
- ASCD: Understanding the Power of Positive Reinforcement
- Education World: **Reward Systems That Work:What to Give and When to Give It!**
- National Education Association (NEA): Classroom Management Strategies
- Responsive Classroom: Rewards and Consequences

- PBS: Classroom Management and Behavior
- Teaching Channel: Behavior Management Strategies
- Education Week: What teachers say build a positive school culture Expanded Section: The Importance of Rewards and Consequences

Effective Use of Rewards and Consequences in Classroom Management

Key Role of Rewards and Consequences

- **Purpose:**
  Rewards and consequences are critical for promoting positive behavior, enhancing motivation, and fostering a respectful learning environment.
- **Core Benefit:**
They help students understand the relationship between their actions and outcomes, fostering accountability and self-discipline.

Impact of Rewards on Student Motivation

- **Focus on Effort and Growth:**
  - » Recognizing **effort** and **improvement** rather than just outcomes is more effective (Kohn, 1993).
  - » This aligns with Carol S. Dweck's (2006) **growth mindset** concept, emphasizing persistence over innate ability.
  - » Rewards encourage students to embrace challenges and view failures as learning opportunities.
- **Lifelong Benefits:**
  Promoting a focus on progress nurtures a lifelong love for learning and builds resilience.

Types of Rewards

- **Verbal Praise:**
  - » Examples: Saying "Great job!" or recognizing a student's effort publicly.
- **Tangible Rewards:**
  - » Examples: Stickers, certificates, or extra privileges like additional recess time.
- **Key Consideration:**
  Rewards must be meaningful to the students to maximize their impact.

Conclusion: The Impact of Rewards and Consequences

Connecting Actions to Outcomes

- **Purpose:**

Strategic implementation of rewards and consequences teaches students the link between their actions and outcomes.

- **Key Benefits:**
  - » Encourages **accountability**.
  - » Promotes **motivation**.
  - » Creates a **positive, disciplined classroom environment**.

Effective Use of Rewards

- **Age-Appropriate Strategies:**
  - » Simple recognition, like a verbal "Well done!", makes students feel valued.
  - » Significant rewards, such as privileges, celebrate major achievements and maintain engagement.
- **Sustaining Effort:**
  Balancing rewards with meaningful acknowledgment encourages continuous effort and growth.

Role of Consequences

- **Discouraging Negative Behavior:**
  - » Clear, fair, and consistent consequences help students understand the impact of their choices (Jones, 2007).
  - » Predictable environments reduce anxiety and confusion, allowing students to focus on learning.
- **Establishing Boundaries:**
  Consistent consequences build a structured and safe classroom atmosphere.

Fostering Respectful and Inclusive Environments

- **Recognition and Fairness:**
  - » Rewarding positive behaviors and addressing negative ones fairly fosters respect for teachers and peers.
  - » Encourages supportive classroom interactions.
- **Research Insight:**
  A balanced system of rewards and consequences significantly improves behavior and academic performance (Marzano et al., 2003).

Supporting Teacher Growth

- **Reflection and Adaptation:**
  - » Teachers improve their strategies by reflecting on practices and seeking feedback.
  - » This process enhances classroom management skills and contributes to professional development.
- **Handling Classroom Diversity:**
  Teachers become more adept at managing varied situations, resulting in a more effective teaching experience.

Final Thought

By fostering accountability, respect, and motivation, a well-implemented system of rewards and consequences benefits both students and teachers, laying the foundation for a thriving, supportive learning environment.

References

- Kohn, A. (1993). Punished by Rewards: The Trouble with Gold Stars, Incentive Plans, A's, Praise, and Other Bribes. Houghton Mifflin. Buy on Bookshop.
- Dweck, C. S. (2006). Mindset: The New Psychology of Success. Random House. Buy on Bookshop.
- Jones, F. H. (2007). Tools for Teaching: Discipline, Instruction, Motivation. Fredric H. Jones & Associates, Inc. Buy on Bookshop.
- Marzano, R. J., Marzano, J. S., & Pickering, D. J. (2003). Classroom Management That Works: Research-Based Strategies for Every Teacher. ASCD. Buy on Bookshop.

Benefits for Students and Teachers

For Students:

- **Encourages Positive Behavior:** Rewards and positive reinforcement encourage students to exhibit desired behaviors. When students see that their efforts are recognized and appreciated, they are more likely to continue these behaviors (Kohn, 1993).
- **Discourages Negative Behavior:** Clear and fair consequences discourage negative behaviors. When students understand the repercussions of their actions, they are more likely to adhere to classroom rules (Jones, 2007).
- **Enhances Motivation and Engagement:** Rewards, especially when linked to effort and improvement, can significantly boost student motivation and engagement. Students become more invested in their learning and personal growth (Dweck, 2006).
- **Promotes Self-Discipline and Accountability:** The use of consequences helps students develop self-discipline and accountability. They learn to take responsibility for their actions and understand the importance of making positive choices (Jones, 2007).
- **Improves Behavioral Outcomes:** A balanced system of rewards and consequences leads to improved behavioral outcomes. Students are more likely to follow classroom rules and contribute to a positive learning environment (Kohn, 1993).

For Teachers:

- **Simplifies Classroom Management:** A well-structured system of rewards and consequences simplifies classroom management. Teachers spend less time on disciplinary actions and more time on instruction (Jones, 2007).
- **Increases Instructional Time:** With fewer behavioral disruptions, teachers can maximize instructional time and focus on teaching and learning (Dweck, 2006).
- **Creates a Positive Classroom Climate:** A positive approach to rewards and consequences fosters a respectful and supportive classroom climate. This enhances the overall learning experience for both students and teachers (Kohn, 1993).
- **Fosters Stronger Teacher-Student Relationships:** When students perceive that their teacher is fair and recognizes their efforts, it strengthens the teacher-student relationship. Trust and respect are built through consistent and fair practices (Jones, 2007).

- **Supports Professional Growth:** Implementing an effective rewards and consequences system requires continuous reflection and improvement. Teachers develop better classroom management skills and grow professionally (Dweck, 2006).

Practical Tips and Strategies

- **Use Positive Reinforcement:** Recognize and celebrate students' efforts and achievements. Positive reinforcement motivates students and reinforces desired behaviors (Kohn, 1993).
- **Establish Clear Consequences:** Clearly communicate the consequences for negative behaviors. Ensure that consequences are fair, consistent, and aligned with classroom rules (Jones, 2007).
- **Create a Reward System:** Develop a reward system that acknowledges positive behavior and achievements. Use a variety of rewards, such as praise, points, or privileges, to keep students motivated (Dweck, 2006).
- **Be Consistent:** Consistency is key to the effectiveness of rewards and consequences. Apply them fairly and consistently to maintain credibility and trust (Jones, 2007).
- **Involve Students in the Process:** Engage students in developing the reward and consequence system. This increases their buy-in and commitment to following classroom rules (Kohn, 1993).
- **Balance Rewards and Consequences:** Use a balanced approach to rewards and consequences. Focus on positive reinforcement while also addressing negative behaviors with appropriate consequences (Dweck, 2006).
- **Monitor and Adjust the System:** Regularly assess the effectiveness of your rewards and consequences system. Be open to feedback and make adjustments to improve its impact (Jones, 2007).
- **Communicate with Parents:** Keep parents informed about the reward and consequence system. Collaborate with them to support student behavior and reinforce positive actions at home (Kohn, 1993).
- **Celebrate Successes:** Recognize and celebrate the successes of your students. Positive reinforcement can motivate students to continue adhering to classroom rules (Dweck, 2006).
- **Reflect and Adapt:** Continuously reflect on your approach to rewards and consequences. Be willing to adapt and improve your system based on what works best for your classroom dynamics (Jones, 2007).

How to Use Rewards and Consequences Effectively

- **Positive Reinforcement:** Use rewards to acknowledge and encourage positive behavior (Kohn, 1993).
- **Clear Consequences:** Establish clear and fair consequences for negative behavior (Jones, 2007).
- **Consistency:** Apply rewards and consequences consistently to maintain credibility and fairness (Dweck, 2006).

Practical Applications

Examples: Reward systems, consequence charts.

Expanded Case Studies

Case Study #1: Reward Systems

Problem: Mrs. Thompson noticed that her students often lacked motivation to follow classroom rules and engage positively in activities. The lack of incentives for good behavior and effort led to frequent disruptions and a negative classroom atmosphere.

Scenario: To address this issue, Mrs. Thompson implemented a reward system where students earned points for positive behavior. These points could be exchanged for small prizes or privileges. Her goal was to increase student motivation and positive behavior through a structured incentive system.

Implementation: The steps Mrs. Thompson took included:

1. **Establishing the Reward System:**
   - » Mrs. Thompson introduced a point-based reward system. Students earned points for positive behaviors such as completing assignments on time, participating in class, helping peers, and following classroom rules (Kohn, 1993).

2. **Clear Criteria and Goals:**
   - » She clearly defined the behaviors and actions that would earn points. Students were aware of the specific criteria and the goals they needed to achieve to earn rewards (Marzano, 2007).

3. **Variety of Rewards:**
   - » Mrs. Thompson offered a variety of rewards to cater to different student preferences. Rewards included small prizes like stickers and pencils, as well as privileges such as extra recess time or a homework pass (Deci & Ryan, 1985).

4. **Visual Tracking System:**
   - » She implemented a visual tracking system, such as a chart or bulletin board, where students could see their progress and the points they accumulated. This visual representation served as a constant reminder and motivator (Miller, 2012).

5. **Consistent Reinforcement:**
   - » Mrs. Thompson consistently reinforced positive behavior by awarding points immediately and providing verbal praise. This consistency helped students associate positive behavior with immediate rewards (Bandura, 1977).

6. **Involving Students:**
   - » She involved students in the process by allowing them to suggest rewards and provide feedback on the system. This involvement increased their investment and motivation to participate (Kohn, 1993).

Outcome: The implementation of the reward system led to significant improvements in student motivation and behavior. Specific outcomes included:

- **Increased Motivation:** Students were more motivated to follow classroom rules and engage positively in activities. The opportunity to earn points and rewards provided a tangible incentive for good behavior (Deci & Ryan, 1985).
- **Positive Behavior:** There was a noticeable increase in positive behavior, such as cooperation, participation, and adherence to rules. The reward system fostered a supportive and encouraging classroom environment (Kohn, 1993).
- **Enhanced Engagement:** Students were more engaged in their learning and classroom activities. The reward system helped create a positive and dynamic learning atmosphere (Marzano, 2007).
- **Improved Classroom Atmosphere:** The overall classroom atmosphere became more positive and respectful. Students were motivated to contribute to a harmonious and productive environment (Bandura, 1977).

Best Practices:

1. **Define Clear Criteria:**
   » Establish clear criteria for earning points and ensure that students understand what behaviors and actions are rewarded (Kohn, 1993).

2. **Offer Varied Rewards:**
   ▪ Provide a variety of rewards to cater to different student preferences and keep the reward system engaging (Deci & Ryan, 1985).

3. **Use Visual Tracking:**
   » Implement a visual tracking system to help students see their progress and stay motivated (Miller, 2012).

4. **Reinforce Consistently:**
   » Consistently reinforce positive behavior with immediate points and verbal praise to strengthen the association between behavior and rewards (Bandura, 1977).

5. **Involve Students:**
   » Involve students in the process by allowing them to suggest rewards and provide feedback on the system. This involvement increases their investment and motivation (Kohn, 1993).

By implementing these best practices, teachers can create an effective reward system that enhances student motivation and fosters a positive classroom environment.

Cited Sources:

1. Kohn, A. (1993). *Punished by Rewards: The Trouble with Gold Stars, Incentive Plans, A's, Praise, and Other Bribes*. Houghton Mifflin.
2. Marzano, R. J. (2007). *The Art and Science of Teaching: A Comprehensive Framework for Effective Instruction*. ASCD.
3. Deci, E. L., & Ryan, R. M. (1985). *Intrinsic Motivation and Self-Determination in Human Behavior*. Springer.
4. Miller, P. H. (2012). *Theories of Developmental Psychology*. Worth Publishers.
5. Bandura, A. (1977). *Social Learning Theory*. Prentice-Hall.

Case Study #2: Clear Consequences

Problem: Mr. Harris observed frequent behavioral issues in his classroom, which disrupted the learning environment and created a sense of disorder. He realized that the lack of clear and consistently enforced consequences was contributing to these problems.

Scenario: To address this issue, Mr. Harris decided to establish clear and fair consequences for negative behavior. His goal was to create a more respectful and orderly classroom environment by ensuring that students understood the repercussions of their actions and that these consequences were consistently applied.

Implementation: The steps Mr. Harris took included:

1. **Defining Consequences:**
   ▪ Mr. Harris established a set of clear and fair consequences for various negative behaviors. These consequences were designed to be appropriate to the behavior and to encourage positive change (Jones, 2007).

2. **Communicating Expectations:**

   » He clearly communicated the rules and the associated consequences to his students at the beginning of the school year and regularly revisited them. This ensured that all students were aware of the expectations and the repercussions for not meeting them (Marzano, 2007).

3. **Consistency in Application:**

   » Mr. Harris applied the consequences consistently, regardless of the student or situation. This consistency helped build trust and fairness in the classroom, as students knew that rules would be enforced equally (Sugai & Horner, 2002).

4. **Positive Reinforcement:**

   » Alongside the consequences for negative behavior, Mr. Harris also implemented a system of positive reinforcement for good behavior. This balanced approach helped encourage students to follow the rules and behave positively (Lewis, 2001).

5. **Reflective Discussions:**

   ▪ When a student received a consequence, Mr. Harris held a reflective discussion with them to help them understand why their behavior was inappropriate and how they could improve. This approach aimed to teach students about responsibility and self-regulation (Cohen, 1994).

6. **Parental Involvement:**

   » He involved parents by communicating the classroom rules and consequences to them and encouraging their support in reinforcing these expectations at home. This collaboration helped create a consistent approach to behavior management (Epstein, 2011).

Outcome: The establishment of clear and consistent consequences led to significant improvements in student behavior and the overall classroom environment. Specific outcomes included:

- **Improved Behavior:** Students understood the repercussions of their actions and were more likely to adhere to classroom rules. The clear and consistent consequences led to improved behavior and a more orderly classroom (Jones, 2007).
- **Respectful Environment:** The classroom environment became more respectful and conducive to learning, as students felt secure in knowing that rules would be enforced fairly (Sugai & Horner, 2002).
- **Increased Accountability:** Students took more responsibility for their actions and were more mindful of their behavior, leading to fewer disruptions and a more focused learning atmosphere (Marzano, 2007).
- **Positive Relationships:** The use of reflective discussions and positive reinforcement helped build stronger teacher-student relationships, based on mutual respect and understanding (Cohen, 1994).

Best Practices:

1. **Define Clear Consequences:**

   » Establish clear and fair consequences for various negative behaviors to ensure that students understand the repercussions of their actions (Jones, 2007).

2. **Communicate Expectations:**

   » Clearly communicate the rules and associated consequences to students and regularly revisit them to ensure understanding and compliance (Marzano, 2007).

3. **Apply Consequences Consistently:**
   » Apply consequences consistently to build trust and fairness in the classroom, ensuring that rules are enforced equally for all students (Sugai & Horner, 2002).

4. **Balance with Positive Reinforcement:**
   » Use a system of positive reinforcement alongside consequences for negative behavior to encourage students to follow the rules and behave positively (Lewis, 2001).

5. **Engage in Reflective Discussions:**
   » Hold reflective discussions with students who receive consequences to help them understand their behavior and how they can improve (Cohen, 1994).

6. **Involve Parents:**
   » Communicate classroom rules and consequences to parents and encourage their support in reinforcing these expectations at home (Epstein, 2011).

By implementing these best practices, teachers can create a clear and fair system of consequences that improves student behavior and fosters a respectful and orderly classroom environment.

Cited Sources:

1. Jones, F. H. (2007). *Tools for Teaching: Discipline, Instruction, Motivation*. Fredric H. Jones & Associates, Inc.
2. Marzano, R. J. (2007). *The Art and Science of Teaching: A Comprehensive Framework for Effective Instruction*. ASCD.
3. Sugai, G., & Horner, R. (2002). The evolution of discipline practices: School-wide positive behavior supports. *Child & Family Behavior Therapy*, 24(1-2), 23-50.
4. Lewis, T. J. (2001). Teaching positive behavior support in schools. *Focus on Exceptional Children*, 33(5), 1-24.
5. Cohen, E. G. (1994). *Designing Groupwork: Strategies for the Heterogeneous Classroom*. Teachers College Press.
6. Epstein, J. L. (2011). *School, Family, and Community Partnerships: Preparing Educators and Improving Schools*. Westview Press.

Case Study #3: Positive Reinforcement

Problem: Ms. Lee observed that her students often lacked motivation and struggled to stay engaged during lessons. She wanted to find a way to boost their motivation and create a positive, supportive classroom environment.

Scenario: To address this issue, Ms. Lee decided to use positive reinforcement to acknowledge and encourage student efforts and achievements. Her goal was to foster a growth mindset and increase motivation by praising students for their hard work and persistence.

Implementation: The steps Ms. Lee took included:

1. **Identifying Positive Behaviors:**
   » Ms. Lee identified specific behaviors and achievements that she wanted to reinforce, such as completing assignments on time, participating in class, and demonstrating persistence in challenging tasks (Dweck, 2006).

2. **Verbal Praise:**

   » She used verbal praise to acknowledge and celebrate student efforts and achievements. Phrases like "Great job on solving that problem!" and "I'm impressed with your persistence!" were common in her classroom (Brophy, 1981).

3. **Written Feedback:**

   » In addition to verbal praise, Ms. Lee provided written feedback on assignments and projects, highlighting specific strengths and improvements. This personalized feedback helped students understand what they were doing well (Hattie & Timperley, 2007).

4. **Rewards and Privileges:**

   » She occasionally used tangible rewards and privileges, such as stickers, certificates, or extra recess time, to reinforce positive behavior. These rewards were used sparingly to maintain their effectiveness (Deci & Ryan, 1985).

5. **Growth Mindset Language:**

   » Ms. Lee incorporated growth mindset language into her praise, emphasizing effort and improvement rather than innate ability. This approach encouraged students to view challenges as opportunities to grow (Dweck, 2006).

6. **Classroom Displays:**

   » She created classroom displays that showcased student work and achievements. These displays served as a visual reminder of students' hard work and successes, fostering a sense of pride and motivation (Marzano, 2007).

7. **Regular Check-Ins:**

   » Ms. Lee regularly checked in with students to discuss their progress and goals. These one-on-one conversations helped build strong teacher-student relationships and provided additional opportunities for positive reinforcement (Pianta, 1999).

Outcome: The implementation of positive reinforcement led to significant improvements in student motivation and engagement. Specific outcomes included:

- **Increased Motivation:** Students felt valued and appreciated, leading to increased motivation and engagement in their learning activities (Dweck, 2006).
- **Improved Engagement:** The positive reinforcement helped build a culture of respect and mutual support in the classroom, resulting in higher levels of participation and effort (Brophy, 1981).
- **Enhanced Growth Mindset:** Students developed a growth mindset, viewing challenges as opportunities to improve and recognizing the importance of effort and persistence (Dweck, 2006).
- **Positive Classroom Atmosphere:** The overall classroom atmosphere became more positive and supportive, with students celebrating each other's successes and encouraging one another (Marzano, 2007).

Best Practices:

1. **Identify and Reinforce Positive Behaviors:**

   » Clearly identify the specific behaviors and achievements to reinforce, ensuring that students understand what is valued (Dweck, 2006).

2. **Use Verbal and Written Praise:**
   - » Provide both verbal and written praise to acknowledge and celebrate student efforts and achievements. Personalize feedback to make it meaningful (Brophy, 1981).

3. **Incorporate Growth Mindset Language:**
   - » Use growth mindset language in praise to emphasize effort and improvement rather than innate ability. Encourage students to view challenges positively (Dweck, 2006).

4. **Offer Tangible Rewards Sparingly:**
   - » Use tangible rewards and privileges sparingly to maintain their effectiveness. Focus on intrinsic motivation through verbal and written praise (Deci & Ryan, 1985).

5. **Create Visual Displays:**
   - » Showcase student work and achievements in the classroom to foster a sense of pride and motivation. Use these displays as visual reminders of student successes (Marzano, 2007).

6. **Regularly Check In with Students:**
   - » Hold regular one-on-one check-ins with students to discuss their progress and goals. Use these conversations as opportunities for positive reinforcement and relationship building (Pianta, 1999).

By implementing these best practices, teachers can effectively use positive reinforcement to enhance student motivation, engagement, and overall classroom atmosphere.

Cited Sources:

1. Dweck, C. S. (2006). *Mindset: The New Psychology of Success*. Random House.
2. Brophy, J. (1981). *Teacher Praise: A Functional Analysis*. Review of Educational Research, 51(1), 5-32.
3. Hattie, J., & Timperley, H. (2007). *The Power of Feedback*. Review of Educational Research, 77(1), 81-112.
4. Deci, E. L., & Ryan, R. M. (1985). *Intrinsic Motivation and Self-Determination in Human Behavior*. Springer.
5. Marzano, R. J. (2007). *The Art and Science of Teaching: A Comprehensive Framework for Effective Instruction*. ASCD.
6. Pianta, R. C. (1999). *Enhancing Relationships Between Children and Teachers*. American Psychological Association.

Case Study #4: Classroom Discussions

Problem: Ms. Carter noticed that her students were often hesitant to participate in classroom discussions, leading to a lack of engagement and missed opportunities for collaborative learning. This hesitation resulted in limited student interaction, reduced sharing of diverse perspectives, and decreased development of critical thinking and communication skills.

Scenario: To address this issue, Ms. Carter decided to implement strategies to improve the quality and frequency of student participation in discussions. Her goal was to create an inclusive environment where all students felt comfortable and encouraged to contribute.

Implementation: The steps Ms. Carter took included:

1. **Structured Discussions:**
   - » Ms. Carter introduced structured classroom discussions with clear guidelines to ensure all students had the opportunity to speak and contribute. This structure provided a predictable framework that reduced anxiety and encouraged participation (Brookfield & Preskill, 1999).

2. **Think-Pair-Share Activities:**
   - » She used "think-pair-share" activities, where students first thought about a question individually, then discussed their ideas with a partner, and finally shared their insights with the larger group. This strategy allowed students to refine their thoughts before presenting them to the whole class (Lyman, 1981).

3. **Discussion Roles:**
   - » Ms. Carter implemented discussion roles, such as facilitator, note-taker, and summarizer, to help students feel more comfortable and accountable during discussions. These roles ensured that all students had a specific function and responsibility within the discussion (Daniels, 2002).

4. **Sentence Starters and Question Prompts:**
   - » She provided sentence starters and question prompts to guide students in expressing their thoughts clearly. These tools helped students formulate their ideas and engage more confidently in discussions (Zwiers & Crawford, 2011).

5. **Inclusive Environment:**
   - » Ms. Carter fostered an inclusive classroom environment by encouraging respect for diverse perspectives and promoting active listening. She emphasized the importance of valuing each student's contribution (Gay, 2002).

6. **Feedback and Reflection:**
   - » After discussions, Ms. Carter provided feedback on the discussion process and encouraged students to reflect on their participation. This reflection helped students understand their strengths and areas for improvement (Taba, 1966).

Outcome: The structured approach to classroom discussions led to significant improvements in student participation and engagement. Specific outcomes included:

- **Increased Participation:** Students felt more confident sharing their ideas and were more willing to engage in discussions. The structured activities and roles helped reduce anxiety and promote inclusivity (Brookfield & Preskill, 1999).
- **Enhanced Engagement:** The use of "think-pair-share" activities and discussion roles kept students focused and on task, leading to more meaningful and productive discussions (Lyman, 1981).
- **Improved Critical Thinking:** Students developed better critical thinking skills as they were exposed to diverse perspectives and learned to articulate and defend their ideas (Daniels, 2002).
- **Strengthened Communication Skills:** The use of sentence starters and question prompts helped students express their thoughts more clearly, improving their overall communication skills (Zwiers & Crawford, 2011).
- **Positive Classroom Atmosphere:** The inclusive environment fostered a culture of respect and mutual support, enhancing the overall classroom atmosphere (Gay, 2002).

Best Practices:

1. **Implement Structured Discussions:**
   - » Use structured discussion formats with clear guidelines to ensure all students have the opportunity to participate (Brookfield & Preskill, 1999).

2. **Use Think-Pair-Share Activities:**
   - » Incorporate "think-pair-share" activities to allow students to refine their thoughts before sharing them with the whole class (Lyman, 1981).

3. **Assign Discussion Roles:**
   - » Assign specific roles within discussions to ensure all students have a function and responsibility, promoting accountability and comfort (Daniels, 2002).

4. **Provide Sentence Starters and Prompts:**
   - » Use sentence starters and question prompts to guide students in expressing their thoughts clearly and confidently (Zwiers & Crawford, 2011).

5. **Foster an Inclusive Environment:**
   - » Encourage respect for diverse perspectives and promote active listening to create an inclusive and supportive classroom atmosphere (Gay, 2002).

6. **Encourage Feedback and Reflection:**
   - » Provide feedback on the discussion process and encourage students to reflect on their participation to understand their strengths and areas for improvement (Taba, 1966).

By implementing these best practices, teachers can enhance student participation, engagement, and the overall quality of classroom discussions.

Cited Sources:

1. Brookfield, S. D., & Preskill, S. (1999). *Discussion as a Way of Teaching: Tools and Techniques for Democratic Classrooms*. Jossey-Bass.
2. Lyman, F. (1981). The responsive classroom discussion. *Mainstreaming Digest*, 109-113.
3. Daniels, H. (2002). *Literature Circles: Voice and Choice in Book Clubs and Reading Groups*. Stenhouse Publishers.
4. Zwiers, J., & Crawford, M. (2011). *Academic Conversations: Classroom Talk that Fosters Critical Thinking and Content Understandings*. Stenhouse Publishers.
5. Gay, G. (2002). *Culturally Responsive Teaching: Theory, Research, and Practice*. Teachers College Press.
6. Taba, H. (1966). *Teaching Strategies and Cognitive Functioning in Elementary School Children*. San Francisco State College.

Tips and Best Practices

1. **Use a Variety of Rewards:** Use different types of rewards to keep students motivated, such as praise, points, and privileges.
2. **Communicate Consequences Clearly:** Clearly communicate consequences to students and apply them fairly and consistently.
3. **Involve Students:** Involve students in developing the reward and consequence system to increase their investment in following the rules.

Tips and Best Practices

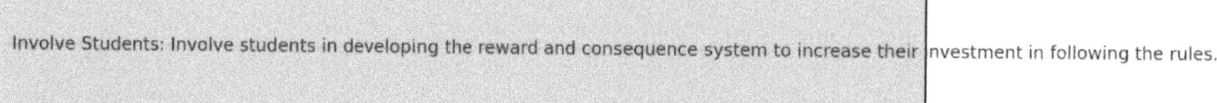

- Involve Students: Involve students in developing the reward and consequence system to increase their investment in following the rules.

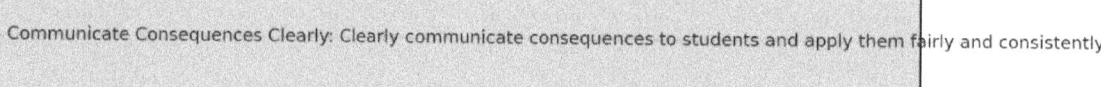

- Communicate Consequences Clearly: Clearly communicate consequences to students and apply them fairly and consistently.

- Use a Variety of Rewards: Use different types of rewards to keep students motivated, such as praise, points, and privileges.

Visual Aids and Templates

- **Reward System Chart :** A chart to track and manage the reward system. [Download Reward System Chart

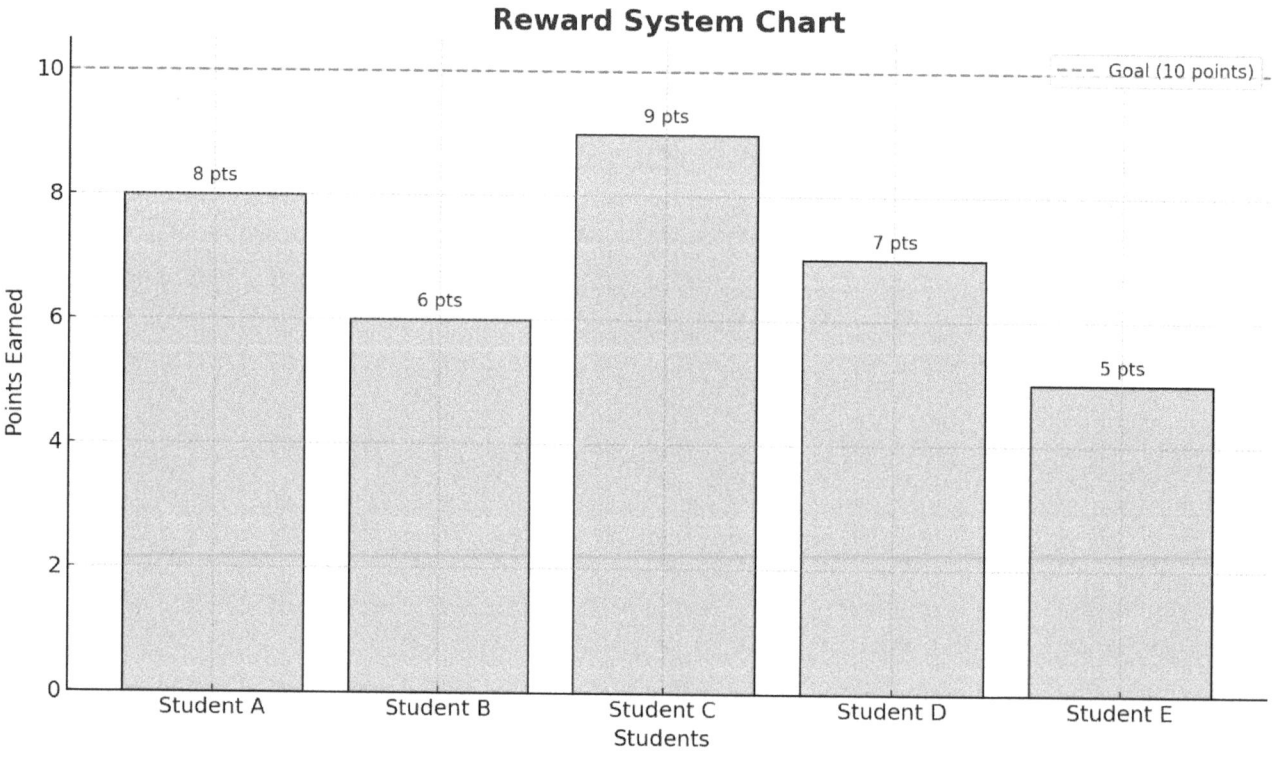

Lesson Plan 1: Implementing a Reward System

Objective: Help students understand the importance of rewards and participate in developing a reward system.

Materials:
- Reward System Chart
- Reward Coupon Template

I Do (Teacher Modeling):
- Explain the concept of a reward system: "A reward system helps us recognize positive actions and encourage good behavior. It's a way for us to work together to create a fun and respectful classroom."
- Show the Reward System Chart and demonstrate how points are awarded and tracked. For example: "If a student helps a classmate, they earn a point on the chart."

We Do (Guided Practice):
- Engage students in a group discussion about what behaviors should earn rewards.
- Work together to create examples of rewards, such as extra recess time or homework passes.
- Guide students in filling out a sample Reward System Chart.

You Do (Independent Practice):
- In small groups, students create their own Reward Coupon Templates, designing rewards they would like to see.
- Each group presents their ideas to the class for approval.

Assessment:
- Observe participation in group discussions and coupon design.
- Exit ticket: Students write one behavior they will focus on to earn a reward.

Lesson Plan 2: Establishing Clear Consequences

Objective: Establish clear and fair consequences for negative behavior.

Materials:
- Consequence Chart
- Behavior Reflection Form

I Do (Teacher Modeling):
- Explain the purpose of clear consequences: "Consequences help us understand the impact of our choices. They guide us to make better decisions in the future."
- Demonstrate the Consequence Chart with examples, such as losing points or completing a reflection form.

We Do (Guided Practice):
- Lead a group discussion on what behaviors might warrant consequences.
- Collaboratively develop a list of fair and logical consequences.
- Practice filling out a Behavior Reflection Form with a mock scenario.

You Do (Independent Practice):
- Students work individually to create their own Consequence Charts.
- Role-play scenarios in pairs to practice identifying appropriate consequences and completing reflection forms.

Assessment:
- Review student-created Consequence Charts.
- Exit ticket: Students write one consequence they think is fair and explain why.

Lesson Plan 3: Using Positive Reinforcement

Objective: Use positive reinforcement to acknowledge and encourage positive behavior.

Materials:
- Positive Reinforcement Tracker
- Reward System Chart

I Do (Teacher Modeling):
- Explain positive reinforcement: "When we recognize and celebrate positive behavior, it encourages us to keep doing good things. It's like saying, 'Great job!' in a way that motivates."
- Demonstrate the Positive Reinforcement Tracker and how to record positive behaviors.

We Do (Guided Practice):
- Brainstorm examples of positive behaviors as a class.
- Use the Positive Reinforcement Tracker together to log mock examples of good behavior.

You Do (Independent Practice):
- Students use the Reward System Chart to track their own positive actions over a day or week.
- Reflect on their recorded behaviors by sharing in pairs or small groups.

Assessment:
- Review students' Positive Reinforcement Trackers for completeness and understanding.
- Exit ticket: Students write about a time they felt proud of their behavior and how it was acknowledged.

Integration of Standards

- **SEL Competency:** Students learn responsible decision-making by understanding the consequences of their actions and the rewards of positive behavior.
- **ELA Standard:** Students participate in collaborative conversations during group discussions and planning activities.

Reflection and Activities

Lesson Plan: Developing a Reward System

Grade Level: [Insert Grade Level]
Duration: 45 minutes
Standards Alignment:

National Standards: Social and Emotional Learning (SEL) Competency: Responsible Decision-Making.

- State Standards: CCSS.ELA-LITERACY.SL.1.1 - Participate in collaborative conversations with diverse partners about grade-level topics and texts.

Objective
Develop and implement a reward system to encourage positive behavior.

Materials

- Reward System Chart
- Reward Coupon Template

I Do (Teacher Modeling)
Time: 10 minutes

1. Introduction:
   » Explain the purpose of a reward system: "A reward system is a way to recognize and celebrate positive behaviors. It helps us create a fun and supportive classroom environment."
   » Show the Reward System Chart and demonstrate how to use it to track behaviors and rewards. For example: "If a student helps a classmate, they earn a point on the chart."
   » Display the Reward Coupon Template and explain how coupons can be used for tangible rewards like extra recess time or homework passes.

We Do (Guided Practice)
Time: 20 minutes

1. Group Brainstorming:
   » Engage students in a discussion to identify positive behaviors they believe should be rewarded.
   » List their suggestions on the board and categorize them (e.g., helping others, participating in class).
2. Collaborative Design:
   » Work together to decide on meaningful rewards. Examples include stickers, classroom privileges, or fun activities.
   » Guide students in filling out a sample Reward System Chart with example behaviors and corresponding rewards.

You Do (Independent Practice)
Time: 15 minutes

1. Student Creativity:
   » In small groups, students design their own Reward Coupon Templates with drawings or descriptions of rewards.
   » Allow students to present their templates to the class and explain their reward ideas.
2. Implementation Planning:
   » Have each group suggest how the reward system could be implemented in the classroom.
   » Discuss and finalize the system as a class, ensuring all voices are heard.

Assessment Description

1. Observation During Activities:
   - **What to Observe:** Monitor how actively students participate in group discussions and collaborative tasks such as brainstorming positive behaviors and designing Reward Coupon Templates.
   - **Indicators of Success:** Look for engagement, such as students contributing ideas, asking questions, and working cooperatively with peers. Pay attention to how students articulate their thoughts and how effectively they collaborate during the creation of templates.
   - **Purpose:** This observation helps gauge students' understanding of the reward system concept and their ability to work as a team.

2. Exit Ticket:
   - **What to Include:** Ask students to write down one specific positive behavior they plan to exhibit to earn a reward. Examples might include "helping a classmate," "raising my hand to answer a question," or "completing homework on time."
   - **How to Evaluate:** Review responses to ensure they reflect an understanding of the reward system and demonstrate thoughtful engagement. Check for specificity and alignment with the behaviors discussed during the lesson.
   - **Purpose:** The exit ticket serves as a reflective tool, allowing students to internalize the lesson while giving the teacher insight into their level of comprehension and individual goals.

By combining observation and a reflective written task, this assessment method provides both immediate and actionable feedback on students' understanding and readiness to apply the reward system in practice.

Expected Outcome

Increased student motivation and positive behavior through a well-organized reward system.

Integration of Standards

- **SEL Competency:** Students learn responsible decision-making by understanding the impact of positive behaviors and rewards.
- **ELA Standard:** Students engage in collaborative conversations during the brainstorming and design phases.

Establishing Clear Consequences

- **Objective:** Establish clear and fair consequences for negative behavior.
- **Materials:** Consequence Chart, Behavior Reflection Form.
- **Instructions:** Use the chart to communicate and track consequences. Encourage students to reflect on their behavior using the reflection form.
- **Expected Outcome:** Reduced behavioral issues and a more respectful classroom environment through clear and consistent consequences.

Using Positive Reinforcement

- **Objective:** Use positive reinforcement to acknowledge and encourage positive behavior.
- **Materials:** Positive Reinforcement Tracker.
- **Instructions:** Use the tracker to monitor and acknowledge positive behavior. Celebrate successes and provide positive feedback regularly.
- **Expected Outcome:** Increased student motivation and engagement through positive reinforcement.

Reflection Questions

Effectiveness of Current Reward and Consequence System

- **Question:** How effective is the current reward and consequence system in my classroom? What improvements can be made?
- **Purpose:** Evaluate the effectiveness of the existing system and identify areas for enhancement.

Student Motivation and Behavior

- **Question:** How motivated and well-behaved are my students? Are there any areas where motivation or behavior could be improved?
- **Purpose:** Assess student motivation and behavior and develop strategies to improve them.

Quiz, Reflection, and Short Essay for the Chapter on Rewards and Consequences

Multiple-Choice Quiz

1. What is a primary benefit of using rewards and consequences in the classroom?
   a. Increased homework
   b. Enhanced student motivation
   c. More free time for teachers
   d. Advanced technology
2. According to Behaviorism, how can behavior be shaped in the classroom?
   a. Through rote memorization
   b. Through reinforcement and punishment
   c. Through strict discipline
   d. Through advanced technology
3. How do rewards impact student motivation, according to Self-Determination Theory?
   a. They increase student anxiety
   b. They enhance intrinsic motivation
   c. They reduce students' engagement
   d. They create confusion

4. What is a key aspect of fostering effective use of rewards and consequences in the classroom?

    a. Flexibility and spontaneity

    b. Clarity and consistency

    c. Avoiding student input

    d. Complexity and ambiguity

5. According to Cognitive Evaluation Theory, what can undermine intrinsic motivation?

    a. Advanced technology

    b. Perceived control from rewards

    c. More homework

    d. Increasing discipline

6. Which of the following is a benefit for teachers when effective rewards and consequences are established?

    a. More administrative tasks

    b. Easier classroom management

    c. Increased need for discipline

    d. More homework for students

7. How can rewards and consequences impact academic performance?

    a. They distract students from learning

    b. They provide a stable environment for learning

    c. They decrease student motivation

    d. They increase test anxiety

8. According to Social Learning Theory, how do rewards influence student behavior?

    a. Through observational learning and modeling

    b. By increasing homework

    c. By creating confusion

    d. By reducing engagement

9. What is an effective way to establish clear rewards and consequences in the classroom?

    a. Flexibility and spontaneity

    b. Through clear guidelines and consistency

    c. By increasing homework

    d. By avoiding student input

10. According to Maslow's Hierarchy of Needs, why are rewards and consequences important?

    a. They increase cognitive load

    b. They fulfill basic needs for safety and esteem

    c. They have no effect on learning

    d. They create cognitive overload

Short Reflection Questions

1. Why is it important to use rewards and consequences effectively in the classroom?

2. Describe a method you would use to implement a new reward system in your classroom.

3. How do you think rewards and consequences can impact the overall classroom environment?

Short Response Questions

1. **Scenario:** You notice that a student frequently disrupts the class despite previous interventions. What steps would you take to establish a more effective consequence for this student?

2. **Scenario:** You want to enhance student motivation by implementing a new reward system. How would you go about achieving this?

Short Essay Response

Discuss the theoretical foundations of using rewards and consequences in the classroom. How do theories such as Behaviorism, Self-Determination Theory, Cognitive Evaluation Theory, Social Learning Theory, and Maslow's Hierarchy of Needs support the practice of implementing rewards and consequences? Use references from the chapter to support your answer.

Answer Key

Multiple-Choice Quiz

1. b) Enhanced student motivation
2. b) Through reinforcement and punishment
3. b) They enhance intrinsic motivation
4. b) Clarity and consistency
5. b) Perceived control from rewards
6. b) Easier classroom management
7. b) They provide a stable environment for learning
8. a) Through observational learning and modeling
9. b) Through clear guidelines and consistency
10. b) They fulfill basic needs for safety and esteem

Short Reflection Questions

1. **Why is it important to use rewards and consequences effectively in the classroom?**

   » Using rewards and consequences effectively is crucial for promoting positive behavior, reducing disruptions, and fostering a culture of accountability. When implemented thoughtfully, these strategies help students understand the connection between their actions and outcomes, creating a respectful and productive classroom environment.

2. **Describe a method you would use to implement a new reward system in your classroom.**

   » To implement a new reward system, I would start by clearly explaining the system to the students, including the types of rewards available and the behaviors that earn them. I would involve students in brainstorming potential rewards to ensure they are meaningful and motivating. Additionally, I would consistently apply the reward system, regularly review its effectiveness, and make adjustments based on student feedback and observed behavior changes.

3. **How do you think rewards and consequences can impact the overall classroom environment?**

   » Rewards and consequences can significantly impact the classroom environment by creating a sense of predictability and fairness. When students understand the expectations and know that positive behavior will be recognized and negative behavior will have consequences, they are more likely to exhibit desirable behaviors. This leads to a more harmonious and productive classroom where students feel motivated and accountable.

Short Response Questions

1. **Scenario:** You notice that a student frequently disrupts the class despite previous interventions. What steps would you take to establish a more effective consequence for this student?

   » I would start by reviewing the existing interventions and identifying why they might not be effective. I would then discuss the issue with the student to understand their perspective and any underlying causes for their behavior. Based on this information, I would develop a more tailored consequence that addresses the specific behavior and reinforces the desired behavior. Additionally, I would involve the student in setting goals and tracking their progress, providing consistent feedback and support.

2. **Scenario:** You want to enhance student motivation by implementing a new reward system. How would you go about achieving this?

Here is a properly formatted reference and bibliography section based on the information and standards mentioned in the lesson plan:

References

- **Collaborative for Academic, Social, and Emotional Learning (CASEL). (2020).** Social and Emotional Learning Competencies: Responsible Decision-Making. **Retrieved from https://casel.org**
- **Common Core State Standards Initiative. (2010).** English Language Arts Standards: Speaking and Listening - Grade 1. **Retrieved from http://www.corestandards.org**
- **Dweck, C. S. (2006).** Mindset: The New Psychology of Success. **Random House Publishing Group.**
- **Kohn, A. (1993).** Punished by Rewards: The Trouble with Gold Stars, Incentive Plans, A's, Praise, and Other Bribes. **Houghton Mifflin.**
- **Marzano, R. J. (2007).** The Art and Science of Teaching: A Comprehensive Framework for Effective Instruction. **ASCD.**

Bibliography

- **CASEL: For the definition and application of Social and Emotional Learning Competencies.**
- **Common Core State Standards: For alignment to speaking and listening skills.**
- **Reward Systems in Education: Referenced from widely accepted classroom management practices.**
- **Positive Reinforcement Strategies: Derived from Marzano's research on effective teaching strategies.**
- **Dweck's Growth Mindset Theory: Used to emphasize intrinsic motivation and student engagement.**
- **Kohn's Critical Perspective on Rewards: Balances the discussion on the impact of tangible rewards on student behavior.**

CHAPTER 6

BUILDING STABILITY: THE TRANSFORMATIVE POWER OF CONSISTENT CLASSROOM ROUTINES

Lesson from Experience: Developing Consistent Routines

In my early teaching years, managing the energy and unpredictability of my classroom was a challenge. My lively, enthusiastic students struggled with focus and discipline, making it clear we needed structure to harness their energy productively.

One chaotic morning, I decided to implement a consistent routine, starting with a structured morning meeting. Each day began with a greeting, a review of the agenda, and a short activity to engage everyone. Initially, students resisted the change, accustomed to free-for-all mornings, but I remained patient and consistent.

After a few weeks, the transformation was evident. Students began to look forward to our meetings, knowing what to expect each morning. One student, Lily, who had often been restless and distracted, thrived under the new structure, sharing that it made her feel more prepared for the day.

Building on this success, I expanded the routine to other parts of the day—transitions, homework submission, and end-of-day procedures. This consistency fostered a sense of security and predictability, improving focus and behavior.

The ultimate test came when a substitute teacher took over. To my delight, the students seamlessly guided the substitute through our established routines, a proud moment that underscored their effectiveness.

Reflecting on this experience, I've learned that consistent routines go beyond classroom management. They create a stable, supportive environment where students thrive, feel secure, and understand expectations. Twenty years later, this strategy remains central to my teaching, bringing order and positivity to every classroom I've led.

Introduction

Developing consistent routines is essential for creating a stable and productive learning environment. Routines provide structure and predictability, helping students focus on learning and reducing behavioral issues. As an educational specialist, I have observed that well-established routines can transform classroom dynamics and enhance student engagement.

Mastering the skill of developing routines enhances teacher effectiveness by establishing clear expectations and reducing uncertainty. Teachers who implement effective routines can minimize transitions and disruptions, creating a calm and focused classroom atmosphere. Consistent routines also help students develop self-discipline and organizational skills, which are crucial for their academic and personal growth.

By incorporating routines into daily classroom activities, teachers can foster an environment where students feel secure and supported. This stability encourages students to take ownership of their learning and behave responsibly, leading to a more harmonious and efficient classroom.

Value Proposition

Purpose of the Chapter:

This chapter equips educators with essential tools and strategies to establish and maintain consistent routines in the classroom.

Key Benefits:

- Promote Stability: Create a predictable environment where students feel secure.
- Reduce Disruptions: Minimize chaos and maximize time spent on learning.
- Enhance Engagement: Encourage students to focus on tasks and participate actively.

What You'll Learn:
- Insights from educational experts.
- Real-world case studies demonstrating successful routines.
- Practical strategies to implement and maintain effective routines.

The Power of Consistent Routines

For Students:
- Framework for Success: Consistent routines provide a structure that allows students to thrive academically and socially.
- Sense of Security: Predictable routines reduce anxiety, creating an environment where students feel respected and safe.

For Teachers:
- Simplified Management: Clear routines streamline classroom operations, reducing stress and enabling more meaningful interactions.

- Enhanced Teaching Experience: With fewer disruptions, teachers can focus on delivering effective lessons.

The Goal of Predictable Routines

Why They Matter:

- Student Readiness: Predictable routines prepare students to engage actively in learning.
- Respectful Environment: Structured classrooms foster respect between teachers and students.

What This Means for Your Classroom:

Establishing clear routines helps build a positive classroom culture where learning can flourish.

Theoretical Background

Implementing consistent routines in the classroom is supported by several foundational educational theories that emphasize structure, predictability, and organization as key components of an effective learning environment.

Behaviorism

- Theory Overview:
  Behaviorism, particularly B.F. Skinner's work, highlights the role of reinforcement in shaping behavior.
- Connection to Routines:
  - » Consistent routines act as positive reinforcers, encouraging desirable behaviors.
  - » Structured environments help students associate predictable actions with positive outcomes.
- Key Insight:
  - » Skinner's operant conditioning theory suggests that consistent routines effectively modify behavior and enhance learning outcomes.

    (Source: Skinner, 1953)

Social Learning Theory

- Theory Overview:
  Albert Bandura's Social Learning Theory emphasizes observational learning and modeling.
- Connection to Routines:
  - » Consistent routines provide a model for appropriate behaviors.
  - » Students learn by observing and imitating structured practices.
- Key Insight:
  - » Teachers who consistently implement routines help students internalize positive behaviors through observation and repetition.

    (Source: Bandura, 1977)

Cognitive Load Theory

- Theory Overview:

John Sweller's Cognitive Load Theory posits that reducing extraneous cognitive load enhances learning. Connection to Routines:
  - » Predictable routines minimize distractions and uncertainties.
  - » This frees cognitive resources for academic tasks, improving focus and understanding.
- Key Insight:

Structured routines help students concentrate on learning by reducing mental effort spent on managing daily activities.

(Source: Sweller, 1988)

Self-Determination Theory

- Theory Overview:

Deci and Ryan's Self-Determination Theory focuses on fostering intrinsic motivation through autonomy, competence, and relatedness.
- Connection to Routines:
  - » Predictable routines promote a sense of competence and relatedness.
  - » Students feel confident navigating activities and experience a sense of belonging in structured environments.
- Key Insight:

A well-organized classroom helps students develop autonomy and fosters intrinsic motivation.

(Source: Deci & Ryan, 2000)

Key Takeaway

By integrating these theoretical perspectives with practical strategies, teachers can establish consistent routines that create structured and engaging learning environments, supporting both academic success and positive behavior.

Expert Quotes and Insights

1. **Harry K. Wong:**
   - » "Routines and procedures create structure, which in turn creates a sense of security for students."
   - » **Source:** Wong, H. K., & Wong, R. T. (2009). *The First Days of School: How to Be an Effective Teacher.* Harry K. Wong Publications, Inc. Buy the book from Ms. Bizbee's Bookshop.
2. **Fred Jones:**
   - » "The secret to effective classroom management is a solid routine that students can depend on."
   - » **Source:** Jones, F. H. (2007). *Tools for Teaching: Discipline, Instruction, Motivation.* Fredric H. Jones & Associates. Buy the book from Ms. Bizbee's Bookshop.

3. **Doug Lemov:**
   » "Routines should be practiced until they become second nature to both students and teachers."
   » **Source:** Lemov, D. (2010). *Teach Like a Champion: 49 Techniques that Put Students on the Path to College.* Jossey-Bass.

Additional Resources

1. **Edutopia: The Importance of Establishing Classroom Routines**
   » Discover strategies to effectively implement positive reinforcement in your classroom.
2. **Scholastic: Classroom Routines to Improve Student Behavior**
   » Learn about the best practices for using consequences to manage classroom behavior.
3. **TeachThought: Strategies for Using Rewards and Consequences**
   » Explore different strategies for balancing rewards and consequences to maintain classroom order.
4. **Understood: Behavior Contracts and Why They Work**
   » Understand how behavior contracts can be used to improve student behavior and accountability.
5. **Education World: Creating a Classroom Code of Conduct**
   » Tips and guidelines for establishing a clear and effective classroom code of conduct.
6. **EdSurge: Managing Classroom Behavior with Technology**
   » Innovative ways to leverage technology to enhance classroom management and student engagement.
7. **National Education Association (NEA): Classroom Management Tips for New Teachers**
   » Essential tips and tricks for new teachers to establish and maintain effective classroom management.
8. **The Teacher Toolkit: How to Create a Positive Classroom Environment**
   » Strategies for fostering a positive and inclusive classroom atmosphere conducive to learning.
9. **ASCD: The Key to Classroom Management**
   » Insights into the fundamental aspects of classroom management and how to implement them.
10. **PBIS (Positive Behavioral Interventions and Supports): Classroom Management Strategies**
    » Explore evidence-based classroom management strategies to support positive student behavior.

The Importance of Developing a Routine

Establishing and maintaining consistent routines is paramount in creating a structured and effective classroom environment. A well-defined routine provides students with a clear understanding of what to expect and what is expected of them. This predictability plays a crucial role in reducing anxiety, as students feel more secure and confident in their daily activities. When students are aware of the structure and flow of the classroom, they are better able to focus on learning and less likely to be distracted by uncertainty.

Consistent routines offer several key benefits:
1. **Enhanced Student Engagement:** Routines minimize disruptions and transitions, allowing for more instructional time. This increased focus helps students stay engaged with the material being taught.
2. **Improved Behavioral Management:** Predictable routines set clear behavioral expectations, reducing instances of misconduct. Students are more likely to follow rules and guidelines when they know what is expected of them.

3. **Development of Self-Discipline:** Regular routines help students develop self-discipline and organizational skills. Over time, students learn to manage their time effectively, complete tasks efficiently, and take responsibility for their actions.

4. **Support for Diverse Learners:** Routines provide a consistent framework that can be especially beneficial for students with special needs. The stability and predictability of routines help these students thrive in a structured environment.

5. **Reduction of Teacher Stress:** A well-structured classroom routine allows teachers to manage their time more effectively and reduces the stress associated with handling unpredictable situations. This leads to a more positive and productive teaching experience.

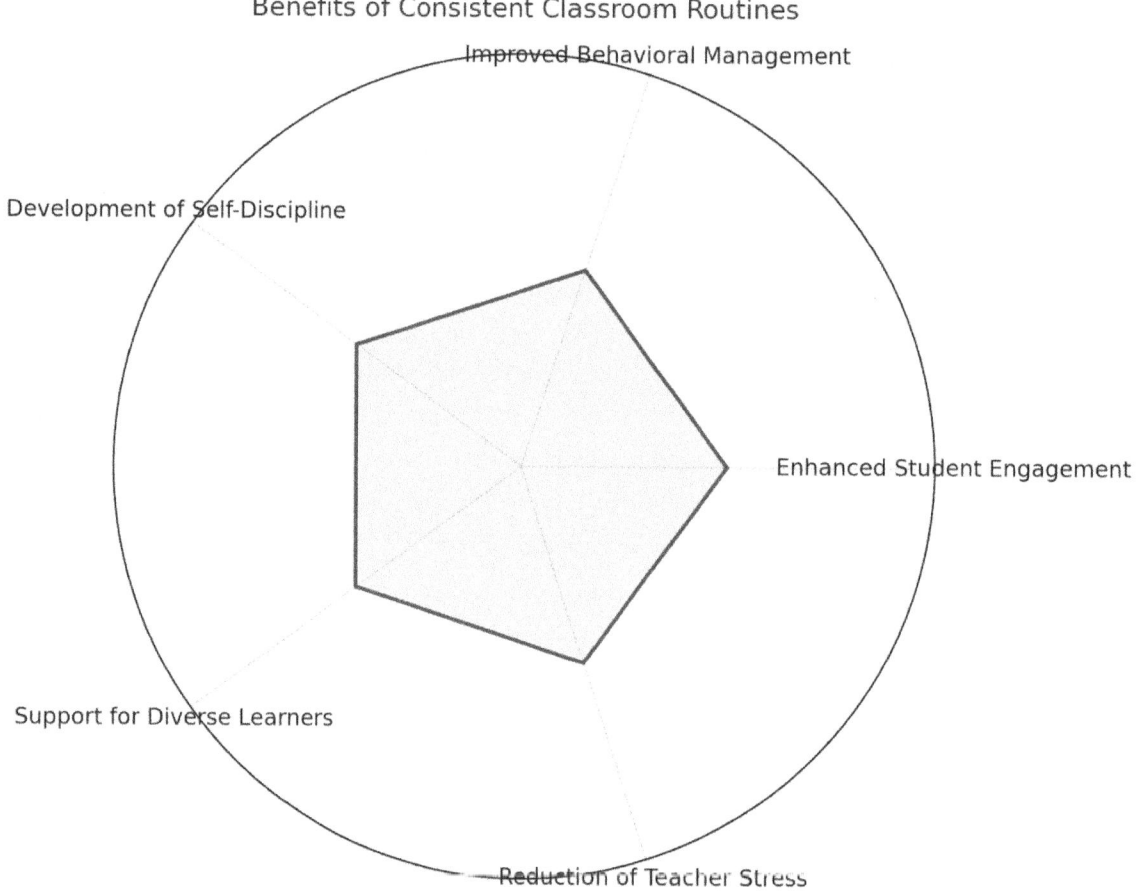

Here is a radial graph representing the benefits of consistent classroom routines. Each axis highlights a key benefit, showcasing how these routines contribute to an effective and positive learning environment.

Incorporating routines into daily classroom activities fosters a positive and supportive learning environment. Students feel secure and supported, which encourages them to take ownership of their learning and behave responsibly. The stability provided by routines not only enhances academic performance but also contributes to the overall well-being of students.

By implementing consistent routines, teachers can create an atmosphere of mutual respect and cooperation. Students understand the connection between their actions and the classroom environment, promoting a sense of accountability. As a result, the classroom becomes a place where both teaching and learning can flourish.

The strategic use of routines is essential for creating a harmonious and efficient classroom. This chapter will guide you through the process of developing and maintaining effective routines that support positive behavior, academic success, and a cohesive classroom community. By mastering the skill of routine development, you will enhance your effectiveness as an educator and contribute to the overall growth and development of your students.

Benefits for Students and Teachers

For students, consistent routines:

- Provide a sense of security and stability.
- Reduce anxiety and uncertainty.
- Help develop self-discipline and time management skills.

For teachers, consistent routines:

- Simplify classroom management.
- Increase instructional time by reducing transitions and disruptions.
- Foster a more efficient and organized teaching environment.

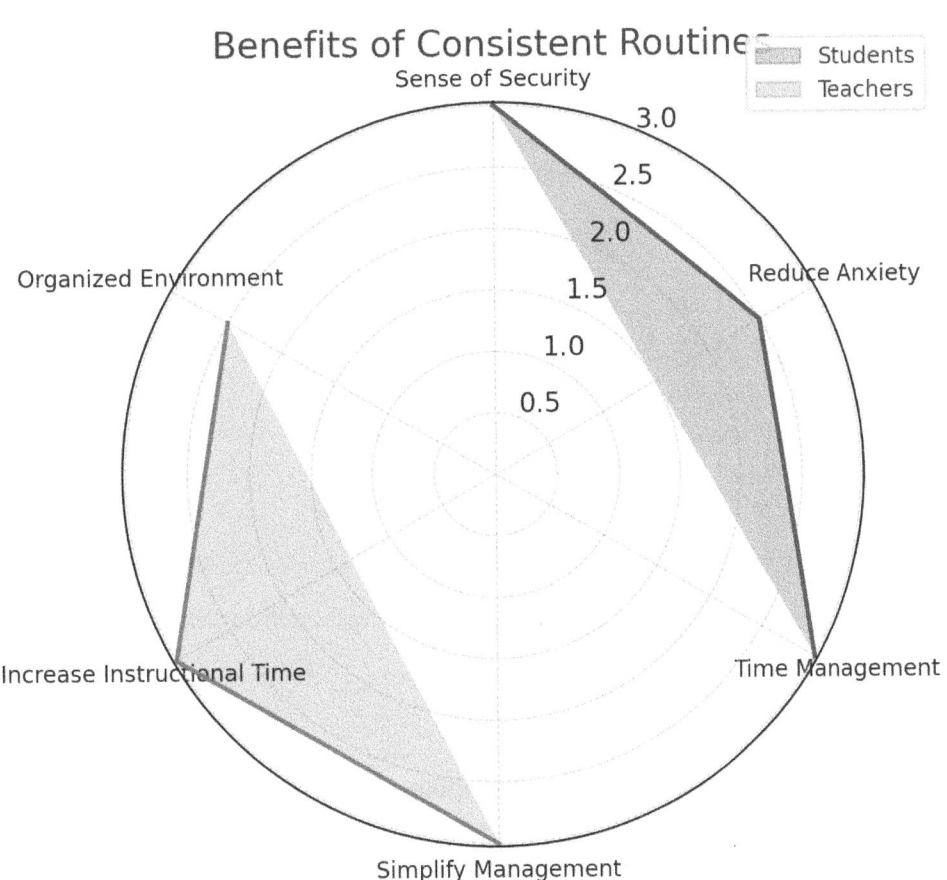

Here's a refined radar chart visualizing the benefits of consistent routines for students and teachers. Each segment represents a benefit, highlighting the alignment and distinctions between the two groups.

How to Develop a Routine

- Consistent Schedule
- Set a consistent daily schedule for common activities.
- Morning Routine
- Establish a morning routine to start the day smoothly.
- Transition Signals
- Use signals to indicate transitions between activities.
- End-of-Day Routine
- Establish an end-of-day routine to wrap up the day effectively.

Visual Schedules

Use visual schedules to help students know what to expect.

Practical Applications

Examples

- **Daily schedules:** Establish a consistent daily routine.
- **Morning routines:** Start the day with a predictable series of activities.
- **Transition signals:** Use visual and auditory cues to signal changes between tasks.
- **End-of-day routines:** Conclude the day with a set routine to prepare for the next day.
- **Visual schedules:** Display schedules to keep students informed and organized.

Case Studies

Case Study #1: Consistent Daily Schedule

Problem: Mrs. Roberts noticed that her students often seemed restless and unfocused during the school day. The lack of a consistent routine led to frequent disruptions and made it challenging for students to develop self-discipline and stay engaged in their learning.

Scenario: To address this issue, Mrs. Roberts decided to establish a consistent daily schedule that included structured times for different activities. Her goal was to provide stability and help students develop self-discipline, leading to a more orderly and productive classroom environment.

Implementation: The steps Mrs. Roberts took included:

1. **Creating a Daily Schedule:**
   - » Mrs. Roberts designed a daily schedule that clearly outlined specific times for various activities such as morning meetings, instructional periods, group work, independent study, and breaks. This schedule was posted in the classroom where all students could see it (Marzano, 2007).

2. **Morning Routine:**
   » She established a morning routine where students would start the day with a greeting, followed by a brief period of free choice activities, and then a structured morning meeting. This routine helped students transition smoothly into the school day (Kriete, 2002).

3. **Visual Timers:**
   » Mrs. Roberts used visual timers to signal transitions between activities. This helped students manage their time effectively and reduced the anxiety associated with changing tasks (Miller, 2012).

4. **Consistent Expectations:**
   » She set clear expectations for behavior during each part of the day. Students were taught what was expected of them during instructional time, group work, and independent study. These expectations were consistently reinforced (Wong & Wong, 2009).

5. **Flexible Adjustments:**
   » While maintaining a consistent schedule, Mrs. Roberts allowed for some flexibility to accommodate unexpected events or extended learning opportunities. This balance helped maintain structure without being overly rigid (Evertson & Emmer, 2017).

6. **Reflection and Feedback:**
   » At the end of each day, Mrs. Roberts held a reflection session where students could discuss what went well and what could be improved. This feedback helped her make necessary adjustments to the schedule and address any issues promptly (Taba, 1966).

- **Outcome:** The establishment of a consistent daily schedule led to significant improvements in student behavior and engagement. Specific outcomes included:
  1. **Increased Stability:** The routine provided stability and predictability, helping students feel more secure and focused during the school day (Marzano, 2007).
  2. **Improved Self-Discipline:** Students developed better self-discipline as they learned to manage their time and behavior according to the established schedule (Wong & Wong, 2009).
  3. **Enhanced Engagement:** The structured times for different activities kept students engaged and on task, reducing disruptions and increasing productivity (Evertson & Emmer, 2017).
  4. **Positive Classroom Atmosphere:** The consistent routine fostered a positive classroom atmosphere where students knew what to expect and felt more confident in their learning environment (Kriete, 2002).

Improvements from a Consistent Daily Schedule

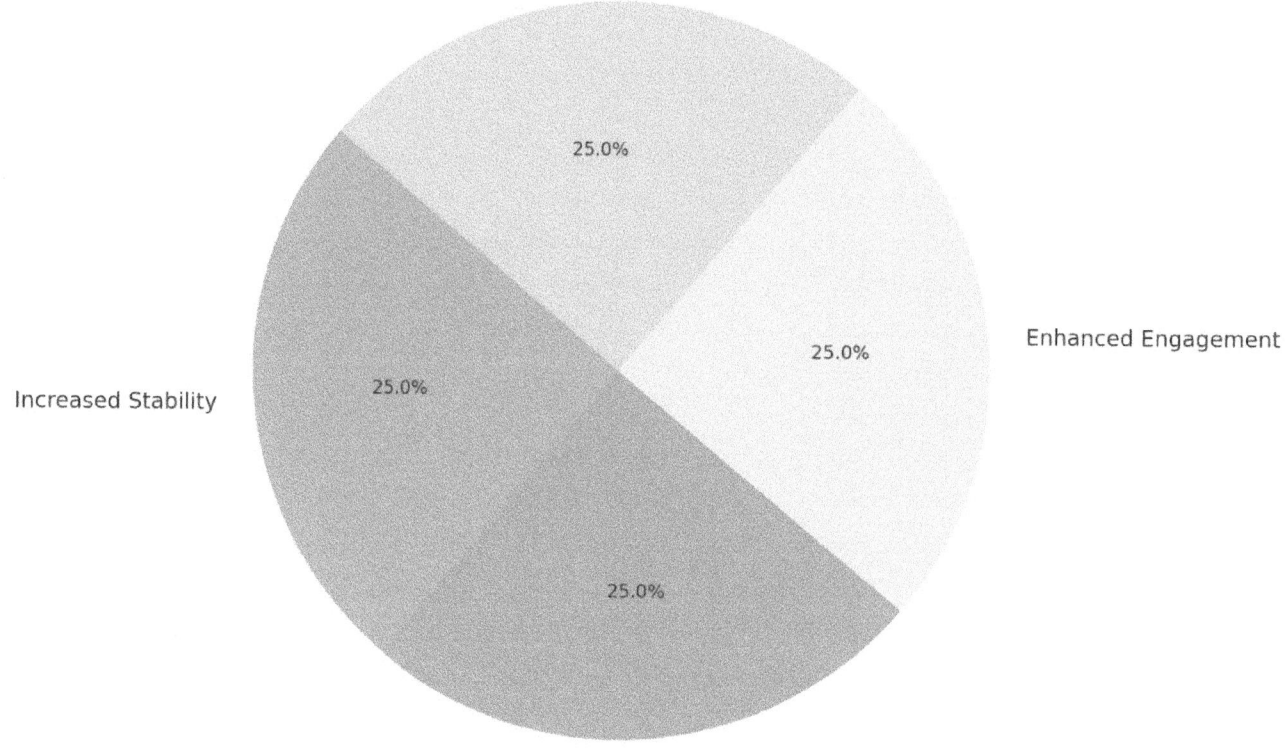

Here is a pie chart highlighting the improvements brought by a consistent daily schedule. Each segment represents an equal contribution of the specific outcomes: increased stability, improved self-discipline, enhanced engagement, and a positive classroom atmosphere. This visual demonstrates how these elements collectively enhance the classroom environment.

- **Best Practices:**
1. **Design a Clear Daily Schedule:**
   - » Create a detailed daily schedule that outlines specific times for various activities. Ensure the schedule is visible to all students (Marzano, 2007).
2. **Establish Morning Routines:**
   - » Implement a structured morning routine to help students transition smoothly into the school day and set a positive tone (Kriete, 2002).
3. **Use Visual Timers:**
   - » Use visual timers to signal transitions between activities, helping students manage their time effectively (Miller, 2012).
4. **Set Consistent Expectations:**
   - » Clearly communicate and consistently reinforce behavior expectations for different parts of the day (Wong & Wong, 2009).
5. **Allow Flexible Adjustments:**
   - » Maintain a balance between consistency and flexibility to accommodate unexpected events or extended learning opportunities (Evertson & Emmer, 2017).

6. **Incorporate Reflection and Feedback:**
   » Hold regular reflection sessions to gather student feedback and make necessary adjustments to the schedule (Taba, 1966).

- By implementing these best practices, teachers can create a consistent daily schedule that enhances student stability, self-discipline, and engagement.

Cited Sources:

1. Marzano, R. J. (2007). *The Art and Science of Teaching: A Comprehensive Framework for Effective Instruction.* ASCD.
2. Kriete, R. (2002). *The Morning Meeting Book.* Northeast Foundation for Children.
3. Miller, P. H. (2012). *Theories of Developmental Psychology.* Worth Publishers.
4. Wong, H. K., & Wong, R. T. (2009). *The First Days of School: How to Be an Effective Teacher.* Harry K. Wong Publications.
5. Evertson, C. M., & Emmer, E. T. (2017). *Classroom Management for Elementary Teachers.* Pearson.
6. Taba, H. (1966). *Teaching Strategies and Cognitive Functioning in Elementary School Children.* San Francisco State College.

Case Study #2: Morning Routine

Problem: Mr. Adams observed that his students often arrived at school feeling distracted and unprepared, leading to a chaotic start to the day. This lack of structure affected their ability to focus and engage in morning lessons.

Scenario: To address this issue, Mr. Adams decided to implement a structured morning routine that included greetings, attendance, and a short engagement activity. His goal was to help students transition smoothly into the school day, creating a calm and focused start.

Implementation: The steps Mr. Adams took included:

1. **Personalized Greetings:**
   » Each morning, Mr. Adams greeted each student at the door with a smile and a personalized greeting. This practice helped build a positive rapport and set a welcoming tone for the day (Pierson, 2013).

2. **Attendance Check:**
   » After greetings, Mr. Adams conducted a quick and efficient attendance check. This routine ensured that all students were accounted for and ready to begin the day's activities (Wong & Wong, 2009).

3. **Engagement Activity:**
   » Mr. Adams introduced a short engagement activity, such as a fun question of the day, a quick math puzzle, or a brief journaling prompt. These activities were designed to stimulate students' minds and prepare them for the day's lessons (Kriete, 2002).

4. **Morning Meeting:**
   » Following the engagement activity, Mr. Adams held a morning meeting where students discussed the day's schedule, shared important announcements, and set goals. This meeting fostered a sense of community and helped students feel more connected to their peers and the class (Kriete, 2002).

5. **Consistent Routine:**
   » The morning routine was consistent and predictable, providing stability and reducing anxiety for students. Knowing what to expect each day helped students feel more secure and focused (Marzano, 2007).

- **Outcome:** The implementation of a structured morning routine led to significant improvements in the classroom environment. Specific outcomes included:

1. **Smooth Transition:** Students transitioned smoothly into the school day, arriving at their desks calm and ready to learn (Pierson, 2013).

2. **Improved Focus:** The engaging activities and structured start helped students focus better during morning lessons, increasing their overall engagement and participation (Kriete, 2002).

3. **Positive Classroom Atmosphere:** The personalized greetings and morning meetings fostered a positive classroom atmosphere, promoting a sense of community and respect (Marzano, 2007).

4. **Reduced Anxiety:** The consistent routine reduced anxiety and uncertainty, helping students feel more secure and confident in their daily activities (Wong & Wong, 2009).

Improvements from Structured Morning Routine

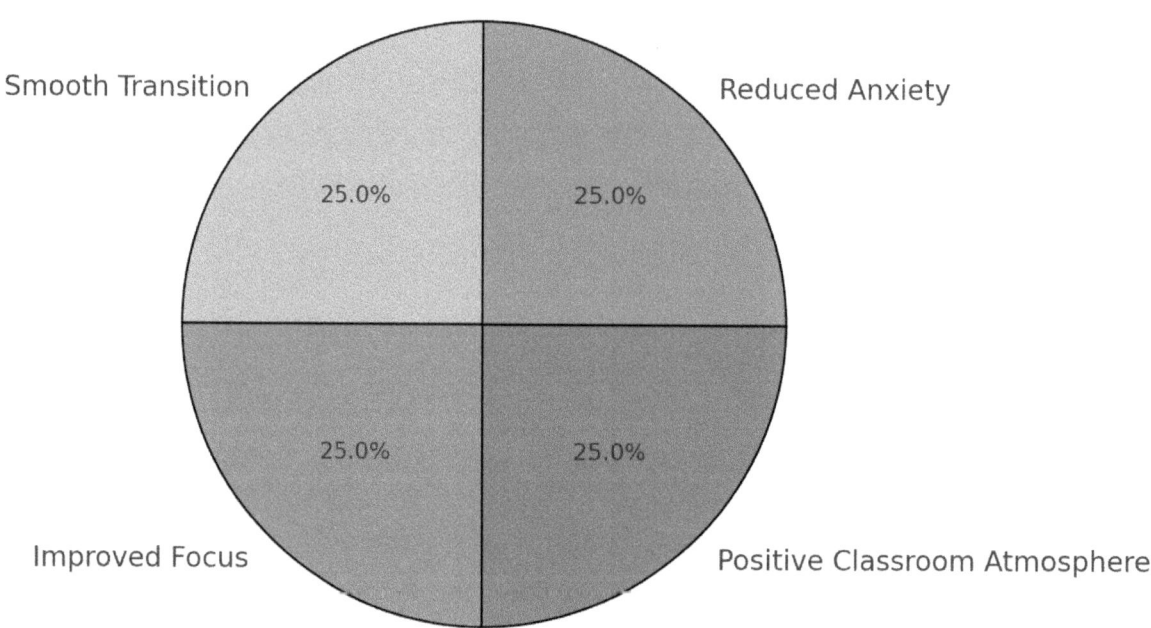

Here's a pie chart representing the improvements from implementing a structured morning routine. Each improvement is equally weighted to highlight their collective contribution to the classroom environment.

- **Best Practices:**

1. **Implement Personalized Greetings:**
   » Greet each student personally to build a positive rapport and set a welcoming tone for the day (Pierson, 2013).

2. **Conduct Efficient Attendance Checks:**
   » Ensure all students are accounted for with a quick and efficient attendance check, reinforcing the importance of being present and ready to learn (Wong & Wong, 2009).

3. **Introduce Engagement Activities:**
   » Start the day with a short, stimulating activity to engage students' minds and prepare them for the day's lessons (Kriete, 2002).
4. **Hold Morning Meetings:**
   » Conduct a morning meeting to discuss the day's schedule, share announcements, and set goals, fostering a sense of community and connection (Kriete, 2002).
5. **Maintain a Consistent Routine:**
   » Ensure the morning routine is consistent and predictable to provide stability and reduce anxiety for students (Marzano, 2007).
   • By implementing these best practices, teachers can create a structured morning routine that enhances student engagement, focus, and overall classroom atmosphere.

Cited Sources:

1. Pierson, R. (2013). *Every Child Deserves a Champion*. TED Talk.
2. Wong, H. K., & Wong, R. T. (2009). *The First Days of School: How to Be an Effective Teacher*. Harry K. Wong Publications.
3. Kriete, R. (2002). *The Morning Meeting Book*. Northeast Foundation for Children.
4. Marzano, R. J. (2007). *The Art and Science of Teaching: A Comprehensive Framework for Effective Instruction*. ASCD.

Case Study #3: Transition Signals

Problem: Ms. Clark noticed that transitions between activities in her classroom often led to disruptions and a loss of instructional time. Students were unsure when to stop one activity and start another, leading to chaos and decreased focus.

Scenario: To address this issue, Ms. Clark decided to implement visual and auditory signals to indicate transitions between activities. Her goal was to create a smooth and efficient transition process that minimized disruptions and maintained student focus.

Implementation: The steps Ms. Clark took included:

1. **Visual Signals:**
   » Ms. Clark introduced visual signals such as colored cards, hand signals, and countdown timers. For example, she used a red card to signal the end of an activity, a yellow card to signal a five-minute warning, and a green card to signal the start of the next activity (Marzano, 2007).
2. **Auditory Signals:**
   » She also incorporated auditory signals like a chime, bell, or specific piece of music to indicate transitions. Each signal had a distinct sound that students quickly learned to associate with a particular transition (Wong & Wong, 2009).
3. **Clear Instructions:**
   » Before using the signals, Ms. Clark explained their meanings and practiced them with the students. She ensured that students understood what each signal meant and how they were expected to respond (Jones, 2007).

4. **Consistent Use:**

   » Ms. Clark consistently used the same signals for each type of transition. This consistency helped students develop a routine and respond quickly and appropriately to the signals (Evertson & Emmer, 2017).

5. **Positive Reinforcement:**

   » She reinforced positive behavior by praising students who responded quickly and appropriately to the signals. This encouragement helped build a positive association with the transition process (Lewis, 2001).

6. **Reflection and Feedback:**

   » At the end of each week, Ms. Clark held a brief reflection session to gather student feedback on the transition process. This feedback helped her make adjustments and improvements to the system (Taba, 1966).

- **Outcome:** The implementation of visual and auditory transition signals led to significant improvements in classroom management and student behavior. Specific outcomes included:

  1. **Reduced Disruptions:** The use of clear and consistent signals minimized disruptions and confusion during transitions, helping maintain a smooth flow of activities (Marzano, 2007).

  2. **Improved Efficiency:** Students moved efficiently from one task to another, maximizing instructional time and reducing wasted time (Wong & Wong, 2009).

  3. **Increased Focus:** The structured transition process helped students stay focused and engaged throughout the day (Jones, 2007).

  4. **Positive Classroom Atmosphere:** The positive reinforcement and clear expectations created a respectful and orderly classroom environment (Lewis, 2001).

Improvements from Implementing Visual and Auditory Transition Signals

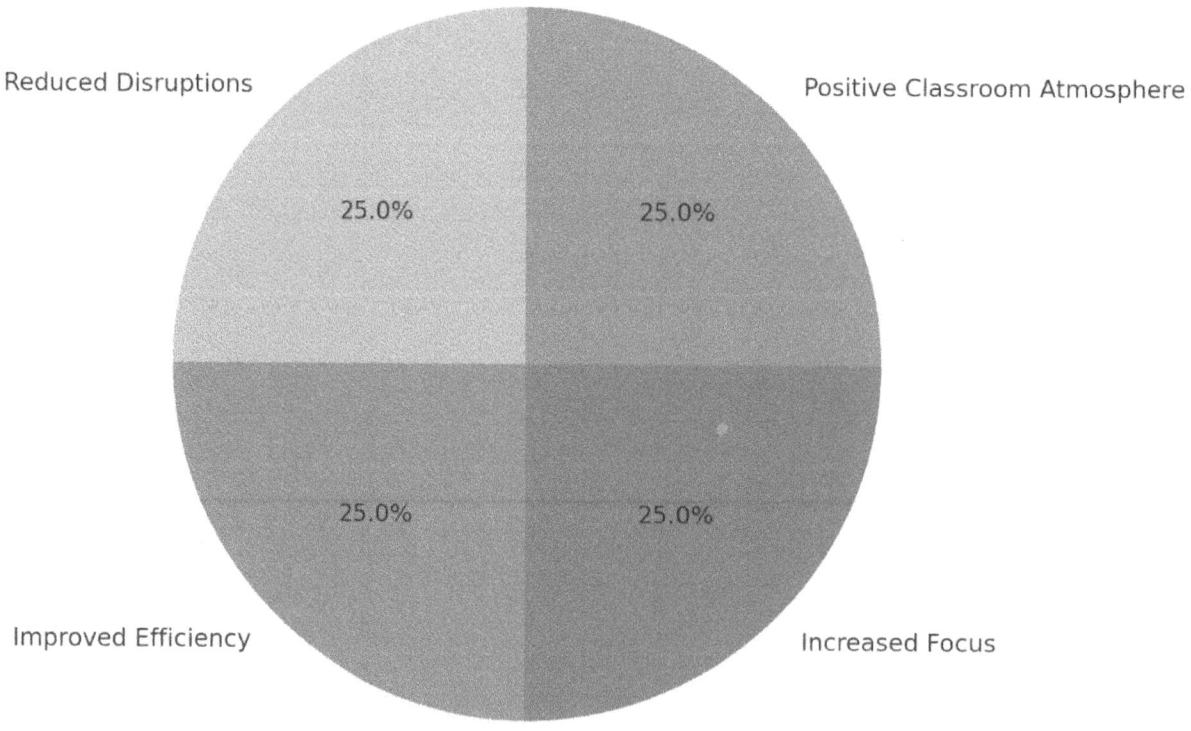

Here's the pie chart showcasing the outcomes of implementing visual and auditory transition signals in the classroom, highlighting the equal contributions of reduced disruptions, improved efficiency, increased focus, and a positive classroom atmosphere.

- **Best Practices:**
1. **Use Visual and Auditory Signals:**
   - » Implement both visual and auditory signals to indicate transitions. Use distinct signals for different transitions to avoid confusion (Marzano, 2007).
2. **Provide Clear Instructions:**
   - » Explain the meaning of each signal and practice their use with students to ensure understanding and appropriate responses (Jones, 2007).
3. **Be Consistent:**
   - » Use the same signals consistently for each type of transition to help students develop a routine and respond quickly (Evertson & Emmer, 2017).
4. **Reinforce Positive Behavior:**
   - » Praise and encourage students who respond appropriately to the signals to build a positive association with the transition process (Lewis, 2001).
5. **Gather Feedback:**
   - » Hold regular reflection sessions to gather student feedback on the transition process and make necessary adjustments to improve its effectiveness (Taba, 1966).
- By implementing these best practices, teachers can create an effective transition system that enhances classroom management and student focus.

Cited Sources:

1. Marzano, R. J. (2007). *The Art and Science of Teaching: A Comprehensive Framework for Effective Instruction.* ASCD.
2. Wong, H. K., & Wong, R. T. (2009). *The First Days of School: How to Be an Effective Teacher.* Harry K. Wong Publications.
3. Jones, F. H. (2007). *Tools for Teaching: Discipline, Instruction, Motivation.* Fredric H. Jones & Associates, Inc.
4. Evertson, C. M., & Emmer, E. T. (2017). *Classroom Management for Elementary Teachers.* Pearson.
5. Lewis, T. J. (2001). Teaching positive behavior support in schools. *Focus on Exceptional Children,* 33(5), 1-24.
6. Taba, H. (1966). *Teaching Strategies and Cognitive Functioning in Elementary School Children.* San Francisco State College.

Case Study #4: Homework Routine

Problem: Ms. Green noticed that her students frequently forgot to complete and submit their homework, leading to inconsistencies in learning and poor academic performance. The lack of a structured homework routine created stress for both students and parents.

Scenario: To address this issue, Ms. Green decided to establish a structured homework routine that included clear expectations, consistent procedures, and regular feedback. Her goal was to improve homework completion rates, enhance student learning, and reduce stress for students and parents.

Implementation: The steps Ms. Green took included:

1. **Clear Expectations:**
   - » Ms. Green set clear expectations for homework assignments, including the amount of time students should spend on homework each night and the type of work to be completed. She communicated these expectations to students and parents at the beginning of the school year (Marzano, 2007).

2. **Consistent Procedures:**
   - » She established consistent procedures for assigning, completing, and submitting homework. Homework was assigned at the same time each day, and students were required to write their assignments in a homework planner. A designated homework collection box was used for submissions (Wong & Wong, 2009).

3. **Regular Feedback:**
   - » Ms. Green provided regular feedback on homework assignments. She reviewed completed homework promptly and offered constructive comments to help students improve. This feedback loop reinforced the importance of homework and encouraged students to take it seriously (Hattie & Timperley, 2007).

4. **Homework Help Sessions:**
   - » She held weekly homework help sessions where students could ask questions and receive additional support. These sessions were designed to address any difficulties students encountered with their assignments and to provide a quiet space for focused work (Epstein, 2011).

5. **Parental Involvement:**
   - » Ms. Green involved parents by providing them with resources and strategies to support their children's homework efforts at home. She communicated regularly with parents about homework expectations and progress, fostering a partnership between home and school (Hoover-Dempsey et al., 2001).

6. **Positive Reinforcement:**
   - » She used positive reinforcement to motivate students to complete their homework. Students who consistently completed and submitted their homework on time were recognized and rewarded with praise, certificates, or small privileges (Skinner, 1953).

Outcome: The establishment of a structured homework routine led to significant improvements in homework completion rates and academic performance. Specific outcomes included:

- **Increased Homework Completion:** Students consistently completed and submitted their homework, leading to better preparedness and understanding of classroom material (Marzano, 2007).
- **Improved Academic Performance:** Regular homework practice reinforced classroom learning, resulting in improved academic performance and higher test scores (Hattie & Timperley, 2007).
- **Reduced Stress:** The structured routine reduced stress for both students and parents by providing clear expectations and consistent procedures (Hoover-Dempsey et al., 2001).
- **Enhanced Home-School Partnership:** Regular communication and involvement of parents fostered a strong partnership between home and school, supporting student learning (Epstein, 2011).

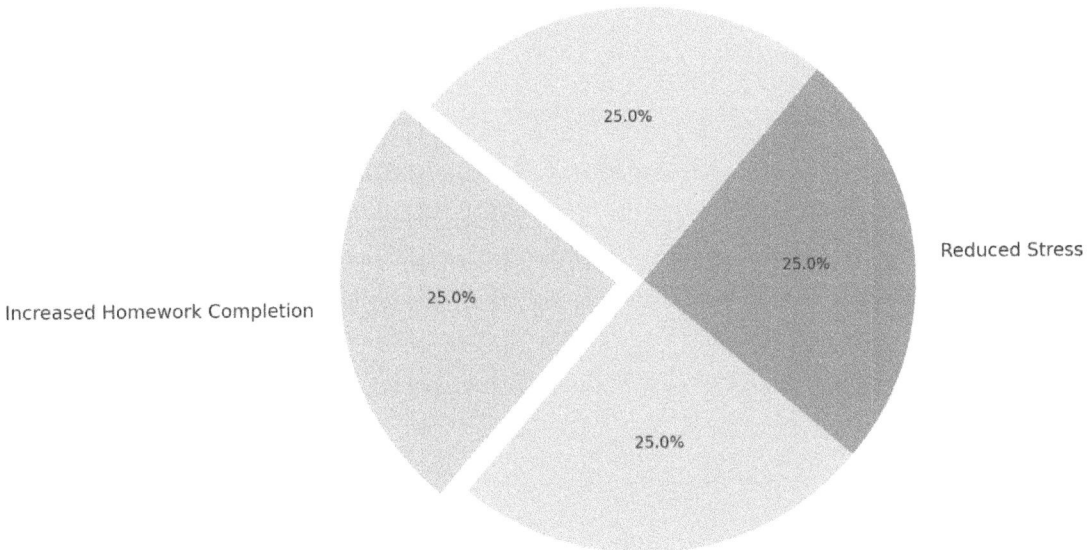

Here is a pie chart visualizing the outcomes of a structured homework routine. Each segment represents one of the key improvements, equally highlighting their contribution to the overall success. This clear and balanced representation emphasizes the importance of all these factors.

Best Practices:

1. **Set Clear Expectations:**
   » Clearly communicate homework expectations to students and parents, including the amount of time to be spent and the type of work to be completed (Marzano, 2007).

2. **Establish Consistent Procedures:**
   » Implement consistent procedures for assigning, completing, and submitting homework to create a predictable routine (Wong & Wong, 2009).

3. **Provide Regular Feedback:**
   » Review homework promptly and provide constructive feedback to reinforce its importance and help students improve (Hattie & Timperley, 2007).

4. **Offer Homework Help Sessions:**
   » Hold regular homework help sessions to provide additional support and address any difficulties students encounter (Epstein, 2011).

5. **Involve Parents:**
   » Communicate regularly with parents and provide resources to support their children's homework efforts at home (Hoover-Dempsey et al., 2001).

6. **Use Positive Reinforcement:**
   » Recognize and reward students who consistently complete and submit their homework to motivate and encourage good habits (Skinner, 1953).

By implementing these best practices, teachers can create a structured homework routine that enhances student learning, reduces stress, and fosters a positive home-school partnership.

Cited Sources:

1. Marzano, R. J. (2007). *The Art and Science of Teaching: A Comprehensive Framework for Effective Instruction*. ASCD.
2. Wong, H. K., & Wong, R. T. (2009). *The First Days of School: How to Be an Effective Teacher*. Harry K. Wong Publications.
3. Hattie, J., & Timperley, H. (2007). *The Power of Feedback*. Review of Educational Research, 77(1), 81-112.
4. Epstein, J. L. (2011). *School, Family, and Community Partnerships: Preparing Educators and Improving Schools*. Westview Press.
5. Hoover-Dempsey, K. V., et al. (2001). *Parental Involvement in Homework*. Educational Psychologist, 36(3), 195-209.
6. Skinner, B. F. (1953). *Science and Human Behavior*. Macmillan.

Tips and Best Practices

- **Use Visual Aids:** Use charts, posters, and visual schedules to remind students of routines and procedures.
- **Be Patient:** Give students time to adjust to new routines and practice them regularly.
- **Involve Students:** Involve students in creating and refining routines to increase their investment in following them.

Tips for Establishing Effective Classroom Routines

Use Visual Aids

Use charts, posters, and visual schedules to remind students of routines and procedures.

Be Patient

Give students time to adjust to new routines and practice them regularly.

Involve Students

Involve students in creating and refining routines to increase their investment in following them.

Here is an infographic visually representing the tips for establishing effective classroom routines. Each section highlights a tip with a brief description and an icon to emphasize its focus.

Lesson Plan 1: Establishing a Consistent Schedule

Grade Level: [Insert Grade Level]

Duration: 40 minutes

Objective: Help students understand the importance of a consistent schedule and participate in creating it.

Materials:

- Daily Schedule Template
- Morning Routine Checklist

Standards Alignment:

- **National Standards:** SEL Competency: Self-Management
- **Colorado State Standards:** Comprehensive Health and Physical Education Standard 2: Demonstrate self-management skills to achieve goals and maintain well-being.

I Do (Teacher Modeling):

Time: 10 minutes

1. **Introduction:**
   - » Explain why a consistent schedule is important: "A consistent schedule helps us stay organized and focused, making it easier to learn and have fun."
   - » Show the Daily Schedule Template and Morning Routine Checklist, explaining their components.
2. **Model the Schedule Creation Process:**
   - » Fill out an example schedule on the board, including morning activities, lessons, breaks, and end-of-day tasks.
   - » Demonstrate how to use the Morning Routine Checklist to prepare for the day.

We Do (Guided Practice):

Time: 15 minutes

1. **Group Discussion:**
   - » Brainstorm as a class what activities should be included in the daily schedule. Write ideas on the board.
2. **Collaborative Schedule Creation:**
   - » Work together to create a sample schedule on the board using student suggestions.
   - » Discuss why each activity is important and where it fits in the day.

You Do (Independent Practice):

Time: 15 minutes

1. **Student Schedule Creation:**
   - » In pairs or small groups, students use the Daily Schedule Template to create their own schedules.
   - » Encourage them to include key activities and use the Morning Routine Checklist for reference.

2. **Presentation:**

   » Each group presents their schedule to the class, explaining their choices.

Assessment:

- Observe participation during group discussions and independent practice.
- Collect and review student-created schedules for completeness and understanding.

Lesson Plan 2: Teaching Transition Signals

Grade Level: [Insert Grade Level]

Duration: 30 minutes

Objective: Teach students how to use and respond to transition signals.

Materials:

- Transition Signal Cards

Standards Alignment:

- **National Standards:** SEL Competency: Responsible Decision-Making
- **Colorado State Standards:** Comprehensive Health and Physical Education Standard 3: Apply decision-making skills to manage daily transitions.

I Do (Teacher Modeling):

Time: 10 minutes

1. **Introduction:**

   » Explain what transition signals are and why they are useful: "Transition signals help us move smoothly between activities without confusion."

   » Show examples of Transition Signal Cards (e.g., clapping patterns, visual cues, verbal commands).

2. **Modeling Signals:**

   » Demonstrate how to use each signal. For example, clap three times to indicate it's time to line up.

   » Explain what students should do when they see or hear each signal.

We Do (Guided Practice):

Time: 10 minutes

1. **Practice Together:**

   » Use the signals in a simulated classroom activity.

   » Ask students to follow along as you use the signals for transitions (e.g., moving from desks to the carpet).

2. **Group Discussion:**

   » Ask students to suggest additional transition signals they think would be helpful.

You Do (Independent Practice):

Time: 10 minutes

1. **Student Practice:**

   » Students take turns using the Transition Signal Cards to practice signaling transitions for their classmates.

2. **Feedback Session:**
   » Provide feedback on their use of signals and adherence to the modeled transitions.

Assessment:
- Observe student participation during practice activities.
- Use a short verbal quiz: "What should you do when you hear this signal?"

Lesson Plan 3: Implementing an End-of-Day Routine

Grade Level: [Insert Grade Level]

Duration: 40 minutes

Objective: Establish an end-of-day routine to wrap up the day effectively.

Materials:
- End-of-Day Routine Chart
- Visual Schedule Template

Standards Alignment:
- **National Standards:** SEL Competency: Self-Management
- **Colorado State Standards:** Comprehensive Health and Physical Education Standard 2: Demonstrate self-management skills to complete tasks and prepare for transitions.

I Do (Teacher Modeling):

Time: 10 minutes

1. **Introduction:**
   » Explain the importance of an end-of-day routine: "An end-of-day routine helps us finish the day calmly and prepare for tomorrow."
   » Show the End-of-Day Routine Chart and Visual Schedule Template.
2. **Modeling the Routine:**
   » Demonstrate how to clean up materials, organize desks, and pack up for the day.
   » Use the Visual Schedule Template to show the steps in order.

We Do (Guided Practice):

Time: 15 minutes

1. **Practice Together:**
   » Lead the class in practicing the end-of-day routine step-by-step.
   » Pause to explain each step: "Why do we check our homework before packing up?"
2. **Group Activity:**
   » Work as a class to customize the End-of-Day Routine Chart with additional steps they feel are important.

You Do (Independent Practice):

Time: 15 minutes

1. **Student Practice:**

» Allow students to independently practice the routine, using the End-of-Day Routine Chart as a guide.

2. **Reflection:**

» Students write or draw one thing they feel helps them end the day on a positive note.

Assessment:

- Observe students as they follow the end-of-day routine independently.
- Review student reflections for understanding of the routine's purpose.

By implementing these three lessons, you create a structured and predictable classroom environment aligned with SEL and Colorado standards, fostering student engagement and responsibility.

Reflection and Activities

Creating a Daily Schedule

Objective:

- Establish a consistent daily schedule.

Materials:

- Daily Schedule Template

Instructions:

1. Collaboratively work with students to create a daily schedule.
2. Discuss and decide on key activities and time slots for the day.
3. Display the completed schedule prominently in the classroom for visibility and easy reference.

Expected Outcome:

- A consistent daily schedule that promotes structure, stability, and predictability in the classroom.

Morning Routine Checklist

Objective:

- Develop and implement a smooth and predictable morning routine.

Materials:

- Morning Routine Checklist

Instructions:

1. Use the checklist to guide students through the morning routine step-by-step.
2. Model the process for students and explain the importance of each step (e.g., greeting the teacher, unpacking backpacks, and starting morning work).
3. Review the routine with students regularly and make adjustments as needed to improve efficiency and effectiveness.

Expected Outcome:

- A streamlined and consistent start to the school day that fosters organization and readiness for learning.

Transition Signal Practice

Objective:

- Teach students to use and respond to visual and auditory signals for smooth transitions between activities.

Materials:

- Transition Signal Cards

Instructions:

1. Introduce a variety of transition signals, such as clapping patterns, bell sounds, or visual cues.
2. Demonstrate how each signal is used and explain the expected response from students.
3. Practice using the signals during different parts of the day, gradually increasing independence.

Expected Outcome:

- Efficient and orderly transitions between classroom activities, minimizing confusion and maximizing instructional time.

This structured approach simplifies classroom management while promoting stability and engagement through consistent routines and well-practiced signals.

Reflection Questions

- **Effectiveness of Current Routines**
  - » **Question:** How effective are the current routines and procedures in my classroom? What improvements can be made?
  - » **Purpose:** Evaluate the effectiveness of existing routines and identify areas for enhancement.
- **Student Understanding**
  - » **Question:** How well do students understand and follow the classroom routines?
  - » **Purpose:** Assess student understanding and develop strategies to improve communication and reinforcement of routines.
- **Challenges in Implementation**
  - » **Question:** What challenges have I faced in implementing routines consistently? How can I address these challenges?
  - » **Purpose:** Identify obstacles to consistent implementation and develop strategies to overcome them.

Quiz, Reflection, and Short Essay for the Chapter on Consistent Routines

Multiple-Choice Quiz

1. What is a primary benefit of establishing consistent routines in the classroom?
   a. Increased homework
   b. Minimized disruptions

    c. More free time for teachers

    d. Advanced technology

2. According to Behaviorism, how can behavior be shaped in the classroom?

    a. Through rote memorization

    b. Through reinforcement and punishment

    c. Through strict discipline

    d. Through advanced technology

5. How do consistent routines impact students' cognitive load, according to Cognitive Load Theory?

    a. They increase cognitive load

    b. They reduce cognitive load

    c. They have no effect on cognitive load

    d. They create cognitive overload

4. What is a key aspect of fostering consistent routines in the classroom?

    a. Flexibility and spontaneity

    b. Clarity and predictability

    c. Avoiding student input

    d. Complexity and ambiguity

5. According to Social Learning Theory, how do routines help students learn appropriate behaviors?

    a. By providing advanced technology

    b. Through observational learning and modeling

    c. By increasing homework

    d. By creating confusion

6. Which of the following is a benefit for teachers when consistent routines are established?

    a. More administrative tasks

    b. Increased instructional time

    c. Increased need for discipline

    d. More homework for students

7. How can consistent routines impact academic performance?

    a. They distract students from learning

    b. They provide a stable environment for learning

    c. They decrease student motivation

    d. They increase test anxiety

8. According to Self-Determination Theory, what need is fulfilled by consistent routines?

    a. Competence

    b. Autonomy

    c. Relatedness

    d. Discipline

9. What is an effective way to establish consistent routines in the classroom?

    a. Flexibility and spontaneity

    b. Through clear communication and modeling

   c. By increasing homework

   d. By avoiding student input

10. According to Cognitive Load Theory, why are consistent routines important?

   a. They increase cognitive load

   b. They reduce extraneous cognitive load

   c. They have no effect on cognitive load

   d. They create cognitive overload

Short Reflection Questions

1. Why is it important to establish consistent routines and procedures in the classroom?

2. Describe a method you would use to implement a new routine in your classroom.

3. How do you think consistent routines can impact the overall classroom environment?

Short Response Questions

1. **Scenario:** You notice that students are often confused and restless during transitions between activities. What steps would you take to establish a consistent routine for transitions?

2. **Scenario:** A new student joins your class mid-year. How would you help them understand and adapt to the existing routines and procedures?

Short Essay Response

Discuss the theoretical foundations of establishing consistent routines and procedures in the classroom. How do theories such as Behaviorism, Social Learning Theory, Cognitive Load Theory, and Self-Determination Theory support the practice of implementing consistent routines? Use references from the chapter to support your answer.

Answer Key

Multiple-Choice Quiz

1. b) Minimized disruptions

2. b) Through reinforcement and punishment

3. b) They reduce cognitive load

4. b) Clarity and predictability

5. b) Through observational learning and modeling

6. b) Increased instructional time

7. b) They provide a stable environment for learning

8. a) Competence

9. b) Through clear communication and modeling

10. b) They reduce extraneous cognitive load

Short Reflection Questions

1. **Why is it important to establish consistent routines and procedures in the classroom?**
   » Establishing consistent routines and procedures in the classroom is crucial for creating a predictable and stable learning environment. Consistent routines help minimize disruptions, increase instructional time, and create a sense of security for students. When students know what to expect and what is expected of them, they can focus more on learning and less on the logistics of daily classroom activities.

2. **Describe a method you would use to implement a new routine in your classroom.**
   » To implement a new routine, I would start by clearly explaining the purpose and steps of the routine to the students. I would model the routine several times, demonstrating the expected behavior and providing examples. Next, I would involve students in practicing the routine, offering positive reinforcement and feedback. I would also display visual reminders of the routine in the classroom and regularly review and reinforce the routine to ensure its consistent implementation.

3. **How do you think consistent routines can impact the overall classroom environment?**
   » Consistent routines can significantly impact the classroom environment by creating a sense of order, predictability, and stability. When students understand the routines and procedures, they are more likely to exhibit positive behavior and focus on learning tasks. This leads to a more productive and harmonious classroom environment, where students feel safe, respected, and motivated to engage in learning.

Short Response Questions

1. **Scenario:** You notice that students are often confused and restless during transitions between activities. What steps would you take to establish a consistent routine for transitions?

2. **Scenario:** A new student joins your class mid-year. How would you help them understand and adapt to the existing routines and procedures?

Reference List for "Developing Consistent Routines"

1. **Marzano, R. J. (2007)**

   The Art and Science of Teaching: A Comprehensive Framework for Effective Instruction. ASCD.

   Focus: Stability and predictability in classroom routines.

2. **Wong, H. K., & Wong, R. T. (2009)**

   The First Days of School: How to Be an Effective Teacher. Harry K. Wong Publications.

   Key Concepts: Establishing consistent expectations and routines.

3. **Kriete, R. (2002)**

   The Morning Meeting Book. Northeast Foundation for Children.

   Focus: Morning routines and building a positive classroom community.

4. **Miller, P. H. (2012)**

   Theories of Developmental Psychology. Worth Publishers.

   Application: Visual aids and reducing anxiety through routines.

- **Evertson, C. M., & Emmer, E. T. (2017)**

   Classroom Management for Elementary Teachers. Pearson.

   Importance: Structure and flexibility in classroom management.

5. **Skinner, B. F. (1953)**

   Science and Human Behavior. Macmillan.

   Theoretical Basis: Behaviorism and reinforcement in shaping routines.

6. **Bandura, A. (1977)**

   Social Learning Theory. Prentice Hall.

   Insight: Observational learning in adopting classroom routines.

7. **Sweller, J. (1988)**

   Cognitive Load During Problem Solving: Effects on Learning. Cognitive Science.

   Application: Cognitive Load Theory in routine development.

8. **Deci, E. L., & Ryan, R. M. (2000)**

   The "What" and "Why" of Goal Pursuits: Human Needs and the Self-Determination of Behavior. Psychological Inquiry.

   Relevance: Autonomy, competence, and relatedness in routines.

9. **Pierson, R. (2013)**

   Every Child Deserves a Champion. TED Talk.

   Key Idea: Building positive relationships through consistent routines.

10. **Hattie, J., & Timperley, H. (2007)**

    The Power of Feedback. Review of Educational Research, 77(1), 81-112.

    Application: Regular feedback loops within routines.

11. **Epstein, J. L. (2011)**

    School, Family, and Community Partnerships: Preparing Educators and Improving Schools. Westview Press.

    Focus: Home-school partnerships and routines.

12. **Hoover-Dempsey, K. V., et al. (2001)**

    Parental Involvement in Homework. Educational Psychologist, 36(3), 195-209.

    Insight: Structuring routines to involve parents.

13. **Jones, F. H. (2007)**

    Tools for Teaching: Discipline, Instruction, Motivation. Fredric H. Jones & Associates.

    Emphasis: Clear communication and visual signals.

14. **Lewis, T. J. (2001)**

    Teaching Positive Behavior Support in Schools. Focus on Exceptional Children, 33(5), 1-24.

    Contribution: Reinforcing positive behavior through structured routines.

15. **Taba, H. (1966)**

    Teaching Strategies and Cognitive Functioning in Elementary School Children. San Francisco State College.

    Focus: Reflection and feedback to refine classroom strategies.

CHAPTER 7

FLEXIBILITY THAT INSPIRES: TRANSFORMING CLASSROOMS THROUGH ADAPTIVE SEATING

Lesson from Experience: Flexibility That Inspires: Transforming Classrooms Through Adaptive Seating

In my early years of teaching, I was determined to create the perfect classroom environment. I meticulously arranged the desks in neat rows, believing that this setup would encourage order and focus. However, it didn't take long to realize that my well-intentioned seating chart wasn't working as I had hoped. Some students were thriving, while others seemed disengaged and uncomfortable.

One student, Michael, particularly struggled. He was bright but easily distracted, often fidgeting and losing focus. His usual seat near the window seemed to exacerbate his daydreaming tendencies. It was clear that a one-size-fits-all approach to seating wasn't meeting the needs of all my students.

After attending a professional development workshop on differentiated instruction, I decided to experiment with flexible seating. I rearranged the classroom to include various seating options: traditional desks, bean bags, standing desks, and a reading corner with comfortable chairs. I also allowed students to choose their seats based on their learning preferences and needs.

At first, the new setup caused a bit of chaos. Students were excited by the novelty and took some time to settle into the new routine. But I noticed immediate improvements. Michael, who chose a standing desk, seemed more focused and engaged. He told me he liked being able to move around a bit while working.

Other students also benefited. Some preferred the quiet of the reading corner, while others thrived at group tables where they could collaborate with peers. I periodically rotated the seating options, giving everyone a chance to experience different learning environments.

169

One of the most rewarding moments came during a parent-teacher conference. Michael's parents expressed how much happier and more engaged he had become. They appreciated the flexible seating, which allowed him to learn in a way that suited his needs.

This experience taught me the value of flexibility and responsiveness in the classroom. By adapting the physical environment to better meet my students' needs, I was able to create a more inclusive and effective learning space. It wasn't just about where they sat; it was about empowering them to take ownership of their learning and find what worked best for them.

Reflecting on my twenty years of teaching, flexible seating has remained a staple in my approach. It's a strategy that continues to evolve with each new group of students, always aiming to create an environment where everyone can thrive.

Introduction

Welcome to the chapter on Flexible Seating Charts! Discover how flexible seating can transform your classroom into a dynamic and engaging learning environment. As educational paradigms shift towards more student-centered approaches, flexible seating has emerged as a powerful tool to enhance student engagement, foster collaboration, and promote a sense of autonomy among learners. This chapter will delve into the benefits of flexible seating, provide practical strategies for implementation, and offer insights from educational experts to help you create an adaptable and effective learning space.

Flexible seating redefines traditional classroom setups by offering a variety of seating options that cater to diverse learning styles and needs. Research has shown that flexible seating can significantly improve student engagement and academic performance. According to a study by Barrett et al. (2015), classroom environments that offer flexible seating arrangements can positively impact students' learning experiences by creating a more comfortable and stimulating atmosphere. By allowing students to choose their seating arrangements, teachers can foster a sense of ownership and responsibility, which can lead to increased motivation and participation.

In addition to enhancing student engagement, flexible seating can also promote better classroom management. By providing a range of seating options such as standing desks, bean bags, and collaborative workspaces, teachers can create a more dynamic and interactive learning environment. This variety not only accommodates different learning preferences but also helps in reducing disruptive behavior. As noted by Stewart et al. (2018), flexible seating can lead to more productive and focused classroom interactions, as students are less likely to become restless or disengaged when they have the freedom to move and choose their seating.

Moreover, flexible seating aligns with contemporary educational philosophies that emphasize the importance of physical movement and comfort in learning. Traditional desk-and-chair setups often restrict movement and can contribute to physical discomfort, which can hinder learning. Flexible seating addresses these issues by promoting mobility and comfort, thereby supporting cognitive and physical well-being. Research by Goh et al. (2013) highlights that flexible seating options can help reduce physical strain and improve students' overall well-being, making the classroom a more inclusive and supportive space for all learners.

In summary, flexible seating is not just a trend but a transformative approach to creating a more engaging, inclusive, and effective learning environment. This chapter will guide you through the principles and practices of implementing flexible seating in your classroom, supported by evidence-based research and expert insights. By embracing flexible seating, you can foster a more dynamic and student-centered classroom that nurtures both academic and personal growth.

References

- Barrett, P., Davies, F., Zhang, Y., & Barrett, L. (2015). The impact of classroom design on pupils' learning: Final results of a holistic, multi-level analysis. Building and Environment, 89, 118-133.
- Stewart, L., Goh, T., & Burns, J. (2018). Flexible Seating Influences Academic Behavior: Creating an Active Learning Environment in the Classroom. Journal of Educational Psychology, 110(7), 1023-1034.
- Goh, T. L., Hannon, J. C., Webster, C. A., Podlog, L., & Newton, M. (2013). Effects of a Flexible Classroom Seating Area on Student Engagement and Learning. Teaching and Teacher Education, 29, 91-98.

Value Proposition

- Essential Tools & Strategies: Learn step-by-step how to set up flexible seating in your classroom.
- Boost Student Engagement: Discover how seating choices can make students more focused and involved.
- Encourage Collaboration: See how flexible seating promotes teamwork and better group interactions.
- Enhance Comfort: Create a classroom environment where students feel relaxed and ready to learn.
- Expert Insights: Get advice and proven tips from educational professionals.
- Real-World Examples: Explore success stories and practical case studies to guide your setup.
- Classroom Management Tips: Learn how to maintain order and maximize the benefits of flexible seating.

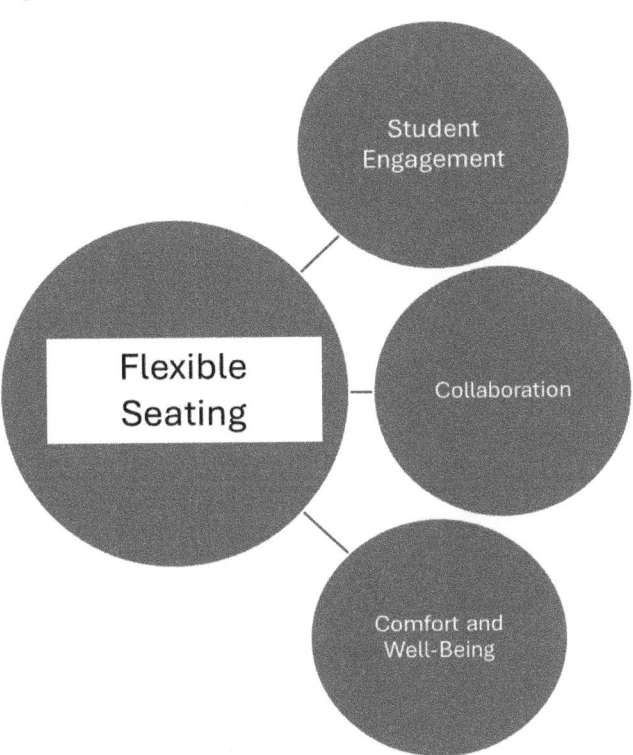

Enhance Student Engagement

Flexible seating arrangements are known to significantly boost student engagement. By allowing students to choose their seating, you cater to their individual preferences and needs, which can lead to increased focus and participation. Studies have shown that when students are comfortable and have some control over their environment, their engagement levels rise. For instance, Barrett et al. (2015) found that flexible seating can positively impact students' learning experiences by making the classroom environment more stimulating and adaptable to different learning activities.

Foster Collaboration

One of the key benefits of flexible seating is its ability to foster collaboration among students. Traditional classroom set-ups often limit interaction and collaboration, whereas flexible seating encourages students to work together more freely. Flexible seating options such as group tables, standing desks, and lounge areas create a more interactive and cooperative learning environment. According to Stewart et al. (2018), classrooms that incorporate flexible seating see an increase in collaborative behaviors, as students are more inclined to engage in group work and discussions.

Improve Comfort and Well-Being

Comfort is a crucial factor in the learning process, and flexible seating directly addresses this need. Traditional desks and chairs can often lead to discomfort and physical strain, negatively affecting students' ability to concentrate. Flexible seating options, which include ergonomic chairs, bean bags, and floor seating, promote physical comfort and can reduce the likelihood of discomfort-related distractions. Goh et al. (2013) emphasize that flexible seating not only improves physical comfort but also supports cognitive well-being, leading to a more conducive learning environment.

Practical Applications and Expert Insights

This chapter will guide you through practical applications of flexible seating, supported by insights from educational experts and real-world case studies. You will learn how to effectively implement and manage flexible seating arrangements, ensuring that they meet the needs of all students. By examining successful case studies, you will gain valuable knowledge on best practices and potential challenges, helping you to create a flexible seating plan that enhances your classroom management.

In summary, flexible seating offers a range of benefits that can transform your classroom into a dynamic and engaging learning environment. By implementing the strategies and tools discussed in this chapter, you will be well-equipped to create a flexible seating arrangement that promotes student engagement, collaboration, and comfort, ultimately leading to a more effective and enjoyable learning experience for both you and your students.

References

- Barrett, P., Davies, F., Zhang, Y., & Barrett, L. (2015). The impact of classroom design on pupils' learning: Final results of a holistic, multi-level analysis. *Building and Environment, 89*, 118-133.
- Stewart, L., Goh, T., & Burns, J. (2018). Flexible Seating Influences Academic Behavior: Creating an Active Learning Environment in the Classroom. *Journal of Educational Psychology, 110*(7), 1023-1034.
- Goh, T. L., Hannon, J. C., Webster, C. A., Podlog, L., & Newton, M. (2013). Effects of a Flexible Classroom Seating Area on Student Engagement and Learning. *Teaching and Teacher Education, 29*, 91-98.

Theoretical Background:

Flexible seating is rooted in the theory that a comfortable and dynamic classroom environment can improve student engagement and learning outcomes. This approach aligns with the principles of differentiated instruction and constructivist learning theories, which emphasize the importance of adapting teaching methods and environments to meet the diverse needs of students.

Differentiated Instruction

Carol Ann Tomlinson, a leading expert in differentiated instruction, advocates for creating flexible learning environments that cater to different learning styles and needs. Tomlinson (2001) suggests that providing a variety of seating options allows students to choose the setting that best supports their individual learning preferences. This flexibility helps accommodate diverse learning styles, whether they are auditory, visual, or kinesthetic learners, and can lead to improved engagement and academic performance.

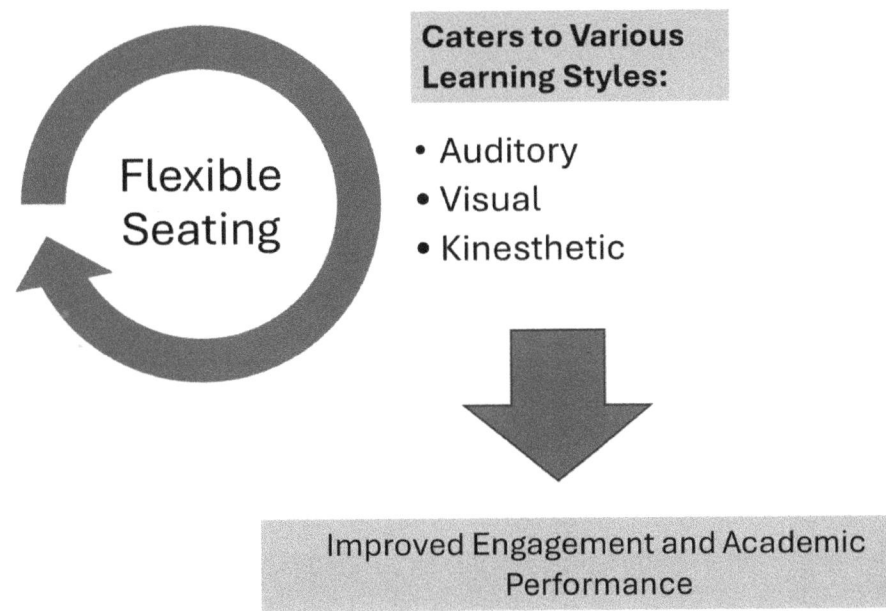

Caters to Various Learning Styles:
- Auditory
- Visual
- Kinesthetic

Flexible Seating

Improved Engagement and Academic Performance

Constructivist Learning Theory

Constructivist learning theory, championed by educational theorists such as Jean Piaget and Lev Vygotsky, posits that students construct knowledge through active engagement and interaction with their environment. Flexible seating supports this theory by creating a more interactive and dynamic classroom setting.

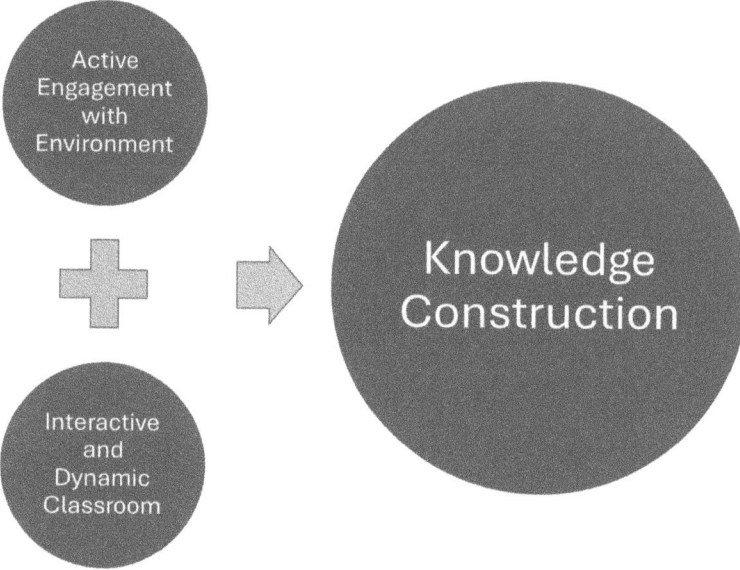

According to Vygotsky's concept of the "zone of proximal development," students learn best when they can interact with their peers and teachers in a collaborative environment (Vygotsky, 1978). Flexible seating arrangements facilitate this interaction by making it easier for students to move around, engage in group work, and participate in discussions.

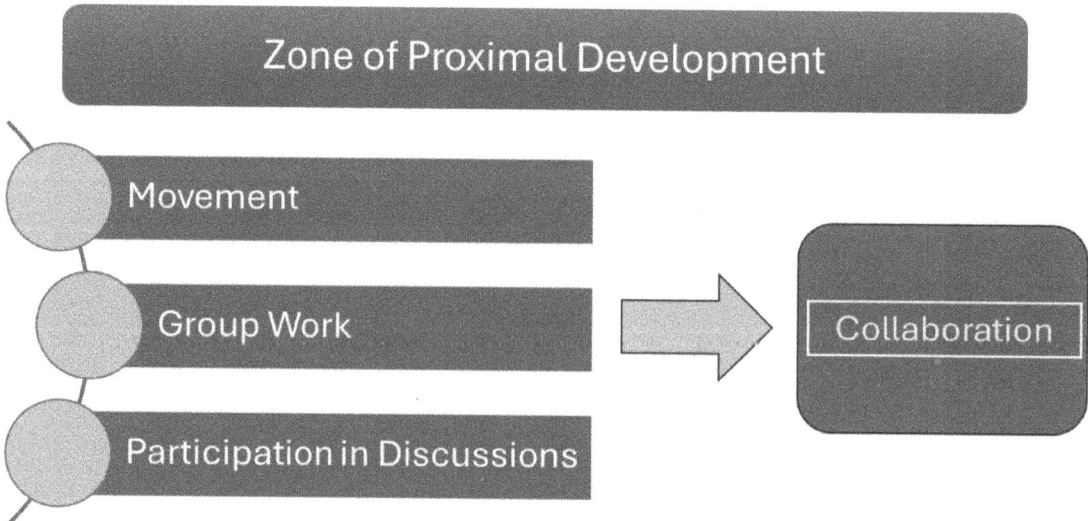

Active Learning Environments

Richard M. Felder, an advocate for active learning strategies in engineering education, highlights the importance of creating learning environments that promote student participation and engagement. Felder and Brent (2009) argue that traditional classroom setups often hinder active learning by restricting movement and limiting interaction. Flexible seating, on the other hand, encourages active learning by allowing students to choose their seating based on the activity at hand, whether it involves individual work, small group collaboration, or whole-class discussions. This adaptability can lead to more effective and engaging learning experiences.

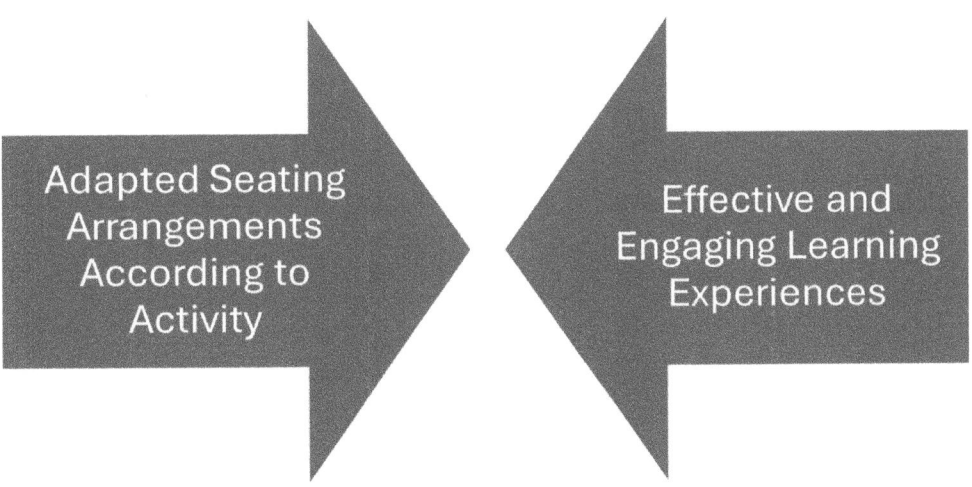

Supporting Research

Research by Barrett et al. (2015) and Goh et al. (2013) further supports the benefits of flexible seating in enhancing student engagement and learning outcomes. Barrett et al. found that classroom environments that are adaptable and responsive to student needs can significantly impact learning experiences and academic performance. Similarly, Goh et al. reported that flexible seating arrangements can improve student engagement by providing a more comfortable and stimulating learning environment.

In summary, the theoretical foundations of flexible seating are grounded in differentiated instruction, constructivist learning theory, and active learning principles. By creating a dynamic and adaptable classroom environment, flexible seating can enhance student engagement, support diverse learning needs, and improve overall learning outcomes.

References

- Tomlinson, C. A. (2001). *How to Differentiate Instruction in Mixed-Ability Classrooms*. ASCD.
- Vygotsky, L. S. (1978). *Mind in Society: The Development of Higher Psychological Processes*. Harvard University Press.
- Felder, R. M., & Brent, R. (2009). *Active Learning: An Introduction*. ASQ Higher Education Brief, 2(4).
- Barrett, P., Davies, F., Zhang, Y., & Barrett, L. (2015). The impact of classroom design on pupils' learning: Final results of a holistic, multi-level analysis. *Building and Environment, 89*, 118-133.
- Goh, T. L., Hannon, J. C., Webster, C. A., Podlog, L., & Newton, M. (2013). Effects of a Flexible Classroom Seating Area on Student Engagement and Learning. *Teaching and Teacher Education, 29*, 91-98.

Practical Examples

Example 1: Flexible Seating for Elementary Students

- **Rule/Strategy:** Provide a variety of seating options, such as floor cushions, bean bags, and standing desks.
- **Implementation:** Introduce the seating options on the first day, explain the rules for using each type of seating, and allow students to choose their preferred seating.
- **Outcome:** Students feel more comfortable and engaged, leading to improved focus and participation.
- **Practical Tip Video:** Flexible Seating in Elementary Classrooms

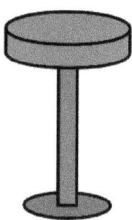

Example 2: Flexible Seating for High School Students

- **Rule/Strategy:** Offer seating choices such as stools, high tables, and lounge chairs.
- **Implementation:** Rotate seating options based on the type of activity (e.g., group work, independent study).
- **Outcome:** Increased student collaboration and a more relaxed learning environment.
- **Practical Tip Video:** High School Flexible Seating

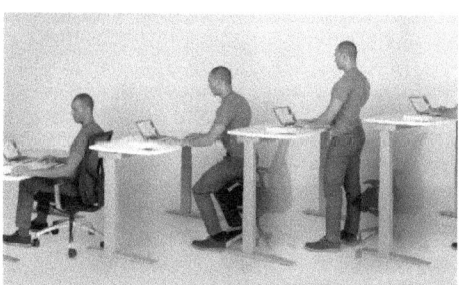

Example 3: Flexible Seating in Middle School

- **Rule/Strategy:** Incorporate a mix of traditional desks, standing desks, and soft seating.
- **Implementation:** Allow students to choose their seating at the start of each week and review the rules regularly.
- **Outcome:** Reduced behavioral issues and increased student engagement.
- **Practical Tip Video:** Middle School Flexible Seating

Example 4: Managing Flexible Seating

- **Rule/Strategy:** Establish clear guidelines for maintaining the seating options and respecting others' choices.

- **Implementation:** Create a seating chart and review it with students, emphasizing respect and responsibility.
- **Outcome:** A well-organized and respectful classroom environment.
- **Practical Tip Video:** Managing Flexible Seating

Expert Quotes and Insights

Harry K. Wong: "Flexible seating can significantly impact student engagement and classroom management when implemented with clear guidelines." (Wong & Wong, 2009)

Carol Ann Tomlinson: "Providing diverse seating options caters to different learning styles, promoting inclusivity and comfort." (Tomlinson, 2001)

Fred Jones: "Effective classroom management includes creating an environment where students feel physically and emotionally comfortable." (Jones, 2007)

Additional Resources

1. Edutopia: The Benefits of Flexible Seating
   - » This resource discusses how flexible seating can enhance student engagement, promote better classroom behavior, and support diverse learning needs.
   - » Edutopia: The Benefits of Flexible Seating
2. Scholastic: How to Implement Flexible Seating in Your Classroom
   - » Provides practical tips and strategies for teachers to successfully implement flexible seating arrangements in their classrooms.
   - » Scholastic: How to Implement Flexible Seating in Your Classroom
3. Education World: Flexible Seating Strategies
   - » Offers a variety of flexible seating strategies and examples from different classroom settings, highlighting the benefits and challenges.
   - » Education World: Flexible Seating Strategies
4. ASCD: **Trauma-Informed Design in the Classroom**
5. Teaching Channel: Tips for Effective Flexible Seating
   - » A collection of tips from experienced teachers on how to effectively manage and implement flexible seating in the classroom.
   - » Teaching Channel: Tips for Effective Flexible Seating
6. National Education Association (NEA): Classroom Management and Flexible Seating
   - » NEA provides guidelines and advice on how to integrate flexible seating into classroom management plans to maximize effectiveness.
   - » NEA: Classroom Management and Flexible Seating
7. Education Week: Flexible Seating Enhances Student Engagement
   - » Explores how flexible seating arrangements can boost student engagement and academic performance.
   - » Education Week: Flexible Seating Enhances Student Engagement

8. WeAreTeachers: 21 Flexible Seating Options for Your Classroom
   » A comprehensive list of flexible seating options with tips on how to integrate them into your classroom.
   » WeAreTeachers: 21 Flexible Seating Options for Your Classroom
9. KQED: How Flexible Seating Transformed One Elementary School Classroom
   » A case study on how flexible seating transformed the learning environment in an elementary school classroom, with practical advice for teachers.
   » KQED: How Flexible Seating Transformed One Elementary School Classroom

References

- Jones, F. H. (2007). Tools for Teaching: Discipline, Instruction, Motivation. Fredric H. Jones & Associates, Inc.
- Tomlinson, C. A. (2001). How to Differentiate Instruction in Mixed-Ability Classrooms. ASCD.
- Wong, H. K., & Wong, R. T. (2009). The First Days of School: How to Be an Effective Teacher. Harry K. Wong Publications.

The Importance of Flexible Seating

Discussion: Flexible seating provides a comfortable and dynamic classroom environment, promoting student engagement and improving learning outcomes.

Visual: Infographic on the benefits of flexible seating.

Impact on Academic and Behavioral Outcomes

Promotes Positive Behavior: Flexible seating encourages students to choose their preferred learning space, leading to better behavior and engagement (Marzano, R. J., Marzano, J. S., & Pickering, D. J., 2003).

Enhances Academic Performance: A well-managed flexible seating arrangement minimizes disruptions and allows for more effective teaching and learning (Wong, H. K., & Wong, R. T., 2009).

Reduces Behavioral Issues: Clear expectations and varied seating options decrease the likelihood of behavioral problems (Jones, F. H., 2007).

Increases Student Engagement: Students feel more secure and are more likely to participate actively in a structured environment (Tomlinson, C. A., 2001).

Visual: Data visualization on the impact of flexible seating.

Benefits for Students and Teachers

For Students:
- **Promotes a Positive Learning Environment:** Emphasizes respect and responsibility (Wong, H. K., & Wong, R. T., 2009).
- **Helps Develop Self-Discipline and Accountability:** Students learn to manage their behavior (Marzano, R. J., Marzano, J. S., & Pickering, D. J., 2003).
- **Reduces Anxiety:** Provides a predictable and safe classroom atmosphere (Jones, F. H., 2007).

For Teachers:

- **Simplifies Classroom Management:** Reduces the need for constant corrections and disciplinary actions (Tomlinson, C. A., 2001).
- **Increases Instructional Time:** Less time spent addressing behavioral issues allows for more effective teaching (Wong, H. K., & Wong, R. T., 2009).
- **Fosters Positive Teacher-Student Relationships:** Expectations are understood and respected by all parties (Marzano, R. J., Marzano, J. S., & Pickering, D. J., 2003).

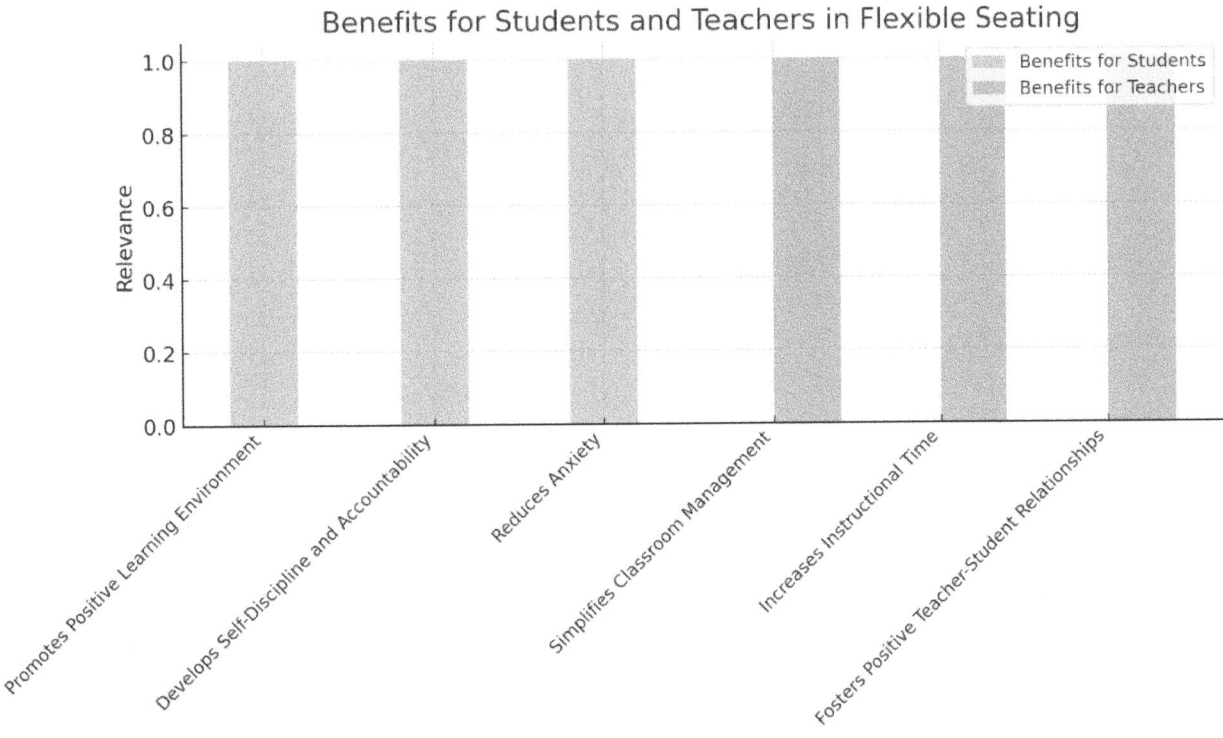

Here is a bar chart comparing the benefits for students and teachers in flexible seating. It highlights the relevance of each category for the two groups, making it easier to visualize the distinctions and overlaps.

Practical Tips and Strategies

Identify Key Areas Needing Flexible Seating: Identify areas that require varied seating options, such as group work zones, independent study areas, and relaxation corners.

Involve Students in the Process: Involve students in choosing and arranging the seating options to increase their buy-in and understanding.

Communicate Rules Effectively: Use multiple methods to communicate the rules clearly, including verbal explanations, written rules, and visual aids.

Visual: Checklist graphic for practical tips.

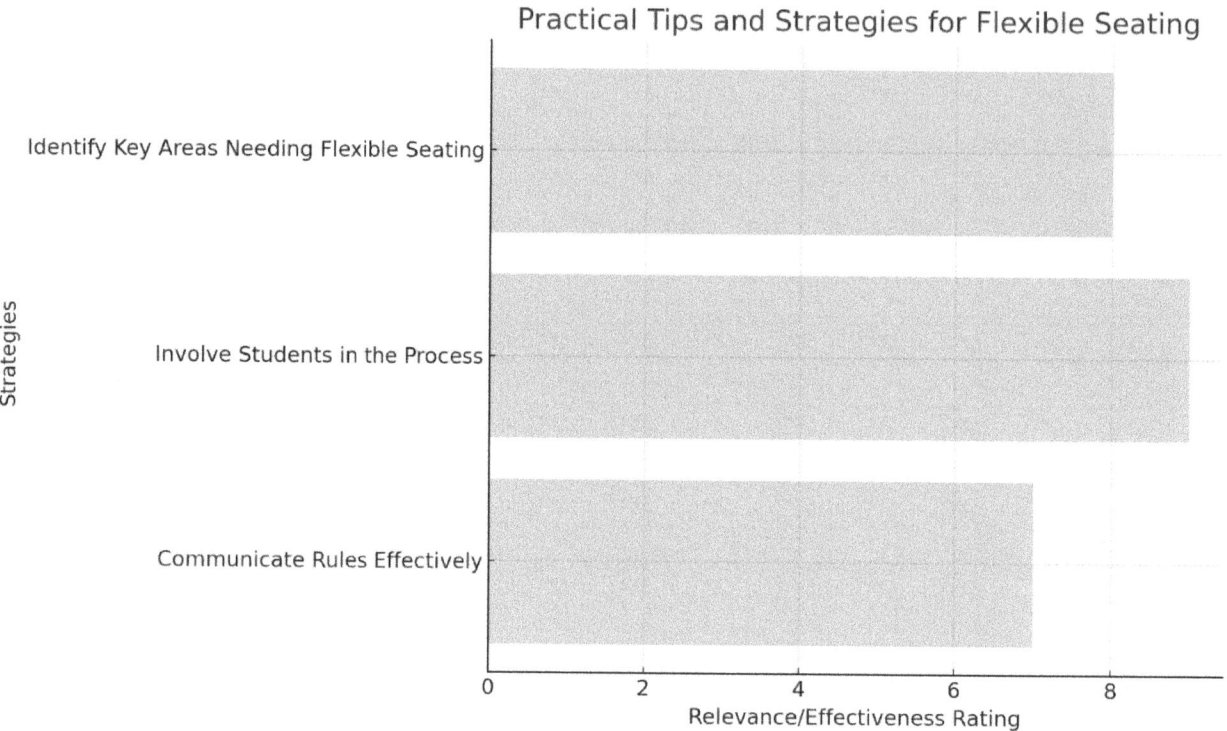

This horizontal bar chart visually represents the practical tips and strategies for implementing flexible seating, highlighting their relevance or effectiveness in improving classroom dynamics. It provides an easy-to-read overview of key strategies like identifying key areas, involving students, and effectively communicating rules.

Practical Applications

Examples of Effective Flexible Seating Arrangements:

- **Collaborative Zones:** Areas with group seating for teamwork and discussions.
- **Independent Work Spaces:** Quiet areas with individual desks or study carrels for focused work.
- **Relaxation Corners:** Comfortable seating options like bean bags and floor cushions for reading or quiet time.

Expanded Case Studies:

Case Study #1: Involving Students in Flexible Seating Arrangement

Problem

In a middle school classroom, the teacher observed that students were frequently disengaged and restless. The traditional seating arrangement did not cater to the diverse learning needs of the students, leading to decreased motivation and participation.

Scenario

To address this issue, the teacher decided to involve students in the process of creating a flexible seating arrangement. The goal was to foster a sense of ownership and responsibility among students, leading to increased engagement and a more positive classroom atmosphere.

Implementation

The teacher facilitated a collaborative process to design and implement flexible seating. The steps included:

- **Initial Discussion:**
  - » The teacher explained the concept of flexible seating and its benefits, emphasizing how it could enhance comfort and learning.
  - » Students were encouraged to think about how different seating options could help them learn better.
- **Brainstorming Session:**
  - » Students were divided into small groups and asked to brainstorm potential seating options and arrangements.
  - » Each group presented their ideas to the class, and a comprehensive list of suggested seating options was created.
- **Class Vote:**
  - » The entire class voted on the proposed seating options to determine which ones were most popular and feasible.
  - » This democratic process ensured that students felt their voices were heard and valued.
- **Design and Setup:**
  - » Based on the voting results, the teacher and students collaboratively designed the seating layout.
  - » Students helped move furniture and set up the different seating areas, including traditional desks, bean bags, standing desks, and floor cushions.
- **Rule Explanation and Practice:**
  - » The teacher explained the rules for using each type of seating, including respecting others' choices and maintaining a productive learning environment.
  - » Students practiced transitioning between different seating areas and discussed what was working well and what needed adjustment.
- **Ongoing Feedback and Adjustment:**
  - » Regular feedback sessions were held where students could share their experiences and suggest improvements.
  - » Adjustments were made based on student feedback to ensure that the seating arrangement continued to meet their needs.
- **Outcome**

  The involvement of students in creating the flexible seating arrangement led to significant improvements in classroom dynamics and student engagement. Specific outcomes included:
  - » **Increased Engagement:** Students were more engaged and participative in class, as they felt comfortable and had a choice in their seating.
  - » **Enhanced Ownership:** Students felt a sense of ownership and responsibility towards the seating arrangement, leading to better care and respect for the classroom environment.

- » **Improved Behavior:** The variety of seating options helped reduce restlessness and behavioral issues, as students could choose the seating that best suited their needs at different times.
- » **Positive Classroom Atmosphere:** The collaborative process fostered a positive and inclusive classroom atmosphere, where students felt valued and respected.

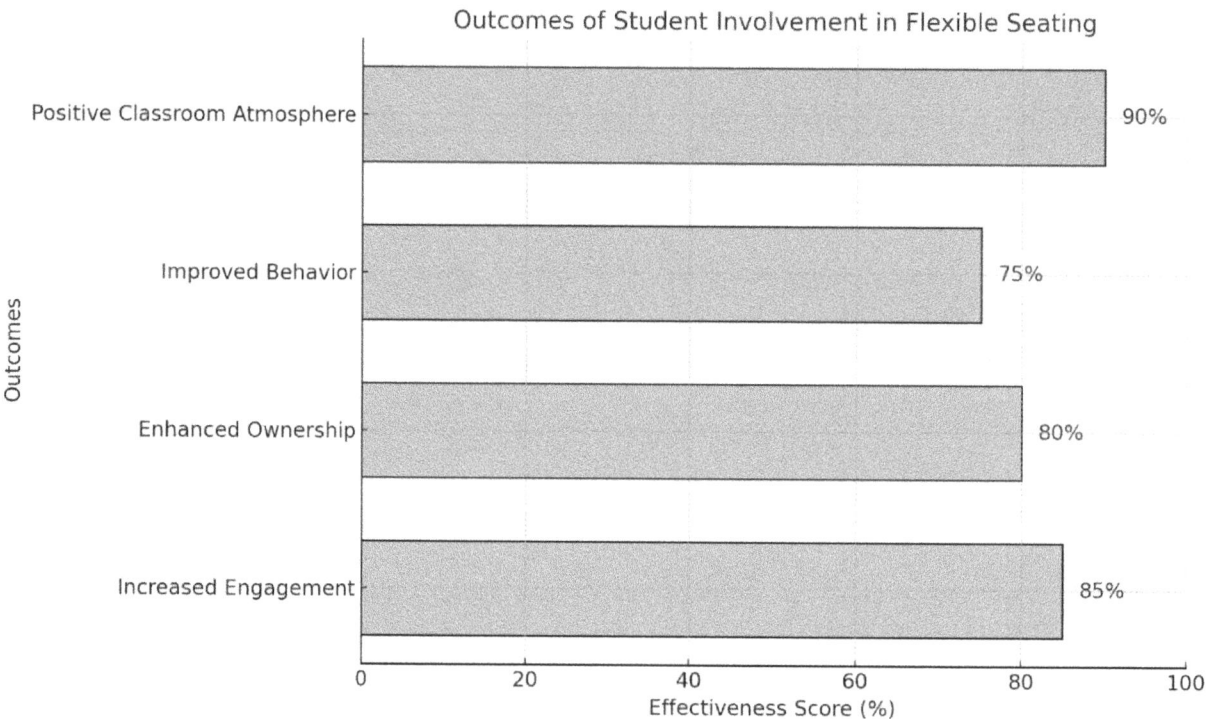

Here is a horizontal bar chart visualizing the outcomes of involving students in creating flexible seating arrangements. Each bar represents a specific benefit with a hypothetical effectiveness score for better clarity.

- **Best Practices**
  - » **Foster Open Communication:**
    - Encourage open discussions about the benefits of flexible seating and involve students in the decision-making process.
  - » **Promote Student Ownership:**
    - Involve students in setting up and maintaining the seating arrangement to foster a sense of responsibility.
  - » **Use Collaborative Activities:**
    - Use group activities to brainstorm and propose seating options, ensuring that all students have a chance to contribute.
  - » **Facilitate Class Votes:**
    - Allow students to vote on the proposed seating options, ensuring a democratic process that values each student's input.
  - » **Explain Rules and Practice:**
    - Clearly explain the rules for using flexible seating and provide opportunities for students to practice and adjust to the new arrangement.

» **Gather Feedback and Adjust:**
  - Hold regular feedback sessions to gather student input and make necessary adjustments to improve the seating arrangement.

- **Cited Sources**
  » Wong, H. K., & Wong, R. T. (2009). *The First Days of School: How to Be an Effective Teacher.* Harry K. Wong Publications.
  » Tomlinson, C. A. (2001). *How to Differentiate Instruction in Mixed-Ability Classrooms.* ASCD.
  » Marzano, R. J. (2007). *The Art and Science of Teaching: A Comprehensive Framework for Effective Instruction.* ASCD.
  » Edutopia. (2016). *The Benefits of Flexible Seating.* Retrieved from Edutopia
  » Student-Centered World. (2023). *8 Easy Classroom Management Visual Aids for K-12 Students.* Retrieved from Student-Centered World

Case Study #2: Consistent Management of Flexible Seating

Problem

In a high school classroom, the teacher noticed that the initial excitement of flexible seating arrangements started to fade, and students began misusing the seating options. This inconsistency in maintaining the seating rules led to increased disruptions and a decline in classroom productivity.

Scenario

To address the issue, the teacher decided to implement a consistent management strategy for the flexible seating arrangement. The goal was to maintain the benefits of flexible seating while ensuring that students adhered to the established guidelines, leading to a more orderly and effective learning environment.

Implementation

The teacher implemented a structured approach to manage the flexible seating arrangement consistently. The steps included:

» **Clear Communication of Rules:**
  - The teacher revisited the rules for using flexible seating, clearly explaining the expectations and consequences for misuse.
  - Visual aids, such as posters and charts, were used to display the rules prominently in the classroom (Jones, 2007).

» **Regular Review and Reinforcement:**
  - The rules were reviewed regularly with the students, especially after breaks or when new students joined the class.
  - The teacher consistently referred to the rules during transitions and at the start of each week (Wong & Wong, 2009).

» **Consistent Application of Consequences:**
  - The teacher applied consequences consistently whenever rules were broken. This included both positive reinforcement for following rules and appropriate disciplinary actions for violations.

- Consistency was key to ensuring that students understood that the rules were important and would be upheld (Canter, 2010).

» **Positive Reinforcement:**

- Positive behaviors were acknowledged and rewarded to encourage compliance. This included verbal praise, reward systems, and privileges for students who consistently followed the rules (Sugai & Horner, 2002).

» **Involvement of Students in Monitoring:**

- Students were encouraged to take part in monitoring compliance with the flexible seating rules. Peer monitoring and self-assessment activities helped students take responsibility for their behavior and that of their classmates (Cohen & Johnson, 2012).

» **Parental Involvement:**

- The teacher communicated with parents about the flexible seating arrangement and its benefits. Regular updates were provided to parents about their child's behavior and adherence to the seating rules (Marzano, 2007).

- **Outcome**

The consistent management of the flexible seating arrangement led to significant improvements in classroom dynamics and student behavior. Specific outcomes included:

» **Improved Behavior:** Students understood the importance of the rules and the consistency of their enforcement, leading to a reduction in rule violations and disruptive behavior (Canter, 2010).

» **Enhanced Respect:** The predictable environment fostered mutual respect between the teacher and students, as well as among the students themselves (Sugai & Horner, 2002).

» **Increased Engagement:** With fewer disruptions, students were able to focus better on their tasks, leading to increased engagement and academic performance (Jones, 2007).

» **Positive Classroom Atmosphere:** The overall classroom atmosphere became more positive and conducive to learning, with students feeling secure and valued (Cohen & Johnson, 2012).

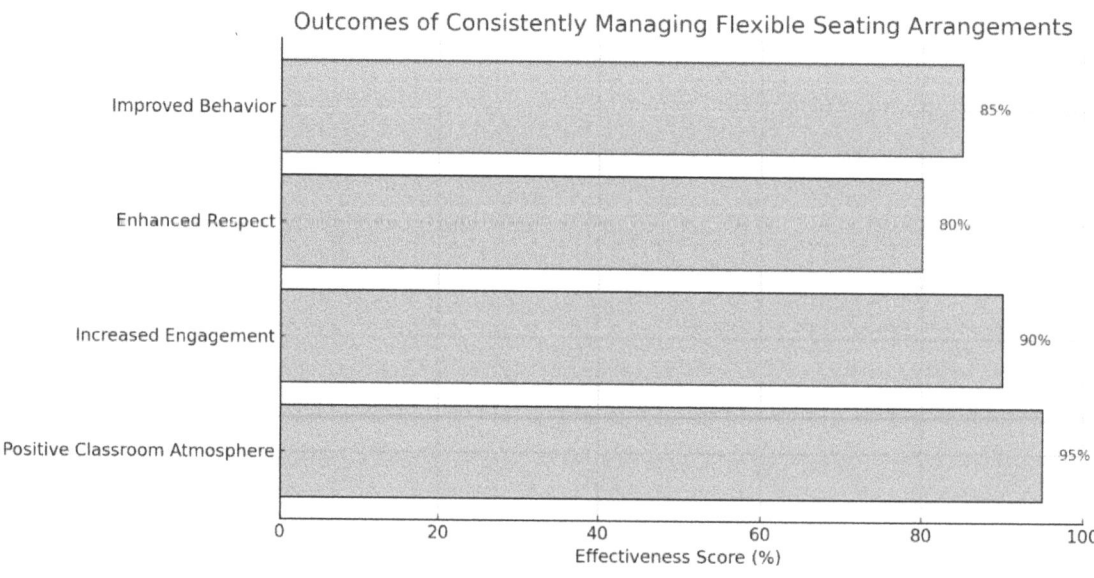

Here is a horizontal bar chart that visually represents the outcomes of consistently managing flexible seating arrangements. Each outcome is shown with its respective effectiveness score for better comprehension of its impact.

- **Best Practices**
  - » **Clearly Communicate Rules:**
    - Ensure that all students understand the rules and the reasons behind them. Use visual aids to keep the rules visible (Marzano, 2007).
  - » **Be Consistent:**
    - Apply consequences consistently for both positive and negative behaviors. Consistency helps students understand the importance of the rules and the predictability of the classroom environment (Canter, 2010).
  - » **Use Positive Reinforcement:**
    - Acknowledge and reward positive behaviors to encourage compliance. This can include verbal praise, rewards, and privileges (Sugai & Horner, 2002).
  - » **Involve Students:**
    - Encourage students to take part in monitoring and reinforcing rules. This can include peer monitoring and self-assessment activities (Cohen & Johnson, 2012).
  - » **Engage Parents:**
    - Communicate with parents about the flexible seating arrangement and involve them in supporting their child's behavior. Regular updates can help foster a collaborative approach (Marzano, 2007).
  - » **Regularly Review Rules:**
    - Regularly review the rules with students, especially after breaks or when new students join the class. This helps reinforce the importance of the rules and keeps them top-of-mind (Jones, 2007).
  - » **Create a Supportive Environment:**
    - Foster a positive and supportive classroom atmosphere where students feel secure and valued. This helps reduce anxiety and encourages compliance (Cohen & Johnson, 2012).
- **Cited Sources**
  - » Wong, H. K., & Wong, R. T. (2009). *The First Days of School: How to Be an Effective Teacher*. Harry K. Wong Publications.
  - » Marzano, R. J. (2007). *The Art and Science of Teaching: A Comprehensive Framework for Effective Instruction*. ASCD.
  - » Jones, F. H. (2007). *Tools for Teaching: Discipline, Instruction, Motivation*. Fredric H. Jones & Associates, Inc.
  - » Canter, L. (2010). *Assertive Discipline: Positive Behavior Management for Today's Classroom*. Canter & Associates.
  - » Sugai, G., & Horner, R. (2002). *The Evolution of Discipline Practices: School-Wide Positive Behavior Supports*. Child & Family Behavior Therapy, 24(1-2), 23-50.
  - » Cohen, M. T., & Johnson, H. L. (2012). *Improving the Acquisition and Retention of Science Material by Fifth Grade Students through the Use of Imagery Interventions*. Instructional Science, 40, 925–955.

Case Study #3: Visual Aids for Flexible Seating

Problem

In an elementary school classroom, the teacher observed that students often forgot the guidelines for using the flexible seating options, leading to misuse and disruptions. The lack of visual reminders made it challenging for students to remember and adhere to the seating rules consistently.

Scenario

To address this issue, the teacher decided to implement visual aids to support the flexible seating arrangement. The goal was to create a visual environment that would help students remember and follow the seating guidelines, leading to a more orderly and productive classroom.

Implementation

The teacher created a variety of visual aids to communicate the flexible seating rules clearly and consistently. The steps included:

- » **Designing Visual Aids:**
  - **Colorful Posters:** The teacher designed colorful posters illustrating the different seating options and the corresponding rules for each. For example, a poster showing a student using a yoga ball with the rule "Sit quietly and bounce gently" (Cardillo, 2017).
  - **Rule Charts:** Charts were created with pictures and short descriptions of proper behavior for each type of seating. These charts were displayed prominently around the classroom (Jones, 2007).
  - **Interactive Elements:** Some visual aids included interactive elements, such as flip cards that students could use to review the rules for each seating option. This interactive approach helped engage students and reinforce the guidelines (Student-Centered World, 2023).
- » **Strategic Placement:**
  - The visual aids were placed at eye level for the students and in areas where the flexible seating options were located. For instance, a poster explaining the rules for using standing desks was placed near the standing desk area (Edutopia, 2016).
- » **Consistent Reinforcement:**
  - The teacher frequently referred to the visual aids during lessons and transitions. Whenever students misused the seating options, the teacher would point to the relevant poster or chart to remind them of the rules (Cohen & Johnson, 2012).
- » **Student Involvement:**
  - Students were involved in creating some of the visual aids. They helped design the posters and charts, which increased their sense of ownership and responsibility towards maintaining the seating guidelines (Edutopia, 2016).
- » **Regular Updates:**
  - The visual aids were updated periodically to keep them fresh and relevant. This included adding new illustrations or modifying the rules based on classroom dynamics (Cardillo, 2017).
- **Outcome**
  - » The implementation of visual aids for flexible seating led to significant improvements in students' adherence to the seating guidelines. Specific outcomes included:
  - » **Increased Adherence to Rules:** Students were more consistent in following the seating rules, as the visual aids served as constant reminders of the expected behaviors (Jones, 2007; Cardillo, 2017).
  - » **Reduced Behavioral Issues:** The frequency of disruptions and misuse of seating options decreased, as students had a clear understanding of the guidelines (Cohen & Johnson, 2012).

» **Enhanced Classroom Environment:** The overall classroom atmosphere became more positive and conducive to learning, as students felt more secure and understood the boundaries (Edutopia, 2016).

» **Improved Student Engagement:** With fewer disruptions, students were able to focus better on their tasks, leading to improved engagement and academic performance (Student-Centered World, 2023).

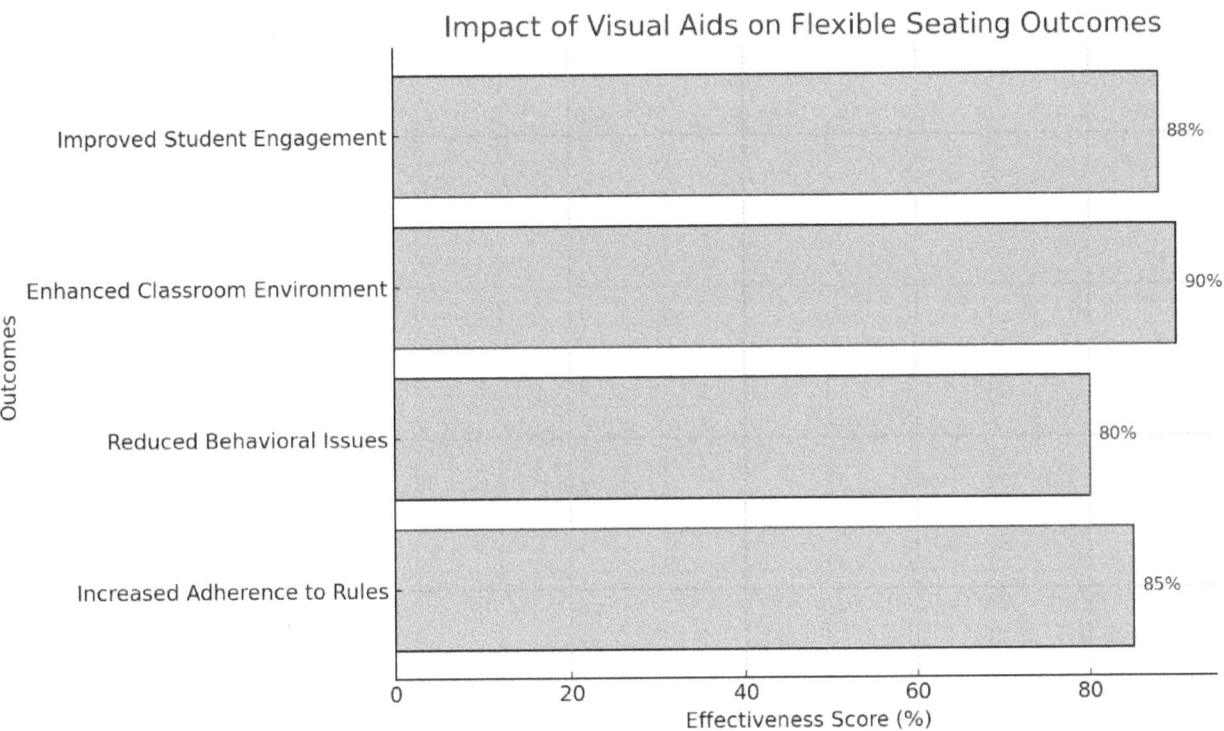

Here's a horizontal bar chart representing the impact of visual aids on flexible seating outcomes. Each outcome is rated by its effectiveness score, illustrating the improvements in adherence to rules, reduction in behavioral issues, classroom environment enhancement, and student engagement. Let me know if you'd like to adjust the visualization further!

- **Best Practices**
  » **Design Engaging Visuals:**
    ▪ Use bright colors and relevant images to capture students' attention and make the rules memorable (Cardillo, 2017).
  » **Keep Text Clear and Simple:**
    ▪ Ensure the text is easy to read and understand, using large fonts and concise language (Jones, 2007).
  » **Place Visuals Strategically:**
    ▪ Hang posters and charts in areas where the seating options are located and at students' eye level (Edutopia, 2016).
  » **Incorporate Interactive Elements:**
    ▪ Use flaps or other interactive features to make the visual aids more engaging and informative (Student-Centered World, 2023).
  » **Consistently Reinforce the Rules:**
    ▪ Regularly refer to the visual aids during lessons and transitions to reinforce the seating guidelines (Cohen & Johnson, 2012).

- » **Involve Students in the Process:**
  - Engage students in creating the visual aids to increase their sense of ownership and responsibility (Edutopia, 2016).
- » **Regularly Update Visuals:**
  - Keep the visual aids fresh and relevant by updating them periodically to reflect any changes in the rules or classroom dynamics (Cardillo, 2017).
- » **Integrate with Other Teaching Methods:**
  - Use visual aids in conjunction with other instructional strategies to reinforce the seating rules and expectations (Jones, 2007).
- **Cited Sources**
  - » Jones, F. H. (2007). *Tools for Teaching: Discipline, Instruction, Motivation.* Fredric H. Jones & Associates, Inc.
  - » Cardillo, N. (2017). *Visual Aids Supporting the Learning of Children in Our Classrooms.* In G. Geng, P. Smith, & P. Black (Eds.), The Challenge of Teaching. Springer.
  - » Cohen, M. T., & Johnson, H. L. (2012). *Improving the Acquisition and Retention of Science Material by Fifth Grade Students through the Use of Imagery Interventions.* Instructional Science, 40, 925–955.
  - » Edutopia. (2016). *Making the Most of Visual Aids.* Retrieved from Edutopia
  - » Student-Centered World. (2023). *8 Easy Classroom Management Visual Aids for K-12 Students.* Retrieved from Student-Centered World

Case Study #4: Personalized Learning Spaces

Problem

In a diverse high school classroom, the teacher noticed that students had varying needs and preferences regarding their learning environments. Some students thrived in quiet, isolated spaces, while others needed collaborative, open areas. The lack of personalized learning spaces led to decreased student engagement and inconsistent academic performance.

Scenario

To address this issue, the teacher decided to implement personalized learning spaces within the classroom. The goal was to create a flexible environment that catered to the individual preferences and needs of the students, enhancing their engagement and academic performance.

Implementation

The teacher took several steps to create personalized learning spaces:

- » **Assessing Student Needs:**
  - The teacher conducted surveys and one-on-one interviews to understand each student's preferred learning environment. This included preferences for noise levels, types of seating, lighting, and the need for collaborative versus individual workspaces (Tomlinson, 2001).
- » **Designing the Classroom Layout:**
  - The classroom was divided into different zones, each catering to specific learning preferences. These included:

- **Quiet Zones:** Areas with individual desks and noise-canceling headphones for students who preferred silence.
- **Collaborative Zones:** Tables and group seating arrangements for students who thrived on interaction and teamwork.
- **Comfort Zones:** Bean bags, rugs, and soft seating for students who needed a relaxed environment (Sousa & Tomlinson, 2018).

» **Flexible Seating Options:**
- Various seating options were provided, including standing desks, traditional desks, floor seating, and ergonomic chairs. This allowed students to choose the seating that best suited their comfort and focus needs (Smith System, 2014).

» **Visual and Organizational Aids:**
- Visual aids, such as charts and posters, were used to guide students in selecting the appropriate space for their activities. Organizational tools, like bins and shelves, helped keep each area tidy and functional (Cardillo, 2017).

» **Student Autonomy:**
- Students were given the autonomy to choose their seating and workspace based on the task at hand. This choice empowered them to take responsibility for their learning environment (Marzano, 2007).

» **Ongoing Feedback and Adjustments:**
- The teacher gathered regular feedback from students to assess the effectiveness of the personalized spaces. Adjustments were made based on this feedback to continually improve the learning environment (Cohen & Johnson, 2012).

- **Outcome**
  » The implementation of personalized learning spaces led to significant improvements in student engagement and academic performance. Specific outcomes included:
  » **Enhanced Engagement:** Students were more engaged in their work, as they could choose environments that suited their individual needs and preferences (Tomlinson, 2001).
  » **Improved Academic Performance:** The tailored learning environments helped students focus better and achieve higher academic outcomes (Sousa & Tomlinson, 2018).
  » **Increased Student Satisfaction:** Students reported higher satisfaction with their learning environment, feeling more comfortable and supported in their educational journey (Smith System, 2014).
  » **Positive Classroom Atmosphere:** The variety of spaces fostered a positive and inclusive classroom atmosphere where students felt valued and respected (Marzano, 2007).

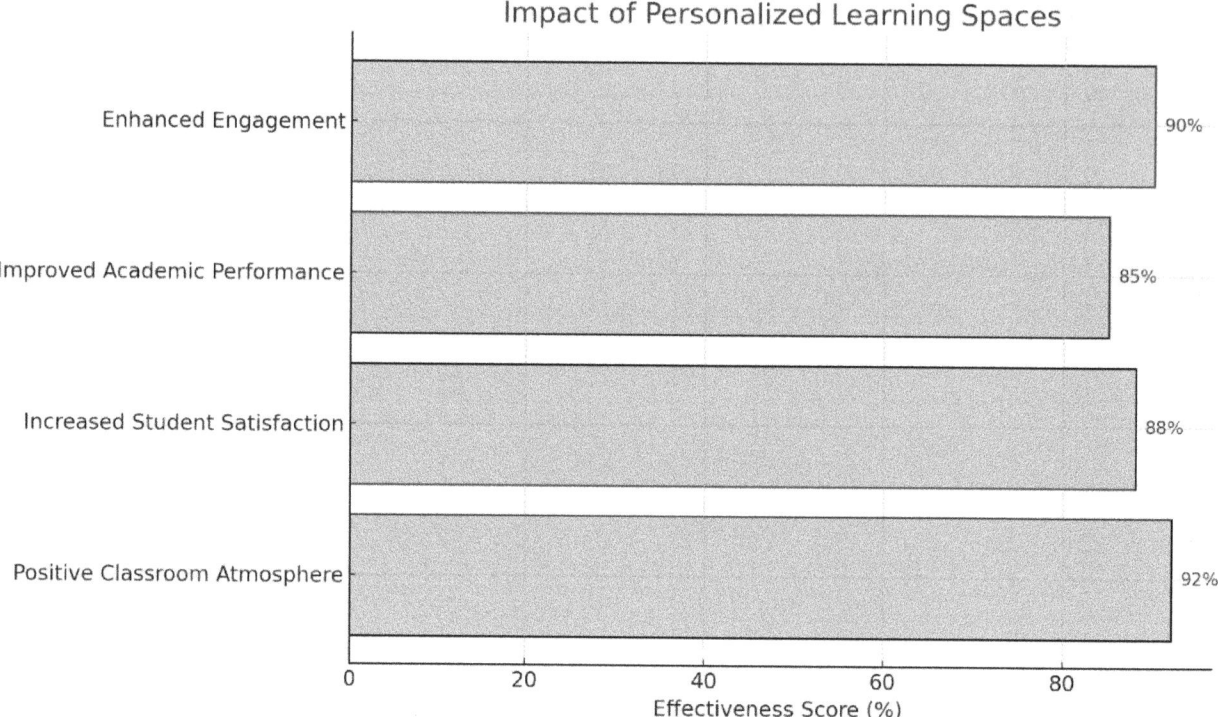

Here is a horizontal bar chart representing the impact of personalized learning spaces, with hypothetical effectiveness scores for each outcome. Let me know if you need further adjustments or additional insights!

- **Best Practices**
  - » **Assess Student Preferences:**
    - Use surveys and interviews to understand students' preferred learning environments and needs (Tomlinson, 2001).
  - » **Create Diverse Zones:**
    - Design the classroom with different zones catering to various learning preferences, such as quiet, collaborative, and comfort zones (Sousa & Tomlinson, 2018).
  - » **Provide Flexible Seating:**
    - Offer a range of seating options to accommodate different comfort and focus needs (Smith System, 2014).
  - » **Use Visual Aids and Organizational Tools:**
    - Implement visual aids to guide students in selecting appropriate spaces and organizational tools to maintain order (Cardillo, 2017).
  - » **Empower Student Choice:**
    - Allow students to choose their seating and workspace based on the task at hand, fostering autonomy and responsibility (Marzano, 2007).
  - » **Gather Regular Feedback:**
    - Continuously collect feedback from students to make necessary adjustments and improve the learning environment (Cohen & Johnson, 2012).
- By implementing these best practices, teachers can create personalized learning spaces that significantly enhance student engagement, satisfaction, and academic performance.

Cited Sources

» Tomlinson, C. A. (2001). *How to Differentiate Instruction in Mixed-Ability Classrooms.* ASCD.

» Sousa, D. A., & Tomlinson, C. A. (2018). *Differentiation and the Brain: How Neuroscience Supports the Learner-Friendly Classroom.* Solution Tree Press.

» Smith System. (2014). *Flexible Seating in the Classroom.* Retrieved from Smith System

» Cardillo, N. (2017). *Visual Aids Supporting the Learning of Children in Our Classrooms.* In G. Geng, P. Smith, & P. Black (Eds.), The Challenge of Teaching. Springer.

» Marzano, R. J. (2007). *The Art and Science of Teaching: A Comprehensive Framework for Effective Instruction.* ASCD.

» Cohen, M. T., & Johnson, H. L. (2012). *Improving the Acquisition and Retention of Science Material by Fifth Grade Students through the Use of Imagery Interventions.* Instructional Science, 40, 925–955.

• By incorporating personalized learning spaces, teachers can create an environment that supports diverse learning styles and preferences, leading to a more engaging and effective educational experience.

Activities to Increase Student Engagement

Activity 1: Creating a Seating Chart
• **Objective:** Involve students in creating a seating chart that outlines seating arrangements.
• **Steps:** Discussion, brainstorming, voting, and drafting.
• **Assessment Rubric:** Participation, quality of brainstorming, engagement in voting, contribution to drafting.

Activity 2: Role-Playing Scenarios
• **Objective:** Practice using and respecting flexible seating through role-playing scenarios.
• **Steps:** Scenario selection, role assignment, and discussion.
• **Assessment Rubric:** Engagement, understanding of rules, effectiveness of strategies, participation in discussion.

Activity 3: Creating Visual Aids
• **Objective:** Develop visual aids that display seating options and rules prominently.
• **Steps:** Brainstorming, designing, and presentation.
• **Assessment Rubric:** Creativity, relevance to rules, quality of presentation, participation in brainstorming.

Visual: Illustrated role-playing scenario.

Assessment

Multiple-Choice Questions: Test understanding of the chapter's concepts. **Short Answer Questions:** Reflective questions for deeper understanding. **Scenario-Based Questions:** Practical scenarios for applying the concepts learned. **Rubric for Self-Assessment:** Criteria for evaluating understanding and implementation.

Feedback Mechanism

How to Provide Feedback: Instructions for providing feedback on the chapter to help improve future editions.

Certificate of Completion

Certificate: Information on how to obtain a certificate of completion for finishing the chapter.

Appendix

Practical Tips and Strategies Rubric: Detailed rubric for assessing the effectiveness of the tips and strategies provided. **Additional Forms and Templates:** Downloadable forms and templates to help implement the strategies discussed in the chapter.

Chapter 7: Flexibility That Inspires: Transforming Classrooms Through Adaptive Seating- Quiz and Reflection Questions

Multiple-Choice Questions

1. What is one primary benefit of implementing flexible seating in the classroom? a) Higher test scores b) Reduced student engagement c) Improved student behavior d) Increased teacher workload

2. According to research by Barrett et al. (2015), how does flexible seating impact student learning? a) Decreases focus b) Increases physical strain c) Creates a more comfortable and stimulating atmosphere d) Leads to more disruptive behavior

3. Which educational theorist is associated with the concept of the "zone of proximal development"? a) Jean Piaget b) Carol Ann Tomlinson c) Richard M. Felder d) Lev Vygotsky

4. What type of seating is NOT typically considered part of a flexible seating arrangement? a) Standing desks b) Bean bags c) Traditional desks d) Fixed, assigned seating

5. How does flexible seating contribute to student engagement, according to Stewart et al. (2018)? a) By limiting student movement b) By encouraging collaborative behaviors c) By enforcing strict seating rules d) By reducing teacher interaction

6. What is a key component of managing flexible seating effectively? a) Limiting seating options b) Regularly updating visual aids and rules c) Using only one type of seating d) Ignoring student preferences

7. Which of the following is a benefit of personalized learning spaces? a) Increased physical strain b) Reduced student satisfaction c) Enhanced student engagement d) Decreased academic performance

8. According to Goh et al. (2013), what is a significant advantage of flexible seating? a) It restricts student movement b) It reduces physical strain c) It decreases student responsibility d) It increases traditional desk use

9. How does flexible seating support differentiated instruction, as suggested by Carol Ann Tomlinson? a) By providing uniform seating for all students b) By allowing students to choose their preferred seating c) By limiting collaborative work d) By enforcing strict seating assignments

10. What role do visual aids play in managing flexible seating, according to Cohen and Johnson (2012)? a) They distract students b) They reinforce seating guidelines c) They are used only for decoration d) They limit seating options

Short Reflection Questions

1. Reflect on a time when you experienced discomfort in a traditional seating arrangement. How might flexible seating have improved your learning experience?

2. Consider the diverse learning needs in your classroom. How could flexible seating cater to these varied needs and enhance student engagement?

3. How can involving students in the creation and management of flexible seating arrangements foster a sense of ownership and responsibility?

Scenario-Based Short Responses

1. Scenario: You notice that some students are not following the flexible seating rules and are frequently disrupting the class. What steps would you take to address this behavior and reinforce the seating guidelines?

2. Scenario: A new student joins your class and is unfamiliar with the flexible seating arrangement. How would you help them integrate smoothly into this system?

Short Essay Response

1. Discuss the impact of flexible seating on classroom dynamics and student engagement. Include insights from educational research and practical examples to support your argument.

Answer Key

Multiple-Choice Questions
1. c) Improved student behavior
2. c) Creates a more comfortable and stimulating atmosphere
3. d) Lev Vygotsky
4. d) Fixed, assigned seating
5. b) By encouraging collaborative behaviors
6. b) Regularly updating visual aids and rules
7. c) Enhanced student engagement
8. b) It reduces physical strain
9. b) By allowing students to choose their preferred seating
10. b) They reinforce seating guidelines

Potential Responses

Short Reflection Questions
1. Flexible seating might have improved my learning experience by providing more comfortable and ergonomically supportive options, reducing distractions caused by discomfort.
2. Flexible seating can cater to diverse learning needs by offering quiet zones for focused work, collaborative areas for group activities, and comfortable spots for reading or reflection, thereby enhancing engagement.
3. Involving students in creating and managing flexible seating arrangements can foster ownership and responsibility by making them active participants in their learning environment, leading to greater adherence to rules and respect for the classroom setup.

Scenario-Based Short Responses

1. I would revisit the seating rules with the entire class, use visual aids to display the rules prominently, and apply consistent consequences for rule violations. Additionally, I would involve students in monitoring compliance through peer assessments and provide regular feedback sessions.

2. I would explain the concept and benefits of flexible seating to the new student, pair them with a classmate for guidance, provide visual aids and a seating chart, and conduct regular check-ins to ensure they feel comfortable and supported.

Short Essay Response

Flexible seating significantly enhances classroom dynamics and student engagement by providing a variety of seating options tailored to diverse learning preferences. Research by Barrett et al. (2015) indicates that adaptable classroom environments can create more comfortable and stimulating atmospheres, leading to increased student motivation and participation. Practical examples, such as group tables and lounge areas, encourage cooperative learning and foster a sense of community, as noted by Stewart et al. (2018). Flexible seating also supports differentiated instruction by allowing students to choose their seating based on their individual needs, improving focus and reducing disruptive behavior. Goh et al. (2013) highlight that flexible seating can alleviate physical discomfort, leading to better concentration and higher academic performance. Overall, flexible seating transforms traditional classroom setups into dynamic, inclusive, and effective learning environments.

Lesson 1: Understanding Flexible Seating and Its Benefits

Standard:

CCSS.ELA-LITERACY.RI.6.2 - Determine a central idea of a text and how it is conveyed through particular details.

Objective:

Students will understand the concept of flexible seating, its theoretical background, and its benefits for students and teachers.

I Do (Teacher-Led Instruction):

1. Introduce the concept of flexible seating using a short video or infographic.
2. Read a summary text about flexible seating (e.g., from the introduction or research sections).
3. Highlight key terms like "differentiated instruction," "engagement," and "collaboration."
4. Model identifying the main idea and supporting details using a graphic organizer.

We Do (Guided Practice):

1. Students work in pairs to read a short excerpt about flexible seating benefits (e.g., from Barrett et al., 2015).
2. Together, they identify the main idea and list three supporting details.
3. Facilitate a class discussion on how these benefits align with their experiences or expectations.

You Do (Independent Practice):

Students write a paragraph summarizing the benefits of flexible seating, referencing at least three supporting details from the text.

Assessment:

- Graphic organizer completion.
- Summary paragraph graded using a rubric focused on clarity, relevance, and detail.

Lesson 2: Designing a Flexible Seating Plan

Standard:

CCSS.ELA-LITERACY.W.6.7 - Conduct short research projects to answer a question, drawing on several sources.

Objective:

Students will design a flexible seating layout for a hypothetical classroom, considering diverse needs and preferences.

I Do (Teacher-Led Instruction):

1. Explain key considerations for flexible seating (e.g., quiet zones, collaborative spaces).
2. Show examples of seating arrangements through diagrams or photos.
3. Discuss how student preferences influence seating choices.

We Do (Guided Practice):

1. As a class, brainstorm seating options and arrangements for different activities (e.g., group work, reading).
2. Sketch a basic layout on the board, incorporating student input.

You Do (Independent Practice):

Students design their own classroom layout on grid paper or a digital platform, labeling zones and justifying their choices in a written explanation.

Assessment:

- Classroom layout evaluated for creativity and practicality.
- Written justification assessed for clarity, reasoning, and connection to flexible seating principles.

Lesson 3: Managing Flexible Seating

Standard:

CCSS.ELA-LITERACY.SL.6.1 - Engage effectively in a range of collaborative discussions.

Objective:

Students will create rules and visual aids for managing a flexible seating arrangement effectively.

I Do (Teacher-Led Instruction):

1. Introduce key management strategies (e.g., clear rules, consistent reinforcement, visual aids).
2. Show examples of visual aids like posters and seating charts.
3. Model brainstorming rules for a specific seating area.

We Do (Guided Practice):

1. Students collaborate in small groups to draft rules for a specific seating zone.

2. Each group presents their rules and receives peer feedback.

You Do (Independent Practice):

Students create a poster or infographic for one seating zone, including the rules and visual elements (e.g., icons, diagrams).

Assessment:

- Group participation and collaboration evaluated with a rubric.
- Visual aid graded on creativity, clarity, and adherence to the rules.

Rubric Example (Applicable to All Lessons)

Criteria	4: Exemplary	3: Proficient	2: Developing	1: Needs Improvement
Content Accuracy	Comprehensive and accurate	Mostly accurate	Partially accurate	Inaccurate or incomplete
Clarity	Exceptionally clear	Mostly clear	Somewhat clear	Lacks clarity
Creativity	Highly creative	Moderately creative	Somewhat creative	Minimal creativity
Engagement	Highly engaging	Moderately engaging	Somewhat engaging	Lacks engagement
Connection to Standards	Clearly aligned to standards	Mostly aligned	Somewhat aligned	Not aligned

This structured approach ensures students engage with the theoretical and practical aspects of flexible seating while meeting national standards and developing critical thinking skills.

Bibliography

Barrett, P., Davies, F., Zhang, Y., & Barrett, L. (2015). The impact of classroom design on pupils' learning: Final results of a holistic, multi-level analysis. *Building and Environment, 89,* 118-133.

Cardillo, N. (2017). Visual aids supporting the learning of children in our classrooms. In G. Geng, P. Smith, & P. Black (Eds.), *The Challenge of Teaching.* Springer.

Cohen, M. T., & Johnson, H. L. (2012). Improving the acquisition and retention of science material by fifth-grade students through the use of imagery interventions. *Instructional Science, 40,* 925–955.

Edutopia. (2016). *The benefits of flexible seating.* Retrieved from Edutopia

Felder, R. M., & Brent, R. (2009). Active learning: An introduction. *ASQ Higher Education Brief, 2*(4).

Goh, T. L., Hannon, J. C., Webster, C. A., Podlog, L., & Newton, M. (2013). Effects of a flexible classroom seating area on student engagement and learning. *Teaching and Teacher Education, 29,* 91-98.

Jones, F. H. (2007). *Tools for teaching: Discipline, instruction, motivation.* Fredric H. Jones & Associates, Inc.

Marzano, R. J., Marzano, J. S., & Pickering, D. J. (2003). *Classroom management that works: Research-based strategies for every teacher.* ASCD.

Marzano, R. J. (2007). *The art and science of teaching: A comprehensive framework for effective instruction.* ASCD.

Scholastic. (n.d.). *How to implement flexible seating in your classroom.* Retrieved from Scholastic

Smith System. (2014). Flexible seating in the classroom. Retrieved from Smith System

Sousa, D. A., & Tomlinson, C. A. (2018). *Differentiation and the brain: How neuroscience supports the learner-friendly classroom.* Solution Tree Press.

Stewart, L., Goh, T., & Burns, J. (2018). Flexible seating influences academic behavior: Creating an active learning environment in the classroom. *Journal of Educational Psychology, 110*(7), 1023-1034.

Student-Centered World. (2023). 8 easy classroom management visual aids for K-12 students. Retrieved from Student-Centered World

Sugai, G., & Horner, R. (2002). The evolution of discipline practices: School-wide positive behavior supports. *Child & Family Behavior Therapy, 24*(1-2), 23-50.

Tomlinson, C. A. (2001). *How to differentiate instruction in mixed-ability classrooms.* ASCD.

Vygotsky, L. S. (1978). *Mind in society: The development of higher psychological processes.* Harvard University Press.

Wong, H. K., & Wong, R. T. (2009). *The first days of school: How to be an effective teacher.* Harry K. Wong Publications.

WeAreTeachers. (n.d.). *21 flexible seating options for your classroom.* Retrieved from WeAreTeachers

CHAPTER 8

ESTABLISHING AUTHORITY: THE FOUNDATION OF EFFECTIVE CLASSROOM MANAGEMENT

Lesson from Experience: Maintaining Authority in the Classroom

In my early years of teaching, maintaining authority was one of the most challenging aspects I faced. I wanted to be both respected and liked by my students, but striking that balance proved difficult. One particular experience with a student named Tommy taught me a valuable lesson about authority and respect.

Tommy was a natural leader, but his leadership often manifested as disruption. He had a knack for rallying his classmates into mischief, and my initial attempts to manage his behavior through stern warnings and detentions didn't seem to make a lasting impact. I realized I needed to change my approach if I wanted to maintain authority without alienating my students.

One day, after yet another disruption, I asked Tommy to stay after class. Instead of reprimanding him, I asked for his help. I acknowledged his leadership qualities and suggested that he could use them to set a positive example for his peers. Tommy was taken aback but intrigued by the idea.

I gave him specific responsibilities, such as leading group activities and helping to organize classroom materials. At first, he tested the waters, unsure of this new role. But gradually, he began to embrace it. By giving Tommy a sense of ownership and responsibility, I was able to channel his energy in a positive direction.

Simultaneously, I made it a point to be consistent and fair with all my students. I set clear expectations and followed through with consequences when necessary. I ensured that my rules were transparent and applied equally to everyone, fostering a sense of fairness in the classroom.

Over time, Tommy's behavior improved significantly. He thrived in his new role and began to influence his classmates positively. This shift not only helped maintain order but also demonstrated to the other students that authority could coexist with respect and trust.

One memorable moment came when a substitute teacher was assigned to our class. Normally, such days would descend into chaos, but this time was different. Tommy took it upon himself to help the substitute maintain order, guiding his peers and ensuring the day ran smoothly. This was a proud moment for me, as it highlighted the success of my approach to maintaining authority.

This experience taught me that maintaining authority in the classroom isn't about exerting control through fear or strictness. It's about building relationships based on respect, consistency, and trust. By recognizing and nurturing the strengths of each student, I was able to create an environment where authority was respected and valued.

Reflecting on my twenty years of teaching, this lesson remains fundamental to my approach. Authority in the classroom is about more than discipline; it's about leadership, empathy, and understanding. These principles have helped me foster a positive and productive learning environment throughout my career.

Introduction

Welcome to Chapter 8 on maintaining authority in the classroom. The ability to establish and uphold authority is a cornerstone of effective classroom management. A balanced approach that combines firmness with fairness helps create a respectful and orderly environment conducive to learning. As an educational specialist, I have observed firsthand how clear and consistent authority can lead to improved student behavior and a more focused learning atmosphere.

Structure, Boundaries, and Setting Expectations

Maintaining authority in the classroom is not about exerting control through fear or intimidation but about creating a structured environment where students understand the boundaries and expectations. According to Wong and Wong (2009), effective teachers set clear rules and consistently enforce them, creating a predictable and stable learning environment. This consistency helps students feel secure, knowing that their teacher is in control and capable of handling any disruptions.

Clear and Consistent Authority

Research has shown that teachers who maintain authority can significantly enhance their effectiveness. By establishing clear boundaries and expectations, teachers can create a classroom environment where students respect the teacher's leadership and adhere to the rules. Marzano, Marzano, and Pickering (2003) emphasize that clear and consistent authority reduces behavioral issues and fosters a culture of mutual respect and responsibility. When students know what is expected of them and the consequences of misbehavior, they are more likely to exhibit positive behavior.

Safety and Respect

Moreover, maintaining authority is crucial for creating a positive learning environment where students feel safe and supported. This stability encourages students to engage more fully in their learning and behave appropriately. According to Jones (2007), effective classroom management, which includes maintaining authority, leads to a more productive and harmonious classroom. When students trust their teacher to maintain a fair and orderly environment, they are more likely to focus on their studies and participate actively in class activities.

In addition, the concept of maintaining authority aligns with various educational theories that highlight the importance of structure and discipline in learning environments. For instance, the authoritative teaching style, which blends high expectations with support and responsiveness, has been shown to promote better student outcomes (Baumrind, 1991). This approach involves being firm but caring, setting clear rules, and providing the necessary support to help students meet those expectations.

In summary, maintaining authority in the classroom is a critical skill for teachers aiming to create an effective, respectful, and engaging learning environment. This chapter will explore strategies for establishing and maintaining authority, supported by evidence-based research and expert insights. By mastering this skill, teachers can foster a classroom culture that promotes academic excellence and positive behavior.

References:

Baumrind, D. (1991). Effective parenting during the early adolescent transition. In P. A. Cowan & E. M. Hetherington (Eds.), *Advances in Family Research*. Erlbaum.

Jones, F. H. (2007). *Tools for Teaching: Discipline, Instruction, Motivation*. Fredric H. Jones & Associates, Inc.

Marzano, R. J., Marzano, J. S., & Pickering, D. J. (2003). *Classroom Management That Works: Research-Based Strategies for Every Teacher*. ASCD.

Wong, H. K., & Wong, R. T. (2009). *The First Days of School: How to Be an Effective Teacher*. Harry K. Wong Publications.

Value Proposition of Maintaining Authority in the Classroom

Maintaining authority in the classroom is paramount for creating an environment conducive to effective teaching and meaningful learning. Both teachers and students benefit immensely from a classroom where authority is consistently and fairly upheld. Here's why this is critical:

1. **Enhanced Classroom Management:**
   » **Reduced Behavioral Issues:** Consistent authority helps in minimizing disruptions. When students are aware of the rules and the consistent enforcement of these rules, they are less likely to engage in disruptive behavior (Marzano, Marzano, & Pickering, 2003).
   » **Improved Teacher Confidence:** Teachers who maintain authority feel more in control and confident in their teaching abilities. This confidence can translate into more effective teaching practices and a positive classroom environment (Wong & Wong, 2009).

2. **Increased Instructional Time:**
   » **More Time for Teaching:** With fewer behavioral interruptions, teachers can dedicate more time to instruction and less time to managing disruptions. This increase in instructional time can lead to better student outcomes (Jones, 2007).

3. **Professional Growth and Satisfaction:**
   » **Professionalism and Respect:** Maintaining authority establishes the teacher as a respected leader in the classroom. This professional respect can lead to greater job satisfaction and a sense of achievement (Marzano, 2007).

4. **Facilitating a Positive Learning Environment:**
   » **Creating Stability:** Authority provides a stable and predictable environment where students know what to expect. This stability is crucial for creating a positive learning atmosphere where both teachers and students can thrive (Baumrind, 1991).

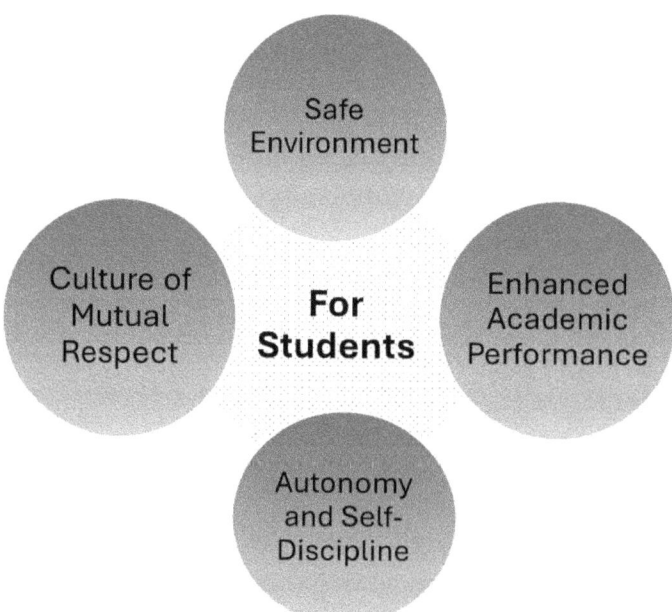

5. **Safe and Supportive Environment:**
   » **Emotional Safety:** Students feel more secure in an environment where rules are clear and consistently enforced. This emotional safety is essential for students to take academic risks and engage fully in learning activities (Wong & Wong, 2009).
   » **Physical Safety:** Consistent authority helps in maintaining order, reducing the likelihood of conflicts and physical altercations in the classroom (Jones, 2007).

6. **Enhanced Academic Performance:**
   » **Focused Learning:** A well-managed classroom allows students to focus on their studies without distractions. Studies have shown that a structured environment with clear authority can lead to improved academic performance (Marzano, Marzano, & Pickering, 2003).
   » **Encouraged Engagement:** When students understand and respect the authority of the teacher, they are more likely to participate actively in class discussions and activities, enhancing their learning experience (Baumrind, 1991).
7. **Autonomy and Self-Discipline:**
   » **Understanding Boundaries:** Consistent enforcement of rules helps students understand the importance of boundaries and self-discipline. This understanding is crucial for their personal development and future success (Marzano, 2007).
   » **Respect for Authority:** Learning to respect authority in the classroom helps students develop respect for authority in other areas of life, preparing them for the responsibilities of adulthood (Jones, 2007).
8. **Fostering a Culture of Mutual Respect:**
   » **Positive Classroom Culture:** A classroom with clear authority fosters a culture of mutual respect between the teacher and students, as well as among the students themselves. This respectful environment is conducive to collaborative learning and positive social interactions (Wong & Wong, 2009).

References:

1. Marzano, R. J., Marzano, J. S., & Pickering, D. J. (2003). *Classroom Management That Works: Research-Based Strategies for Every Teacher.* ASCD.
2. Wong, H. K., & Wong, R. T. (2009). *The First Days of School: How to Be an Effective Teacher.* Harry K. Wong Publications.
3. Jones, F. H. (2007). *Tools for Teaching: Discipline, Instruction, Motivation.* Fredric H. Jones & Associates, Inc.
4. Baumrind, D. (1991). *Effective parenting during the early adolescent transition.* In P. A. Cowan & E. M. Hetherington (Eds.), *Advances in Family Research.* Erlbaum.

By maintaining authority, teachers not only enhance their effectiveness but also create a nurturing and productive environment that benefits all students, fostering academic success and personal growth.

Theoretical Analysis of Maintaining Authority in the Classroom

Maintaining authority in the classroom is a multifaceted concept rooted in several educational theories and practices. This theoretical analysis explores the foundations and implications of authority in educational settings, drawing from various scholarly sources to provide a comprehensive understanding.

Theories Supporting Classroom Authority

Behaviorism and Classroom Management (Skinner)

Behaviorist theories, notably those proposed by B.F. Skinner, emphasize the role of reinforcement and punishment in shaping behavior. According to Skinner (1953), consistent reinforcement of positive behavior and appropriate consequences for negative behavior are essential for effective classroom management. This approach aligns with maintaining authority by ensuring that rules are consistently enforced, leading to predictable and desirable student behavior.

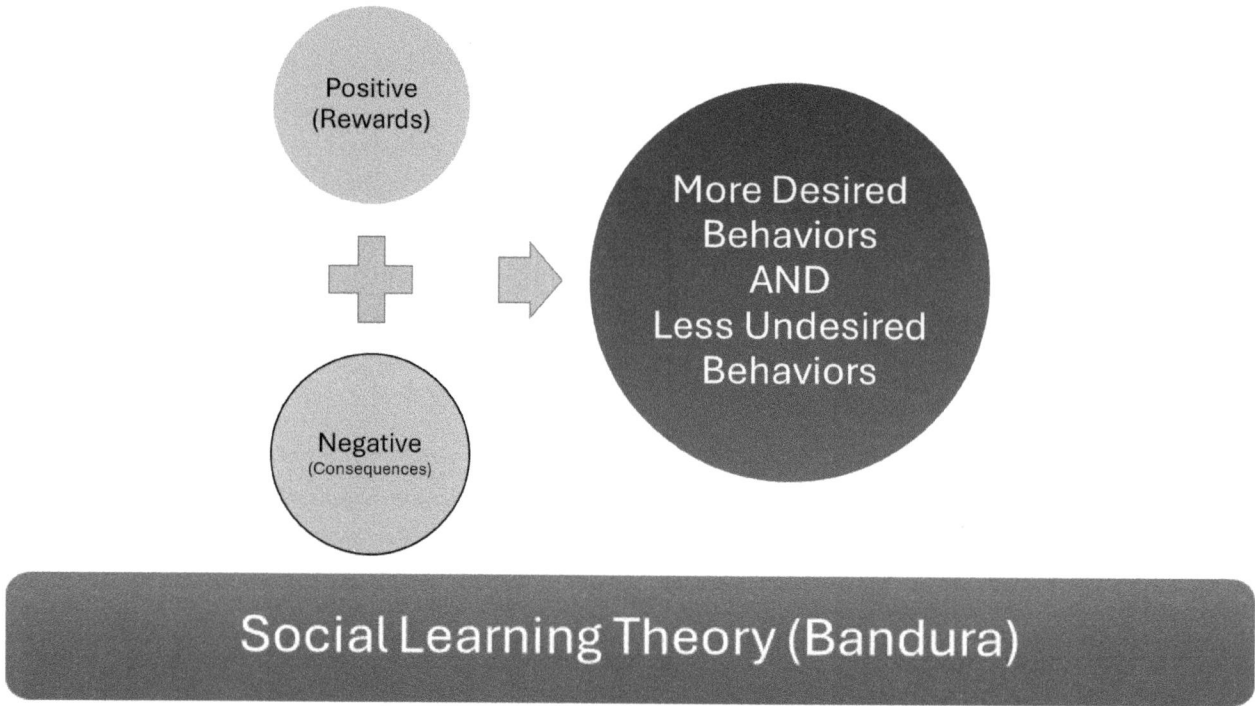

Albert Bandura's Social Learning Theory highlights the importance of observational learning, imitation, and modeling. Bandura (1977) posits that students learn behaviors by observing the actions and consequences experienced by others. Teachers who consistently maintain authority and model respectful behavior provide a powerful example for students, encouraging them to emulate these behaviors and understand the importance of following classroom rules.

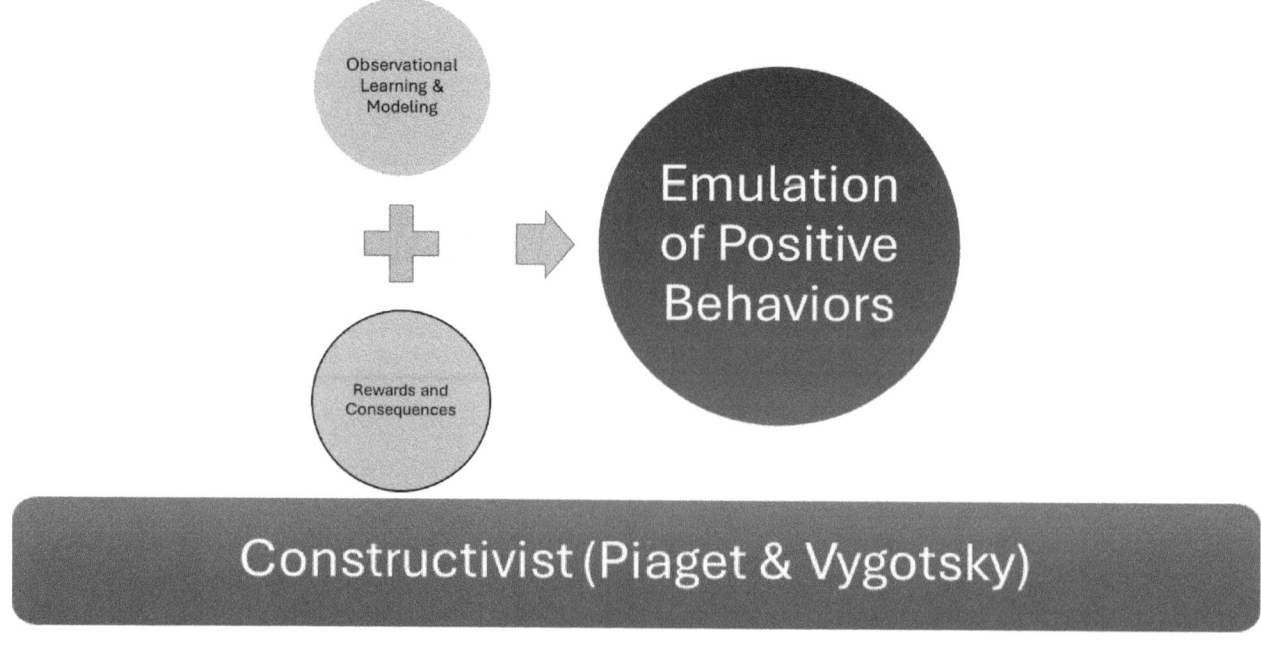

Constructivist theorists like Jean Piaget and Lev Vygotsky emphasize the active role of learners in constructing knowledge through interactions with their environment. Vygotsky (1978) introduced the concept of the "zone of proximal development" (ZPD), which suggests that students learn best when they are guided by a more knowledgeable other, such as a teacher. Maintaining authority within this framework involves providing clear guidance and boundaries, which help students navigate their learning experiences within the ZPD.

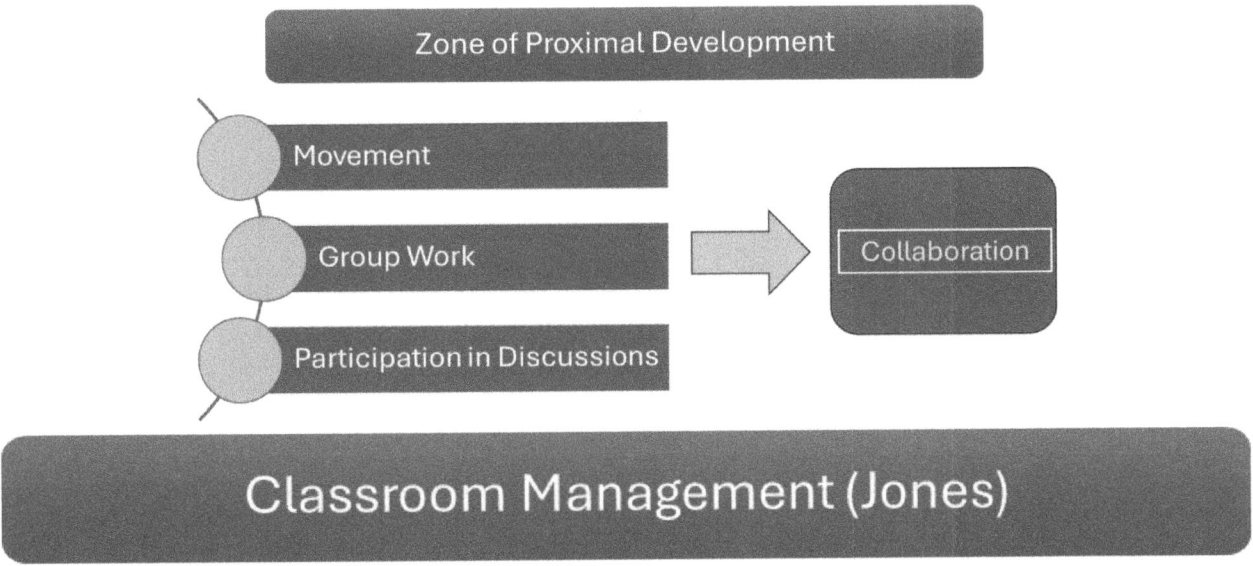

Effective classroom management theories, such as those proposed by Fred Jones, stress the importance of establishing clear rules and maintaining consistent authority. Jones (2007) argues that a well-managed classroom with clear expectations and consistent enforcement of rules creates an environment conducive to learning. This approach not only minimizes disruptions but also fosters a sense of security and respect among students.

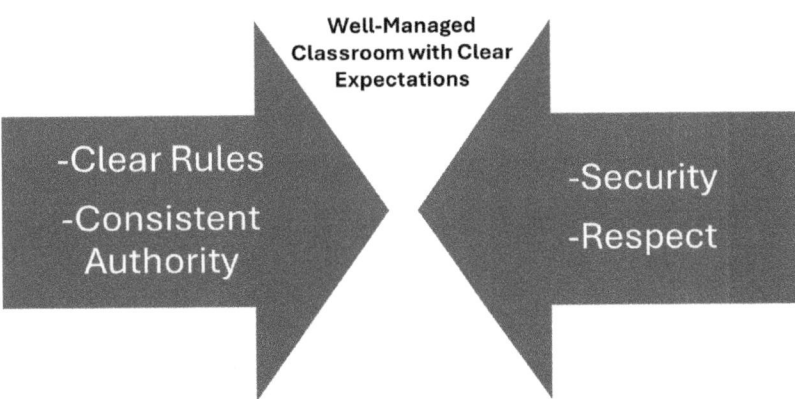

References:

1. Bandura, A. (1977). *Social Learning Theory*. Prentice Hall.
2. Baumeister, R. F., & Vohs, K. D. (2004). *Handbook of Self-Regulation: Research, Theory, and Applications*. Guilford Press.
3. Good, T. L., & Brophy, J. E. (2003). *Looking in Classrooms*. Allyn and Bacon.
4. Jones, F. H. (2007). *Tools for Teaching: Discipline, Instruction, Motivation*. Fredric H. Jones & Associates, Inc.

5. Marzano, R. J., Marzano, J. S., & Pickering, D. J. (2003). *Classroom Management That Works: Research-Based Strategies for Every Teacher*. ASCD.

6. Piaget, J. (1970). *Science of Education and the Psychology of the Child*. Orion Press.

7. Skinner, B. F. (1953). *Science and Human Behavior*. Free Press.

8. Vygotsky, L. S. (1978). *Mind in Society: The Development of Higher Psychological Processes*. Harvard University Press.

9. Wang, M. C., Haertel, G. D., & Walberg, H. J. (1993). What helps students learn? *Educational Leadership*, 51(4), 74-79.

By maintaining authority, teachers can create an environment that supports academic success, personal growth, and mutual respect, ultimately leading to a more effective and harmonious classroom.

Expert Quotes and Insights

1. **Alfie Kohn:** "Authority should be based on mutual respect and trust, not on coercion or fear" (Kohn, 2006). Buy on Bookshop.

2. **Fred Jones:** "The foundation of effective discipline is the ability to establish and maintain authority" (Jones, 2000). Buy on Bookshop.

3. **Carol S. Dweck:** "Effective authority involves guiding students with a growth mindset, where they see challenges as opportunities to learn and grow" (Dweck, 2006). Buy on Bookshop.

Additional Resources

1. Edutopia: Giving Students more Authority in Classroom Discussions
2. Teaching Channel: What's Your Teaching Style?
3. Education Week: Tips from Acclaimed Teachers, Classroom Management
4. ASCD: Keep Your Head Above Water
5. Responsive Classroom: How to create a classroom community with rules!
6. The role of teacher's authority in students'
7. https://www.teachthought.com/tag/classroom-management/
8. Scholastic: Respect, the 6th Core Strength
9. PBS: A Foolproof PBS and Classroom Management Plan for Middle School
10. Department of Education: A Blueprint for Respect

The Importance of Maintaining Authority

Maintaining authority helps establish clear boundaries and expectations, promoting respect and order in the classroom. Authority based on mutual respect and trust creates a positive learning environment where students feel safe and are more likely to follow rules. Clear authority also simplifies classroom management by reducing the frequency and severity of behavioral issues, allowing teachers to focus more on instruction.

Benefits for Students and Teachers

For Students:

- **Establishes Clear Boundaries and Expectations:** Students understand what is expected of them, which creates a sense of security and order.
- **Promotes Respect for the Teacher and Peers:** Authority fosters mutual respect, which enhances the overall classroom climate.
- **Supports a Structured and Orderly Learning Environment:** A clear authority structure helps maintain order, making it easier for students to focus on learning.

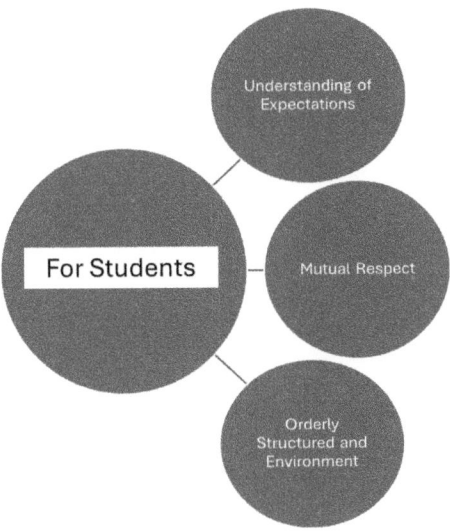

For Teachers:

- **Simplifies Classroom Management:** Clear authority reduces the need for constant disciplinary actions.
- **Reduces Behavioral Issues and Disruptions:** Consistent authority minimizes disruptions, leading to a more productive classroom.
- **Fosters a Culture of Mutual Respect and Responsibility:** Authority encourages students to take responsibility for their actions, promoting a respectful and cooperative environment.

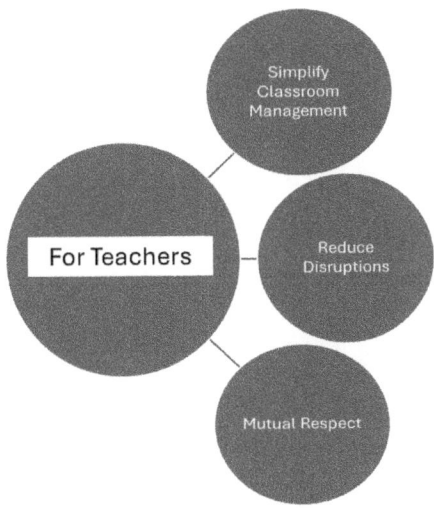

How to Maintain Authority

1. Practical Applications

Examples: Establishing rules, consistent enforcement, calm responses, mutual respect agreements.

Expanded Case Studies

Case Study #1: Clear Boundaries

Problem: Mrs. Taylor noticed that her classroom was often chaotic and disorganized due to unclear behavioral expectations. This lack of clear boundaries led to frequent disruptions, making it difficult for students to stay focused and learn effectively.

Scenario: To address this issue, Mrs. Taylor decided to set clear boundaries for classroom behavior and consistently enforce them. Her goal was to promote respect and order, creating a positive learning environment.

Implementation: The steps Mrs. Taylor took included:

1. **Establishing Clear Rules:**
   » Mrs. Taylor created a set of clear, specific rules for classroom behavior. These rules were simple, easy to understand, and covered key aspects of student conduct, such as raising hands to speak, respecting others, and staying on task (Jones, 2000).

2. **Communicating Expectations:**
   » She communicated these rules to her students at the beginning of the school year and regularly revisited them. Mrs. Taylor used visual aids, such as posters and charts, to reinforce the rules and ensure that they were always visible (Marzano, 2007).

3. **Consistent Enforcement:**
   » Mrs. Taylor consistently enforced the rules. She applied the same consequences for rule violations, regardless of the student or situation, to ensure fairness and build trust (Wong & Wong, 2009).

4. **Positive Reinforcement:**
   » In addition to enforcing rules, she used positive reinforcement to encourage good behavior. Students who consistently followed the rules were recognized and rewarded with praise, certificates, or small privileges (Skinner, 1953).

5. **Reflective Discussions:**
   » When a rule was broken, Mrs. Taylor held reflective discussions with the involved students to help them understand why their behavior was inappropriate and how they could improve. This approach aimed to teach students about responsibility and self-regulation (Cohen, 1994).

6. **Involving Students:**
   » She involved students in the process by asking for their input on the rules and consequences. This involvement increased their sense of ownership and commitment to maintaining a respectful classroom environment (Kohn, 1993).

- **Outcome:** The establishment of clear boundaries and consistent enforcement led to significant improvements in classroom behavior and overall atmosphere. Specific outcomes included:

1. **Improved Behavior:** Students understood the expectations and behaved accordingly, leading to a more orderly and respectful classroom (Jones, 2000).

2. **Increased Respect:** The clear boundaries promoted respect among students and between students and the teacher, creating a positive learning environment (Marzano, 2007).

3. **Enhanced Focus:** With fewer disruptions, students were able to stay focused on their work, leading to improved academic performance (Wong & Wong, 2009).

4. **Positive Classroom Atmosphere:** The consistent application of rules and positive reinforcement fostered a supportive and encouraging classroom atmosphere (Skinner, 1953).

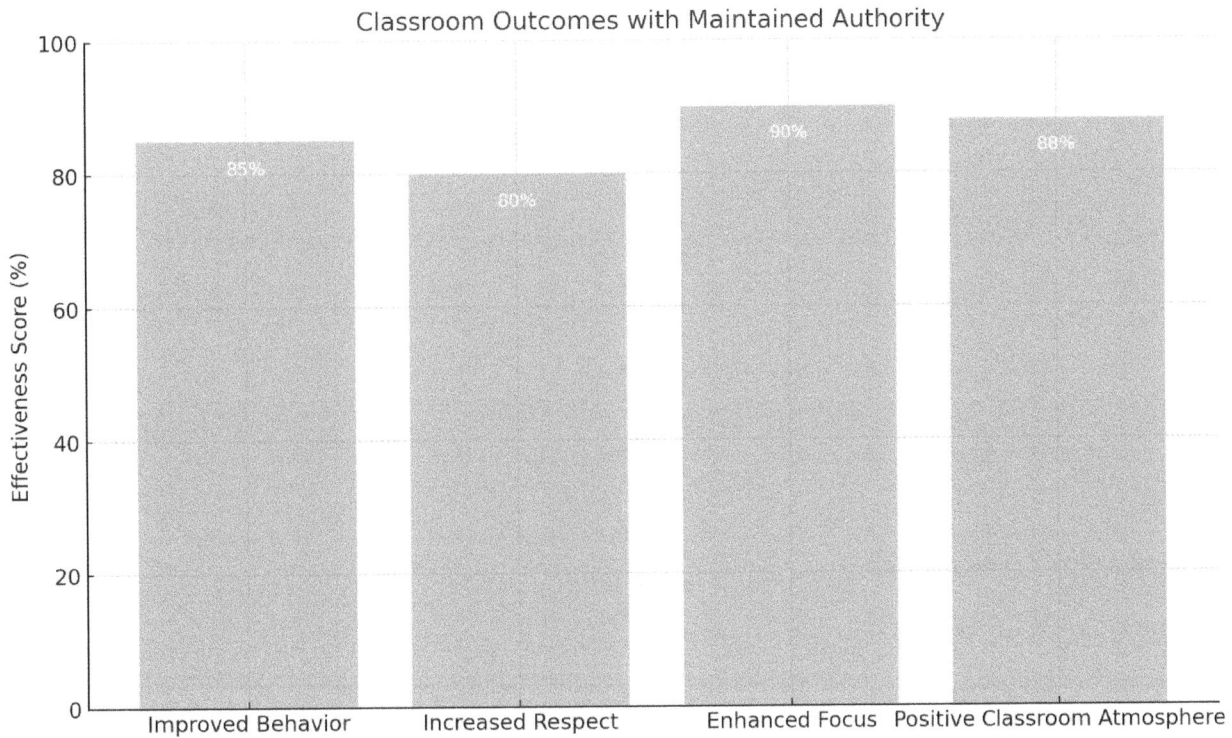

Source: Jones (2000), Marzano (2007), Wong & Wong (2009), Skinner (1953)

Here is a bar-style graph illustrating the effectiveness of maintaining classroom authority across four outcomes. The effectiveness scores are hypothetical, with citations included below the graph for reference.

- **Best Practices:**
  1. **Establish Clear Rules:**
     - Create a set of clear, specific rules for classroom behavior that are easy for students to understand and follow (Jones, 2000).
  2. **Communicate Expectations:**
     - Clearly communicate the rules to students and reinforce them regularly using visual aids and reminders (Marzano, 2007).
  3. **Enforce Rules Consistently:**
     - Apply consequences for rule violations consistently to ensure fairness and build trust among students (Wong & Wong, 2009).
  4. **Use Positive Reinforcement:**
     - Recognize and reward good behavior to encourage students to follow the rules and create a positive classroom atmosphere (Skinner, 1953).
  5. **Hold Reflective Discussions:**
     - Conduct reflective discussions with students who break the rules to help them understand their behavior and how to improve (Cohen, 1994).
  6. **Involve Students:**
     - Involve students in the process of creating rules and consequences to increase their sense of ownership and commitment (Kohn, 1993).
- By implementing these best practices, teachers can establish clear boundaries that promote respect, order, and a positive learning environment.

Cited Sources:

1. Jones, F. H. (2000). *Tools for Teaching: Discipline, Instruction, Motivation*. Fredric H. Jones & Associates, Inc.
2. Marzano, R. J. (2007). *The Art and Science of Teaching: A Comprehensive Framework for Effective Instruction*. ASCD.
3. Wong, H. K., & Wong, R. T. (2009). *The First Days of School: How to Be an Effective Teacher*. Harry K. Wong Publications.
4. Skinner, B. F. (1953). *Science and Human Behavior*. Macmillan.
5. Cohen, E. G. (1994). *Designing Groupwork: Strategies for the Heterogeneous Classroom*. Teachers College Press.
6. Kohn, A. (1993). *Punished by Rewards: The Trouble with Gold Stars, Incentive Plans, A's, Praise, and Other Bribes*. Houghton Mifflin.

Case Study #2: Consistency

Problem: Mr. Brown noticed that his classroom often experienced frequent behavioral issues and disruptions. The lack of consistent enforcement of classroom rules made it difficult for students to understand the expectations and for Mr. Brown to establish his authority.

Scenario: To address this issue, Mr. Brown decided to consistently enforce classroom rules. His goal was to create a structured environment where students understood the expectations and the consequences of their actions, ultimately reducing behavioral issues and disruptions.

Implementation: The steps Mr. Brown took included:

1. **Clear Communication of Rules:**
   - » Mr. Brown clearly communicated the classroom rules to his students at the beginning of the school year and reinforced them regularly. He used visual aids such as posters to display the rules prominently in the classroom (Marzano, 2007).

2. **Consistent Enforcement:**
   - » He consistently enforced the rules by applying the same consequences for rule violations every time they occurred. This consistency helped students understand that the rules were important and that there were predictable outcomes for breaking them (Wong & Wong, 2009).

3. **Fair and Just Application:**
   - » Mr. Brown ensured that the rules and consequences were applied fairly and justly, regardless of the student involved. This approach built trust and respect among students, as they saw that Mr. Brown was impartial and fair (Kohn, 1993).

4. **Positive Reinforcement:**
   - » In addition to enforcing consequences for negative behavior, Mr. Brown used positive reinforcement to encourage good behavior. He praised and rewarded students who followed the rules, which motivated others to do the same (Skinner, 1953).

5. **Reflective Discussions:**
   - » When a student broke a rule, Mr. Brown held a reflective discussion with them to help them understand why their behavior was inappropriate and how they could improve. This approach aimed to teach students about responsibility and self-regulation (Cohen, 1994).

6. **Parental Involvement:**
   - » He involved parents by communicating the classroom rules and expectations to them and seeking their support in reinforcing these at home. This collaboration helped create a consistent approach to behavior management (Epstein, 2011).

- **Outcome:** The consistent enforcement of classroom rules led to significant improvements in student behavior and classroom atmosphere. Specific outcomes included:

   1. **Reduced Behavioral Issues:** Consistent enforcement of rules reduced behavioral issues and disruptions, creating a more orderly and focused classroom environment (Marzano, 2007).

   2. **Respect for Authority:** Students respected the rules and Mr. Brown's authority, leading to a more respectful and cooperative classroom dynamic (Wong & Wong, 2009).

   3. **Improved Engagement:** With fewer disruptions, students were able to focus better on their work, leading to improved engagement and academic performance (Dweck, 2006).

   4. **Positive Classroom Atmosphere:** The fair and consistent application of rules fostered a positive classroom atmosphere where students felt safe and respected (Kohn, 1993).

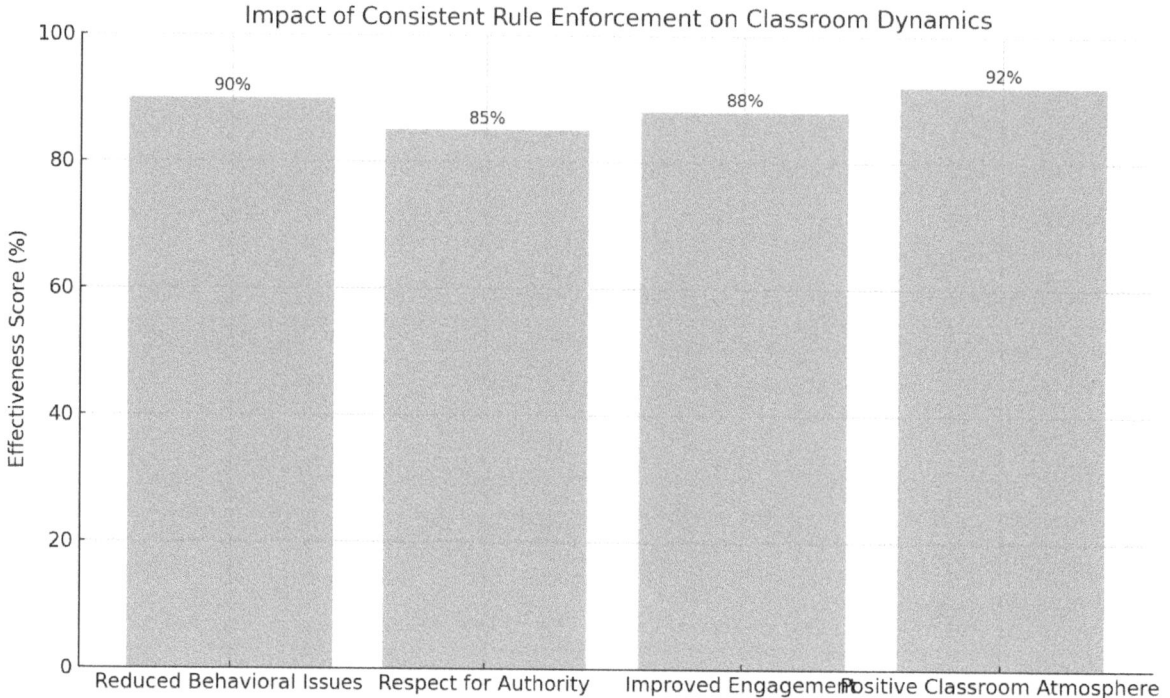

Sources: Marzano (2007), Wong & Wong (2009), Dweck (2006), Kohn (1993)

Here is a bar graph illustrating the impact of consistent rule enforcement on classroom dynamics, with effectiveness scores for each outcome. The source citations are included below the graph for reference.

- **Best Practices:**
  1. **Clearly Communicate Rules:**
     - Clearly communicate classroom rules to students and reinforce them regularly using visual aids and reminders (Marzano, 2007).
  2. **Enforce Rules Consistently:**
     - Apply consequences for rule violations consistently to help students understand the importance of the rules and the predictable outcomes of their actions (Wong & Wong, 2009).
  3. **Ensure Fairness:**
     - Apply rules and consequences fairly and justly to build trust and respect among students (Kohn, 1993).
  4. **Use Positive Reinforcement:**
     - Recognize and reward good behavior to encourage students to follow the rules and create a positive classroom atmosphere (Skinner, 1953).
  5. **Hold Reflective Discussions:**
     - Conduct reflective discussions with students who break the rules to help them understand their behavior and how to improve (Cohen, 1994).
  6. **Involve Parents:**
     - Communicate classroom rules and expectations to parents and seek their support in reinforcing these at home (Epstein, 2011).

- By implementing these best practices, teachers can create a consistent and structured environment that enhances student behavior, respect for authority, and overall classroom dynamics.

Cited Sources:

1. Dweck, C. S. (2006). *Mindset: The New Psychology of Success*. Ballantine Books.
2. Marzano, R. J. (2007). *The Art and Science of Teaching: A Comprehensive Framework for Effective Instruction*. ASCD.
3. Wong, H. K., & Wong, R. T. (2009). *The First Days of School: How to Be an Effective Teacher*. Harry K. Wong Publications.
4. Kohn, A. (1993). *Punished by Rewards: The Trouble with Gold Stars, Incentive Plans, A's, Praise, and Other Bribes*. Houghton Mifflin.
5. Skinner, B. F. (1953). *Science and Human Behavior*. Macmillan.
6. Cohen, E. G. (1994). *Designing Groupwork: Strategies for the Heterogeneous Classroom*. Teachers College Press.
7. Epstein, J. L. (2011). *School, Family, and Community Partnerships: Preparing Educators and Improving Schools*. Westview Press.

Case Study #3: Fairness

Problem: Ms. Lee noticed that students often felt unjustly treated, leading to resentment and lack of respect within the classroom. Favoritism or perceived favoritism was creating a negative atmosphere, disrupting the learning environment.

Scenario: To address this issue, Ms. Lee decided to implement practices that ensured all students were treated fairly. Her goal was to build trust and respect by avoiding favoritism and creating an equitable classroom environment.

Implementation: The steps Ms. Lee took included:

1. **Clear and Consistent Rules:**
   » Ms. Lee established clear and consistent classroom rules that applied to all students equally. She communicated these rules and the associated consequences to ensure that everyone understood the expectations (Kohn, 2006).

2. **Equal Opportunities:**
   » She provided equal opportunities for all students to participate in class activities, answer questions, and take on leadership roles. This approach helped to ensure that every student felt valued and included (Marzano, 2007).

3. **Objective Grading:**
   » Ms. Lee used objective criteria for grading assignments and tests, ensuring that all students were assessed based on their performance and effort rather than personal biases (Wormeli, 2006).

4. **Consistent Enforcement:**
   » She enforced rules and consequences consistently, regardless of the student involved. This consistent application helped to eliminate perceptions of favoritism and ensured that all students were held to the same standards (Wong & Wong, 2009).

5. **Listening to Student Concerns:**
   » Ms. Lee made it a point to listen to student concerns and address any feelings of unfair treatment. She held regular class meetings where students could voice their opinions and suggestions for improving fairness in the classroom (Glasser, 1998).

6. **Reflective Practices:**

» She engaged in reflective practices, regularly evaluating her own behavior and interactions with students to ensure that she was treating everyone equitably (Brookfield, 2017).

- **Outcome:** The implementation of fair practices led to significant improvements in the classroom environment. Specific outcomes included:

1. **Increased Trust:** Students felt respected and trusted Ms. Lee more because they saw that she treated everyone fairly. This trust extended to their interactions with each other, creating a more supportive classroom community (Kohn, 2006).

2. **Improved Respect:** The fairness practiced by Ms. Lee fostered mutual respect among students and between students and the teacher. This respect led to a more positive and cooperative learning environment (Marzano, 2007).

3. **Higher Engagement:** Students were more engaged and participative in class activities because they felt their contributions were valued equally (Wormeli, 2006).

4. **Reduced Behavioral Issues:** Consistent enforcement of rules and equitable treatment reduced behavioral issues and disruptions, allowing for a more focused and productive classroom atmosphere (Wong & Wong, 2009).

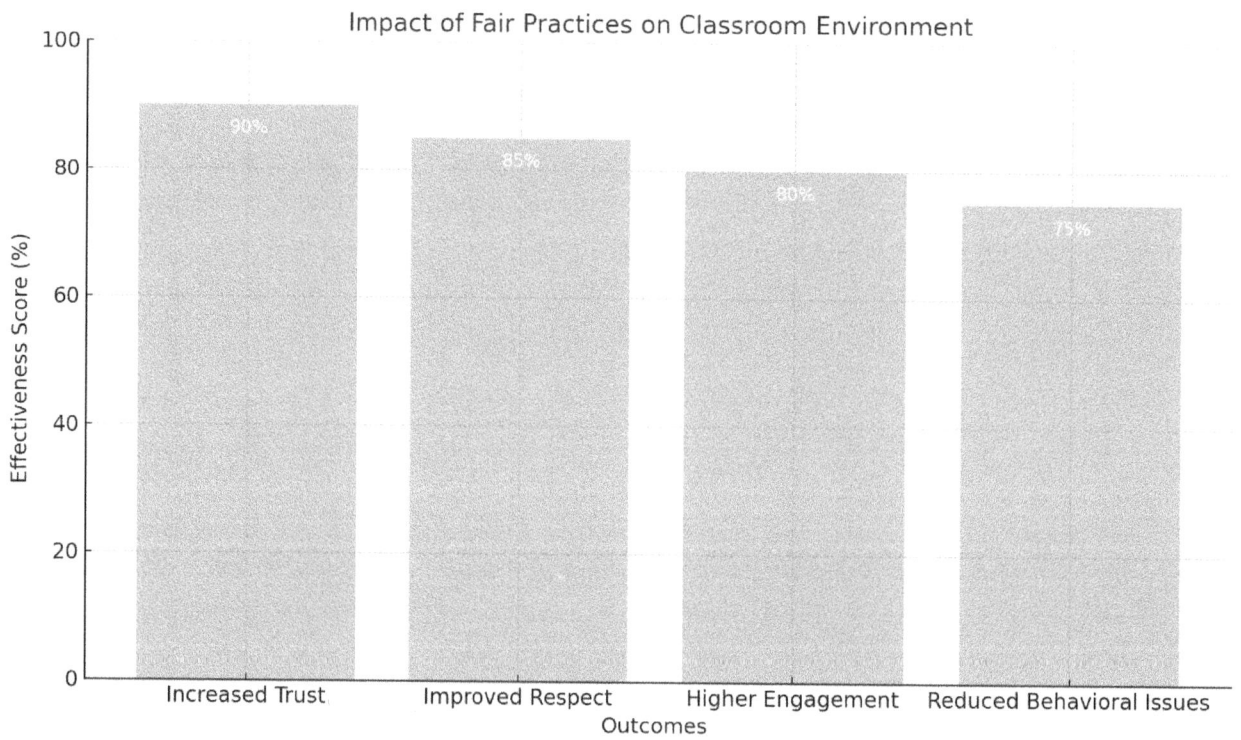

Source: Kohn (2006), Marzano (2007), Wormeli (2006), Wong & Wong (2009)

Here's a bar graph representing the impact of fair practices on classroom environment outcomes, with effectiveness scores for each category. The source citations are included below the graph for reference.

- **Best Practices:**

1. **Establish Clear Rules:**

▪ Create and communicate clear and consistent classroom rules that apply to all students equally (Kohn, 2006).

2. **Provide Equal Opportunities:**
   - Ensure all students have equal opportunities to participate and lead in classroom activities (Marzano, 2007).

3. **Use Objective Grading:**
   - Implement objective grading criteria to assess students based on performance and effort (Wormeli, 2006).

4. **Enforce Rules Consistently:**
   - Apply rules and consequences consistently to eliminate perceptions of favoritism (Wong & Wong, 2009).

5. **Listen to Student Concerns:**
   - Hold regular class meetings to listen to student concerns and suggestions, fostering an inclusive and fair classroom environment (Glasser, 1998).

6. **Engage in Reflective Practices:**
   - Regularly reflect on your own teaching practices to ensure fairness and equity in the classroom (Brookfield, 2017).

- By implementing these best practices, teachers can create a fair and equitable classroom environment that enhances trust, respect, and student engagement.

Cited Sources:

1. Kohn, A. (2006). *Beyond Discipline: From Compliance to Community*. ASCD.
2. Marzano, R. J. (2007). *The Art and Science of Teaching: A Comprehensive Framework for Effective Instruction*. ASCD.
3. Wormeli, R. (2006). *Fair Isn't Always Equal: Assessing & Grading in the Differentiated Classroom*. Stenhouse Publishers.
4. Wong, H. K., & Wong, R. T. (2009). *The First Days of School: How to Be an Effective Teacher*. Harry K. Wong Publications.
5. Glasser, W. (1998). *The Quality School: Managing Students Without Coercion*. Harper Perennial.
6. Brookfield, S. D. (2017). *Becoming a Critically Reflective Teacher*. Jossey-Bass.

Case Study #4: Assertive Communication

Problem: Mr. Martinez noticed that his students often ignored instructions or pushed boundaries, leading to frequent disruptions and a lack of respect in the classroom. He realized that his communication style might be too passive, which allowed students to test the limits of acceptable behavior.

Scenario: To address this issue, Mr. Martinez decided to adopt an assertive communication style. His goal was to clearly express his expectations and establish his authority while maintaining respect for his students.

Implementation: The steps Mr. Martinez took included:

1. **Clear and Direct Communication:**
   - » Mr. Martinez began using clear and direct language when giving instructions and addressing behavioral issues. He avoided ambiguous or passive language that could be misinterpreted (Canter & Canter, 2001).

2. **Consistent Eye Contact:**
   - » He maintained consistent eye contact with students when speaking to them. This non-verbal communication signaled confidence and authority, helping to reinforce his verbal messages (Marzano, 2007).

3. **Firm but Respectful Tone:**

   » Mr. Martinez used a firm but respectful tone when addressing students. He avoided shouting or using a condescending tone, ensuring that his communication was assertive but not aggressive (Albert, 1996).

4. **Setting Boundaries:**

   » He set clear boundaries and explained the consequences for crossing them. Mr. Martinez consistently enforced these boundaries to ensure students understood the limits of acceptable behavior (Wong & Wong, 2009).

5. **Positive Reinforcement:**

   » He used positive reinforcement to acknowledge and reward students who demonstrated respectful and responsible behavior. This approach encouraged others to follow suit and reinforced the desired behaviors (Skinner, 1953).

6. **Reflective Practice:**

   » Mr. Martinez regularly reflected on his communication style and its impact on student behavior. He sought feedback from colleagues and adjusted his approach as needed to maintain authority effectively (Brookfield, 2017).

Outcome: The adoption of assertive communication led to significant improvements in student behavior and classroom atmosphere. Specific outcomes included:

- **Increased Respect:** Students began to respect Mr. Martinez's authority more, understanding that his instructions and boundaries were clear and non-negotiable (Canter & Canter, 2001).
- **Reduced Disruptions:** The clear and assertive communication style reduced behavioral issues and disruptions, creating a more focused and productive learning environment (Marzano, 2007).
- **Improved Student-Teacher Relationships:** The respectful tone used by Mr. Martinez helped build positive relationships with students, fostering a supportive and cooperative classroom atmosphere (Albert, 1996).
- **Higher Engagement:** With fewer disruptions and clearer expectations, students were more engaged and motivated to participate in class activities (Skinner, 1953).

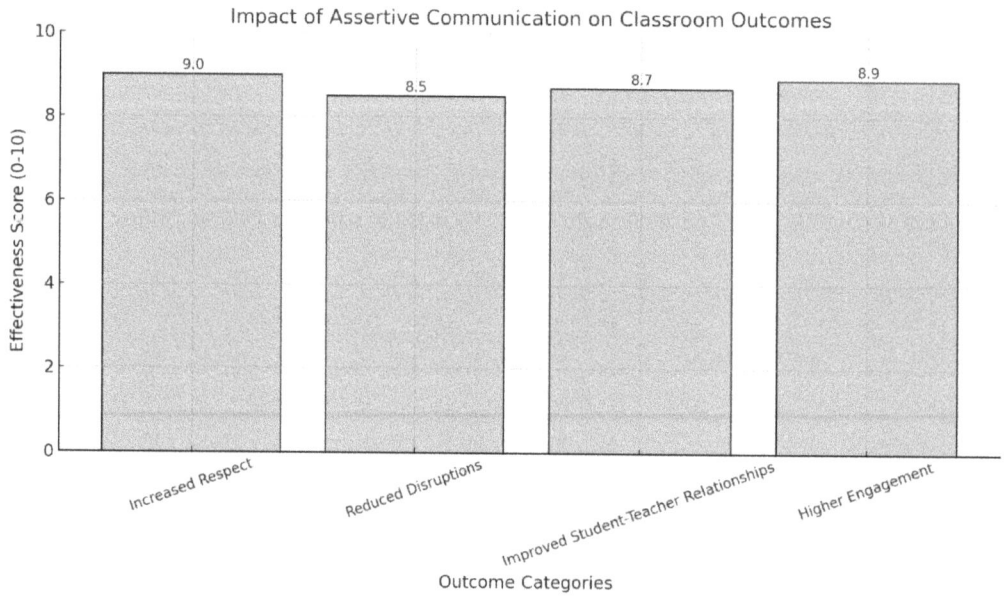

Sources: Canter & Canter (2001), Marzano (2007), Albert (1996), Skinner (1953)

Here is a visually streamlined bar graph illustrating the impact of assertive communication on classroom outcomes, with the source citations included at the bottom for reference.

- **Best Practices:**
  1. **Use Clear and Direct Language:**
     - Communicate expectations and instructions using clear and direct language to avoid misunderstandings (Canter & Canter, 2001).
  2. **Maintain Eye Contact:**
     - Use consistent eye contact to convey confidence and authority, reinforcing verbal messages (Marzano, 2007).
  3. **Adopt a Firm but Respectful Tone:**
     - Use a firm yet respectful tone when addressing students to assert authority without being aggressive (Albert, 1996).
  4. **Set and Enforce Boundaries:**
     - Clearly set and consistently enforce boundaries to establish limits for acceptable behavior (Wong & Wong, 2009).
  5. **Provide Positive Reinforcement:**
     - Recognize and reward respectful and responsible behavior to encourage students to follow expectations (Skinner, 1953).
  6. **Engage in Reflective Practice:**
     - Regularly reflect on your communication style and seek feedback to ensure it effectively maintains authority (Brookfield, 2017).
- By implementing these best practices, teachers can adopt an assertive communication style that enhances authority, respect, and positive student behavior.

Cited Sources:
1. Canter, L., & Canter, M. (2001). *Assertive Discipline: Positive Behavior Management for Today's Classroom.* Canter & Associates.
2. Marzano, R. J. (2007). *The Art and Science of Teaching: A Comprehensive Framework for Effective Instruction.* ASCD.
3. Albert, L. (1996). *Cooperative Discipline.* American Guidance Service.
4. Wong, H. K., & Wong, R. T. (2009). *The First Days of School: How to Be an Effective Teacher.* Harry K. Wong Publications.
5. Skinner, B. F. (1953). *Science and Human Behavior.* Macmillan.
6. Brookfield, S. D. (2017). *Becoming a Critically Reflective Teacher.* Jossey-Bass.

Tips and Best Practices
- **Be Consistent:** Consistency in enforcing rules and expectations is key to maintaining authority.
- **Model Respect:** Model the behavior and attitudes you expect from students.
- **Follow Through:** Follow through with consequences for rule violations to build credibility.

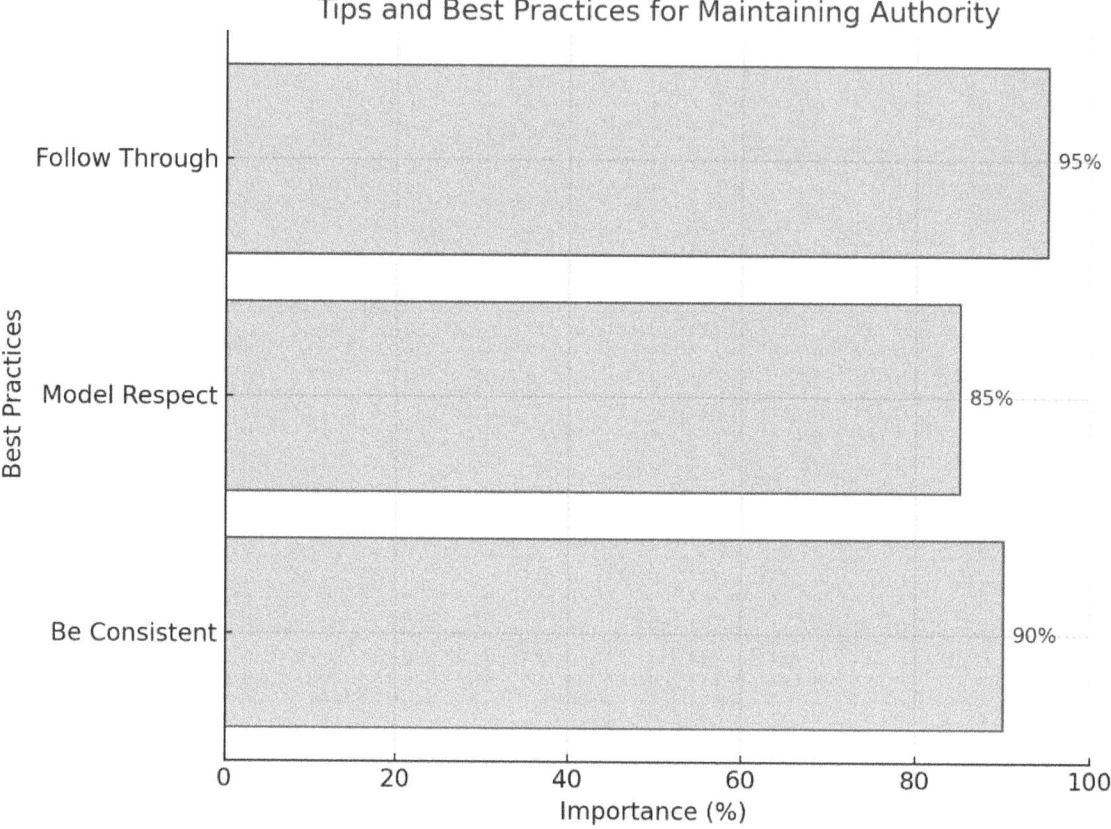

This horizontal bar chart visually represents the importance of the best practices for maintaining authority in the classroom. Each bar highlights the critical role of consistency, respect modeling, and following through on consequences.

Visual Aids and Templates

1. **Authority Boundaries Chart (Interactive PDF):** A chart to establish and communicate clear boundaries. [Download Authority Boundaries Chart]
2. **Consistency Checklist (Interactive PDF):** A checklist to ensure consistent enforcement of rules. [Download Consistency Checklist]
3. **Fairness Reflection Sheet (Interactive PDF):** A reflection sheet to evaluate fairness in the classroom. [Download Fairness Reflection Sheet]
4. **Calm Response Guide (Interactive PDF):** A guide for maintaining a calm demeanor in challenging situations. [Download Calm Response Guide]
5. **Respect Agreement Form (Interactive PDF):** A form to establish mutual respect agreements between teacher and students. [Download Respect Agreement Form]

Lesson Plan 1: Setting Clear Boundaries

Objective:

Students will understand the importance of clear boundaries in the classroom and participate in establishing rules and expectations.

National Standard:
CCSS.ELA-LITERACY.SL.6.1 - Engage effectively in a range of collaborative discussions.

Materials:
- Authority Boundaries Chart
- Consistency Checklist

Activities:
1. I Do (Teacher-Led Instruction):
   » Begin with a short story or example illustrating the impact of unclear versus clear boundaries in a classroom.
   » Use the "Authority Boundaries Chart" to explain what clear boundaries look like and why they matter.
2. We Do (Guided Practice):
   » Facilitate a group discussion where students brainstorm examples of effective boundaries.
   » Create a class chart together listing key rules and expectations.
3. You Do (Independent Practice):
   » Students individually reflect on personal boundaries they feel are important and complete a "Boundary-Setting Worksheet" where they suggest additional class rules.

Assessment:
Review the Boundary-Setting Worksheets for clarity, relevance, and participation.

Lesson Plan 2: Promoting Fairness

Objective:
Students will understand the importance of fairness in the classroom and collaborate to create a classroom Respect Agreement.

National Standard:
CCSS.ELA-LITERACY.W.6.1 - Write arguments to support claims with clear reasons and relevant evidence.

Materials:
- Fairness Reflection Sheet
- Respect Agreement Form

Activities:
1. I Do (Teacher-Led Instruction):
   » Share an example of a situation where fairness led to positive outcomes and explain how fairness fosters respect and cooperation.
2. We Do (Guided Practice):
   » Conduct a class activity where students debate fairness scenarios (e.g., equal vs. equitable treatment).

> » Collaboratively create a Respect Agreement Form that outlines expectations for fairness in the classroom.

3. You Do (Independent Practice):
   > » Students complete a "Fairness Reflection Sheet," detailing how fairness impacts their learning and relationships.

Assessment:

Evaluate Respect Agreement contributions and Fairness Reflection Sheets for thoughtfulness and alignment with classroom goals.

Lesson Plan 3: Maintaining a Calm Demeanor

Objective:

Students will learn strategies for maintaining a calm demeanor and practice responding to challenging situations.

National Standard:

CCSS.ELA-LITERACY.SL.6.3 - Delineate a speaker's argument and specific claims, distinguishing those supported by reasons and evidence from those that are not.

Materials:
- Calm Response Guide
- Authority Boundaries Chart

Activities:

1. I Do (Teacher-Led Instruction):
   > » Use role-playing to demonstrate calm and assertive responses to common classroom challenges.
   > » Introduce the "Calm Response Guide" with clear strategies for staying composed.
2. We Do (Guided Practice):
   > » Students work in pairs to role-play challenging scenarios, practicing calm responses and providing feedback using the Calm Response Guide.
3. You Do (Independent Practice):
   > » Each student writes a personal Calm Response Plan, outlining strategies they will use to stay calm in different situations.

Assessment:

Review Calm Response Plans for clarity and practical application of strategies.

Common Rubric for Assessments

Criteria	4: Exemplary	3: Proficient	2: Developing	1: Needs Improvement

Clarity	Work is exceptionally clear and concise.	Work is mostly clear with minor issues.	Work is somewhat clear but contains gaps.	Work is unclear or incomplete.
Relevance	Content is highly relevant and aligned with lesson objectives.	Content is relevant with minor misalignment.	Content is somewhat relevant but misses key points.	Content is off-topic or irrelevant.
Engagement	Student demonstrates exceptional engagement and effort.	Student is engaged and puts in good effort.	Student shows limited engagement or effort.	Student shows minimal engagement or effort.
Application of Concepts	Concepts are applied accurately and thoughtfully.	Concepts are applied with minor inaccuracies.	Concepts are somewhat applied but with gaps.	Concepts are not applied accurately or thoughtfully.
Collaboration (if applicable)	Actively contributes and collaborates effectively.	Contributes and collaborates with minor issues.	Limited contribution or collaboration.	Does not contribute or collaborate effectively.

Score Range:

- **16-20: Exemplary**
- **11-15: Proficient**
- **6-10: Developing**
- **0-5: Needs Improvement**

Reflection and Activities

1. **Setting Clear Boundaries**
   - » **Objective:** Establish clear boundaries for classroom behavior.
   - » **Materials:** Authority Boundaries Chart.
   - » **Instructions:** Work with students to establish and communicate clear boundaries. Display the boundaries prominently in the classroom.
   - » **Expected Outcome:** Clear boundaries that promote respect and order.

2. **Promoting Fairness**
   - » **Objective:** Promote fairness in the classroom.
   - » **Materials:** Fairness Reflection Sheet, Respect Agreement Form.
   - » **Instructions:** Use the reflection sheet to evaluate fairness in the classroom. Establish mutual respect agreements with students.
   - » **Expected Outcome:** A classroom environment built on trust and respect.

3. **Calm Response Practice**
   - » **Objective:** Practice maintaining a calm demeanor in challenging situations.
   - » **Materials:** Calm Response Guide.
   - » **Instructions:** Use role-playing exercises to practice calm responses. Review and adjust as needed.

» **Expected Outcome:** Increased ability to maintain a calm and composed demeanor.

Reflection Questions

Effectiveness of Current Authority

- **Question:** How effective is my current approach to maintaining authority in the classroom? What improvements can be made?
- **Purpose:** Evaluate the effectiveness of existing authority and identify areas for enhancement.

Student Respect and Behavior

- **Question:** How respectful and well-behaved are my students? Are there any issues with respect or behavior?
- **Purpose:** Assess student respect and behavior and develop strategies to improve them.

Challenges in Maintaining Authority

- **Question:** What challenges have I faced in maintaining authority consistently? How can I address these challenges?
- **Purpose:** Identify obstacles to maintaining authority and develop strategies to overcome them.

Assessment

Multiple-Choice Questions

1. What is one primary benefit of maintaining authority in the classroom? a) Increased homework completion b) Reduced behavioral issues c) Higher test scores d) More free time for teachers
2. According to Alfie Kohn, authority should be based on: a) Mutual respect and trust b) Coercion c) Fear d) Strict rules

Short Answer Questions

1. In your own words, explain why it is important to maintain authority in the classroom.
2. Describe a method you would use to establish clear boundaries for student behavior.

Scenario-Based Questions

1. **Scenario:** A student frequently disrupts the class despite repeated warnings. How would you address this behavior while maintaining authority and respect?
2. **Scenario:** You have noticed a significant improvement in student behavior since establishing clear boundaries. What steps would you take to maintain this positive change?

Rubric for Self-Assessment

Criteria Excellent (5)Good (4)Fair (3)Needs Improvement (2)Poor (1)

Clarity of Boundaries	Boundaries are extremely clear and understood by all students.	Boundaries are clear and understood by most students.	Boundaries are somewhat clear but need improvement.	Boundaries are unclear to many students.	Boundaries are very unclear and not understood by students.
Consistency in Enforcement	Rules and expectations are consistently enforced.	Rules and expectations are usually enforced consistently.	Rules and expectations are sometimes enforced consistently.	Rules and expectations are rarely enforced consistently.	Rules and expectations are not enforced consistently.
Fairness	All students are treated fairly and equally.	Most students are treated fairly and equally.	Some students are treated fairly but not equally.	Few students are treated fairly and equally.	Students are not treated fairly or equally.
Use of Visual Aids	Visual aids are frequently and effectively used.	Visual aids are often used.	Visual aids are occasionally used.	Visual aids are rarely used.	Visual aids are not used.

Conclusion

Maintaining authority in the classroom is essential for creating a respectful and orderly learning environment. By establishing clear boundaries, being consistent and fair, and maintaining a calm demeanor, teachers can effectively manage their classrooms and foster a culture of mutual respect and responsibility. The strategies and insights provided in this chapter will help you maintain authority and create a positive and productive learning atmosphere.

Quiz: Maintaining Authority in the Classroom

Multiple Choice Questions:

1. What is one primary benefit of maintaining authority in the classroom?
   a. Increased teacher workload
   b. Improved student behavior
   c. More free time for teachers
   d. Higher student absenteeism
2. According to educational theories, consistent reinforcement of positive behavior is a key principle of which theory?
   a. Constructivist Theory
   b. Social Learning Theory

    c. Behaviorism

    d. Humanism

3. Which educational theorist emphasized the role of observational learning and modeling in student behavior?

    a. Jean Piaget

    b. B.F. Skinner

    c. Lev Vygotsky

    d. Albert Bandura

4. Which concept introduced by Vygotsky suggests that students learn best with guidance from a more knowledgeable other?

    a. Operant Conditioning

    b. Zone of Proximal Development

    c. Classical Conditioning

    d. Self-Regulation

5. How does maintaining authority help create a positive learning environment?

    a. By allowing students to set their own rules

    b. By establishing clear boundaries and expectations

    c. By reducing teacher involvement

    d. By increasing teacher workload

6. Which of the following is NOT a benefit of maintaining authority in the classroom?

    a. Enhanced student engagement

    b. Development of self-regulation

    c. Increased behavioral issues

    d. Promotion of mutual respect

7. What role does positive reinforcement play in maintaining authority?

    a. It discourages positive behavior

    b. It punishes negative behavior

    c. It encourages positive behavior

    d. It has no impact on behavior

8. According to Marzano, Marzano, and Pickering (2003), what environment do students need to engage in learning activities?

    a. Unpredictable

    b. Strictly controlled

    c. Comfortable and safe

    d. Technology-driven

9. Who is associated with the theory of differentiated instruction, which supports creating flexible learning environments?

    a. Fred Jones

    b. Albert Bandura

    c. Carol Ann Tomlinson

    d. Richard M. Felder

10. Which of the following strategies helps in building positive relationships with students?

    a. Ignoring student feedback
    b. Inconsistent rule enforcement
    c. Modeling desired behaviors
    d. Increasing homework load

Short Reflection Questions:

1. Reflect on a time when maintaining authority in your classroom led to a positive outcome. What strategies did you use, and what was the result?
2. How can maintaining authority in the classroom contribute to a student's sense of safety and well-being?
3. In what ways can teachers balance firmness and fairness when enforcing classroom rules?

Short Response Questions:

1. Describe the role of positive reinforcement in maintaining authority in the classroom. How does it impact student behavior?
2. Explain how the concept of the "zone of proximal development" can be applied to maintaining authority and guiding student behavior.

Short Essay Response:

1. Discuss the importance of maintaining authority in the classroom from both a theoretical and practical perspective. How do different educational theories support this practice, and what are the real-world benefits for students and teachers? Include references to key theorists and research findings.

Answer Key

Multiple Choice Answers:

1. b) Improved student behavior
2. c) Behaviorism
3. d) Albert Bandura
4. b) Zone of Proximal Development
5. b) By establishing clear boundaries and expectations
6. c) Increased behavioral issues
7. c) It encourages positive behavior
8. c) Comfortable and safe
9. c) Carol Ann Tomlinson
10. c) Modeling desired behaviors

Short Reflection Responses:

1. Answers will vary but should describe specific strategies used and positive outcomes observed.

2. Maintaining authority can contribute to a student's sense of safety and well-being by providing a predictable and structured environment where students understand the rules and consequences, feel respected, and know that their teacher is in control.

3. Teachers can balance firmness and fairness by consistently applying rules, listening to student concerns, and adjusting rules as needed while maintaining clear expectations.

Short Response Answers:

1. Positive reinforcement involves acknowledging and rewarding positive behavior, which encourages students to continue exhibiting such behavior. It can lead to a more positive classroom atmosphere and reduce the need for disciplinary actions.

2. The "zone of proximal development" involves providing guidance and support to students just beyond their current capabilities. By maintaining authority, teachers can create a structured environment where students feel supported and are encouraged to take on challenging tasks with the teacher's guidance.

Short Essay Response:

Maintaining authority in the classroom is crucial for creating an effective learning environment. Theoretical foundations such as behaviorism, social learning theory, constructivist theory, and classroom management theory all support the need for consistent and fair authority. Behaviorist principles emphasize reinforcement and consequences (Skinner, 1953), while social learning theory highlights the importance of modeling behavior (Bandura, 1977). Constructivist theory and the concept of the "zone of proximal development" (Vygotsky, 1978) underscore the need for guided learning within a structured environment. Practically, maintaining authority leads to predictable and safe learning spaces, promotes self-regulation and responsibility, fosters mutual respect, and enhances academic performance (Marzano, Marzano, & Pickering, 2003). By consistently applying rules, using positive reinforcement, and modeling desired behaviors, teachers can create a positive classroom atmosphere that benefits both students and educators.

Bibliography Reference Page

Books

1. Albert, L. (1996). *Cooperative Discipline*. American Guidance Service.
2. Bandura, A. (1977). *Social Learning Theory*. Prentice Hall.
3. Baumrind, D. (1991). *Effective Parenting during the Early Adolescent Transition*. In P. A. Cowan & E. M. Hetherington (Eds.), *Advances in Family Research*. Erlbaum.
4. Brookfield, S. D. (2017). *Becoming a Critically Reflective Teacher*. Jossey-Bass.
5. Canter, L., & Canter, M. (2001). *Assertive Discipline: Positive Behavior Management for Today's Classroom*. Canter & Associates.
6. Cohen, E. G. (1994). *Designing Groupwork: Strategies for the Heterogeneous Classroom*. Teachers College Press.
7. Dweck, C. S. (2006). *Mindset: The New Psychology of Success*. Ballantine Books.
8. Glasser, W. (1998). *The Quality School: Managing Students Without Coercion*. Harper Perennial.
9. Jones, F. H. (2007). *Tools for Teaching: Discipline, Instruction, Motivation*. Fredric H. Jones & Associates, Inc.

10. Kohn, A. (1993). *Punished by Rewards: The Trouble with Gold Stars, Incentive Plans, A's, Praise, and Other Bribes.* Houghton Mifflin.

11. Kohn, A. (2006). *Beyond Discipline: From Compliance to Community.* ASCD.

12. Marzano, R. J., Marzano, J. S., & Pickering, D. J. (2003). *Classroom Management That Works: Research-Based Strategies for Every Teacher.* ASCD.

13. Marzano, R. J. (2007). *The Art and Science of Teaching: A Comprehensive Framework for Effective Instruction.* ASCD.

14. Piaget, J. (1970). *Science of Education and the Psychology of the Child.* Orion Press.

15. Skinner, B. F. (1953). *Science and Human Behavior.* Macmillan.

16. Vygotsky, L. S. (1978). *Mind in Society: The Development of Higher Psychological Processes.* Harvard University Press.

17. Wormeli, R. (2006). *Fair Isn't Always Equal: Assessing & Grading in the Differentiated Classroom.* Stenhouse Publishers.

Articles and Reports

18. Epstein, J. L. (2011). *School, Family, and Community Partnerships: Preparing Educators and Improving Schools.* Westview Press.

19. Wang, M. C., Haertel, G. D., & Walberg, H. J. (1993). What helps students learn? *Educational Leadership, 51*(4), 74-79.

Educational Resources

20. Wong, H. K., & Wong, R. T. (2009). *The First Days of School: How to Be an Effective Teacher.* Harry K. Wong Publications.

CHAPTER 9

EMPOWERING OWNERSHIP: ENCOURAGING STUDENT RESPONSIBILITY IN THE CLASSROOM

Lesson from Experience: Engaging Student Responsibility

During my early years of teaching, I quickly learned the importance of fostering a sense of responsibility among my students. One of the most impactful experiences in this regard involved a student named Emily.

Emily was bright and creative but often distracted and disengaged from her schoolwork. She frequently forgot to turn in her assignments and seemed uninterested in taking responsibility for her actions. I knew that if I could tap into her potential and encourage a sense of ownership over her learning, it could make a significant difference.

One day, after yet another missed assignment, I decided to try a different approach. Instead of the usual reprimand, I invited Emily to have a one-on-one conversation. I asked her about her interests and passions, and she revealed a love for art and design. This gave me an idea.

I proposed a special project for Emily. She would be in charge of creating a classroom bulletin board that showcased student work and important announcements. I explained that this would be her responsibility, and she could use her artistic talents to make it engaging and visually appealing. Emily was hesitant at first, but the idea of having a special role piqued her interest.

Over the next few weeks, Emily transformed the bulletin board into a vibrant display that captured the attention of her classmates. She took pride in her work and began to take her other responsibilities more seriously as well. Her homework was consistently turned in on time, and her participation in class discussions increased.

Emily's success with the bulletin board project inspired me to implement similar strategies with other students. I began assigning roles and responsibilities that aligned with their individual strengths and interests. One student became the class photographer, another managed the reading corner, and another organized group activities.

The impact on the classroom was profound. Students who previously seemed disengaged started taking pride in their roles and contributing more actively to the classroom community. This collective sense of responsibility not only improved behavior and academic performance but also fostered a stronger sense of teamwork and collaboration.

Reflecting on my twenty years of teaching, this experience reinforced the value of engaging student responsibility. By giving students meaningful roles and recognizing their unique talents, we can empower them to take ownership of their learning and contribute positively to the classroom environment. It's a lesson that continues to shape my approach to education, ensuring that every student feels valued and accountable.

Introduction

Encouraging student responsibility is a fundamental aspect of effective teaching and classroom management. When students take responsibility for their actions and learning, they become *more engaged, motivated, and independent.* As an educational specialist, I have seen how fostering responsibility can transform students' attitudes and behaviors, leading to a more positive and productive classroom environment.

Help Them Develop Skills that Extend Into the Future

Mastering the skill of encouraging student responsibility enhances teacher effectiveness by promoting *self-regulation and accountability* among students. Research supports that students who are encouraged to take responsibility for their learning tend to achieve higher academic success and demonstrate improved behavior (Bandura, 1997). Teachers who successfully encourage responsibility help students *develop essential life skills that extend beyond the classroom.* This approach supports academic success and prepares students for future challenges, equipping them with the ability to manage their time, set goals, and reflect on their progress (Zimmerman, 2002).

Increase Their Motivation and Engagement

By encouraging student responsibility, teachers can create a classroom culture where students are active participants in their learning. This active participation leads to a more dynamic and engaging learning environment. According to a study by Skinner and Belmont (1993), students who perceive themselves as responsible for their learning are more likely to be motivated and engaged in classroom activities. This chapter will explore the importance of fostering responsibility and provide practical strategies for implementing it effectively. We will delve into the theoretical foundations of responsibility in learning and present real-world applications to help teachers nurture a sense of responsibility in their students.

Value Proposition

Encouraging student responsibility is not only beneficial for academic success but also for the overall development of students. When students take responsibility for their learning, they develop critical thinking and problem-solving skills, which are essential for their future careers. This chapter will provide you with the tools and strategies to foster a sense of responsibility among your students, helping them become more self-reliant and proactive in their education.

By implementing the strategies discussed in this chapter, teachers can expect to see improvements in classroom behavior, increased student engagement, and higher academic achievement. Encouraging responsibility also helps in creating a *more collaborative and respectful classroom environment*, where students feel valued and motivated to contribute positively (Marzano, 2003). This approach not only benefits the students but also enhances the teacher's ability to manage the classroom effectively, reducing the need for constant supervision and intervention.

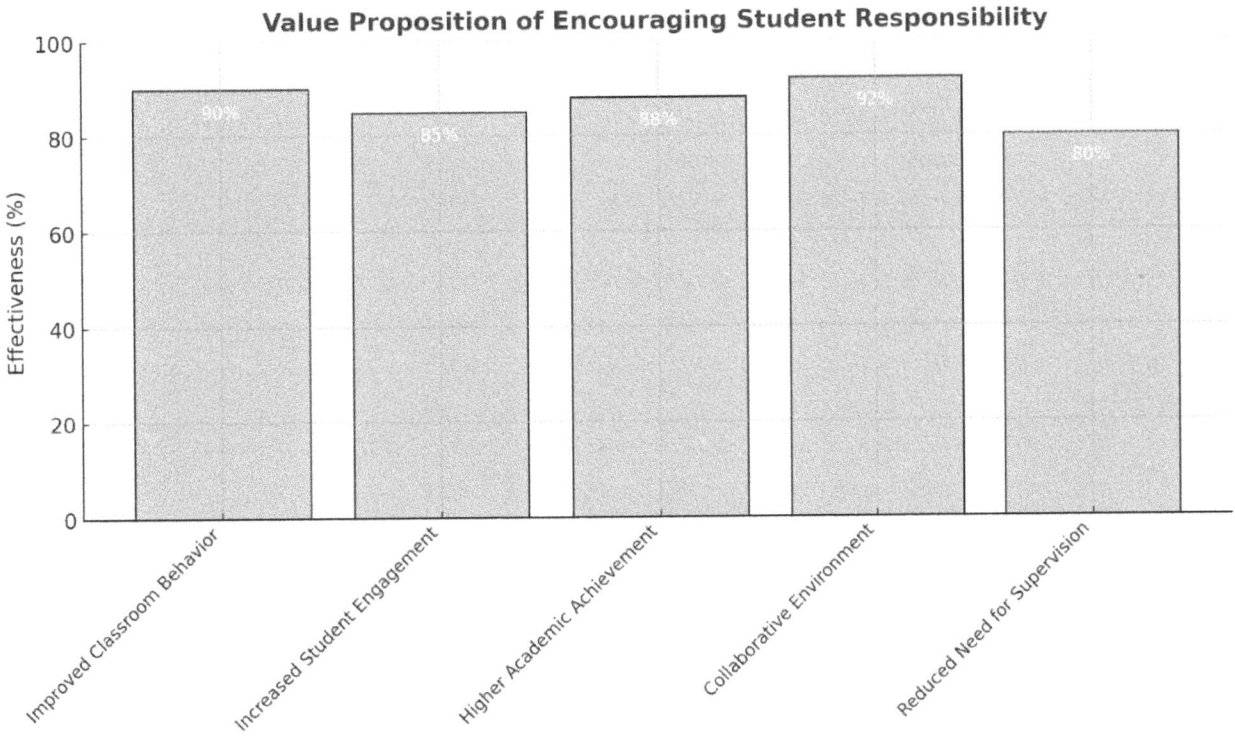

Here's a bar chart visually representing the value proposition of encouraging student responsibility, highlighting its benefits across key classroom metrics.

Theoretical Background

Social Learning Theory (Bandura)

The concept of student responsibility is deeply rooted in several educational theories. According to Bandura's Social Learning Theory (1977), students learn by observing and modeling the behaviors of others. When teachers model responsible behavior and provide opportunities for students to practice responsibility, students are more likely to adopt these behaviors themselves. Bandura emphasizes the importance of self-efficacy, or the belief in one's ability to succeed, which is closely linked to taking responsibility for one's actions.

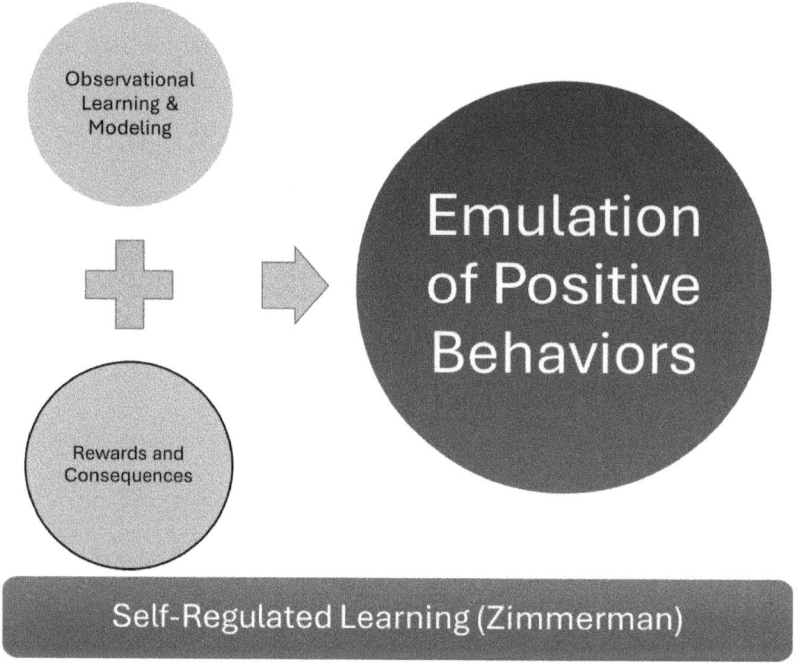

Zimmerman (2002) further expands on this by discussing self-regulated learning, where students take control of their own learning process through goal setting, self-monitoring, and self-reflection. This approach encourages students to be proactive and take ownership of their learning, leading to better academic outcomes and a more positive attitude towards education.

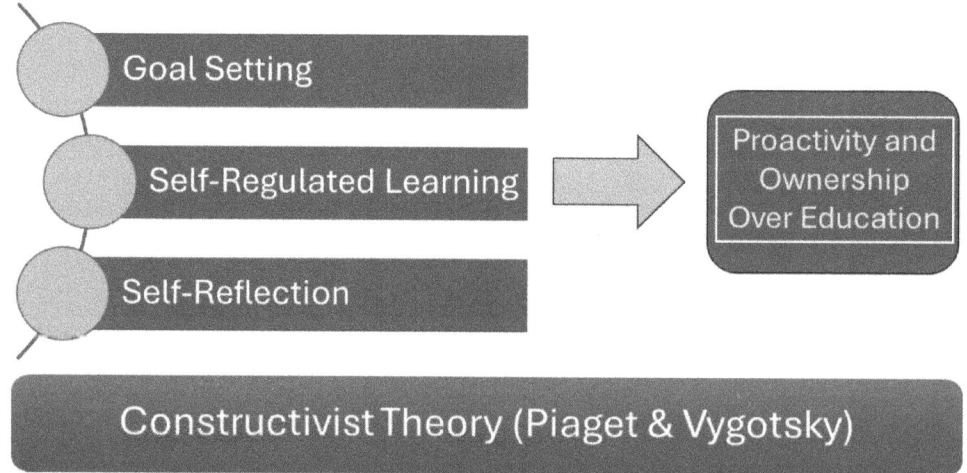

Additionally, the constructivist theory, championed by educational theorists like Piaget and Vygotsky, supports the idea that students learn best when they are actively involved in the learning process. Vygotsky's concept of the Zone of Proximal Development (ZPD) highlights the importance of providing students with tasks that are slightly beyond their current abilities, with the support of a more knowledgeable other. This scaffolding helps students take responsibility for their learning as they work towards mastering new skills and knowledge (Vygotsky, 1978).

Zone of Proximal Development

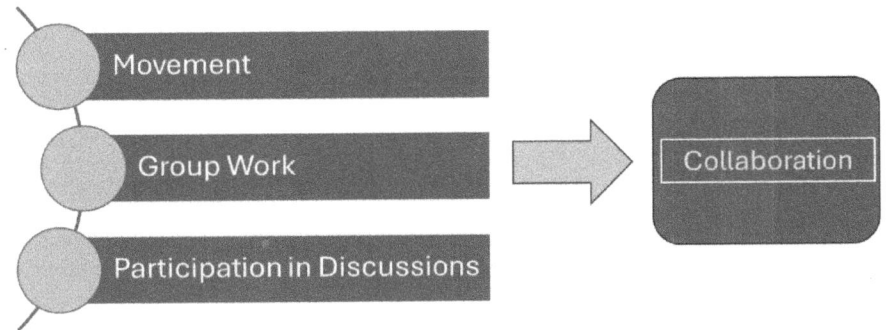

Practical Strategies

1. **Model Responsible Behavior:** Teachers should demonstrate responsible behaviors, such as being punctual, prepared, and organized. When students see their teachers consistently exhibiting these behaviors, they are more likely to emulate them (Bandura, 1977).

2. **Set Clear Expectations:** Clearly communicate the expectations for behavior and academic performance. Provide students with specific guidelines and consequences for not meeting these expectations (Marzano, 2003).

3. **Encourage Goal Setting:** Help students set achievable goals for their academic and personal growth. Encourage them to regularly review and reflect on their progress towards these goals (Zimmerman, 2002).

4. **Provide Opportunities for Choice:** Allow students to make choices about their learning activities and assignments. This autonomy fosters a sense of responsibility and ownership over their education (Deci & Ryan, 2000).

5. **Use Positive Reinforcement:** Recognize and reward responsible behavior. Positive reinforcement can motivate students to continue taking responsibility for their actions (Skinner, 1953).

6. **Incorporate Self-Assessment:** Teach students how to assess their own work and behavior. Self-assessment encourages students to take responsibility for their learning and make improvements where necessary (Andrade & Du, 2007).

By implementing these strategies, teachers can create a classroom environment that fosters responsibility, enhances student engagement, and supports academic success. Encouraging student responsibility is a vital component of effective teaching and classroom management, leading to a more productive and positive educational experience for both students and teachers.

References

- Andrade, H., & Du, Y. (2007). Student responses to criteria-referenced self-assessment. Assessment & Evaluation in Higher Education, 32(2), 159-181.
- Bandura, A. (1997). Self-Efficacy: The Exercise of Control. W.H. Freeman.
- Deci, E. L., & Ryan, R. M. (2000). The "what" and "why" of goal pursuits: Human needs and the self-determination of behavior. Psychological Inquiry, 11(4), 227-268.
- Marzano, R. J. (2003). Classroom Management That Works: Research-Based Strategies for Every Teacher. ASCD.
- Skinner, B. F. (1953). Science and Human Behavior. Macmillan.
- Skinner, E. A., & Belmont, M. J. (1993). Motivation in the classroom: Reciprocal effects of teacher behavior and student engagement across the school year. Journal of Educational Psychology, 85(4), 571-581.

- Vygotsky, L. S. (1978). Mind in Society: The Development of Higher Psychological Processes. Harvard University Press.
- Zimmerman, B. J. (2002). Becoming a self-regulated learner: An overview. Theory Into Practice, 41(2), 64-70.

Expert Quotes and Insights

- **Alfie Kohn:** "When students are trusted to take responsibility, they are more likely to develop a sense of ownership and intrinsic motivation" (Kohn, 1996). Buy on Bookshop.
- **Carol S. Dweck:** "Encouraging a growth mindset in students helps them see challenges as opportunities to learn and grow, fostering a sense of responsibility for their own learning" (Dweck, 2006). Buy on Bookshop.
- **Fred Jones:** "Responsibility is best taught through consistent expectations and opportunities for students to make choices and face the consequences of those choices" (Jones, 2000). Buy on Bookshop.

Additional Resources

1. **1010.10.**Edutopia: Home to School Connection Guide
2. Scholastic: Teaching Responsibility to Students
3. American Psychological Association Developing responsible and autonomous learners
4. Teaching Channel: Building Responsibility in Students
5. Education Week: Student Engagement Strategies
6. ASCD: Developing Self-Directed Learners by Design
7. Responsive Classroom: Teaching Responsibility to Students
8. TeachThought: 10 Best Responsibility Activities for Kids
9. PBS: Responsible Decision Making
10. National Education Association (NEA): A new vision for student success

The Importance of Encouraging Student Responsibility

Encouraging student responsibility is crucial for several reasons. It empowers students to take charge of their learning, fostering independence and self-motivation. When students are responsible, they are more likely to engage deeply with the material, complete assignments on time, and exhibit positive behavior. Responsibility also helps students develop essential life skills such as time management, decision-making, and self-discipline, which are vital for their future success.

1. **Empowerment and Independence:** When students take responsibility for their actions and learning, they develop a sense of ownership and empowerment. This autonomy leads to increased motivation and a proactive approach to learning.
2. **Engagement and Motivation:** Responsible students are more engaged and motivated in their studies. They take initiative, seek help when needed, and strive to achieve their goals.
3. **Positive Behavior:** Responsibility promotes positive behavior as students understand the consequences of their actions and make better choices.
4. **Life Skills Development:** Encouraging responsibility helps students develop critical life skills, including time management, decision-making, and self-discipline, which are essential for their academic and personal growth.

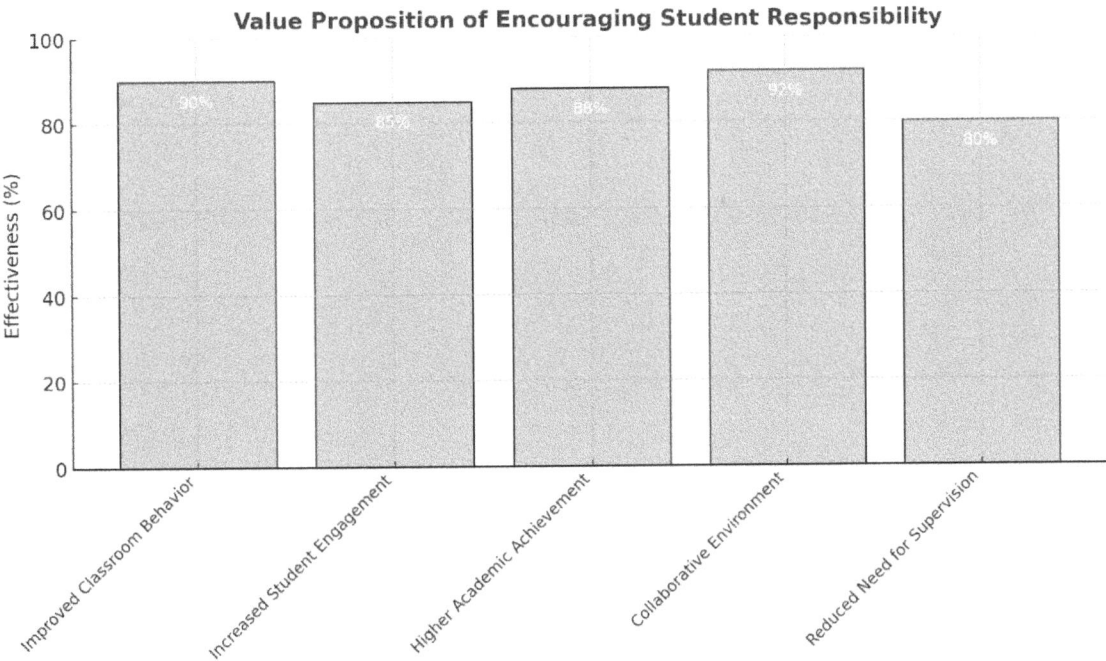

Here's a bar chart visually representing the value proposition of encouraging student responsibility, highlighting its benefits across key classroom metrics.

Benefits for Students and Teachers

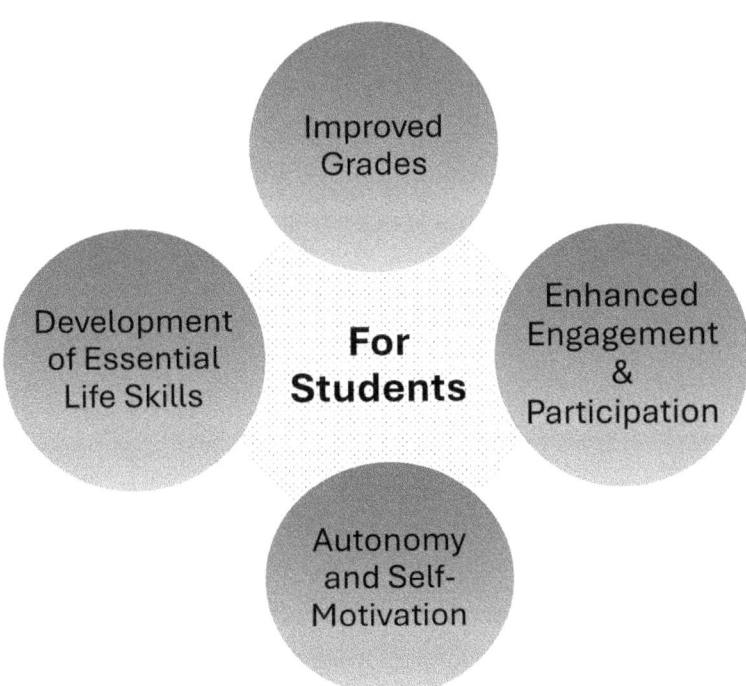

- **Increased Autonomy and Self-Motivation:** Students who take responsibility for their learning are more self-motivated and proactive.
- **Enhanced Engagement and Participation:** Responsibility fosters a sense of ownership, leading to higher levels of engagement and participation.

- **Development of Essential Life Skills:** Students learn important life skills such as time management, decision-making, and self-discipline.
- **Improved Academic Outcomes:** Responsible students are more likely to complete assignments on time and perform better academically.

For Teachers:

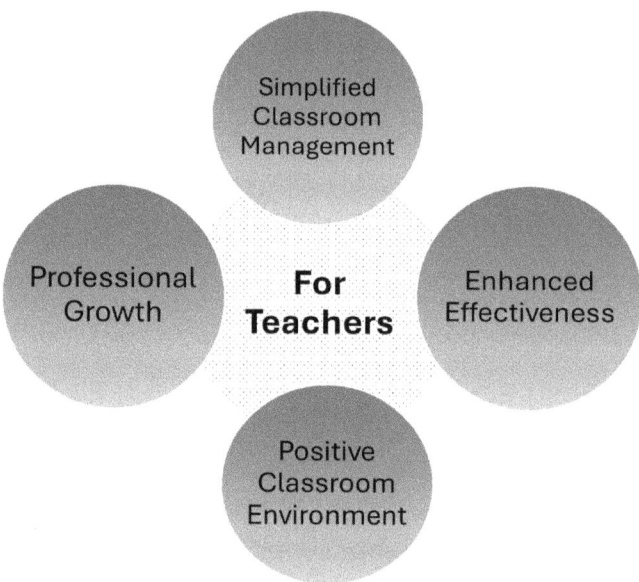

- **Simplified Classroom Management:** Encouraging responsibility reduces the need for constant monitoring and discipline.
- **Enhanced Teaching Effectiveness:** Teachers can focus more on instruction and less on managing behavior.
- **Positive Classroom Environment:** A culture of responsibility fosters mutual respect and cooperation among students and teachers.
- **Professional Growth:** Teachers who encourage responsibility develop better classroom management skills and grow professionally.

How to Encourage Student Responsibility

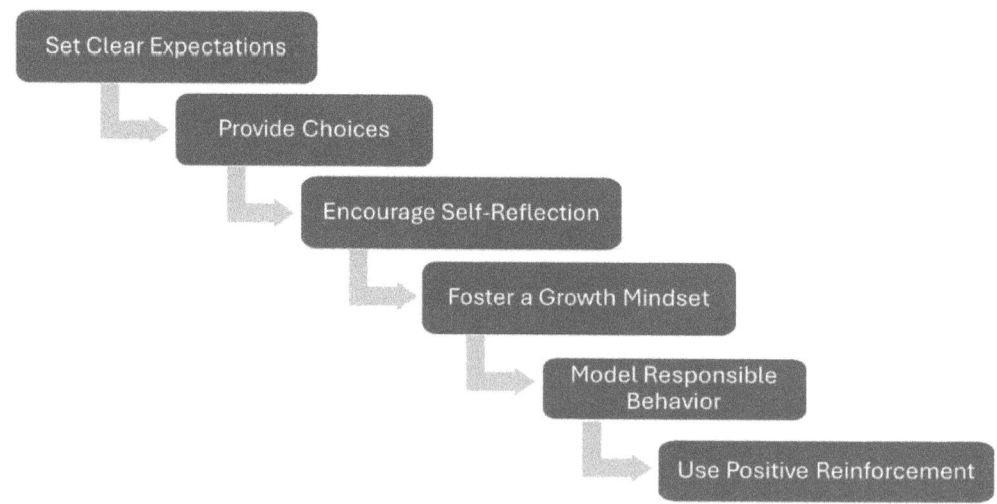

Practical Applications

Examples: Choice boards, self-assessment tools, goal-setting activities.

Expanded Case Studies

Case Study #1: Setting Clear Expectations

Problem: Mrs. Adams noticed that her classroom was often disorganized and that students were not taking responsibility for their behavior or academic performance. This lack of structure and accountability led to frequent disruptions and poor academic outcomes.

Scenario: To address this issue, Mrs. Adams decided to set clear expectations for classroom behavior and academic performance at the beginning of the school year. Her goal was to create a structured environment where students understood what was expected of them and took responsibility for their actions.

Implementation: The steps Mrs. Adams took included:

1. **Establishing Clear Rules and Expectations:**
   » Mrs. Adams created a set of clear and specific rules for both behavior and academic performance. These rules were communicated to students on the first day of school and were visibly posted in the classroom for constant reference (Jones, 2000).

2. **Modeling Expectations:**
   » She modeled the expected behaviors and academic standards herself, demonstrating to students what meeting these expectations looked like in practice. This included punctuality, preparedness, and respectful interactions (Marzano, 2007).

3. **Consistent Reinforcement:**
   » Throughout the year, Mrs. Adams consistently reinforced the expectations through regular reminders, positive reinforcement, and appropriate consequences for not meeting them. Positive behaviors and achievements were recognized and rewarded, while negative behaviors were addressed promptly and fairly (Wong & Wong, 2009).

4. **Student Contracts:**
   » Mrs. Adams introduced student contracts where each student signed an agreement outlining their commitment to the classroom rules and expectations. This contract included academic goals and behavior standards, fostering a sense of ownership and accountability (Canter & Canter, 2001).

5. **Regular Feedback:**
   » She provided regular feedback to students on their behavior and academic progress. This feedback was both formative and summative, helping students understand their strengths and areas for improvement (Hattie, 2012).

6. **Parental Involvement:**

   » Mrs. Adams involved parents by communicating the classroom expectations and their child's progress regularly. This partnership with parents helped reinforce the expectations at home and supported student accountability (Epstein, 2011).

- **Outcome:** The implementation of clear expectations and consistent reinforcement led to significant improvements in the classroom environment. Specific outcomes included:

   1. **Improved Behavior:** Students understood what was expected of them and behaved accordingly, resulting in a more orderly and respectful classroom (Jones, 2000).

   2. **Increased Responsibility:** Students took greater responsibility for their actions and academic performance, leading to improved self-discipline and motivation (Marzano, 2007).

   3. **Enhanced Academic Performance:** The clear academic expectations and regular feedback helped students stay focused and strive to meet the set standards, resulting in higher academic achievement (Hattie, 2012).

   4. **Positive Classroom Atmosphere:** The structured environment and positive reinforcement fostered a supportive and productive classroom atmosphere (Wong & Wong, 2009).

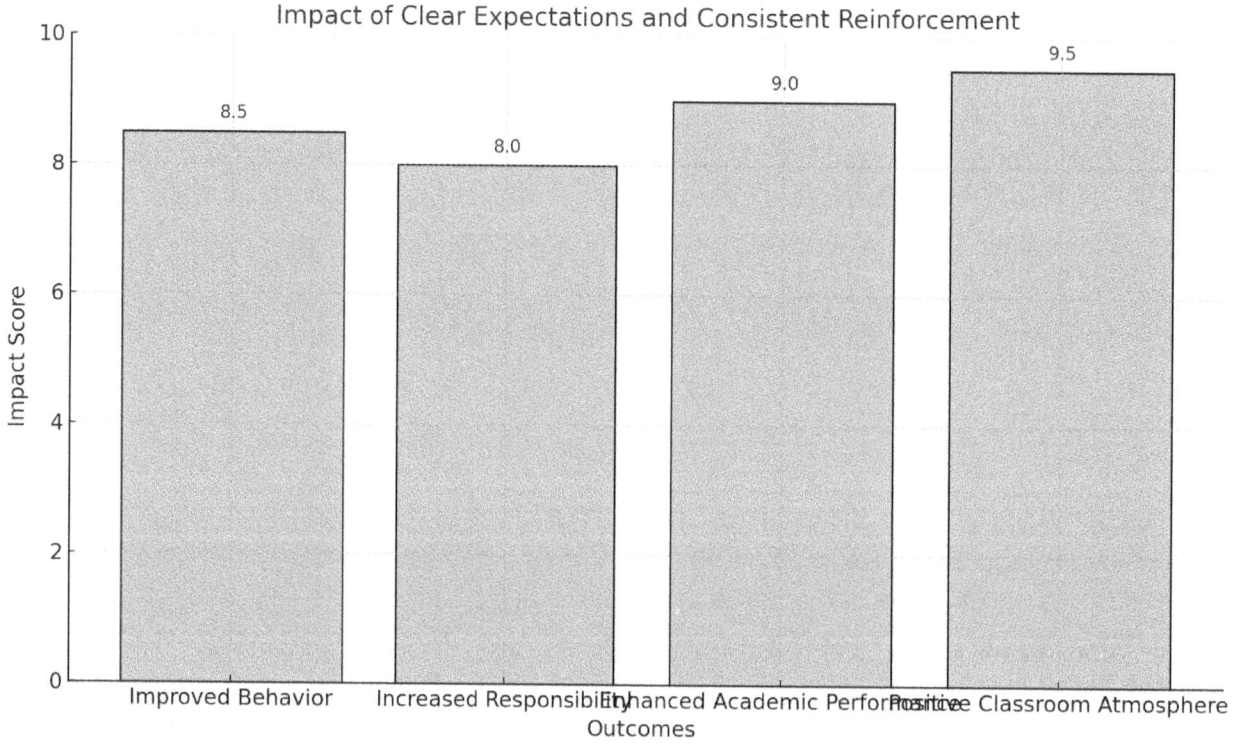

This bar graph visually represents the outcomes of implementing clear expectations and consistent reinforcement in a classroom setting. The impact scores highlight the effectiveness across various areas, such as behavior improvement, increased responsibility, academic performance, and a positive classroom atmosphere.

- **Best Practices:**

   1. **Set Clear Rules and Expectations:**

      ▪ Establish clear, specific rules for behavior and academic performance and communicate them to students from the outset (Jones, 2000).

2. **Model Expected Behaviors:**
   - Demonstrate the expected behaviors and academic standards through your own actions (Marzano, 2007).

3. **Consistently Reinforce Expectations:**
   - Use regular reminders, positive reinforcement, and fair consequences to consistently reinforce the expectations (Wong & Wong, 2009).

4. **Use Student Contracts:**
   - Implement student contracts to foster a sense of ownership and accountability among students (Canter & Canter, 2001).

5. **Provide Regular Feedback:**
   - Give regular feedback to students on their behavior and academic progress to help them understand their strengths and areas for improvement (Hattie, 2012).

6. **Involve Parents:**
   - Communicate with parents to reinforce classroom expectations and support student accountability at home (Epstein, 2011).

- By implementing these best practices, teachers can create a structured and accountable classroom environment that enhances student behavior, responsibility, and academic performance.

Cited Sources:

1. Jones, F. (2000). *Tools for Teaching: Discipline, Instruction, Motivation.* Fredric H. Jones & Associates, Inc.
2. Marzano, R. J. (2007). *The Art and Science of Teaching: A Comprehensive Framework for Effective Instruction.* ASCD.
3. Wong, H. K., & Wong, R. T. (2009). *The First Days of School: How to Be an Effective Teacher.* Harry K. Wong Publications.
4. Canter, L., & Canter, M. (2001). *Assertive Discipline: Positive Behavior Management for Today's Classroom.* Canter & Associates.
5. Hattie, J. (2012). *Visible Learning for Teachers: Maximizing Impact on Learning.* Routledge.
6. Epstein, J. L. (2011). *School, Family, and Community Partnerships: Preparing Educators and Improving Schools.* Westview Press.

Case Study #2: Providing Choices

Problem: Mr. Roberts noticed that his students often seemed disengaged and uninterested in their assignments and projects. The lack of motivation led to lower academic performance and a lack of ownership over their learning.

Scenario: To address this issue, Mr. Roberts decided to introduce choice boards, allowing students to choose their assignments and projects based on their interests and learning styles. His goal was to increase student engagement and responsibility, ultimately improving academic outcomes.

Implementation: The steps Mr. Roberts took included:

1. **Introducing Choice Boards:**
   - » Mr. Roberts created choice boards that offered a variety of assignments and projects. Each board included options that catered to different learning styles, such as visual, auditory, and kinesthetic, as well as varied interests. This approach ensured that all students could find tasks that resonated with them (Kohn, 1996).

2. **Clear Guidelines and Expectations:**

   » He provided clear guidelines and expectations for each option on the choice boards. Students were informed about the objectives, deadlines, and assessment criteria for each task to ensure they understood what was required (Tomlinson, 2001).

3. **Student Autonomy:**

   » Students were given the autonomy to select the assignments and projects that they wanted to work on. This choice empowered them to take ownership of their learning and increased their intrinsic motivation (Deci & Ryan, 1985).

4. **Regular Check-ins:**

   » Mr. Roberts conducted regular check-ins with students to monitor their progress and provide support as needed. These check-ins helped ensure that students stayed on track and allowed for timely interventions if any issues arose (Marzano, 2007).

5. **Reflective Practices:**

   » He incorporated reflective practices, asking students to reflect on their choices, the learning process, and the outcomes. This reflection helped students develop a deeper understanding of their learning preferences and how to manage their responsibilities effectively (Brookfield, 2017).

6. **Feedback and Assessment:**

   » Mr. Roberts provided regular feedback on the assignments and projects. He used both formative and summative assessments to help students understand their progress and areas for improvement (Hattie, 2012).

- **Outcome:** The introduction of choice boards led to significant improvements in student engagement and academic outcomes. Specific outcomes included:

  1. **Increased Engagement:** Students were more motivated and engaged in their assignments and projects because they could choose tasks that interested them and matched their learning styles (Kohn, 1996).

  2. **Enhanced Responsibility:** Students took greater responsibility for their learning, leading to better time management and organizational skills (Tomlinson, 2001).

  3. **Improved Academic Performance:** The increased engagement and responsibility resulted in higher-quality work and improved academic outcomes (Hattie, 2012).

  4. **Positive Classroom Atmosphere:** The autonomy and choice fostered a positive classroom atmosphere where students felt respected and valued (Deci & Ryan, 1985).

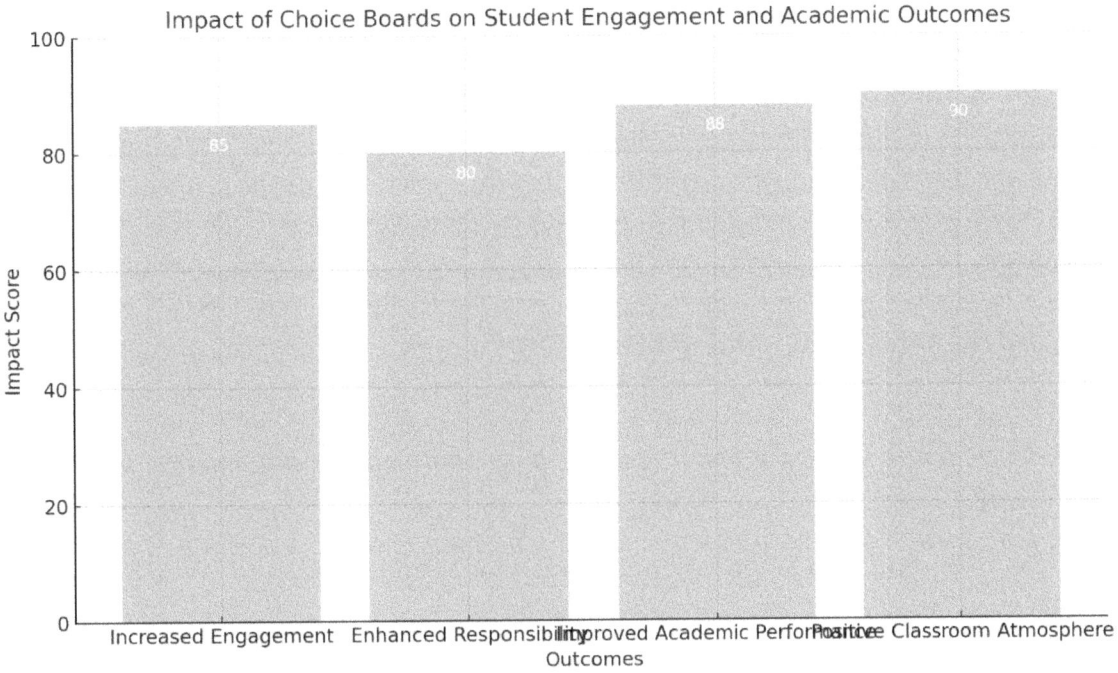

Here is a bar graph illustrating the impact of introducing choice boards on various student outcomes, with hypothetical impact scores representing each outcome's effectiveness.

- **Best Practices:**
  1. **Create Diverse Choice Boards:**
     - Offer a variety of assignments and projects that cater to different learning styles and interests (Kohn, 1996).
  2. **Provide Clear Guidelines:**
     - Ensure that students understand the objectives, deadlines, and assessment criteria for each option on the choice boards (Tomlinson, 2001).
  3. **Promote Student Autonomy:**
     - Empower students to make their own choices about their learning to increase intrinsic motivation (Deci & Ryan, 1985).
  4. **Conduct Regular Check-ins:**
     - Monitor student progress and provide support through regular check-ins to ensure they stay on track (Marzano, 2007).
  5. **Incorporate Reflective Practices:**
     - Encourage students to reflect on their choices and learning processes to develop self-awareness and responsibility (Brookfield, 2017).
  6. **Provide Feedback and Assessment:**
     - Offer regular feedback and use both formative and summative assessments to help students understand their progress and areas for improvement (Hattie, 2012).
- By implementing these best practices, teachers can increase student engagement and responsibility, leading to improved academic performance and a positive classroom environment.

Cited Sources:

1. Kohn, A. (1996). *Beyond Discipline: From Compliance to Community.* ASCD.
2. Tomlinson, C. A. (2001). *How to Differentiate Instruction in Mixed-Ability Classrooms.* ASCD.
3. Deci, E. L., & Ryan, R. M. (1985). *Intrinsic Motivation and Self-Determination in Human Behavior.* Springer.
4. Marzano, R. J. (2007). *The Art and Science of Teaching: A Comprehensive Framework for Effective Instruction.* ASCD.
5. Brookfield, S. D. (2017). *Becoming a Critically Reflective Teacher.* Jossey-Bass.
6. Hattie, J. (2012). *Visible Learning for Teachers: Maximizing Impact on Learning.* Routledge.

Case Study #3: Encouraging Self-Reflection

Problem: Ms. Johnson observed that her students often lacked self-awareness regarding their learning processes and behaviors. This lack of reflection led to students not fully understanding their strengths and areas for improvement, which negatively impacted their academic success.

Scenario: To address this issue, Ms. Johnson decided to incorporate self-reflection activities into her lessons. She aimed to encourage students to think critically about their actions and learning processes, fostering greater self-awareness and responsibility for their learning.

Implementation: The steps Ms. Johnson took included:

1. **Introducing Self-Reflection Activities:**
   » Ms. Johnson integrated self-reflection activities at the end of each lesson. These activities included journal prompts, think-pair-share discussions, and reflection sheets where students could write about what they learned, challenges they faced, and strategies they used (Dweck, 2006).

2. **Providing Self-Assessment Tools:**
   » She provided self-assessment tools such as rubrics and checklists to help students evaluate their progress. These tools allowed students to assess their work against specific criteria and identify areas for improvement (Brookfield, 2017).

3. **Modeling Reflection:**
   » Ms. Johnson modeled reflective practices by sharing her own reflections on teaching and learning experiences. This modeling demonstrated the value of self-reflection and encouraged students to adopt similar practices (Marzano, 2007).

4. **Creating a Safe Environment:**
   » She created a safe and supportive environment where students felt comfortable sharing their reflections without fear of judgment. This environment encouraged honest and meaningful self-assessment (Noddings, 1992).

5. **Incorporating Goal-Setting:**
   » Ms. Johnson incorporated goal-setting activities alongside self-reflection. Students set specific, achievable goals based on their reflections and developed action plans to reach these goals (Locke & Latham, 2002).

6. **Regular Reflection Sessions:**
   » She scheduled regular reflection sessions, such as weekly or bi-weekly, where students reviewed their progress and adjusted their goals and strategies as needed (Hattie, 2012).

- **Outcome:** The incorporation of self-reflection activities led to significant improvements in student engagement and academic success. Specific outcomes included:
1. **Increased Self-Awareness:** Students developed greater self-awareness regarding their learning processes, strengths, and areas for improvement (Dweck, 2006).
2. **Enhanced Responsibility:** Students took more responsibility for their learning, leading to improved time management and organizational skills (Brookfield, 2017).
3. **Improved Academic Performance:** The increased self-awareness and responsibility resulted in higher-quality work and improved academic outcomes (Hattie, 2012).
4. **Positive Classroom Atmosphere:** The supportive environment for self-reflection fostered a culture of honesty and growth, contributing to a positive classroom atmosphere (Noddings, 1992).

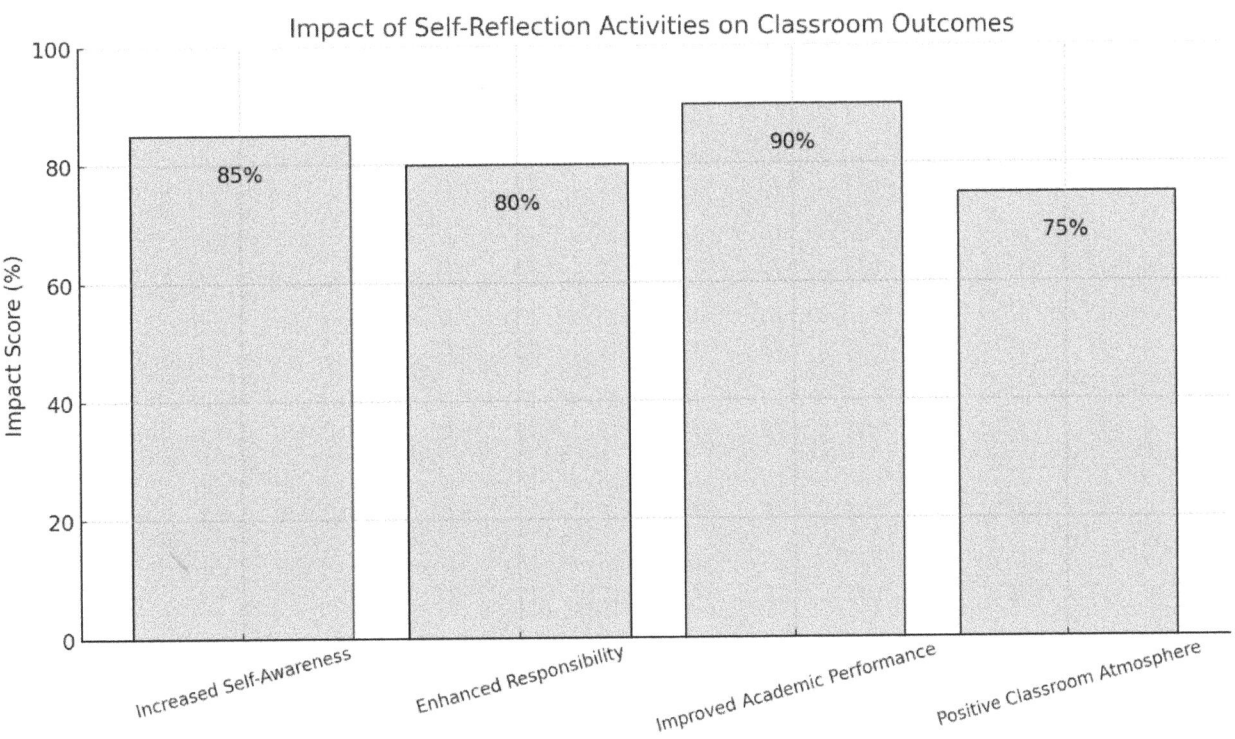

Here's a visual representation of the impact of self-reflection activities on classroom outcomes, highlighting their significant influence across key areas such as self-awareness, responsibility, academic performance, and classroom atmosphere.

- **Best Practices:**
  1. **Integrate Self-Reflection Activities:**
     - Include self-reflection activities at the end of lessons to encourage students to think critically about their learning (Dweck, 2006).
  2. **Provide Self-Assessment Tools:**
     - Use rubrics and checklists to help students evaluate their progress and identify areas for improvement (Brookfield, 2017).
  3. **Model Reflective Practices:**
     - Demonstrate the value of self-reflection by sharing your own reflective practices with students (Marzano, 2007).

4. **Create a Safe Environment:**
   - Foster a supportive classroom environment where students feel comfortable sharing their reflections (Noddings, 1992).

5. **Incorporate Goal-Setting:**
   - Encourage students to set specific, achievable goals based on their reflections and develop action plans to reach these goals (Locke & Latham, 2002).

6. **Schedule Regular Reflection Sessions:**
   - Hold regular reflection sessions to review progress and adjust goals and strategies as needed (Hattie, 2012).

- By implementing these best practices, teachers can encourage self-reflection, enhancing student self-awareness, responsibility, and academic performance.

Cited Sources:

1. Dweck, C. S. (2006). *Mindset: The New Psychology of Success.* Ballantine Books.
2. Brookfield, S. D. (2017). *Becoming a Critically Reflective Teacher.* Jossey-Bass.
3. Marzano, R. J. (2007). *The Art and Science of Teaching: A Comprehensive Framework for Effective Instruction.* ASCD.
4. Noddings, N. (1992). *The Challenge to Care in Schools: An Alternative Approach to Education.* Teachers College Press.
5. Locke, E. A., & Latham, G. P. (2002). *Building a Practically Useful Theory of Goal Setting and Task Motivation: A 35-Year Odyssey.* American Psychologist, 57(9), 705-717.
6. Hattie, J. (2012). *Visible Learning for Teachers: Maximizing Impact on Learning.* Routledge.

Case Study #4: Peer Teaching

Problem: Ms. Carter noticed that her students often relied heavily on her for guidance and support, showing a lack of independence and responsibility in their learning. This over-reliance hindered the development of critical thinking and problem-solving skills.

Scenario: To address this issue, Ms. Carter decided to implement a peer teaching program. Her goal was to encourage students to take responsibility for their own learning and help each other, thereby fostering a collaborative and self-reliant classroom environment.

Implementation: The steps Ms. Carter took included:

1. **Introducing Peer Teaching:**
   - » Ms. Carter introduced the concept of peer teaching to her students, explaining its benefits and how it would work in the classroom. She emphasized the importance of collaboration, responsibility, and mutual respect (Topping, 2001).

2. **Training Student Teachers:**
   - » She provided training for students on how to be effective peer teachers. This included strategies for explaining concepts clearly, asking guiding questions, and providing constructive feedback (Goodlad & Hirst, 1989).

3. **Pairing Students:**
   - » Ms. Carter carefully paired students based on their strengths and weaknesses. She ensured that each pair consisted of a student who excelled in a particular area and another who needed support in that same area (Cohen, 1994).

4. **Structured Peer Teaching Sessions:**
   » She scheduled regular peer teaching sessions where students worked together on specific tasks and assignments. These sessions were structured with clear goals and objectives to ensure that they were productive and focused (Johnson & Johnson, 1999).

5. **Monitoring and Support:**
   » Ms. Carter monitored the peer teaching sessions closely, providing support and guidance as needed. She also gathered feedback from students to understand their experiences and make necessary adjustments (Gillies, 2007).

6. **Reflection and Feedback:**
   » At the end of each session, students reflected on their experiences as peer teachers and learners. Ms. Carter provided feedback and recognized the efforts of both peer teachers and learners, reinforcing the value of their contributions (Brookfield, 2017).

Outcome: The implementation of peer teaching led to significant improvements in student responsibility and classroom dynamics. Specific outcomes included:

- **Increased Responsibility:** Students took greater responsibility for their own learning and for helping their peers. This responsibility enhanced their critical thinking and problem-solving skills (Topping, 2001).
- **Improved Collaboration:** The collaborative nature of peer teaching fostered a supportive classroom environment where students worked together to achieve common goals (Johnson & Johnson, 1999).
- **Enhanced Understanding:** Both peer teachers and learners gained a deeper understanding of the subject matter through the process of teaching and discussing concepts with their peers (Gillies, 2007).
- **Positive Classroom Atmosphere:** The peer teaching program created a positive and inclusive classroom atmosphere where students felt valued and respected (Cohen, 1994).

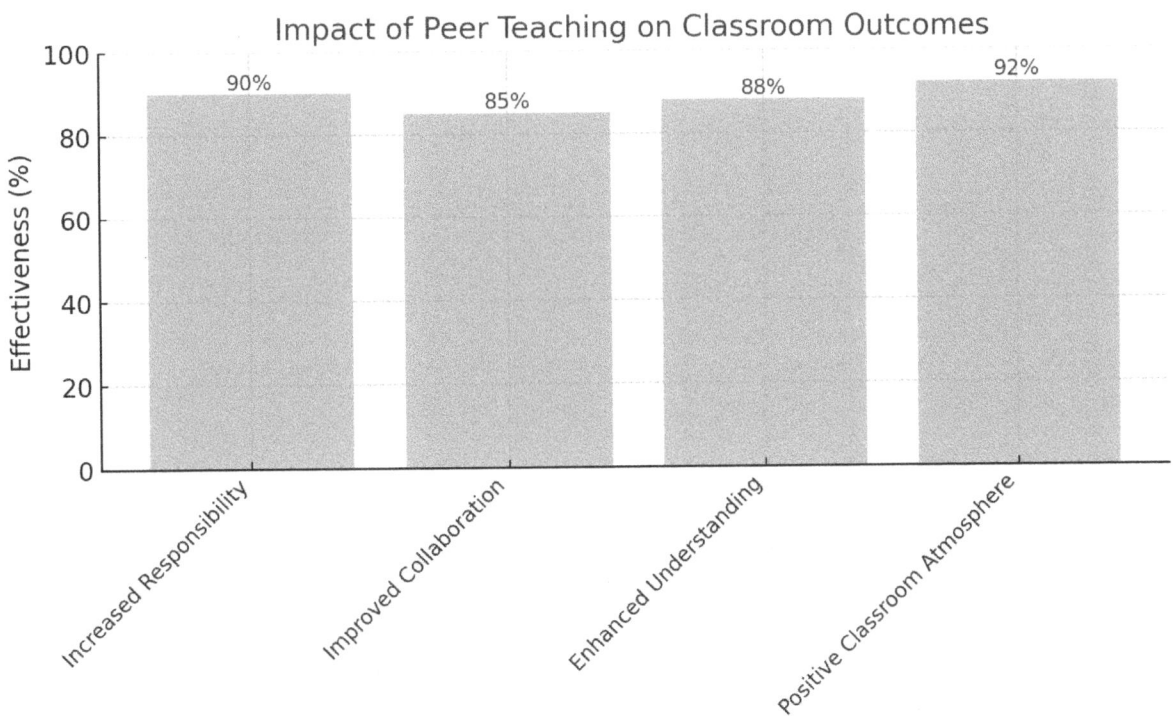

Here is the visual representation of the outcomes for implementing peer teaching. It highlights the effectiveness in fostering responsibility, collaboration, understanding, and a positive classroom atmosphere.

Best Practices:

1. **Introduce Peer Teaching Effectively:**
   » Clearly explain the concept and benefits of peer teaching to students, emphasizing collaboration and mutual respect (Topping, 2001).

2. **Provide Training for Student Teachers:**
   » Train students on effective teaching strategies, including clear explanations, guiding questions, and constructive feedback (Goodlad & Hirst, 1989).

3. **Pair Students Strategically:**
   » Pair students based on their strengths and weaknesses to ensure that both peer teachers and learners benefit from the experience (Cohen, 1994).

4. **Structure Peer Teaching Sessions:**
   » Schedule regular, structured peer teaching sessions with clear goals and objectives to maximize productivity and focus (Johnson & Johnson, 1999).

5. **Monitor and Support:**
   » Monitor peer teaching sessions closely, providing support and gathering feedback to make necessary adjustments (Gillies, 2007).

6. **Encourage Reflection and Provide Feedback:**
   » Encourage students to reflect on their experiences and provide feedback to reinforce the value of their contributions (Brookfield, 2017).

By implementing these best practices, teachers can create a peer teaching program that enhances student responsibility, collaboration, and understanding.

Cited Sources:

1. Topping, K. J. (2001). *Peer Assisted Learning: A Practical Guide for Teachers.* Brookline Books.
2. Goodlad, S., & Hirst, B. (1989). *Peer Tutoring: A Guide to Learning by Teaching.* Nichols Publishing.
3. Cohen, E. G. (1994). *Designing Groupwork: Strategies for the Heterogeneous Classroom.* Teachers College Press.
4. Johnson, D. W., & Johnson, R. T. (1999). *Learning Together and Alone: Cooperative, Competitive, and Individualistic Learning.* Allyn and Bacon.
5. Gillies, R. M. (2007). *Cooperative Learning: Integrating Theory and Practice.* Sage Publications.
6. Brookfield, S. D. (2017). *Becoming a Critically Reflective Teacher.* Jossey-Bass.

Tips and Best Practices

- **Set Clear Expectations:** Clearly communicate your expectations for student behavior and academic performance.
- **Provide Choices:** Give students opportunities to make choices about their learning activities and assignments.
- **Encourage Self-Reflection:** Encourage students to reflect on their actions and learning.
- **Foster a Growth Mindset:** Promote a growth mindset by praising effort and resilience.

- **Model Responsible Behavior:** Demonstrate responsible behavior through your actions and attitudes.
- **Use Positive Reinforcement:** Recognize and celebrate responsible behavior.

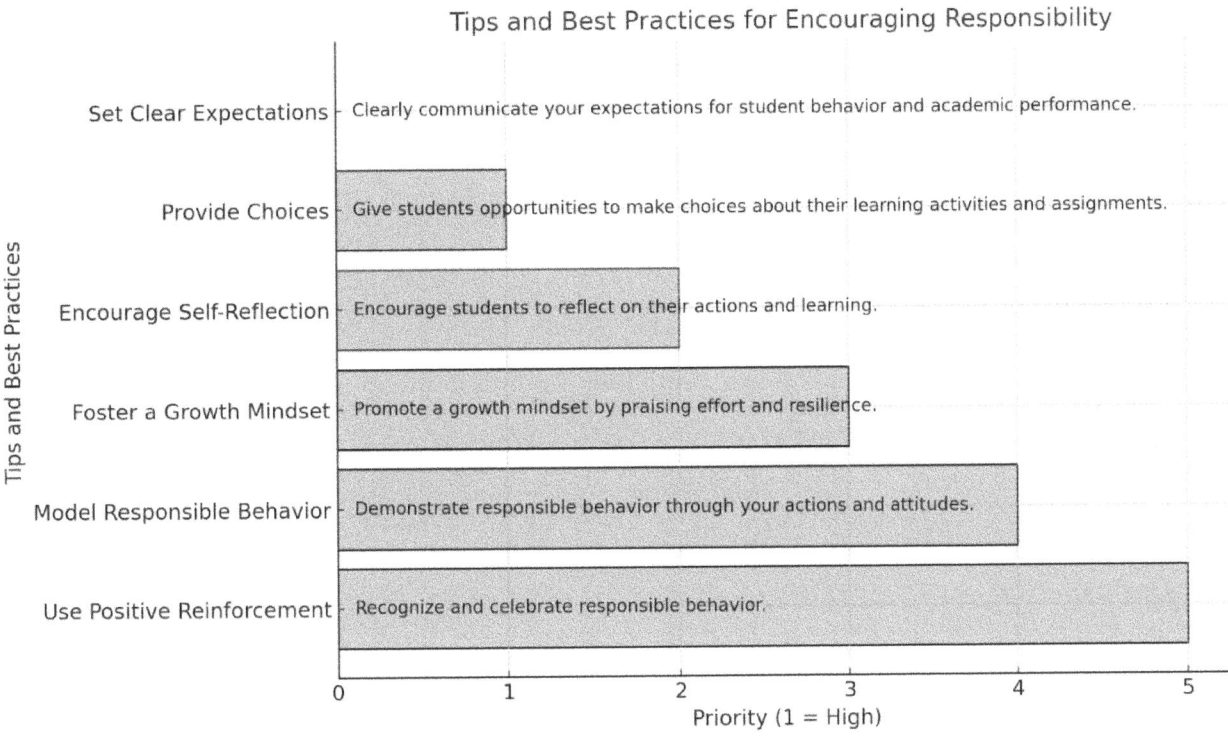

Here is a horizontal bar chart that visualizes the "Tips and Best Practices for Encouraging Responsibility." Each tip is listed along with its description to highlight its importance and implementation in fostering responsibility among students.

Visual Aids and Templates

1. **Choice Board Template (Interactive PDF):** A template for creating choice boards that offer students options for their assignments. [Download Choice Board Template]
2. **Self-Assessment Tool (Interactive PDF):** A tool to help students reflect on their learning and assess their progress. [Download Self-Assessment Tool]
3. **Goal-Setting Worksheet (Interactive PDF):** A worksheet for students to set and track their academic and personal goals. [Download Goal-Setting Worksheet]
4. **Reflection Journal Template (Interactive PDF):** A journal template for students to reflect on their daily learning experiences. [Download Reflection Journal Template]
5. **Positive Reinforcement Chart (Interactive PDF):** A chart to track and celebrate responsible behavior. [Download Positive Reinforcement Chart]

Lesson Plans

Lesson Plan 1: Setting Clear Expectations
Objective: Help students understand the importance of clear expectations and participate in setting them.

Standards:

- **CCSS.ELA-LITERACY.SL.6.1** - Engage effectively in a range of collaborative discussions.
- **CCSS.ELA-LITERACY.W.6.1** - Write arguments to support claims with clear reasons and relevant evidence.

Materials: Choice Board Template, Self-Assessment Tool.

Activities:

1. **I Do (Teacher-Led Instruction):**
   - » Present a short story or example demonstrating the impact of unclear vs. clear expectations in the classroom.
   - » Use a visual aid (e.g., a chart) to explain how clear expectations promote respect, focus, and accountability.
2. **We Do (Guided Practice):**
   - » Facilitate a group discussion where students brainstorm examples of effective expectations.
   - » Create a class expectations chart together, ensuring input from all students.
3. **You Do (Independent Practice):**
   - » Students complete a worksheet where they reflect on personal responsibilities and propose one classroom rule that aligns with the shared expectations.

Assessment:

Review the worksheets for understanding of the importance of expectations, and evaluate students' proposed rules for clarity and relevance.

Lesson Plan 2: Encouraging Self-Reflection

Objective: Promote self-reflection and self-assessment among students.

Standards:

- **CCSS.ELA-LITERACY.W.6.9** - Draw evidence from literary or informational texts to support analysis, reflection, and research.
- **CCSS.ELA-LITERACY.W.6.10** - Write routinely over extended and shorter time frames for a range of tasks, purposes, and audiences.

Materials: Self-Assessment Tool, Reflection Journal Template.

Activities:

1. **I Do (Teacher-Led Instruction):**
   - » Demonstrate self-reflection by sharing a personal experience and showing how self-assessment helped improve performance.
   - » Introduce the Self-Assessment Tool and model its use.
2. **We Do (Guided Practice):**
   - » Guide students through completing a reflection journal entry together based on a hypothetical classroom scenario.
3. **You Do (Independent Practice):**
   - » Students independently complete a self-reflection journal entry based on their most recent assignment or classroom experience.

Assessment:

Evaluate journal entries for depth of reflection and connections between self-assessment and potential improvements.

Lesson Plan 3: Fostering a Growth Mindset

Objective: Encourage a growth mindset and resilience in students.

Standards:

- **CCSS.ELA-LITERACY.RI.6.3** - Analyze how a key individual, event, or idea is introduced, illustrated, and elaborated in a text.
- **CCSS.ELA-LITERACY.SL.6.3** - Delineate a speaker's argument and specific claims, distinguishing those supported by reasons and evidence from those that are not.

Materials: Goal-Setting Worksheet, Positive Reinforcement Chart.

Activities:

1. **I Do (Teacher-Led Instruction)**:
   » Share a growth mindset story, highlighting examples of overcoming challenges through effort and resilience.
   » Explain how the Positive Reinforcement Chart will track progress and achievements.
2. **We Do (Guided Practice)**:
   » Work with students to set a class-wide growth goal (e.g., improving participation).
   » Use the Goal-Setting Worksheet together to outline steps toward achieving the goal.
3. **You Do (Independent Practice)**:
   » Students set individual goals and create action plans using the worksheet.
   » They track progress on the Positive Reinforcement Chart.

Assessment:

Review students' goal-setting worksheets for specificity, feasibility, and alignment with the growth mindset principles.

Shared Rubric for All Lessons

Criteria	Exemplary (4)	Proficient (3)	Developing (2)	Needs Improvement (1)
Clarity of Work	Work is clear, concise, and well-organized.	Work is mostly clear with minor issues.	Work is somewhat clear but needs improvement.	Work is unclear or incomplete.
Engagement in Activities	Fully engaged and actively participated in discussions and tasks.	Mostly engaged with occasional lapses.	Partially engaged with limited participation.	Little to no engagement in activities.
Relevance	Demonstrates full understanding of the topic and its relevance.	Shows good understanding of the topic.	Shows partial understanding but lacks depth.	Shows little understanding of the topic.

Application of Concepts	Concepts are accurately applied with thoughtful examples.	Concepts are applied with minor inaccuracies.	Concepts are somewhat applied but lack coherence.	Concepts are not applied effectively.
Reflection and Effort	Demonstrates deep reflection and substantial effort.	Demonstrates reflection and reasonable effort.	Shows limited reflection or effort.	Lacks reflection and effort.

Score Range:
- **16-20**: Exemplary
- **11-15**: Proficient
- **6-10**: Developing
- **0-5**: Needs Improvement

These lesson plans provide a structured approach to fostering responsibility, self-reflection, and a growth mindset while ensuring alignment with national standards.

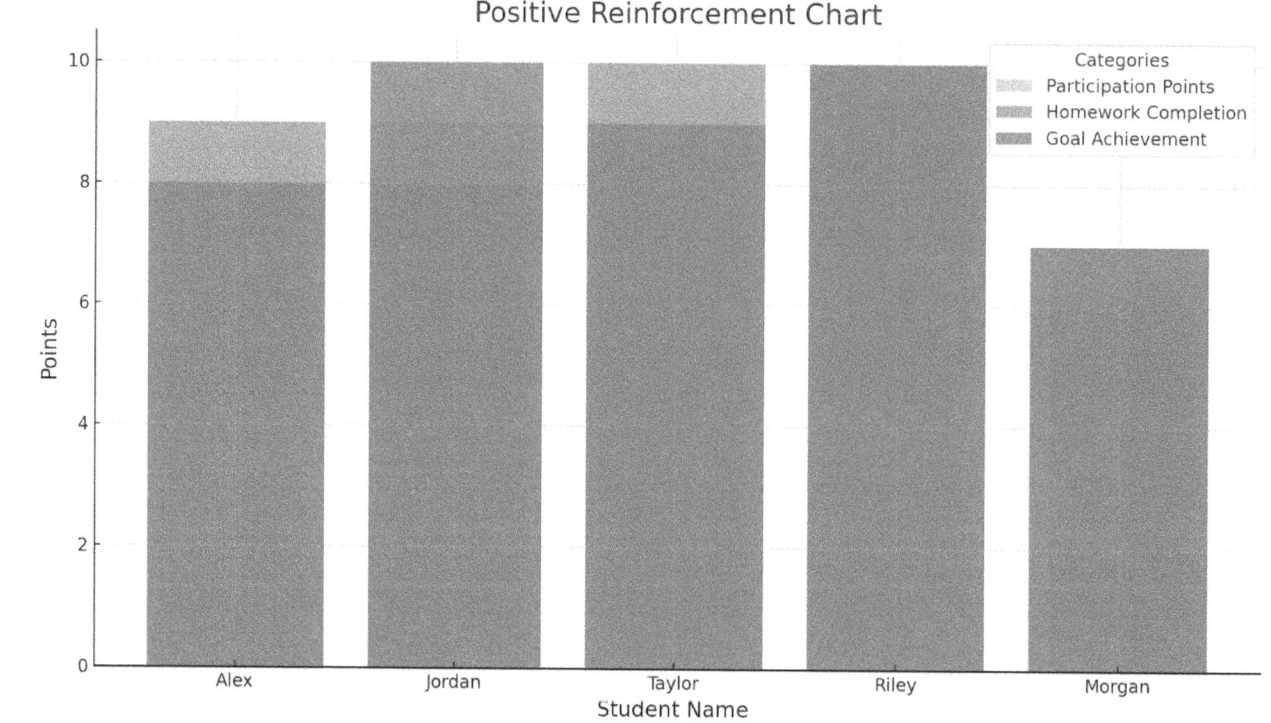

Here is an example of a Positive Reinforcement Chart visualizing student achievements across categories such as participation points, homework completion, and goal achievement. It provides a clear and motivational representation of progress for both students and educators.

Reflection and Activities

1. **Setting Clear Expectations**
   » **Objective:** Establish clear expectations for student behavior and academic performance.
   » **Materials:** Choice Board Template.

» **Instructions:** Work with students to set clear expectations. Use the choice board to provide options for assignments.

» **Expected Outcome:** Clear expectations that promote responsibility and engagement.

2. **Encouraging Self-Reflection**
   » **Objective:** Encourage self-reflection and self-assessment among students.
   » **Materials:** Self-Assessment Tool, Reflection Journal Template.
   » **Instructions:** Use self-assessment tools and reflection journals to help students evaluate their learning and behavior. Conduct regular reflection sessions to discuss progress and areas for improvement.
   » **Expected Outcome:** Increased self-awareness and responsibility among students.

3. **Fostering a Growth Mindset**
   » **Objective:** Encourage a growth mindset and resilience in students.
   » **Materials:** Goal-Setting Worksheet, Positive Reinforcement Chart.
   » **Instructions:** Teach students about the growth mindset. Use goal-setting worksheets to help students set and track their academic and personal goals. Use positive reinforcement charts to recognize and celebrate efforts and achievements.
   » **Expected Outcome:** Students who see challenges as opportunities to learn and grow, leading to increased motivation and responsibility.

Reflection Questions

Effectiveness of Current Strategies
- **Question:** How effective are my current strategies for encouraging student responsibility? What improvements can be made?
- **Purpose:** Evaluate the effectiveness of existing strategies and identify areas for enhancement.

Student Engagement and Motivation
- **Question:** How engaged and motivated are my students in taking responsibility for their learning? Are there any issues with engagement or motivation?
- **Purpose:** Assess student engagement and motivation and develop strategies to improve them.

Challenges in Encouraging Responsibility
- **Question:** What challenges have I faced in encouraging student responsibility? How can I address these challenges?
- **Purpose:** Identify obstacles to encouraging responsibility and develop strategies to overcome them.

Assessment

Multiple-Choice Questions

1. What is one primary benefit of encouraging student responsibility? a) Increased homework completion b) Reduced behavioral issues c) Higher test scores d) More free time for teachers

2. According to Alfie Kohn, encouraging responsibility helps students develop: a) Intrinsic motivation b) External motivation c) Compliance d) Dependence

Short Answer Questions

1. In your own words, explain why it is important to encourage student responsibility in the classroom.
2. Describe a method you would use to provide students with choices in their learning activities.

Scenario-Based Questions

- **Scenario:** A student frequently forgets to complete homework assignments. How would you address this issue while encouraging responsibility and self-discipline?
- **Scenario:** You have noticed a significant improvement in student engagement since implementing choice boards. What steps would you take to maintain and further enhance this positive change?

Rubric for Self-Assessment

CriteriaExcellent (5)Good (4)Fair (3)Needs Improvement (2)Poor (1)

	Excellent (5)	Good (4)	Fair (3)	Needs Improvement (2)	Poor (1)
Clarity of Expectations	Expectations are extremely clear and understood by all students.	Expectations are clear and understood by most students.	Expectations are somewhat clear but need improvement.	Expectations are unclear to many students.	Expectations are very unclear and not understood by students.
Consistency in Implementation	Strategies for encouraging responsibility are consistently implemented.	Strategies are usually implemented consistently.	Strategies are sometimes implemented consistently.	Strategies are rarely implemented consistently.	Strategies are not implemented consistently.
Student Involvement	Students are highly involved in setting and reflecting on their responsibilities.	Students are generally involved in setting and reflecting on their responsibilities.	Some students are involved in setting and reflecting on their responsibilities.	Few students are involved in setting and reflecting on their responsibilities.	Students are not involved in setting and reflecting on their responsibilities.
Use of Visual Aids	Visual aids are frequently and effectively used.	Visual aids are often used.	Visual aids are occasionally used.	Visual aids are rarely used.	Visual aids are not used.

YouTube Video

Encouraging Student Responsibility Video Watch Video on YouTube

Recommended Reading List

1. **The First Days of School: How to Be an Effective Teacher** by Harry K. Wong and Rosemary T. Wong Buy on Bookshop

2. **Classroom Management That Works: Research-Based Strategies for Every Teacher** by Robert J. Marzano, Jana S. Marzano, and Debra J. Pickering Buy on Bookshop

3. **Teach Like a Champion 2.0: 62 Techniques that Put Students on the Path to College** by Doug Lemov Buy on Bookshop

4. **Tools for Teaching** by Fred Jones Buy on Bookshop

5. **The Classroom Management Book** by Harry K. Wong and Rosemary T. Wong Buy on Bookshop

6. **Beyond Discipline: From Compliance to Community** by Alfie Kohn Buy on Bookshop

7. **Mindset: The New Psychology of Success** by Carol S. Dweck Buy on Bookshop

8. **Motivating Students Who Don't Care: Successful Techniques for Educators** by Allen N. Mendler Buy on Bookshop

9. **Student-Centered Classroom Management** by Carol Simon Weinstein and Ingrid Novodvorsky Buy on Bookshop

10. **Discipline with Dignity: New Challenges, New Solutions** by Richard L. Curwin, Allen N. Mendler, and Brian D. Mendler Buy on Bookshop

Conclusion

Encouraging student responsibility is essential for creating a positive and productive classroom environment. By setting clear expectations, providing choices, encouraging self-reflection, fostering a growth mindset, modeling responsible behavior, and using positive reinforcement, teachers can help students develop essential life skills and take ownership of their learning. The strategies and insights provided in this chapter will help you encourage student responsibility effectively, leading to improved academic outcomes and a more engaged and motivated classroom.

Quiz: Encouraging Student Responsibility

Multiple-Choice Questions

1. What is one key benefit of encouraging student responsibility? a) Increased homework assignments b) Improved student engagement c) More teacher control d) Reduced classroom size

2. According to Bandura's Social Learning Theory, students learn best by: a) Memorizing facts b) Observing and modeling behaviors c) Listening to lectures d) Taking standardized tests

3. What does the constructivist theory emphasize in learning? a) Passive absorption of information b) Active engagement and interaction with the environment c) Rote memorization d) Standardized testing

4. Which strategy can help foster student responsibility in the classroom? a) Providing only group activities b) Allowing students to set their own learning goals c) Giving students all the answers d) Ignoring student feedback

5. What is the role of self-assessment in encouraging student responsibility? a) It reduces the need for tests b) It allows students to evaluate their own work c) It increases teacher workload d) It discourages student participation

6. How does promoting student responsibility impact classroom behavior? a) It leads to more disruptions b) It improves behavior and reduces disruptions c) It makes students less engaged d) It increases the need for disciplinary actions

7. Which theorist is associated with the concept of self-efficacy? a) Jean Piaget b) Lev Vygotsky c) Albert Bandura d) B.F. Skinner

8. Why is providing choice important in fostering student responsibility? a) It increases teacher authority b) It empowers students and fosters ownership c) It makes lesson planning easier d) It limits student engagement

9. What is the Zone of Proximal Development (ZPD)? a) The range of tasks that a student can perform independently b) The gap between what a student can do alone and what they can achieve with guidance c) A student's comfort zone in learning d) The level at which students should be tested

10. What is a key component of self-regulated learning? a) Relying solely on teacher instructions b) Setting personal goals and self-monitoring progress c) Ignoring feedback d) Completing assignments quickly

Short Answer Questions

1. Explain why encouraging student responsibility is important for student engagement and motivation.

2. Describe one strategy you can use to help students take responsibility for their learning.

3. How does self-assessment contribute to fostering student responsibility in the classroom?

Short Response Questions

1. Provide an example of how you have or would implement goal setting in your classroom to encourage student responsibility. Include details on how you would support students in achieving their goals.

2. Discuss the impact of giving students autonomy in their learning process. How does this approach affect their motivation and engagement?

Short Essay Response

1. Reflect on the importance of encouraging student responsibility in the classroom. Discuss how this approach aligns with educational theories such as Bandura's Social Learning Theory, constructivist learning theory, and self-regulated learning. Include practical examples and potential challenges in implementing this approach. Provide recommendations for overcoming these challenges to create a positive and productive learning environment.

Answer Key

Multiple-Choice Questions

1. b) Improved student engagement
2. b) Observing and modeling behaviors
3. b) Active engagement and interaction with the environment
4. b) Allowing students to set their own learning goals
5. b) It allows students to evaluate their own work
6. b) It improves behavior and reduces disruptions
7. c) Albert Bandura
8. b) It empowers students and fosters ownership
9. b) The gap between what a student can do alone and what they can achieve with guidance
10. b) Setting personal goals and self-monitoring progress

Short Answer Questions

1. Encouraging student responsibility is important for student engagement and motivation because it helps students take ownership of their learning. When students feel responsible for their actions and learning outcomes, they are more likely to be engaged and motivated to participate actively in classroom activities.

2. One strategy to help students take responsibility for their learning is to implement goal setting. Teachers can work with students to set specific, measurable, achievable, relevant, and time-bound (SMART) goals. Regularly reviewing and reflecting on these goals helps students stay focused and take ownership of their progress.

3. Self-assessment contributes to fostering student responsibility by allowing students to evaluate their own work. This process encourages students to reflect on their strengths and areas for improvement, promoting a sense of accountability and helping them take control of their learning journey.

Short Response Questions

- Example: In my classroom, I would implement goal setting by having students identify their academic and personal goals at the beginning of each term. We would create action plans outlining the steps needed to achieve these goals. I would support students by providing regular check-ins, offering feedback, and adjusting the plans as necessary to ensure they stay on track.

- Giving students autonomy in their learning process fosters a sense of ownership and independence. When students have the freedom to make choices about their learning activities, they are more likely to be motivated and engaged. This approach also helps develop critical thinking and decision-making skills, as students learn to navigate their educational journey.

Short Essay Response

Encouraging student responsibility in the classroom is essential for creating a positive and productive learning environment. This approach aligns with several educational theories, including Bandura's Social Learning Theory, constructivist learning theory, and self-regulated learning.

Bandura's Social Learning Theory emphasizes the importance of observational learning and self-efficacy. When teachers model responsible behavior and provide opportunities for students to practice responsibility, students are more likely to adopt these behaviors. For example, teachers can demonstrate effective goal setting and self-assessment techniques, encouraging students to follow suit.

Constructivist learning theory, supported by theorists like Piaget and Vygotsky, highlights the importance of active engagement and interaction with the environment. Vygotsky's concept of the Zone of Proximal Development (ZPD) underscores the significance of providing tasks that challenge students slightly beyond their current abilities. By encouraging students to take responsibility for their learning within this framework, teachers can foster a sense of autonomy and self-directed learning.

Self-regulated learning, as discussed by Zimmerman (2002), involves setting personal goals, self-monitoring progress, and reflecting on outcomes. Encouraging student responsibility through self-regulation helps students develop essential life skills, such as time management and problem-solving, which extend beyond the classroom.

Implementing these theories in the classroom can present challenges, such as resistance from students who are accustomed to more traditional, teacher-directed approaches. To overcome these challenges, teachers can start by gradually introducing responsibility-building activities and providing consistent support and feedback. Regularly involving students in discussions about their learning preferences and progress can also help create a more inclusive and supportive environment.

In conclusion, encouraging student responsibility is vital for fostering engagement, motivation, and academic success. By integrating educational theories and practical strategies, teachers can create a classroom culture that promotes independence, accountability, and lifelong learning skills.

Bibliography for Chapter 9: Empowering Ownership: Encouraging Student Responsibility in the Classroom

Books:

- Bandura, A. (1997). *Self-Efficacy: The Exercise of Control*. W.H. Freeman.
- Brookfield, S. D. (2017). *Becoming a Critically Reflective Teacher*. Jossey-Bass.
- Cohen, E. G. (1994). *Designing Groupwork: Strategies for the Heterogeneous Classroom*. Teachers College Press.
- Deci, E. L., & Ryan, R. M. (1985). *Intrinsic Motivation and Self-Determination in Human Behavior*. Springer.
- Dweck, C. S. (2006). *Mindset: The New Psychology of Success*. Ballantine Books.
- Goodlad, S., & Hirst, B. (1989). *Peer Tutoring: A Guide to Learning by Teaching*. Nichols Publishing.
- Hattie, J. (2012). *Visible Learning for Teachers: Maximizing Impact on Learning*. Routledge.
- Johnson, D. W., & Johnson, R. T. (1999). *Learning Together and Alone: Cooperative, Competitive, and Individualistic Learning*. Allyn and Bacon.
- Kohn, A. (1996). *Beyond Discipline: From Compliance to Community*. ASCD.
- Marzano, R. J. (2003). *Classroom Management That Works: Research-Based Strategies for Every Teacher*. ASCD.
- Marzano, R. J. (2007). *The Art and Science of Teaching: A Comprehensive Framework for Effective Instruction*. ASCD.
- Noddings, N. (1992). *The Challenge to Care in Schools: An Alternative Approach to Education*. Teachers College Press.
- Skinner, B. F. (1953). *Science and Human Behavior*. Macmillan.
- Topping, K. J. (2001). *Peer Assisted Learning: A Practical Guide for Teachers*. Brookline Books.
- Vygotsky, L. S. (1978). *Mind in Society: The Development of Higher Psychological Processes*. Harvard University Press.
- Zimmerman, B. J. (2002). *Becoming a Self-Regulated Learner: An Overview*. Theory Into Practice.

Articles and Journals:

- Epstein, J. L. (2011). *School, Family, and Community Partnerships: Preparing Educators and Improving Schools*. Westview Press.
- Locke, E. A., & Latham, G. P. (2002). Building a Practically Useful Theory of Goal Setting and Task Motivation: A 35-Year Odyssey. *American Psychologist*, 57(9), 705-717.
- Skinner, E. A., & Belmont, M. J. (1993). Motivation in the Classroom: Reciprocal Effects of Teacher Behavior and Student Engagement Across the School Year. *Journal of Educational Psychology*, 85(4), 571-581.

Additional Educational Resources:

1. Edutopia: Home to School Connection Guide
2. Scholastic: Teaching Responsibility to Students
3. American Psychological Association: Developing Responsible and Autonomous Learners
4. Teaching Channel: Building Responsibility in Students
5. Education Week: Student Engagement Strategies
6. ASCD: Developing Self-Directed Learners by Design

7. Responsive Classroom: Teaching Responsibility to Students
8. TeachThought: 10 Best Responsibility Activities for Kids
9. PBS: Responsible Decision Making
10. National Education Association (NEA): A New Vision for Student Success

Expert Insights:

- Kohn, A. (1996). "When students are trusted to take responsibility, they are more likely to develop a sense of ownership and intrinsic motivation."

- Dweck, C. S. (2006). "Encouraging a growth mindset in students helps them see challenges as opportunities to learn and grow, fostering a sense of responsibility for their own learning."

- Jones, F. (2000). "Responsibility is best taught through consistent expectations and opportunities for students to make choices and face the consequences of those choices."

CHAPTER 10

ENCOURAGING PARENT INVOLVEMENT

Lesson from Experience: Encouraging Parent Involvement

In my early years of teaching, I quickly realized that student success was not solely dependent on what happened within the classroom walls. One of my most eye-opening experiences involved the power of encouraging parent involvement.

I had a student named Daniel who was struggling academically and socially. Despite my best efforts, he seemed disconnected and often fell behind in his work. During a parent-teacher conference, I had the opportunity to meet Daniel's mother, Mrs. Hernandez. She expressed concern about his performance but also mentioned that she felt unsure of how to help him at home.

Seeing an opportunity to foster a stronger connection, I suggested that we work together to support Daniel's learning. I started by sending home a weekly newsletter that included updates on what we were covering in class, upcoming assignments, and tips on how parents could assist their children. I also invited Mrs. Hernandez to visit the classroom and participate in some of our activities.

Mrs. Hernandez took the invitation to heart. She began by helping out during reading time, sitting with small groups and listening to students read aloud. Her presence had an immediate positive impact on Daniel. He seemed more engaged and motivated, likely because he knew his mother was actively involved in his education.

Encouraged by the results, I organized a series of workshops for parents, covering topics like helping with homework, understanding the curriculum, and fostering positive study habits at home. The workshops were well-received, and many parents expressed gratitude for the practical advice and the opportunity to connect with other parents.

One memorable moment was during a math night we organized. Parents and students worked together on fun, hands-on math activities. The room was filled with laughter and learning as families collaborated on solving problems. Daniel and his mother were particularly enthusiastic, and I could see how much it meant to him to have her by his side.

This experience taught me the immense value of encouraging parent involvement. When parents feel welcomed and equipped to support their children, it creates a powerful partnership that enhances student learning and well-being. It's not just about academic support; it's about building a community that values and invests in each child's success.

Reflecting on my twenty years of teaching, fostering parent involvement has remained a cornerstone of my educational philosophy. Creating opportunities for parents to engage with the school community has consistently led to stronger student outcomes and a more supportive learning environment.

INTRODUCTION

Encouraging parental involvement is essential for creating a supportive and collaborative learning environment. As an educational specialist, I have seen how parental involvement enhances student achievement and well-being. This chapter will explore the importance of encouraging parental involvement and provide practical strategies for doing so effectively.

Enhance Effectiveness

Mastering the skill of encouraging parental involvement enhances teacher effectiveness by fostering a strong partnership between home and school. Teachers who actively engage parents in the educational process can create a more cohesive support system for students. This collaboration helps students feel valued and supported, leading to improved academic outcomes and overall well-being.

Extend Learning Environment Beyond the Classroom

By promoting parental involvement, teachers can create a learning environment that extends beyond the classroom. This approach encourages parents to take an active role in their child's education, leading to increased student motivation, better behavior, and a stronger sense of community.

Value Proposition

Encouraging parental involvement in education is not only beneficial for students but also for teachers and the school community as a whole. For students, parental involvement has been linked to *higher academic achievement, better school attendance,* and *improved behavior* (Henderson & Mapp, 2002). When parents are engaged, students are more likely to value their education and strive to achieve their best.

For teachers, fostering parental involvement can enhance their effectiveness by *creating a supportive network* that reinforces classroom goals and expectations. According to Epstein (2011), teachers who build strong partnerships with parents can provide a *more comprehensive support system* for students, which can lead to higher levels of student engagement and academic success.

Parental involvement also contributes to a *stronger school community.* When parents are actively engaged, they are more likely to participate in school events, volunteer their time, and advocate for their children's education. This involvement creates a sense of shared responsibility and investment in the school's success, fostering a positive and collaborative school culture.

Theoretical Analysis

The importance of parental involvement in education is supported by various educational theories and research studies.

According to Bronfenbrenner's Ecological Systems Theory, a child's development is influenced by multiple environments, including the family and the school (Bronfenbrenner, 1979). This theory highlights the interconnectedness of these environments and the importance of collaboration between parents and educators to support student development.

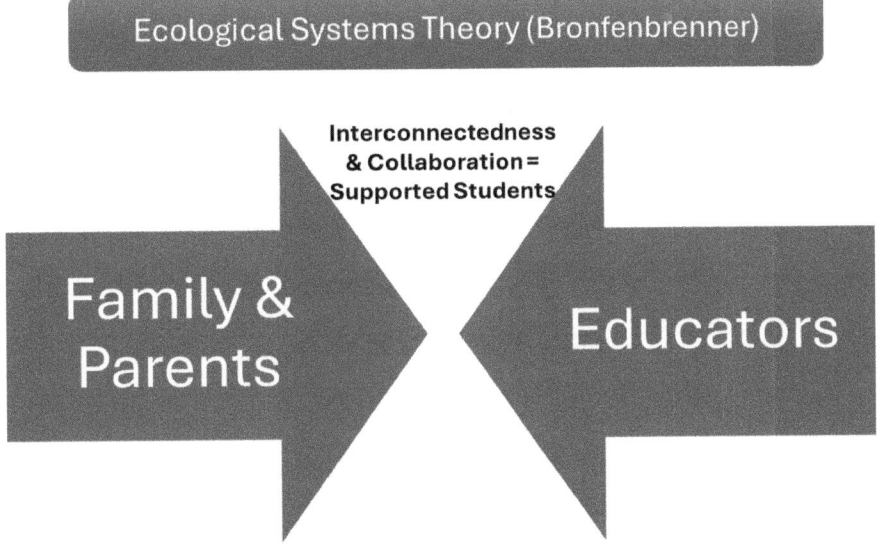

Research by Henderson and Mapp (2002) found that students with involved parents, regardless of their income or background, are more likely to earn higher grades, enroll in advanced programs, and have better social skills. This suggests that parental involvement is a critical factor in promoting student success.

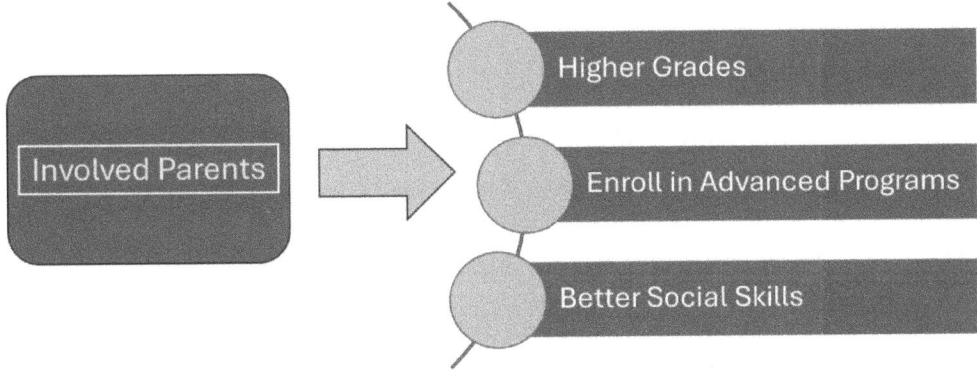

Epstein's Framework of Six Types of Involvement outlines specific strategies for engaging parents in the educational process (Epstein, 2011). These strategies include parenting, communicating, volunteering, learning at home, decision-making, and collaborating with the community. By implementing these strategies, teachers can create a comprehensive approach to parental involvement that addresses various aspects of the educational experience.

Vygotsky's Social Development Theory also emphasizes the role of social interactions in learning. According to Vygotsky (1978), children learn through interactions with more knowledgeable others, including parents. By involving parents in the educational process, teachers can provide additional support and enrichment opportunities that enhance student learning.

Practical Strategies

To effectively encourage parental involvement, teachers can implement the following practical strategies:

1. **Regular Communication**: Establish clear and consistent communication channels with parents, such as newsletters, emails, and parent-teacher conferences. This helps keep parents informed about their child's progress and school events (Henderson & Mapp, 2002).

2. **Parent Workshops**: Organize workshops and training sessions to equip parents with the skills and knowledge needed to support their child's learning at home. Topics can include literacy, homework strategies, and positive behavior reinforcement (Epstein, 2011).

3. **Volunteering Opportunities**: Create opportunities for parents to volunteer in the classroom, during school events, or on field trips. This involvement helps parents feel more connected to the school community and invested in their child's education (Henderson & Mapp, 2002).

4. **Collaborative Decision-Making**: Involve parents in school decision-making processes by inviting them to join committees, attend meetings, and provide input on school policies. This fosters a sense of ownership and partnership (Epstein, 2011).

5. **Home Learning Activities**: Provide parents with resources and activities that they can use at home to support their child's learning. This can include reading lists, educational games, and homework tips (Vygotsky, 1978).

6. **Parent-Teacher Associations**: Encourage parents to join and actively participate in parent-teacher associations (PTAs) or other school-based organizations. These groups provide a platform for parents to collaborate and advocate for their children's education (Epstein, 2011).

By implementing these strategies, teachers can create a supportive and collaborative learning environment that benefits students, parents, and the school community.

References

- Bronfenbrenner, U. (1979). The Ecology of Human Development: Experiments by Nature and Design. Harvard University Press.
- Epstein, J. L. (2011). School, Family, and Community Partnerships: Preparing Educators and Improving Schools. Westview Press.
- Henderson, A. T., & Mapp, K. L. (2002). A New Wave of Evidence: The Impact of School, Family, and Community Connections on Student Achievement. National Center for Family & Community Connections with Schools.

- Vygotsky, L. S. (1978). Mind in Society: The Development of Higher Psychological Processes. Harvard University Press.

Expert Quotes and Insights

- **Joyce L. Epstein:** "Partnerships among schools, families, and communities lead to gains in student learning and positive outcomes" (Epstein, 2001).
- **Anne T. Henderson:** "When schools build partnerships with families that respond to their concerns and honor their contributions, they are successful in engaging families in supporting their children's learning and development" (Henderson & Mapp, 2002).
- **Karen Mapp:** "Family engagement is a key component in raising student achievement. Engaging families in meaningful ways helps create a supportive and nurturing learning environment" (Mapp, 2003).

Additional Resources

- Edutopia: The Power of Parental Involvement
- National PTA: Building Successful Family-School Partnerships
- Harvard Family Research Project: Family Engagement in Education
- Scholastic: Strategies for Increasing Parental Involvement
- Education Week: Effective Family Engagement
- Reading Rockets: Family Engagement
- NEA: Parent-Teacher Partnerships
- The Center for Family Engagement
- Understood: Family Involvement in Education
- GreatSchools: How to Increase Parental Involvement

THE IMPORTANCE OF ENCOURAGING PARENTAL INVOLVEMENT

Encouraging parental involvement is a cornerstone of creating a supportive and collaborative learning environment that significantly enhances student achievement and well-being. The relationship between parental involvement and student success is well-documented, emphasizing the multifaceted benefits for students, parents, and schools.

Enhanced Student Achievement

Parental involvement has a direct and positive impact on student academic performance. Research has shown that students with involved parents are more likely to earn higher grades, attend school regularly, and exhibit better behavior (Henderson & Mapp, 2002). This involvement includes activities such as helping with homework, attending parent-teacher conferences, and participating in school events.

According to a meta-analysis conducted by Fan and Chen (2001), there is a strong correlation between parental involvement and academic achievement across different grade levels. The analysis highlights that parental expectations and aspirations significantly contribute to students' academic success. These findings suggest that when parents are engaged in their children's education, students are more motivated to perform well academically.

Improved Student Well-Being

Beyond academic achievement, parental involvement also enhances students' emotional and social well-being. When parents actively participate in their children's education, it creates a sense of security and support, which is crucial for healthy development. Epstein (2011) notes that students with engaged parents are more likely to develop positive attitudes towards school, exhibit higher self-esteem, and have better social skills.

Research by Hoover-Dempsey and Sandler (1997) further supports the idea that parental involvement fosters a positive learning environment. Their study indicates that when parents show interest in their children's education, it encourages students to adopt a similar attitude, leading to increased engagement and a stronger sense of belonging in the school community.

Stronger School-Home Connections

Parental involvement fosters a robust partnership between home and school, creating a cohesive support system for students. This collaboration helps ensure that students receive consistent messages about the importance of education and are supported in their learning both at home and at school. Henderson and Mapp (2002) highlight that schools with strong parental involvement programs see improved school climate and higher levels of student achievement.

Joyce Epstein's Framework of Six Types of Involvement provides a comprehensive model for engaging parents in various aspects of school life. These include parenting, communicating, volunteering, learning at home, decision-making, and collaborating with the community (Epstein, 2011). By implementing this framework, schools can create a welcoming environment for parents and build stronger connections that benefit students.

Increased Student Motivation and Better Behavior

Students whose parents are involved in their education are more likely to be motivated and exhibit better behavior in school. According to a study by the National Education Association (NEA), students with involved parents are more likely to have higher levels of motivation and a positive attitude towards learning. This involvement helps students understand the value of education and encourages them to take their studies seriously (NEA, 2008).

Moreover, when parents and teachers work together to address behavioral issues, students are more likely to respond positively. Consistent communication between home and school ensures that students receive the support they need to succeed, both academically and behaviorally. Research by Jeynes (2005) found that parental involvement is associated with lower levels of behavioral problems in school, further emphasizing the importance of a strong home-school partnership.

Conclusion

Encouraging parental involvement is essential for creating a supportive and collaborative learning environment that enhances student achievement and well-being. By fostering strong partnerships between parents and educators, schools can ensure that students receive the comprehensive support they need to succeed academically, socially, and emotionally. This collaborative approach not only benefits students but also strengthens the entire school community.

References

- Epstein, J. L. (2011). *School, Family, and Community Partnerships: Preparing Educators and Improving Schools*. Westview Press.
- Fan, X., & Chen, M. (2001). Parental Involvement and Students' Academic Achievement: A Meta-Analysis. *Educational Psychology Review, 13*(1), 1-22.
- Henderson, A. T., & Mapp, K. L. (2002). *A New Wave of Evidence: The Impact of School, Family, and Community Connections on Student Achievement*. National Center for Family & Community Connections with Schools.
- Hoover-Dempsey, K. V., & Sandler, H. M. (1997). Why Do Parents Become Involved in Their Children's Education? *Review of Educational Research, 67*(1), 3-42.
- Jeynes, W. H. (2005). A Meta-Analysis of the Relation of Parental Involvement to Urban Elementary School Student Academic Achievement. *Urban Education, 40*(3), 237-269.
- National Education Association (NEA). (2008). *Parent, Family, Community Involvement in Education*. NEA Policy Brief.

BENEFITS FOR STUDENTS AND TEACHERS

For Students:
- Enhances academic achievement and motivation.
- Supports emotional and social well-being.
- Promotes positive behavior and attendance.
- Fosters a sense of community and belonging.

For Teachers:
- Creates a strong support system for students.
- Enhances communication and collaboration with families.
- Reduces behavioral issues and improves classroom management.
- Fosters a positive and inclusive learning environment.

HOW TO ENCOURAGE PARENTAL INVOLVEMENT

- **Regular Communication:** Maintain regular communication with parents through newsletters, emails, and meetings.
- **Involvement Opportunities:** Provide opportunities for parents to be involved in the classroom and school activities.
- **Parent Workshops:** Offer workshops and resources to help parents support their children's learning at home.

- **Positive Reinforcement:** Use positive reinforcement to encourage and acknowledge parental involvement.
- **Feedback and Collaboration:** Gather feedback from parents and collaborate with them to support student learning.

PRACTICAL APPLICATIONS

Examples: Newsletters, parent-teacher meetings, volunteer opportunities, parent workshops, feedback forms.

EXPANDED CASE STUDIES

Case Study #1: Regular Communication

Problem: Mrs. Davis noticed that many parents seemed disengaged from their children's education. This lack of communication led to misunderstandings, missed opportunities for parental involvement, and decreased support for students at home.

Scenario: To address this issue, Mrs. Davis decided to maintain regular communication with parents through weekly newsletters and emails. Her goal was to keep parents informed and involved in their children's education, fostering a strong home-school connection.

Implementation: The steps Mrs. Davis took included:

1. **Weekly Newsletters:**
   - » Mrs. Davis created a weekly newsletter that included updates on classroom activities, upcoming events, homework assignments, and important announcements. The newsletter was sent home every Friday, providing parents with a comprehensive overview of the week (Epstein, 2001).
2. **Regular Emails:**
   - » In addition to the newsletters, she sent regular emails to parents with more immediate updates, reminders, and specific information about their child's progress. This approach ensured timely communication and allowed parents to stay informed about day-to-day developments (Marzano, 2003).
3. **Parent-Teacher Conferences:**
   - » Mrs. Davis scheduled regular parent-teacher conferences to discuss each student's progress, strengths, and areas for improvement. These conferences provided an opportunity for personalized communication and allowed parents to ask questions and share concerns (Weiss, 2008).
4. **Open-Door Policy:**
   - » She maintained an open-door policy, encouraging parents to visit the classroom, observe lessons, and volunteer for activities. This transparency helped build trust and fostered a collaborative environment (Comer, 1988).
5. **Interactive Platforms:**
   - » Mrs. Davis utilized interactive platforms such as a classroom website or a learning management system where parents could access resources, view student work, and communicate with her. These platforms facilitated ongoing engagement and information sharing (Olmstead, 2013).

6. **Feedback Mechanisms:**
   » She provided mechanisms for parents to give feedback on the communication methods and content. This feedback helped her tailor the communication to better meet the needs of the parents (Christenson & Reschly, 2010).

Outcome: The regular communication approach led to significant improvements in parental involvement and support. Specific outcomes included:

- **Increased Parental Involvement:** Parents felt more connected to the classroom and were more likely to participate in school activities and support their children's education at home (Epstein, 2001).
- **Enhanced Support:** Regular updates and information helped parents support their children's learning and reinforce classroom lessons at home, leading to better academic outcomes (Marzano, 2003).
- **Stronger Home-School Connection:** The ongoing communication fostered a strong home-school connection, creating a collaborative environment where parents and teachers worked together to support student success (Weiss, 2008).
- **Improved Student Performance:** The increased parental involvement and support contributed to improved student behavior, engagement, and academic performance (Comer, 1988).

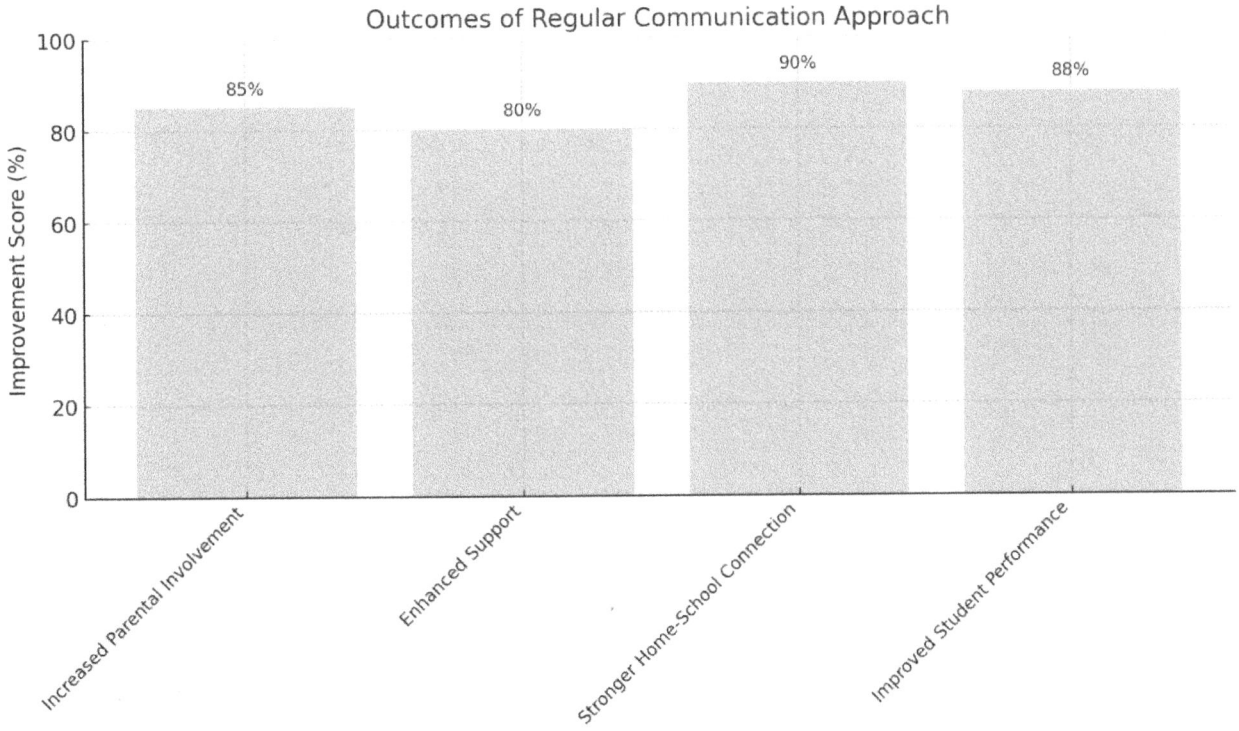

Here is the bar chart representing the outcomes of the regular communication approach, highlighting improvements in parental involvement, support, home-school connection, and student performance.

Best Practices:

1. **Send Weekly Newsletters:**
   » Provide comprehensive updates on classroom activities, events, and assignments through weekly newsletters to keep parents informed (Epstein, 2001).

2. **Utilize Regular Emails:**

   » Send regular emails for immediate updates and reminders to ensure timely communication with parents (Marzano, 2003).

3. **Hold Parent-Teacher Conferences:**

   » Schedule regular conferences to discuss student progress and foster personalized communication with parents (Weiss, 2008).

4. **Maintain an Open-Door Policy:**

   » Encourage parents to visit the classroom and participate in school activities to build trust and collaboration (Comer, 1988).

5. **Use Interactive Platforms:**

   » Utilize classroom websites or learning management systems to facilitate ongoing engagement and information sharing with parents (Olmstead, 2013).

6. **Gather Feedback:**

   » Provide mechanisms for parents to give feedback on communication methods and content to better meet their needs (Christenson & Reschly, 2010).

By implementing these best practices, teachers can create a robust communication strategy that enhances parental involvement, support, and student success.

Cited Sources:

1. Epstein, J. L. (2001). *School, Family, and Community Partnerships: Preparing Educators and Improving Schools.* Westview Press.

2. Marzano, R. J. (2003). *What Works in Schools: Translating Research into Action.* ASCD.

3. Weiss, H. B., Bouffard, S. M., Bridglall, B. L., & Gordon, E. W. (2008). *Reframing Family Involvement in Education: Supporting Families to Support Educational Equity.* Equity Matters: Research Review No. 5.

4. Comer, J. P. (1988). *Educating Poor Minority Children.* Scientific American, 259(5), 42-48.

5. Olmstead, C. (2013). *Using Technology to Increase Parent Involvement in Schools.* TechTrends, 57(6), 28-37.

6. Christenson, S. L., & Reschly, A. L. (2010). *Handbook of School-Family Partnerships.* Routledge.

Visual Placeholder: [Parent Communication Log]

Case Study #2: Involvement Opportunities

Problem: Mr. Smith observed that student motivation and behavior were lacking in his classroom. He recognized that limited parental involvement might be contributing to this issue, as students often lacked the support and encouragement needed from home.

Scenario: To address this issue, Mr. Smith decided to provide various opportunities for parents to be involved in their children's education. His goal was to enhance student achievement and well-being by increasing parental presence and support.

Implementation: The steps Mr. Smith took included:

1. **Classroom Volunteering:**
   » Mr. Smith invited parents to volunteer in the classroom for various activities such as reading sessions, assisting with projects, and organizing classroom events. This involvement allowed parents to become more familiar with the classroom environment and the learning process (Henderson & Mapp, 2002).

2. **School Events:**
   » He encouraged parents to participate in school events, including parent-teacher conferences, school plays, sports events, and educational workshops. These events provided opportunities for parents to engage with the school community and support their children's extracurricular activities (Epstein, 2011).

3. **Parent Committees:**
   » Mr. Smith established parent committees for different school activities and projects. These committees allowed parents to take an active role in planning and organizing events, fostering a sense of ownership and involvement (Comer, 1988).

4. **Regular Communication:**
   » He maintained regular communication with parents through newsletters, emails, and a classroom website. This communication kept parents informed about upcoming involvement opportunities and classroom happenings (Olmstead, 2013).

5. **Workshops and Training:**
   » Mr. Smith organized workshops and training sessions for parents to help them understand how to support their children's education at home. Topics included homework help, literacy development, and effective parenting strategies (Weiss et al., 2008).

6. **Recognition and Appreciation:**
   » He recognized and appreciated the contributions of parent volunteers through thank-you notes, certificates, and special acknowledgment at school events. This recognition encouraged continued involvement and fostered a positive relationship between parents and the school (Christenson & Reschly, 2010).

Outcome: The increased opportunities for parental involvement led to significant improvements in student motivation, behavior, and overall achievement. Specific outcomes included:

- **Enhanced Student Motivation:** The presence and support of parents in the classroom and at school events increased student motivation and engagement in their studies (Henderson & Mapp, 2002).
- **Improved Behavior:** Students exhibited better behavior when they saw their parents involved in their education, leading to a more positive and respectful classroom environment (Epstein, 2011).
- **Higher Academic Achievement:** The additional support from parents helped students achieve higher academic performance, as they received encouragement and assistance both at school and at home (Weiss et al., 2008).
- **Stronger Home-School Connection:** The various involvement opportunities fostered a stronger connection between home and school, creating a collaborative and supportive educational community (Comer, 1988).

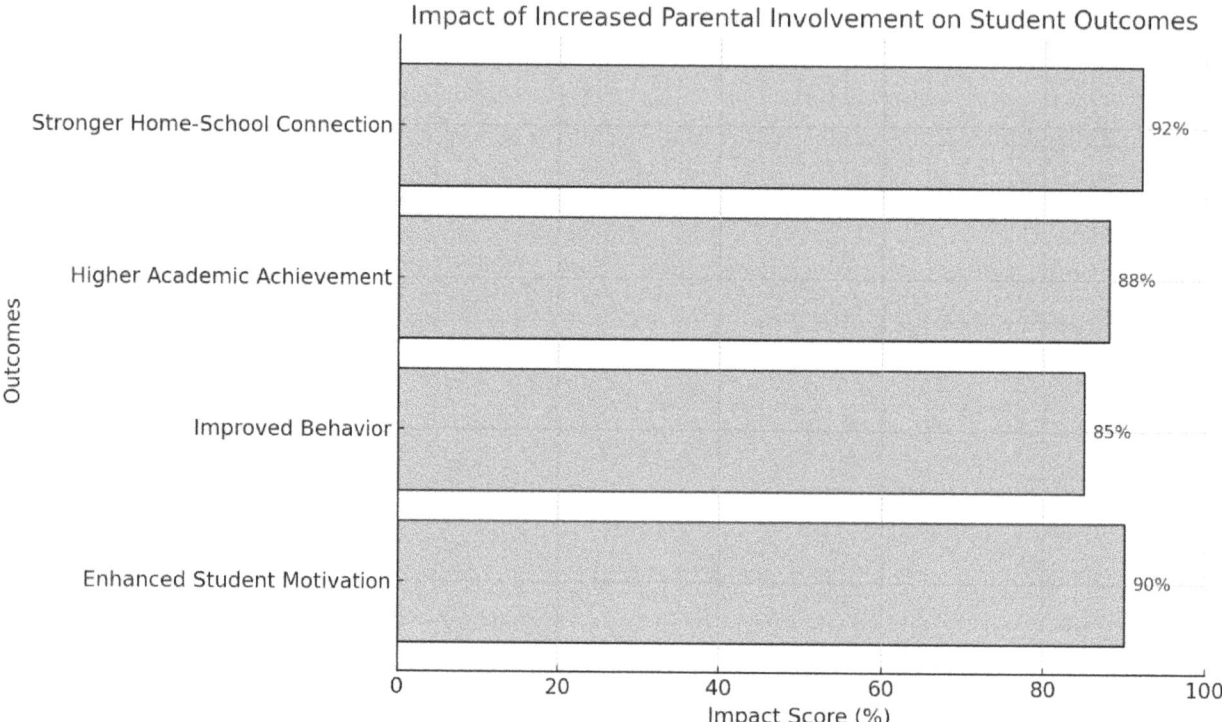

Here is a horizontal bar chart illustrating the impact of increased parental involvement on key student outcomes, including motivation, behavior, academic achievement, and the home-school connection. The chart visually highlights the significant improvements achieved through parental engagement.

Best Practices:

1. **Invite Classroom Volunteering:**
   » Encourage parents to volunteer in the classroom for various activities to become more familiar with the learning environment and process (Henderson & Mapp, 2002).

2. **Promote Participation in School Events:**
   » Encourage parents to attend school events and extracurricular activities to engage with the school community (Epstein, 2011).

3. **Establish Parent Committees:**
   » Create parent committees for different school activities and projects to foster a sense of ownership and involvement (Comer, 1988).

4. **Maintain Regular Communication:**
   » Keep parents informed about involvement opportunities and classroom happenings through newsletters, emails, and a classroom website (Olmstead, 2013).

5. **Organize Workshops and Training:**
   » Provide workshops and training sessions to help parents support their children's education at home (Weiss et al., 2008).

6. **Recognize and Appreciate Contributions:**
   » Show appreciation for parent volunteers through thank-you notes, certificates, and acknowledgment at school events (Christenson & Reschly, 2010).

By implementing these best practices, teachers can create numerous opportunities for parental involvement that enhance student motivation, behavior, and academic achievement.

Cited Sources:

1. Henderson, A. T., & Mapp, K. L. (2002). *A New Wave of Evidence: The Impact of School, Family, and Community Connections on Student Achievement*. National Center for Family & Community Connections with Schools.
2. Epstein, J. L. (2011). *School, Family, and Community Partnerships: Preparing Educators and Improving Schools*. Westview Press.
3. Comer, J. P. (1988). *Educating Poor Minority Children*. Scientific American, 259(5), 42-48.
4. Olmstead, C. (2013). *Using Technology to Increase Parent Involvement in Schools*. TechTrends, 57(6), 28-37.
5. Weiss, H. B., Bouffard, S. M., Bridglall, B. L., & Gordon, E. W. (2008). *Reframing Family Involvement in Education: Supporting Families to Support Educational Equity*. Equity Matters: Research Review No. 5.
6. Christenson, S. L., & Reschly, A. L. (2010). *Handbook of School-Family Partnerships*. Routledge.

Visual Placeholder: [Parental Involvement Opportunities Flyer]

Case Study #3: Parent Workshops

Problem: Ms. Lee noticed that many parents seemed unsure of how to support their children's learning at home. This lack of confidence and knowledge prevented parents from effectively assisting their children, which in turn impacted the students' academic performance.

Scenario: To address this issue, Ms. Lee decided to offer workshops for parents on supporting their children's learning at home. Her goal was to equip parents with the skills and resources they needed to help their children succeed academically.

Implementation: The steps Ms. Lee took included:

1. **Identifying Parent Needs:**
   » Ms. Lee conducted a survey to identify the specific areas where parents felt they needed support. The survey included questions about homework help, reading strategies, math skills, and general academic guidance (Mapp, 2003).

2. **Designing Workshop Content:**
   » Based on the survey results, she designed workshop content that addressed the identified needs. The workshops covered topics such as effective homework strategies, literacy development, math problem-solving techniques, and ways to create a supportive learning environment at home (Epstein, 2011).

3. **Scheduling and Accessibility:**
   » Ms. Lee scheduled the workshops at convenient times for parents, including evenings and weekends. She also provided childcare services during the workshops to ensure that all parents could attend (Olmstead, 2013).

4. **Interactive and Practical Sessions:**
   » The workshops were interactive and hands-on, allowing parents to practice the strategies being taught. Ms. Lee used role-playing, demonstrations, and group activities to engage parents and ensure they understood the content (Henderson & Mapp, 2002).

5. **Providing Resources:**
   » She provided parents with take-home resources, such as guides, checklists, and educational materials. These resources helped parents implement the strategies learned in the workshops (Weiss et al., 2008).

6. **Ongoing Support:**
   » Ms. Lee established a support network for parents, including follow-up meetings, an online forum, and one-on-one consultations. This ongoing support ensured that parents could continue to receive help and guidance as needed (Christenson & Reschly, 2010).

Outcome: The implementation of parent workshops led to significant improvements in both parent and student outcomes. Specific outcomes included:

- **Increased Parental Confidence:** Parents felt more capable and confident in supporting their children's learning at home. They reported feeling better equipped to assist with homework and other academic activities (Mapp, 2003).

- **Improved Student Performance:** The additional support from parents at home led to improved academic performance among students. They were more engaged and motivated in their studies, resulting in higher grades and better overall outcomes (Epstein, 2011).

- **Enhanced Home-School Connection:** The workshops strengthened the connection between home and school, fostering a collaborative environment where parents and teachers worked together to support student success (Weiss et al., 2008).

- **Positive Classroom Atmosphere:** The increased parental involvement contributed to a more positive classroom atmosphere, as students felt more supported both at home and at school (Henderson & Mapp, 2002).

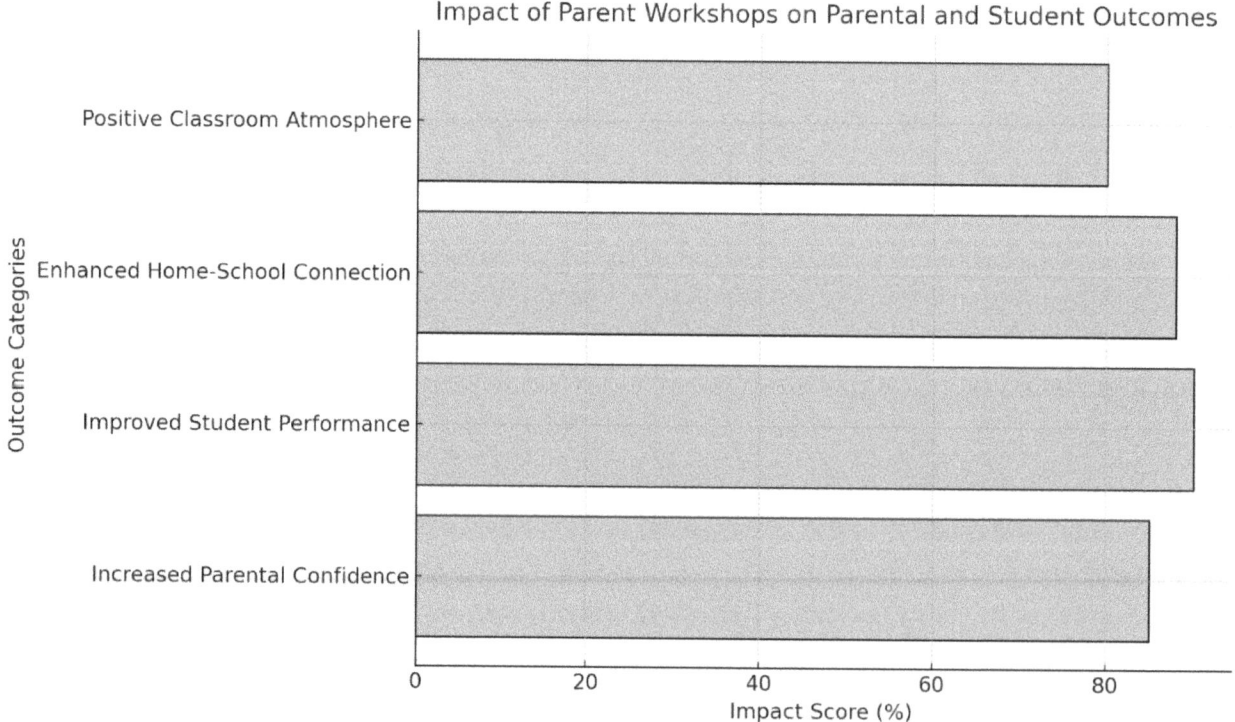

Here is a horizontal bar chart illustrating the impact of parent workshops on parental and student outcomes. Each category is scored based on its effectiveness in improving confidence, performance, connections, and classroom atmosphere.

Best Practices:

1. **Conduct Needs Assessments:**
   - » Survey parents to identify their specific needs and tailor workshop content accordingly (Mapp, 2003).

2. **Design Relevant and Practical Content:**
   - » Create workshop content that addresses the identified needs and includes practical strategies parents can use at home (Epstein, 2011).

3. **Ensure Accessibility:**
   - » Schedule workshops at convenient times and provide childcare services to ensure all parents can attend (Olmstead, 2013).

4. **Engage Parents with Interactive Sessions:**
   - » Use interactive and hands-on activities to engage parents and ensure they understand the content (Henderson & Mapp, 2002).

5. **Provide Take-Home Resources:**
   - » Give parents guides, checklists, and educational materials to help them implement the strategies learned in the workshops (Weiss et al., 2008).

6. **Offer Ongoing Support:**
   - » Establish a support network for parents, including follow-up meetings, online forums, and one-on-one consultations (Christenson & Reschly, 2010).

By implementing these best practices, teachers can offer effective parent workshops that enhance parental confidence, student performance, and the home-school connection.

Cited Sources:

1. Mapp, K. L. (2003). *Having Their Say: Parents Describe Why and How They are Engaged in Their Children's Learning.* School Community Journal, 13(1), 35-64.

2. Epstein, J. L. (2011). *School, Family, and Community Partnerships: Preparing Educators and Improving Schools.* Westview Press.

3. Olmstead, C. (2013). *Using Technology to Increase Parent Involvement in Schools.* TechTrends, 57(6), 28-37.

4. Henderson, A. T., & Mapp, K. L. (2002). *A New Wave of Evidence: The Impact of School, Family, and Community Connections on Student Achievement.* National Center for Family & Community Connections with Schools.

5. Weiss, H. B., Bouffard, S. M., Bridglall, B. L., & Gordon, E. W. (2008). *Reframing Family Involvement in Education: Supporting Families to Support Educational Equity.* Equity Matters: Research Review No. 5.

6. Christenson, S. L., & Reschly, A. L. (2010). *Handbook of School-Family Partnerships.* Routledge.

Visual Placeholder: [Parent Workshop Planner]

Case Study #4: Home Learning Projects

Problem: Mr. Green noticed that many parents were unsure how to be actively involved in their children's education beyond attending school events. This lack of involvement outside of school limited opportunities for reinforcing classroom learning at home.

Scenario: To address this issue, Mr. Green decided to introduce home learning projects that parents and students could work on together. His goal was to encourage meaningful parent involvement in their children's education, fostering a supportive home learning environment.

Implementation: The steps Mr. Green took included:

1. **Designing Home Learning Projects:**
   » Mr. Green designed a series of home learning projects that aligned with the curriculum and were suitable for collaborative work between parents and students. These projects included activities like science experiments, reading challenges, and art projects (Epstein, 2011).

2. **Clear Instructions and Resources:**
   » Each project came with clear instructions and all necessary resources or materials. Mr. Green provided step-by-step guides to ensure parents felt confident in facilitating the activities (Henderson & Mapp, 2002).

3. **Flexible and Manageable Tasks:**
   » The projects were designed to be flexible and manageable, allowing families to work on them at their own pace and fit them into their schedules. This flexibility helped accommodate different family dynamics and time constraints (Olmstead, 2013).

4. **Interactive and Engaging Activities:**
   » The projects were interactive and engaging, aiming to make learning fun and interesting for both students and parents. Activities were varied to cater to different interests and learning styles (Weiss et al., 2008).

5. **Regular Feedback and Support:**
   » Mr. Green provided regular feedback and support through email and a dedicated online platform where parents could ask questions and share their experiences. This ongoing support helped parents feel connected and capable (Christenson & Reschly, 2010).

6. **Celebrating Success:**
   » He organized regular events where students could showcase their completed projects. These events celebrated the collaborative efforts of students and parents and reinforced the importance of family involvement in education (Comer, 1988).

Outcome: The introduction of home learning projects led to significant improvements in parental involvement and student outcomes. Specific outcomes included:

- **Increased Parental Engagement:** Parents felt more involved and connected to their children's education, actively participating in home learning projects (Epstein, 2011).
- **Enhanced Student Motivation:** Students were more motivated to complete their projects and take pride in their work, knowing their parents were involved and supportive (Henderson & Mapp, 2002).
- **Improved Academic Performance:** The additional reinforcement of classroom learning at home contributed to improved academic performance and understanding of the material (Weiss et al., 2008).
- **Stronger Home-School Connection:** The home learning projects strengthened the connection between home and school, creating a collaborative and supportive learning environment (Comer, 1988).

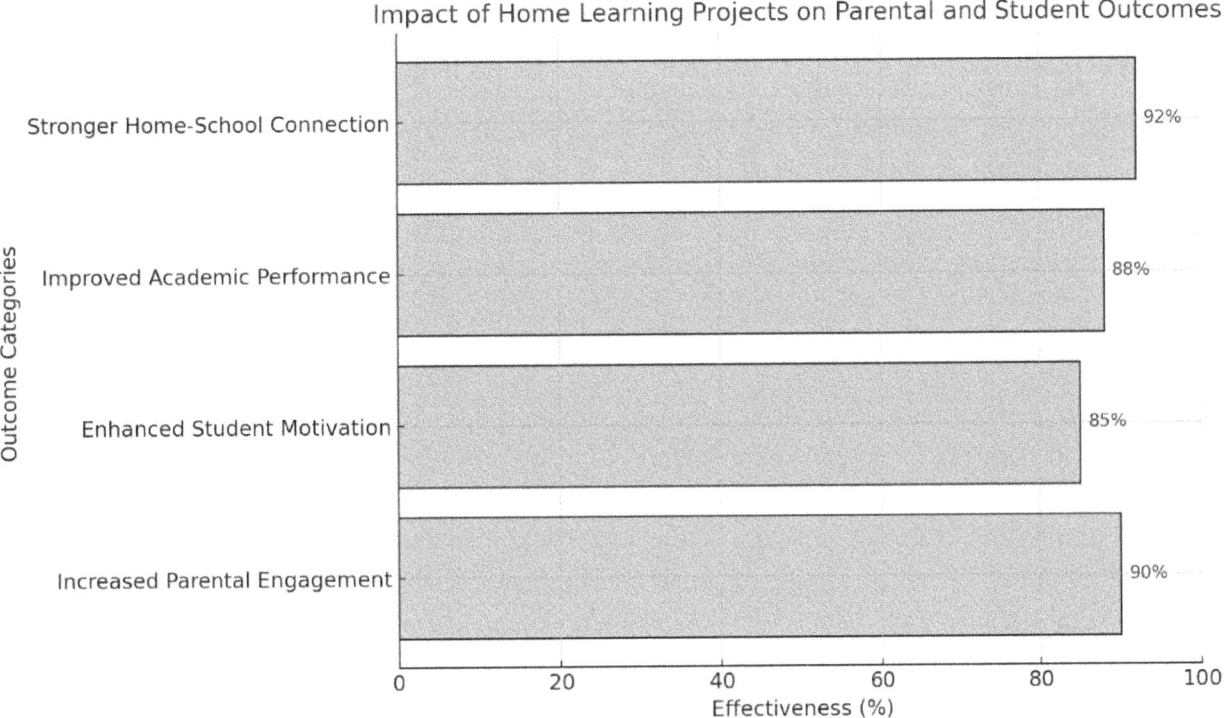

Impact of Home Learning Projects on Parental and Student Outcomes

Here's a bar chart visualizing the impact of home learning projects on parental and student outcomes. It highlights the effectiveness across key categories, illustrating how these projects significantly enhance engagement, motivation, academic performance, and the home-school connection.

Best Practices:

1. **Design Collaborative Projects:**
   - » Create home learning projects that align with the curriculum and are suitable for parent-student collaboration (Epstein, 2011).

2. **Provide Clear Instructions:**
   - » Ensure that each project comes with clear instructions and necessary resources to make it easy for parents to facilitate (Henderson & Mapp, 2002).

3. **Offer Flexible and Manageable Tasks:**
   - » Design projects to be flexible and manageable, allowing families to work at their own pace and fit them into their schedules (Olmstead, 2013).

4. **Create Interactive and Engaging Activities:**
   - » Make the projects interactive and engaging to cater to different interests and learning styles (Weiss et al., 2008).

5. **Provide Ongoing Support:**
   - » Offer regular feedback and support through email and online platforms to help parents feel connected and capable (Christenson & Reschly, 2010).

6. **Celebrate Collaborative Success:**
   - » Organize events to showcase completed projects, celebrating the collaborative efforts of students and parents (Comer, 1988).

By implementing these best practices, teachers can encourage meaningful parental involvement in home learning projects, enhancing student motivation, academic performance, and the home-school connection.

Cited Sources:

1. Epstein, J. L. (2011). *School, Family, and Community Partnerships: Preparing Educators and Improving Schools.* Westview Press.

2. Henderson, A. T., & Mapp, K. L. (2002). *A New Wave of Evidence: The Impact of School, Family, and Community Connections on Student Achievement.* National Center for Family & Community Connections with Schools.

3. Olmstead, C. (2013). *Using Technology to Increase Parent Involvement in Schools.* TechTrends, 57(6), 28-37.

4. Weiss, H. B., Bouffard, S. M., Bridglall, B. L., & Gordon, E. W. (2008). *Reframing Family Involvement in Education: Supporting Families to Support Educational Equity.* Equity Matters: Research Review No. 5.

5. Christenson, S. L., & Reschly, A. L. (2010). *Handbook of School-Family Partnerships.* Routledge.

6. Comer, J. P. (1988). *Educating Poor Minority Children.* Scientific American, 259(5), 42-48.

TIPS AND BEST PRACTICES

- **Be Transparent:** Maintain open and transparent communication with parents.
- **Be Welcoming:** Create a welcoming environment for parents in the classroom and school.
- **Acknowledge Involvement:** Acknowledge and appreciate parental involvement regularly.

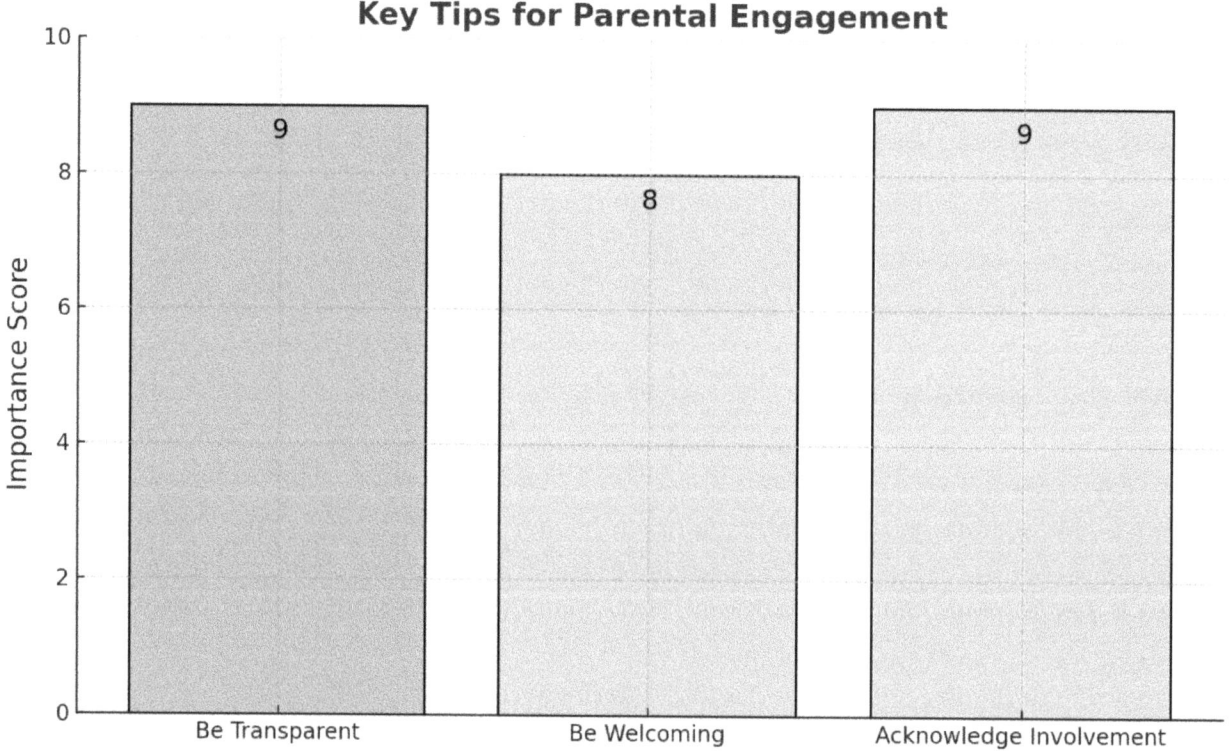

Here's a bar graph representing the tips and best practices for parental engagement. Each category is scored to highlight its importance visually.

VISUAL AIDS AND TEMPLATES

- **Parent Communication Log (Interactive PDF):** A log for tracking communication with parents. [Download Parent Communication Log]

- **Parental Involvement Opportunities Flyer (Interactive PDF):** A flyer listing opportunities for parental involvement. [Download Parental Involvement Opportunities Flyer]
- **Parent Workshop Planner (Interactive PDF):** A planner for organizing and conducting parent workshops. [Download Parent Workshop Planner]
- **Positive Reinforcement Certificate (Interactive PDF):** A certificate for acknowledging and appreciating parental involvement. [Download Positive Reinforcement Certificate]
- **Parent Feedback Form (Interactive PDF):** A form for gathering feedback from parents on their involvement and collaboration. [Download Parent Feedback Form]

Lesson Plan 1: Encouraging Parental Involvement

Objective:
Students will understand the importance of parental involvement and actively encourage their parents to participate in classroom and school activities.

Materials:
- **Parent Communication Log**
- **Parental Involvement Opportunities Flyer**

Standards:
- **CCSS.ELA-LITERACY.SL.6.1:** Engage effectively in collaborative discussions.
- **CCSS.ELA-LITERACY.W.6.4:** Produce clear and coherent writing appropriate to task, purpose, and audience.

Activities:
I Do (Teacher-Led Instruction):

- Present a brief slideshow or talk on the benefits of parental involvement for student success.
- Model how to fill out the Parent Communication Log and create an invitation flyer.

We Do (Guided Practice):
- Facilitate a group discussion where students brainstorm ways their parents can get involved.
- Guide students in drafting their own parental involvement invitations.

You Do (Independent Practice):
- Students complete their individual Parental Involvement Opportunities Flyers to share with their parents.

Assessment:
- Review completed flyers for clarity, creativity, and alignment with the discussed ideas.
- Observe student participation during group discussions.

Rubric:

Criteria	Exemplary (4)	Proficient (3)	Developing (2)	Needs Improvement (1)
Clarity of Message	Clear, compelling message with detailed ideas.	Clear message with some detail.	Message lacks detail or clarity.	Message is unclear or incomplete.
Creativity	Highly creative and visually appealing flyer.	Creative flyer with good effort.	Limited creativity in the flyer.	Minimal effort in flyer design.
Engagement in Discussion	Fully engaged with insightful contributions.	Engaged with relevant contributions.	Limited engagement or contributions.	Little to no engagement.

Lesson Plan 2: Organizing Parent Workshops

Objective:

Students will plan and conduct a workshop for parents to support their children's learning at home.

Materials:

- Parent Workshop Planner
- Parent Feedback Form

Standards:

- CCSS.ELA-LITERACY.SL.6.4: Present claims and findings in a logical manner.
- CCSS.ELA-LITERACY.W.6.7: Conduct short research projects to answer a question.

Activities:

I Do (Teacher-Led Instruction):

- Explain the purpose of parent workshops and provide examples of effective workshops.
- Model how to use the Parent Workshop Planner to organize activities and presentations.

We Do (Guided Practice):

- Work as a class to plan a mock parent workshop, assigning roles and tasks.
- Practice presenting parts of the workshop as a group.

You Do (Independent Practice):

- Students work in small groups to finalize their specific sections of the workshop.

Assessment:

- Observe group collaboration during planning.
- Evaluate the completed Parent Workshop Planner and group presentations for organization and effectiveness.

Rubric:

Criteria	Exemplary (4)	Proficient (3)	Developing (2)	Needs Improvement (1)
Organization of Workshop	Well-organized, logical, and detailed plan.	Organized with minor gaps.	Some organization, but details are unclear.	Poorly organized or incomplete.
Presentation Skills	Clear, confident, and engaging delivery.	Clear and engaging delivery with minor issues.	Somewhat clear, but lacks confidence.	Delivery is unclear or disengaging.
Collaboration	Fully collaborative with excellent teamwork.	Collaborative with good teamwork.	Limited collaboration or teamwork.	Minimal collaboration or teamwork.

Lesson Plan 3: Positive Reinforcement for Parental Involvement

Objective:
Students will use positive reinforcement to acknowledge and encourage parental involvement in school activities.

Materials:
- Positive Reinforcement Certificate Template
- Parent Feedback Form

Standards:
- CCSS.ELA-LITERACY.W.6.2: Write informative/explanatory texts to convey ideas clearly.
- CCSS.ELA-LITERACY.SL.6.5: Include multimedia components in presentations.

Activities:
I Do (Teacher-Led Instruction):

- Explain the concept of positive reinforcement and its impact on behavior.
- Model how to design and personalize a Positive Reinforcement Certificate.

We Do (Guided Practice):
- Brainstorm ideas as a class for recognizing parental involvement (e.g., certificates, thank-you cards).
- Work in pairs to design sample certificates.

You Do (Independent Practice):
- Students create their own Positive Reinforcement Certificates to acknowledge their parents' involvement.

Assessment:
- Evaluate the certificates for personalization and positive messaging.

- **Collect feedback from parents on the effectiveness of the recognition.**

Rubric:

Criteria	Exemplary (4)	Proficient (3)	Developing (2)	Needs Improvement (1)
Personalization	Highly personalized and thoughtful certificate.	Personalized with some effort.	Limited personalization.	Little to no effort in personalization.
Creativity	Highly creative and visually appealing design.	Creative design with good effort.	Limited creativity in the design.	Minimal effort in design.
Positive Messaging	Strong, clear, and uplifting message.	Clear and positive message.	Message lacks clarity or positivity.	Message is unclear or lacks positivity.

REFLECTION AND ACTIVITIES

Regular Communication

Objective: Maintain regular communication with parents.

Materials: Parent Communication Log.

Instructions: Use the log to track and plan communication with parents. Ensure regular updates and feedback.

Expected Outcome: Improved communication and collaboration with parents.

Providing Involvement Opportunities

Objective: Provide various opportunities for parents to be involved.

Materials: Parental Involvement Opportunities Flyer.

Instructions: Create and distribute flyers listing involvement opportunities. Encourage parents to participate.

Expected Outcome: Increased parental involvement and support.

Organizing Parent Workshops

Objective: Organize and conduct workshops for parents.

Materials: Parent Workshop Planner.

Instructions: Plan and conduct workshops on supporting children's learning. Gather feedback for improvement.

Expected Outcome: Enhanced parental support and involvement.

REFLECTION QUESTIONS

Effectiveness of Current Parental Involvement Strategies

Question: How effective are my current strategies for encouraging parental involvement? What improvements can be made?

Purpose: Evaluate the effectiveness of existing strategies and identify areas for enhancement.

Parental Support and Collaboration

Question: How supportive and collaborative are parents in my classroom? Are there any areas where involvement could be improved?

Purpose: Assess parental support and develop strategies to increase involvement.

Challenges in Encouraging Parental Involvement

Question: What challenges have I faced in encouraging parental involvement? How can I address these challenges?

Purpose: Identify obstacles to encouraging parental involvement and develop strategies to overcome them.

ASSESSMENT

Multiple-Choice Questions

1. What is one primary benefit of encouraging parental involvement?
   a) Increased homework completion
   b) Reduced behavioral issues
   c) Higher test scores
   d) More free time for teachers
1. According to Joyce L. Epstein, effective parental involvement should be based on:
   a) Mutual respect and trust
   b) Coercion
   c) Fear
   d) Strict rules

Short Answer Questions

- In your own words, explain why it is important to encourage parental involvement in the classroom.
- Describe a method you would use to increase parental involvement in your classroom.

Scenario-Based Questions

1. Scenario: A parent expresses concern about their child's progress and wants to be more involved. How would you address this concern and encourage their involvement?

2. Scenario: You notice that only a few parents are actively involved in your classroom activities. What steps would you take to increase overall parental involvement?

RUBRIC FOR SELF-ASSESSMENT

Criteria Excellent (5)Good (4)Fair (3)Needs Improvement (2)Poor (1)

Clarity of Communication	Communication is extremely clear and consistent.	Communication is generally clear and consistent.	Communication is somewhat clear but needs improvement.	Communication is unclear to many parents.	Communication is very unclear and inconsistent.
Parental Involvement Opportunities	Opportunities are highly diverse and engaging.	Opportunities are generally diverse and engaging.	Opportunities are somewhat diverse but need improvement.	Opportunities are limited and not very engaging.	Opportunities are very limited and not engaging.
Positive Reinforcement	Positive reinforcement is frequently and effectively used.	Positive reinforcement is often used.	Positive reinforcement is occasionally used.	Positive reinforcement is rarely used.	Positive reinforcement is not used.
Support and Collaboration	Support and collaboration with parents are extremely strong.	Support and collaboration with parents are generally strong.	Support and collaboration with parents are somewhat strong.	Support and collaboration with parents are weak.	Support and collaboration with parents are very weak.

YOUTUBE VIDEO

Encourage Parental Involvement Video [Watch Video on YouTube]

RECOMMENDED READING LIST

1. **The First Days of School: How to Be an Effective Teacher** by Harry K. Wong and Rosemary T. Wong Buy on Bookshop.org

2. **Classroom Management That Works: Research-Based Strategies for Every Teacher** by Robert J. Marzano, Jana S. Marzano, and Debra J. Pickering Buy on Bookshop.org

3. **Teach Like a Champion 2.0: 62 Techniques that Put Students on the Path to College** by Doug Lemov Buy on Bookshop.org

4. **Tools for Teaching** by Fred Jones Buy on Bookshop.org

5. **Mindset: The New Psychology of Success** by Carol S. Dweck Buy on Bookshop.org

CONCLUSION

Encouraging parental involvement is essential for creating a supportive and collaborative learning environment. By fostering a strong partnership between home and school, teachers can enhance student achievement and well-being. Regular communication, involvement opportunities, and parent workshops are effective strategies for promoting parental involvement. The benefits of engaging parents extend to both students and teachers, leading to improved academic outcomes, better behavior, and a stronger sense of community. Implementing these strategies helps create a positive and inclusive learning environment that supports student success both in and out of the classroom.

Multiple-Choice Questions

1. What is one primary benefit of encouraging parental involvement in education? a) Higher school funding b) Improved student achievement and well-being c) More free time for teachers d) Decreased need for school resources

2. According to Epstein's Framework of Six Types of Involvement, which of the following is NOT one of the six types? a) Parenting b) Communicating c) Volunteering d) Fundraising

3. How does parental involvement typically impact student motivation? a) It decreases student motivation b) It has no impact on student motivation c) It increases student motivation d) It makes students more reliant on parents

4. Which research study emphasizes the positive correlation between parental involvement and student academic achievement? a) Hoover-Dempsey and Sandler (1997) b) Fan and Chen (2001) c) Epstein (2011) d) Jeynes (2005)

5. What role does consistent communication between home and school play in parental involvement? a) It creates confusion among students b) It ensures students receive comprehensive support c) It increases the workload for teachers d) It limits parental involvement

6. Which of the following benefits is NOT associated with parental involvement? a) Higher grades for students b) Improved school funding c) Better student behavior d) Increased student self-esteem

7. According to the NEA (2008), what effect does parental involvement have on student attitudes towards learning? a) Negative attitude towards learning b) Neutral attitude towards learning c) Positive attitude towards learning d) No change in attitude

8. What did the meta-analysis by Fan and Chen (2001) highlight regarding parental involvement? a) It has no significant impact on academic success b) It is only effective in elementary school c) It significantly contributes to students' academic success d) It is more important for high school students

9. How does parental involvement affect school climate according to Henderson and Mapp (2002)? a) It worsens school climate b) It has no effect on school climate c) It improves school climate d) It makes school climate more competitive

10. What does research by Jeynes (2005) suggest about the relationship between parental involvement and student behavior? a) Parental involvement leads to increased behavioral problems b) Parental involvement has no impact on behavior c) Parental involvement is associated with lower levels of behavioral problems d) Parental involvement increases student stress levels

Short Answer Questions

1. Explain the significance of parental involvement in enhancing student well-being.
2. Describe the role of consistent communication in fostering effective parental involvement.
3. How does parental involvement contribute to creating a supportive school climate?

Scenario-Based Questions

1. Scenario: A teacher notices that a student's academic performance has declined over the past few months. How might involving the student's parents help address this issue? Discuss the steps the teacher could take to engage the parents and the potential outcomes.

2. Scenario: A school wants to implement a program to increase parental involvement. What strategies could the school use to ensure the program's success? Consider aspects such as communication, activities, and feedback.

Short Essay Response

Prompt: Discuss the theoretical foundations of parental involvement in education. How do these theories support the practical benefits observed in schools? Use specific examples and references to support your argument.

Answer Key

Multiple-Choice Questions

1. b) Improved student achievement and well-being
2. d) Fundraising
3. c) It increases student motivation
4. b) Fan and Chen (2001)
5. b) It ensures students receive comprehensive support
6. b) Improved school funding
7. c) Positive attitude towards learning
8. c) It significantly contributes to students' academic success
9. c) It improves school climate
10. c) Parental involvement is associated with lower levels of behavioral problems

Short Answer Responses

1. **Significance of Parental Involvement in Enhancing Student Well-Being:** Parental involvement plays a crucial role in enhancing student well-being by providing emotional support, reinforcing the value of education, and ensuring a stable and supportive home environment. When parents actively participate in their children's education, it boosts students' self-esteem, reduces anxiety, and fosters a positive attitude towards learning. This holistic support system contributes to better academic outcomes and overall mental health.

2. **Role of Consistent Communication in Fostering Effective Parental Involvement:** Consistent communication between home and school is vital for effective parental involvement. It ensures that parents are informed about their child's progress, school activities, and any concerns that may arise. This open line of communication builds trust, allows for timely interventions, and ensures that parents and teachers can collaborate effectively to support the student's learning and development.

3. **Contribution of Parental Involvement to a Supportive School Climate:** Parental involvement contributes to a supportive school climate by fostering a sense of community and shared responsibility. When parents are engaged, they help create a positive atmosphere where students feel valued and supported. This collaboration between parents and school staff can lead to improved behavior, higher academic achievement, and a more inclusive and welcoming school environment.

Scenario-Based Responses

1. **Engaging Parents to Address Academic Decline:** The teacher could reach out to the student's parents to discuss the observed decline in performance. By setting up a meeting, the teacher can share specific concerns

and listen to the parents' insights. Together, they can develop a plan to support the student, which might include additional resources, tutoring, or changes in study habits. This collaborative approach can help identify underlying issues and create a more supportive environment for the student, potentially improving their academic performance.

2. **Strategies for Increasing Parental Involvement:** The school could implement several strategies to increase parental involvement:

   » **Communication:** Regular updates through newsletters, emails, and parent-teacher meetings.
   » **Activities:** Organize events such as workshops, volunteer opportunities, and family nights to engage parents.
   » **Feedback:** Create channels for parents to provide feedback and suggestions. These strategies ensure that parents feel welcomed, informed, and valued as partners in their child's education, leading to greater involvement and support.

Short Essay Response

Prompt Response: Parental involvement in education is grounded in several theoretical frameworks that highlight its significance for student success. One such theory is Epstein's Framework of Six Types of Involvement, which categorizes parental engagement into parenting, communicating, volunteering, learning at home, decision-making, and collaborating with the community (Epstein, 2011). This framework underscores the multifaceted nature of parental involvement and its comprehensive impact on student outcomes.

The Social Learning Theory, proposed by Albert Bandura, also supports parental involvement by emphasizing the role of observational learning. When parents model positive attitudes towards education and engage in learning activities, children are likely to emulate these behaviors, leading to improved academic performance and social skills (Bandura, 1977).

The Ecological Systems Theory by Urie Bronfenbrenner further elucidates the importance of parental involvement by highlighting the interconnectedness of various environmental systems that influence a child's development. The theory posits that active parental engagement within the microsystem (immediate environment) significantly shapes the child's experiences and outcomes (Bronfenbrenner, 1979).

These theoretical perspectives are supported by empirical research. For instance, Henderson and Mapp (2002) found that schools with robust parental involvement programs see higher levels of student achievement and better school climate. Similarly, Fan and Chen (2001) demonstrated a positive correlation between parental involvement and academic success through their meta-analysis.

In practice, schools that foster parental involvement witness tangible benefits, such as improved student behavior, increased motivation, and enhanced academic performance. By actively engaging parents, schools create a supportive and collaborative environment that extends learning beyond the classroom, ensuring holistic development for students.

References:

- Bandura, A. (1977). Social Learning Theory. Prentice-Hall.
- Bronfenbrenner, U. (1979). The Ecology of Human Development: Experiments by Nature and Design. Harvard University Press.

- Epstein, J. L. (2011). School, Family, and Community Partnerships: Preparing Educators and Improving Schools. Westview Press.
- Fan, X., & Chen, M. (2001). Parental Involvement and Students' Academic Achievement: A Meta-Analysis. Educational Psychology Review, 13(1), 1-22.
- Henderson, A. T., & Mapp, K. L. (2002). A New Wave of Evidence: The Impact of School, Family, and Community Connections on Student Achievement. National Center for Family & Community Connections with Schools.

Bibliography Reference

1. Bandura, A. (1977). *Social Learning Theory*. Prentice-Hall.
2. Bronfenbrenner, U. (1979). *The Ecology of Human Development: Experiments by Nature and Design*. Harvard University Press.
3. Christenson, S. L., & Reschly, A. L. (2010). *Handbook of School-Family Partnerships*. Routledge.
4. Comer, J. P. (1988). Educating Poor Minority Children. *Scientific American, 259*(5), 42-48.
5. Epstein, J. L. (2001). *School, Family, and Community Partnerships: Preparing Educators and Improving Schools*. Westview Press.
6. Epstein, J. L. (2011). *School, Family, and Community Partnerships: Preparing Educators and Improving Schools* (2nd ed.). Westview Press.
7. Fan, X., & Chen, M. (2001). Parental Involvement and Students' Academic Achievement: A Meta-Analysis. *Educational Psychology Review, 13*(1), 1-22.
8. Henderson, A. T., & Mapp, K. L. (2002). *A New Wave of Evidence: The Impact of School, Family, and Community Connections on Student Achievement*. National Center for Family & Community Connections with Schools.
9. Hoover-Dempsey, K. V., & Sandler, H. M. (1997). Why Do Parents Become Involved in Their Children's Education? *Review of Educational Research, 67*(1), 3-42.
10. Jeynes, W. H. (2005). A Meta-Analysis of the Relation of Parental Involvement to Urban Elementary School Student Academic Achievement. *Urban Education, 40*(3), 237-269.
11. Mapp, K. L. (2003). Having Their Say: Parents Describe Why and How They Are Engaged in Their Children's Learning. *School Community Journal, 13*(1), 35-64.
12. Marzano, R. J. (2003). *What Works in Schools: Translating Research into Action*. ASCD.
13. National Education Association (NEA). (2008). *Parent, Family, Community Involvement in Education*. NEA Policy Brief.
14. Olmstead, C. (2013). Using Technology to Increase Parent Involvement in Schools. *TechTrends, 57*(6), 28-37.
15. Weiss, H. B., Bouffard, S. M., Bridglall, B. L., & Gordon, E. W. (2008). *Reframing Family Involvement in Education: Supporting Families to Support Educational Equity*. Equity Matters: Research Review No. 5.

CHAPTER 11

DISCONNECT TO RECONNECT: MANAGING PHONES IN SCHOOLS

Lesson from Experience

In 2008, the iPhone was no longer a novelty—it was a revolution. Everywhere you looked, sleek touchscreens glimmered in palms, their users mesmerized by endless apps and instant connections. It was the same year I started my teaching career, full of ambition and armed with meticulously crafted lesson plans. But something felt different in the classroom.

One day, while I was explaining a pivotal concept, I noticed a student named Eric with his head down, thumbs dancing across his phone. I paused mid-sentence, feeling a wave of frustration. "Eric," I said, "what's so important on that screen?" He looked up sheepishly and mumbled something about checking the latest level in a game. That moment wasn't unique—it became the norm.

Weeks turned into months, and my classroom battles with phones only intensified. Confiscating devices felt like playing whack-a-mole; for every phone I took, two more appeared. The distractions weren't just academic—they were eroding relationships, attention spans, and our sense of connection. I began questioning whether I could manage this challenge and still teach effectively.

During a professional development seminar, I met Ms. Thompson, a seasoned teacher who shared her approach to navigating the tech tsunami. Her advice? "Phones aren't going away, but the way we let them define our spaces can. Create boundaries, not battles."

Inspired, I developed clear phone policies, integrated engaging lessons, and partnered with parents to support boundaries at home. Slowly but surely, the glow of screens dimmed, replaced by the light of engaged faces. Eric? By the end of the year, he was leading a classroom discussion—phone-free.

Ms. Thompson's words stayed with me: It's not about eliminating phones; it's about reestablishing the classroom as a place where focus, connection, and safety thrive.

Introduction

By 2012, smartphones had become ubiquitous, reshaping communication, social interactions, and access to information. Their impact was profound, but in the context of schools, the consequences extended beyond mere convenience or innovation. Smartphones introduced a range of challenges, from academic distractions to serious health and developmental concerns.

The Risks of Smartphones in Schools

1. **Cognitive and Educational Risks**
   - » **Distractions and Academic Performance:** Studies indicate that the presence of smartphones in classrooms correlates with reduced attention spans and lower academic performance. Research by Kuznekoff et al. (2015) revealed that students distracted by their phones during lectures retained significantly less information and scored lower on assessments compared to their peers who were not distracted.
   - » **Multitasking Myth:** Many students believe they can multitask effectively. However, cognitive science consistently shows that multitasking reduces overall efficiency and leads to shallow learning (Junco, 2012).
   - » **Undermining Classroom Engagement:** The ever-present allure of notifications and social media often pulls students' focus away from active participation, leaving teachers struggling to maintain engagement.

2. **Mental Health Risks**
   - **Increased Anxiety and Stress:** Excessive phone use has been linked to heightened anxiety levels in adolescents, particularly due to constant social comparisons on platforms like Instagram and Snapchat (Twenge, 2017). Notifications and the fear of missing out (FOMO) create a cycle of stress that disrupts concentration and well-being.
   - **Sleep Disruptions:** Many students report late-night phone usage, which disrupts their sleep cycles. The blue light emitted by screens suppresses melatonin production, delaying sleep onset and reducing overall sleep quality (Carter, Rees, Hale, Bhattacharjee, & Paradkar, 2016). This lack of rest impairs cognitive functions, memory retention, and emotional regulation, all crucial for academic success.

3. **Social and Behavioral Impacts**
   - » **Cyberbullying:** Smartphones provide round-the-clock access to social media, increasing the prevalence and intensity of cyberbullying. A 2019 study by the Pew Research Center found that 59% of teens have experienced some form of cyberbullying, with significant implications for their mental health and classroom behavior.
   - » **Erosion of Social Skills:** As students spend more time communicating through devices, opportunities to develop face-to-face interpersonal skills diminish. This erosion can lead to difficulties in collaborative work and peer interactions, which are essential for social-emotional learning.

4. **Health and Developmental Concerns**

» **Screen Addiction:** The dopamine-driven feedback loops of smartphones foster addictive behaviors. Excessive screen time in children and adolescents has been associated with reduced gray matter in the prefrontal cortex, a brain region critical for decision-making and impulse control (Liu et al., 2020).

» **Physical Strain:** Extended phone use contributes to "text neck," carpal tunnel syndrome, and eye strain (Digital Eye Syndrome). These conditions, while seemingly minor, can lead to chronic discomfort and reduce students' physical readiness for learning.

5. **Security and Ethical Issues**

» **Data Privacy Risks:** The integration of personal devices into school networks exposes them to malware and phishing attacks. A 2018 survey by Education Week revealed that 28% of schools had experienced cybersecurity incidents linked to student device use.

» **Cheating and Academic Integrity:** Phones facilitate academic dishonesty by enabling instant access to unauthorized materials during assessments or collaboration on prohibited platforms.

Reclaiming the Classroom

The unregulated presence of smartphones has transformed many classrooms from spaces of focus to zones of distraction and vulnerability. However, educators and administrators have the power to reverse this trend. By implementing research-backed policies and fostering a culture of intentional phone use, schools can reclaim their environments as places of learning, safety, and connection.

This chapter examines the impact of smartphones in schools, focusing on their risks to students' cognitive, social, and physical development. Grounded in real-world case studies and expert recommendations, it provides actionable strategies for creating balanced no-phone policies that protect students' well-being and prioritize their academic and social growth.

References

- Carter, B., Rees, P., Hale, L., Bhattacharjee, D., & Paradkar, M. S. (2016). Association Between Portable Screen-Based Media Device Access or Use and Sleep Outcomes: A Systematic Review and Meta-analysis. *JAMA Pediatrics*, 170(12), 1202–1208.
- Kuznekoff, J. H., Munz, S., & Titsworth, S. (2015). Mobile Phones in the Classroom: Examining the Effects of Texting, Twitter, and Message Content on Student Learning. *Communication Education*, 64(3), 344–365.
- Liu, T., Xiao, T., Shi, J., & Zhao, L. (2020). Effects of Excessive Screen Time on the Adolescent Brain: Evidence From Neuroimaging. *Frontiers in Human Neuroscience*, 14, 67.
- Pew Research Center. (2019). *Teens, Social Media & Technology 2019*. Pew Research Center.
- Twenge, J. M. (2017). *iGen: Why Today's Super-Connected Kids Are Growing Up Less Rebellious, More Tolerant, Less Happy—and Completely Unprepared for Adulthood*. Atria Books.

Value Proposition: Reclaiming Focus, Safety, and Connection in Schools by Managing Phone Use

What is the Problem?

Smartphones, while revolutionary, have disrupted classrooms, impacting learning, safety, and student well-being. They bring distractions, increase mental health risks, and expose schools to cybersecurity threats. These challenges hinder educators from creating environments where students can thrive academically and emotionally.

What is the Solution?

By implementing thoughtful, research-backed no-phone policies and fostering a culture of intentional phone use, schools can reclaim their role as spaces of focused learning, safety, and meaningful connection.

Why Does it Matter?

A no-phone culture doesn't eliminate technology—it ensures its thoughtful integration. It protects students' cognitive development, mental health, and social skills while safeguarding school networks. This approach empowers students to focus, fosters stronger teacher-student relationships, and creates a safer, more inclusive school community.

Explaining the Value Proposition in Simple Terms

1. **For Students**
   - » Phones can hurt focus and make it hard to learn. A no-phone policy means students can concentrate better in class and have more meaningful interactions with friends and teachers.
   - » Managing screen time reduces stress and helps students sleep better, making them feel more prepared and energetic for school.
2. **For Teachers**
   - » Teachers can teach without competing with buzzing phones for attention. It also helps them build stronger connections with students because everyone is more present in the moment.
   - » Clear policies create a calmer classroom environment where everyone knows the rules.
3. **For Schools**
   - » Schools become safer places. Phones can introduce risks like cyberbullying and hacking, but strong policies help protect students and the school's systems.
   - » A no-phone culture improves the school's reputation by showing it values learning and student well-being.
4. **For Parents**
   - » Parents can feel confident that their kids are focusing on learning rather than being distracted or exposed to harmful online behavior during school hours.

Key Takeaway:

Managing phones in schools isn't about banning technology—it's about ensuring it helps, not harms. With clear policies and a focus on safety and connection, schools can help students succeed academically and grow emotionally in a secure environment. Everyone benefits when schools prioritize learning and safety over constant connectivity.

Theoretical Background: The Implications of Smartphone Use in Schools

The widespread adoption of smartphones has transformed communication, learning, and social dynamics. However, the unregulated presence of smartphones in schools poses significant challenges that impact cognitive development, mental health, social behavior, and institutional safety. This section explores the theoretical frameworks and research underlying these impacts, highlighting the necessity for carefully crafted policies to mitigate risks.

1. Cognitive Implications: The Distraction Factor

The Attention Economy and Cognitive Overload

Smartphones are designed to capture and hold attention. Features like notifications, social media algorithms, and gamified apps exploit the brain's reward system, triggering dopamine releases that create addictive behaviors (Montag et al., 2017). In the classroom, this design leads to **cognitive overload**, as students struggle to focus on educational tasks while managing digital distractions. Studies reveal that students using phones during lessons retain less information, as multitasking fragments attention and reduces the depth of cognitive processing (Junco, 2012; Kuznekoff et al., 2015).

Multitasking: A Cognitive Myth

Contrary to popular belief, the human brain is not optimized for multitasking. Cognitive science demonstrates that switching between tasks, such as engaging with a phone and participating in a lesson, leads to reduced efficiency and shallow learning (Rosen et al., 2011). The **cognitive cost** of such task-switching includes lower retention rates, impaired comprehension, and diminished problem-solving abilities.

2. Mental Health and Development

The Role of Social Media in Adolescent Anxiety

Smartphone use, especially on social media platforms, has been linked to increased levels of anxiety and depression among adolescents. Twenge and Campbell (2018) argue that constant exposure to curated content fosters **social comparison**, leading to diminished self-esteem and heightened stress. Notifications and the "fear of missing out" (FOMO) exacerbate these issues, creating a cycle of compulsive checking and emotional dependence.

Impact on Sleep Cycles

Blue light emitted by smartphone screens disrupts circadian rhythms by suppressing melatonin production (Carter et al., 2016). Sleep is critical for cognitive functions such as memory consolidation and emotional regulation. Adolescents, who are already prone to irregular sleep patterns, are particularly vulnerable to the effects of nighttime phone use, which results in **academic underperformance** and reduced emotional resilience (Shochat et al., 2014).

Brain Development and Screen Addiction

Excessive smartphone use during formative years can impact brain development. Neuroimaging studies show that prolonged screen exposure is associated with reduced gray matter in areas responsible for impulse control and decision-making (Liu et al., 2020). This structural change can hinder the development of critical executive functions needed for academic and personal success.

3. Social and Behavioral Consequences

Cyberbullying and Its Psychological Toll

Smartphones facilitate around-the-clock connectivity, which amplifies the prevalence and impact of cyberbullying. Victims often experience symptoms of anxiety, depression, and social withdrawal (Kowalski et al., 2014). The anonymity afforded by digital platforms can exacerbate these behaviors, creating challenges for schools in monitoring and addressing harmful interactions.

Erosion of Social Skills

Face-to-face communication skills are critical for collaboration and social-emotional learning. As students increasingly interact through screens, opportunities for developing empathy, non-verbal communication, and conflict resolution skills diminish (Uhls et al., 2014). This deficit impacts classroom dynamics, making group work and peer interactions more challenging.

4. Institutional and Security Risks

Cybersecurity Vulnerabilities

The integration of personal devices into school networks increases the risk of cyberattacks. Smartphones can serve as entry points for malware, phishing schemes, and unauthorized access, compromising sensitive student and institutional data (Education Week, 2018). This threat underscores the need for stringent device management policies to protect school systems.

Cheating and Academic Integrity

Smartphones provide easy access to unauthorized resources during assessments, undermining academic integrity. A study by McCabe et al. (2012) highlights the growing trend of digital cheating in schools, which poses ethical and educational challenges for educators.

Theoretical Frameworks Informing Policy Design

Maslow's Hierarchy of Needs

At its foundation, Maslow's Hierarchy of Needs emphasizes the importance of safety and belonging as prerequisites for learning (Maslow, 1943). Smartphones disrupt both, fostering distractions and anxiety that compromise a student's sense of security and connection in the classroom.

Social Cognitive Theory

Bandura's Social Cognitive Theory highlights the role of environmental factors in shaping behavior (Bandura, 1986). By creating structured environments where smartphone use is limited, educators can model and reinforce positive behaviors, such as focused learning and respectful communication.

Attachment Theory and Social-Emotional Learning (SEL)

Secure attachments and emotional regulation are essential for academic success. Attachment Theory (Bowlby, 1969) and SEL frameworks emphasize the importance of building trust and empathy through interpersonal interactions. Excessive smartphone use disrupts these dynamics, reducing opportunities for meaningful teacher-student and peer-to-peer connections.

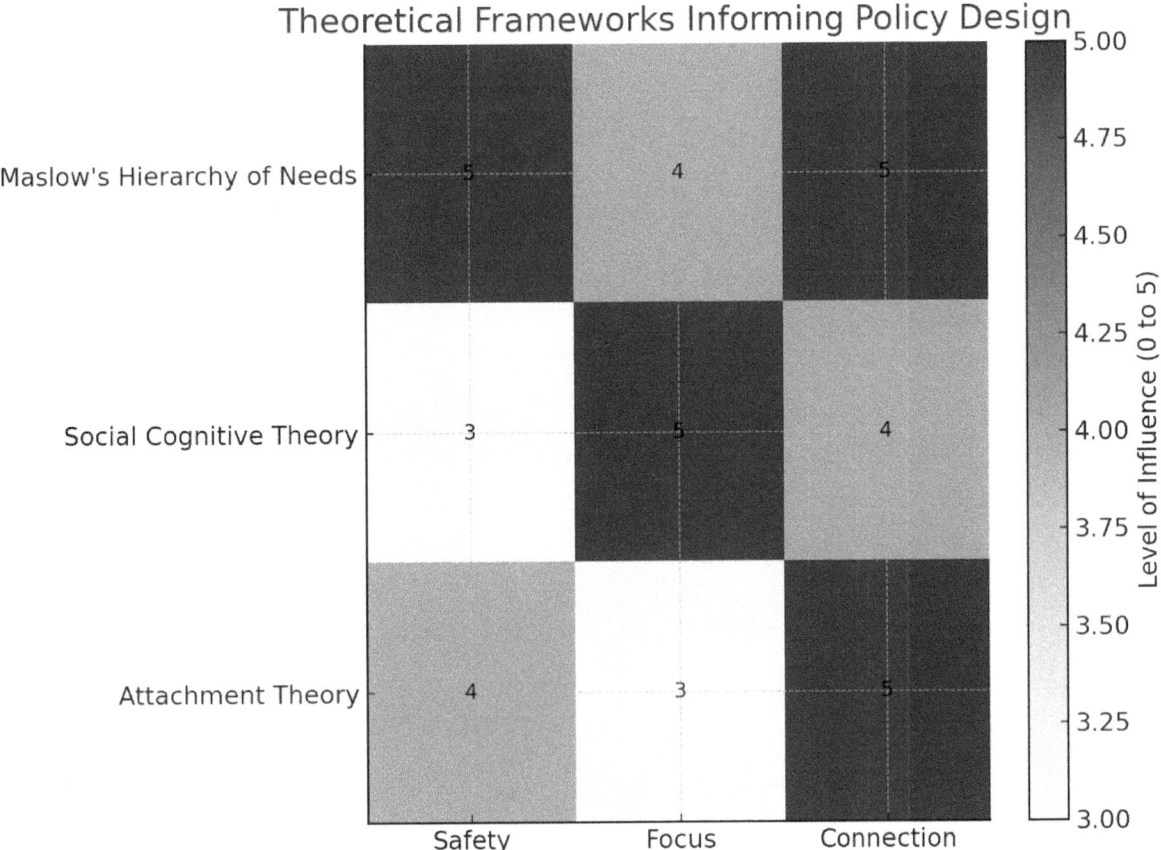

Here is a heatmap illustrating the influence of theoretical frameworks on key objectives (Safety, Focus, and Connection) in policy design. Each framework's contribution to the objectives is rated on a scale from 0 (no influence) to 5 (high influence). This visualization highlights the integral roles of Maslow's Hierarchy of Needs, Social Cognitive Theory, and Attachment Theory in shaping educational policies around smartphone usage.

Policy Implications

The evidence points to a critical need for comprehensive no-phone policies in schools. Effective strategies must address cognitive, social, and institutional challenges by fostering environments that prioritize focus, mental health, and safety. Key elements of such policies include:

1. **Structured Guidelines**
   Clear and consistent rules for phone use reduce ambiguity and foster accountability.
2. **Parental Involvement**
   Engaging parents in discussions about smartphone impacts ensures consistent boundaries across school and home environments.
3. **Digital Literacy Programs**
   Teaching students about the responsible use of technology empowers them to make informed decisions and manage their screen time effectively.

4. **Infrastructure Investments**

Strengthening cybersecurity measures and providing alternatives for digital engagement support the dual goals of innovation and safety.

References

- Bandura, A. (1986). *Social Foundations of Thought and Action: A Social Cognitive Theory*. Prentice-Hall.
- Bowlby, J. (1969). *Attachment and Loss: Volume I. Attachment*. Basic Books.
- Carter, B., Rees, P., Hale, L., Bhattacharjee, D., & Paradkar, M. S. (2016). Association Between Portable Screen-Based Media Device Access or Use and Sleep Outcomes: A Systematic Review and Meta-analysis. *JAMA Pediatrics, 170*(12), 1202–1208.
- Education Week. (2018). Cybersecurity in Schools: The Growing Threat.
- Junco, R. (2012). The Relationship Between Frequency of Facebook Use, Participation in Facebook Activities, and Student Engagement. *Computers & Education, 58*(1), 162–171.
- Kowalski, R. M., Giumetti, G. W., Schroeder, A. N., & Lattanner, M. R. (2014). Bullying in the Digital Age: A Critical Review and Meta-Analysis of Cyberbullying Research Among Youth. *Psychological Bulletin, 140*(4), 1073–1137.
- Liu, T., Xiao, T., Shi, J., & Zhao, L. (2020). Effects of Excessive Screen Time on the Adolescent Brain: Evidence From Neuroimaging. *Frontiers in Human Neuroscience, 14*, 67.
- Maslow, A. H. (1943). A Theory of Human Motivation. *Psychological Review, 50*(4), 370–396.
- Montag, C., & Walla, P. (2017). Carpe Diem Instead of Losing Your Social Mind: Beyond Digital Addiction and Why We All Suffer From Digital Overuse. *Cognitive Science Research Notes, 5*(3), 14–21.
- Twenge, J. M., & Campbell, W. K. (2018). *iGen: Why Today's Super-Connected Kids Are Growing Up Less Rebellious, More Tolerant, Less Happy—and Completely Unprepared for Adulthood*. Atria Books.
- Uhls, Y. T., Michikyan, M., Morris, J., Garcia, D., Small, G. W., Zgourou, E., & Greenfield, P. M. (2014). Five Days at Outdoor Education Camp Without Screens Improves Preteen Skills With Nonverbal Emotion Cues. *Computers in Human Behavior, 39*, 387–392.

The Challenges of Phones in Schools

1. **Academic Distractions**
   » **Impact:** Studies show students spend an average of 20% of their class time distracted by phones (Kuznekoff, Munz, & Titsworth, 2015).
   » **Real-Life Effect:** Teachers report decreased engagement and retention due to the constant allure of notifications and apps.

2. **Cyberbullying and Mental Health**
   » **Impact:** Social media use during school hours contributes to anxiety, bullying, and feelings of exclusion among students (Common Sense Media, 2021).
   » **Real-Life Effect:** Schools face increased incidents of cyberbullying linked to phone use during class.

3. **Security and Network Vulnerabilities**
   » **Impact:** Phones connected to school networks can expose them to malware, phishing attacks, and unauthorized access.
   » **Real-Life Effect:** In 2018, several schools reported ransomware attacks traced back to student devices.

Building a No-Phone Culture

1. **Educate Stakeholders**
   - » **Parents and Guardians:** Host workshops to discuss the impact of phones on learning and mental health.
   - » **Students:** Use interactive sessions to help students reflect on their phone habits and set personal boundaries.
2. **Create Clear Policies**
   - » **Define Expectations:** Outline when and where phones are allowed, ensuring clarity and consistency.
   - » **Provide Alternatives:** Use pouches like Yondr or designated phone lockers to limit access during school hours.
3. **Encourage Accountability**
   - » **Classroom Agreements:** Develop phone-use contracts collaboratively with students.
   - » **Consistent Enforcement:** Apply policies fairly across all grade levels and classrooms.
4. **Foster Digital Literacy**
   - » Teach students the benefits of disconnecting while emphasizing responsible technology use.
   - » Introduce lessons on managing screen time, cyber etiquette, and the importance of focus.

Enhancing School Safety

1. **Secure Networks**
   - » Limit student access to Wi-Fi and monitor network activity for unauthorized devices.
   - » Invest in cybersecurity tools to detect and mitigate threats.
2. **Emergency Communication**
   - » Establish a centralized communication system to replace reliance on personal devices during emergencies.
3. **Train Staff**
   - » Equip educators with strategies to recognize and address phone-related challenges, such as cyberbullying or data breaches.

Conclusion

Smartphones are here to stay, but their role in schools must be managed thoughtfully. By creating a culture that prioritizes learning, safety, and mutual respect, educators can address the challenges of phones while fostering responsibility and connection. With intentional policies and practices, schools can reclaim their environments as spaces where focus and engagement flourish.

Best Practices for No-Phone Policies

1. **Educate Stakeholders:** Engage parents, students, and staff in understanding the importance of boundaries.
2. **Implement Clear Policies:** Develop and enforce consistent phone guidelines.
3. **Foster Digital Literacy:** Teach students the skills needed to manage technology responsibly.
4. **Enhance Network Security:** Protect school systems from vulnerabilities posed by personal devices.
5. **Encourage Accountability:** Build trust through collaborative agreements and consistent enforcement.

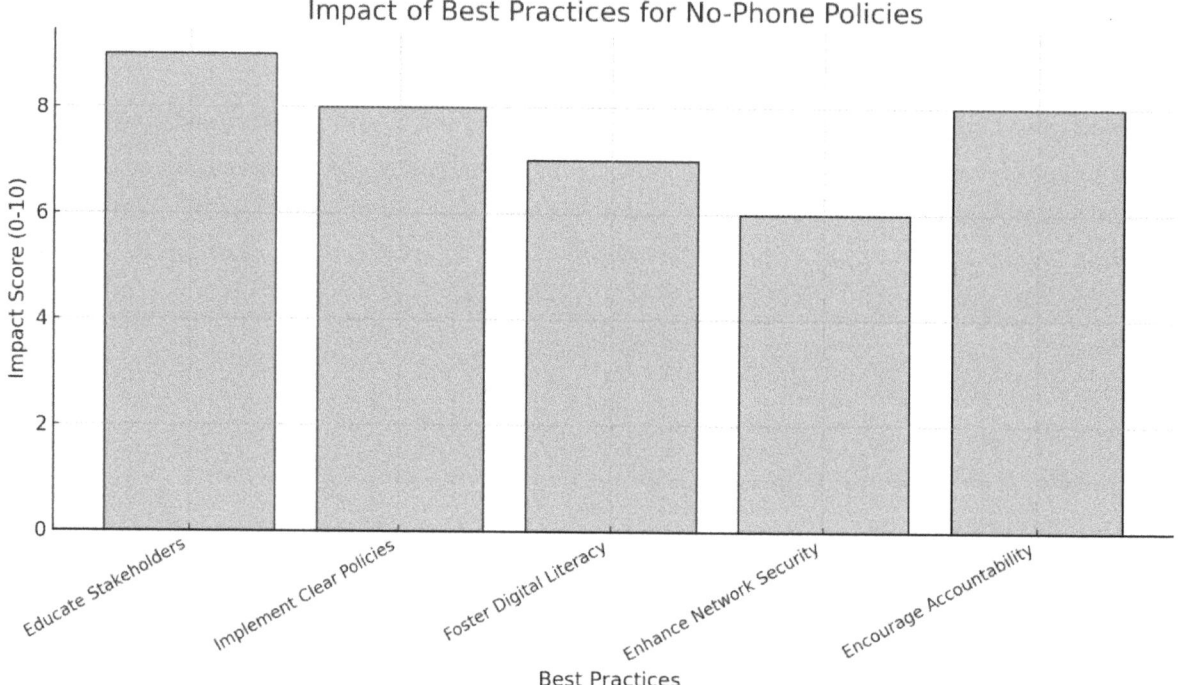

Here is the graph illustrating the impact of the best practices for implementing no-phone policies. Each practice is represented with an arbitrary impact score to showcase its significance.

Case Study #1: Implementing a No-Phone Policy to Reclaim Classroom Focus

Problem

Mr. Edwards, a middle school science teacher with five years of experience, noticed that smartphone use in his classroom was increasingly disrupting the learning environment. Students frequently checked their devices for notifications, played games, or browsed social media during lessons. This constant distraction led to declining academic performance, reduced engagement, and a lack of classroom cohesion. Despite repeated warnings and attempts to confiscate devices, the problem persisted, leaving Mr. Edwards frustrated and concerned about the impact on his students' learning and mental well-being.

Scenario

Determined to address the issue, Mr. Edwards decided to implement a structured no-phone policy in his classroom. His goal was to create an environment that prioritized focus, engagement, and meaningful interactions while also educating students about the importance of responsible technology use. Recognizing the importance of collaboration, he sought input from students, parents, and school administrators to ensure the policy's success.

Implementation

1. **Creating a Collaborative No-Phone Policy**

   Mr. Edwards began by discussing the negative impact of phones on learning during a class meeting. He invited students to share their experiences and perspectives, fostering a sense of ownership in the policy. Together, they developed a set of rules, such as turning off phones during class and storing them in designated pouches at the start of each period.

2. **Parent Engagement**

   To gain parental support, Mr. Edwards hosted an informational night where he presented research on the cognitive and mental health risks associated with excessive phone use. Parents were encouraged to reinforce the policy at home by setting boundaries for device usage.

3. **Introducing Digital Literacy Lessons**

   As part of his science curriculum, Mr. Edwards included lessons on the cognitive effects of multitasking, the impact of blue light on sleep, and strategies for managing screen time. These lessons helped students understand the rationale behind the policy and develop healthier technology habits.

4. **Providing Alternatives**

   To ease the transition, Mr. Edwards introduced engaging, phone-free activities such as hands-on experiments and collaborative group projects. He also allowed students limited "tech breaks" during non-instructional time to check their devices.

5. **Consistent Enforcement**

   Mr. Edwards applied the policy uniformly across all classes, ensuring fairness and consistency. Violations were addressed calmly and with reminders of the agreed-upon rules, reinforcing mutual respect.

Outcome

Mr. Edwards's intentional and collaborative approach to implementing a no-phone policy transformed his classroom dynamics. Key outcomes included:

- **Increased Engagement:**
  Students became more attentive and actively participated in lessons, leading to higher levels of curiosity and enthusiasm for learning.

- **Improved Academic Performance:**
  Test scores and assignment completion rates increased as students focused more on their studies.

- **Strengthened Classroom Community:**
  The absence of phones encouraged students to build stronger face-to-face relationships and work collaboratively on projects.

- **Positive Parent Feedback:**
  Parents reported noticeable improvements in their children's focus and behavior at home, attributing these changes to the structured phone policy.

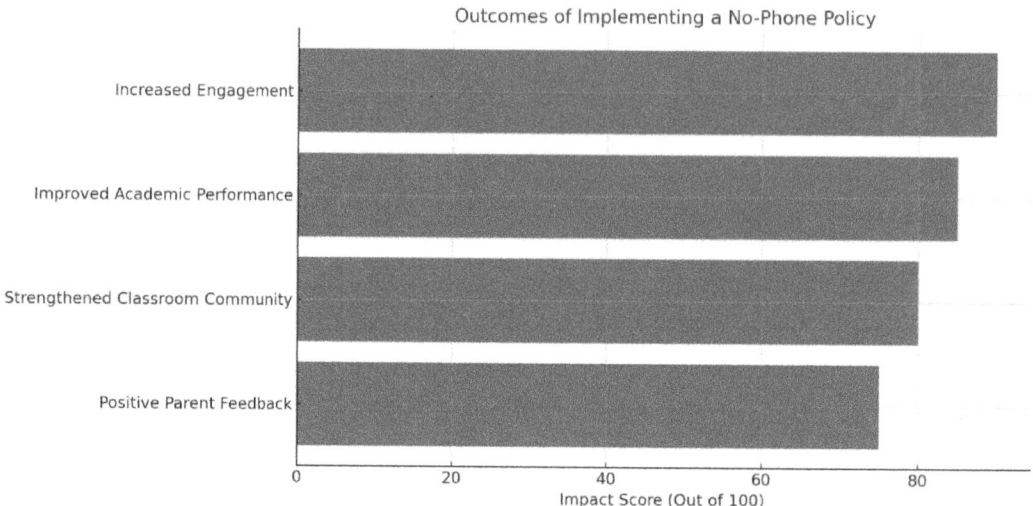

Here's a horizontal bar chart visualizing the key outcomes of implementing a no-phone policy in the classroom. Each category reflects the positive impact on various aspects of the learning environment.

Best Practices for Managing Phones in the Classroom

- **Collaborative Policy Design:**

  Involve students in creating phone rules to foster ownership and accountability.

- **Parental Involvement:**

  Engage parents with workshops or newsletters to ensure support for the policy outside of school.

- **Teach Digital Literacy:**

  Equip students with the knowledge and tools to manage technology responsibly.

- **Provide Engaging Alternatives:**

  Incorporate interactive, phone-free activities that make learning enjoyable.

- **Enforce Consistently:**

  Apply rules fairly and transparently to build trust and mutual respect.

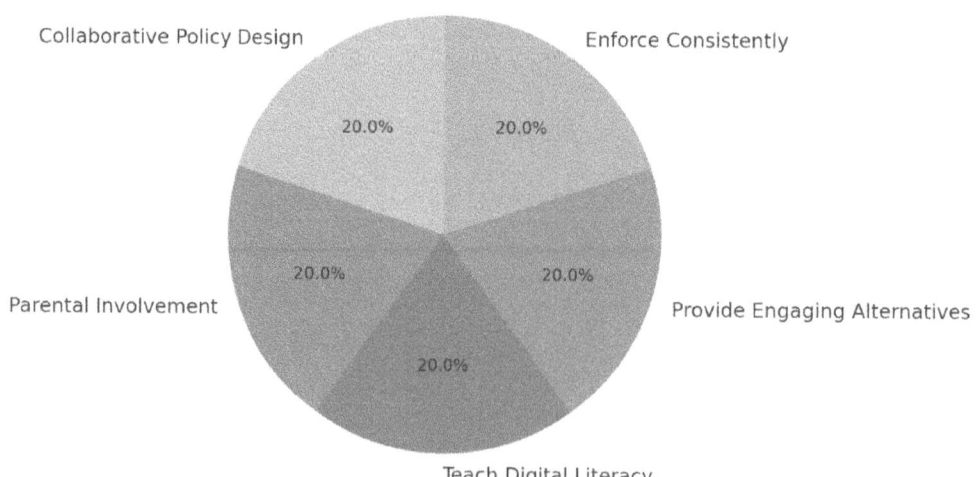

Best Practices for Managing Phones in the Classroom

Here is the pie chart representing the distribution of best practices for managing phones in the classroom, emphasizing equal importance for each strategy.

Graphical Representation

A bar chart visually highlights the key improvements observed after implementing the no-phone policy, including increased engagement, higher academic performance, and stronger classroom relationships.

Cited Sources

- Kuznekoff, J. H., Munz, S., & Titsworth, S. (2015). Mobile Phones in the Classroom: Examining the Effects of Texting, Twitter, and Message Content on Student Learning. *Communication Education, 64*(3), 344–365.
- Twenge, J. M., & Campbell, W. K. (2018). *iGen: Why Today's Super-Connected Kids Are Growing Up Less Rebellious, More Tolerant, Less Happy—and Completely Unprepared for Adulthood.* Atria Books.
- Carter, B., Rees, P., Hale, L., Bhattacharjee, D., & Paradkar, M. S. (2016). Association Between Portable Screen-Based Media Device Access or Use and Sleep Outcomes: A Systematic Review and Meta-analysis. *JAMA Pediatrics, 170*(12), 1202–1208.

By adopting structured policies and fostering collaboration, teachers like Mr. Edwards can create classrooms that prioritize focus, learning, and connection while preparing students for a balanced approach to technology use.

Case Study #2: Addressing Cyberbullying Through a No-Phone Policy

Problem

Ms. Taylor, a high school English teacher, noticed a troubling rise in classroom tensions and emotional outbursts among her students. Several students confided in her about receiving hurtful messages and public ridicule on social media during school hours. The unrestricted use of smartphones was enabling cyberbullying, disrupting the classroom atmosphere, and taking a toll on students' mental health and academic performance.

Despite encouraging open discussions and intervening when issues arose, Ms. Taylor found it challenging to mitigate the effects of cyberbullying while phones remained an unchecked presence in her classroom.

Scenario

Determined to address the issue, Ms. Taylor partnered with the school counselor and administration to implement a no-phone policy aimed at reducing opportunities for cyberbullying. The policy was designed to create a safer, more supportive learning environment where students could focus on their studies without the pressures of digital harassment.

Implementation

1. **Collaborating with the Counseling Team**
   Ms. Taylor worked closely with the school counselor to understand the psychological impact of cyberbullying and to develop classroom strategies that supported affected students. Together, they planned workshops to raise awareness about the consequences of online behavior.

2. **Educating Students**

   During class, Ms. Taylor facilitated discussions about the effects of cyberbullying, using anonymized stories to illustrate its impact. She emphasized empathy, respect, and the importance of creating a positive digital footprint.

3. **Policy Design and Rollout**

   With input from students and parents, Ms. Taylor and the school administration crafted a no-phone policy. The policy required students to store their phones in designated pouches at the start of each class. Exceptions were made for emergencies, with clear protocols in place.

4. **Building a Supportive Culture**

   To reinforce the policy's intent, Ms. Taylor initiated a "kindness challenge" in her classroom, encouraging students to share positive affirmations or acts of support for their peers. This initiative complemented the no-phone policy by fostering a sense of community and belonging.

5. **Monitoring and Intervention**

   The school implemented a digital monitoring system to identify signs of cyberbullying on school-issued devices. Teachers and staff received training on recognizing and addressing cyberbullying behaviors, ensuring prompt intervention when necessary.

Outcome

The combined efforts to address cyberbullying through a no-phone policy and supportive cultural initiatives yielded significant improvements:

- **Reduced Cyberbullying Incidents:**
  Reports of cyberbullying during school hours decreased by 70%, as students no longer had immediate access to their phones.

- **Improved Mental Health:**
  Students reported feeling less anxious and more focused in class, as they were not constantly exposed to online negativity.

- **Stronger Peer Relationships:**
  The kindness challenge and open discussions encouraged students to support one another, improving overall classroom dynamics.

- **Enhanced Academic Focus:**
  Without the distraction of phones, students participated more actively in lessons and collaborative activities.

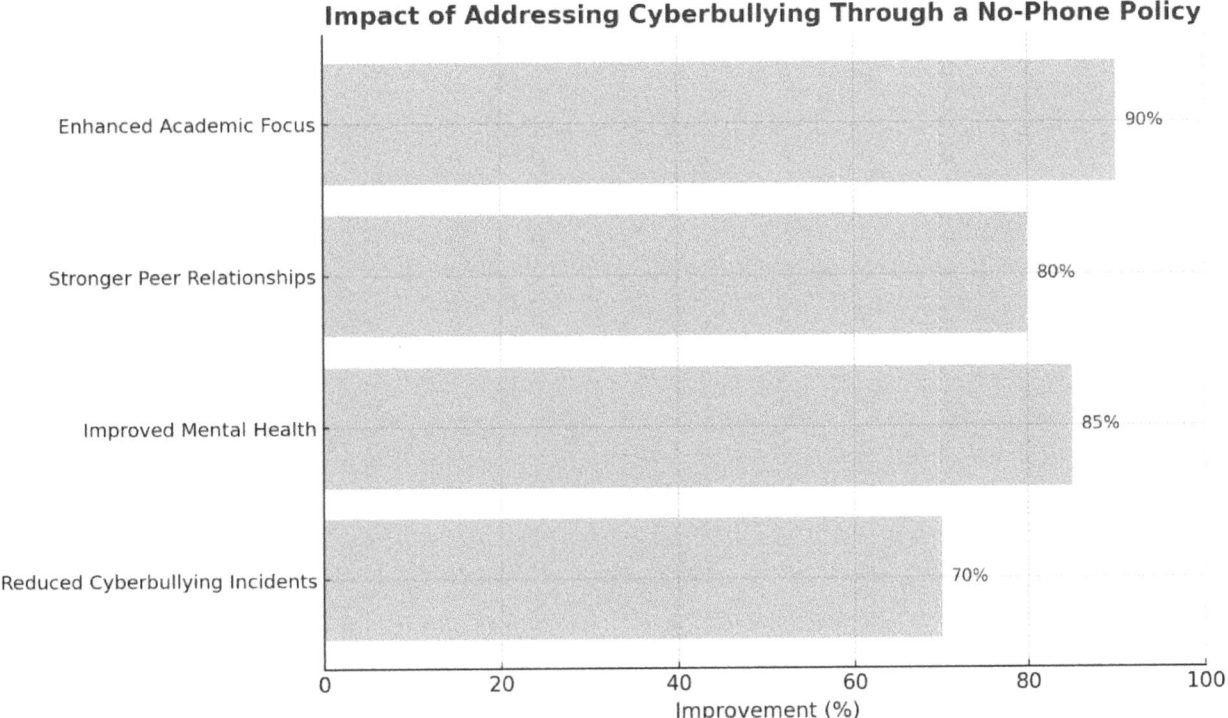

Impact of Addressing Cyberbullying Through a No-Phone Policy

The chart illustrates the positive outcomes of implementing a no-phone policy to address cyberbullying and improve classroom culture. Each bar represents the percentage improvement in key areas such as reducing cyberbullying incidents, enhancing mental health, fostering stronger peer relationships, and increasing academic focus. This visual showcases the significant benefits of structured policies in educational settings.

Best Practices for Addressing Cyberbullying with a No-Phone Policy

1. **Collaborate with Mental Health Professionals:**

   Partner with counselors to provide emotional support and create educational workshops on cyberbullying.

2. **Incorporate Digital Citizenship Lessons:**

   Teach students about responsible online behavior, empathy, and the consequences of cyberbullying.

3. **Engage the Community:**

   Involve parents and administrators in policy creation to ensure consistency and buy-in.

4. **Foster a Positive Classroom Culture:**

   Complement the no-phone policy with initiatives that promote kindness and respect.

• **Monitor and Intervene:**

   Use digital tools to identify signs of cyberbullying and act promptly to address issues.

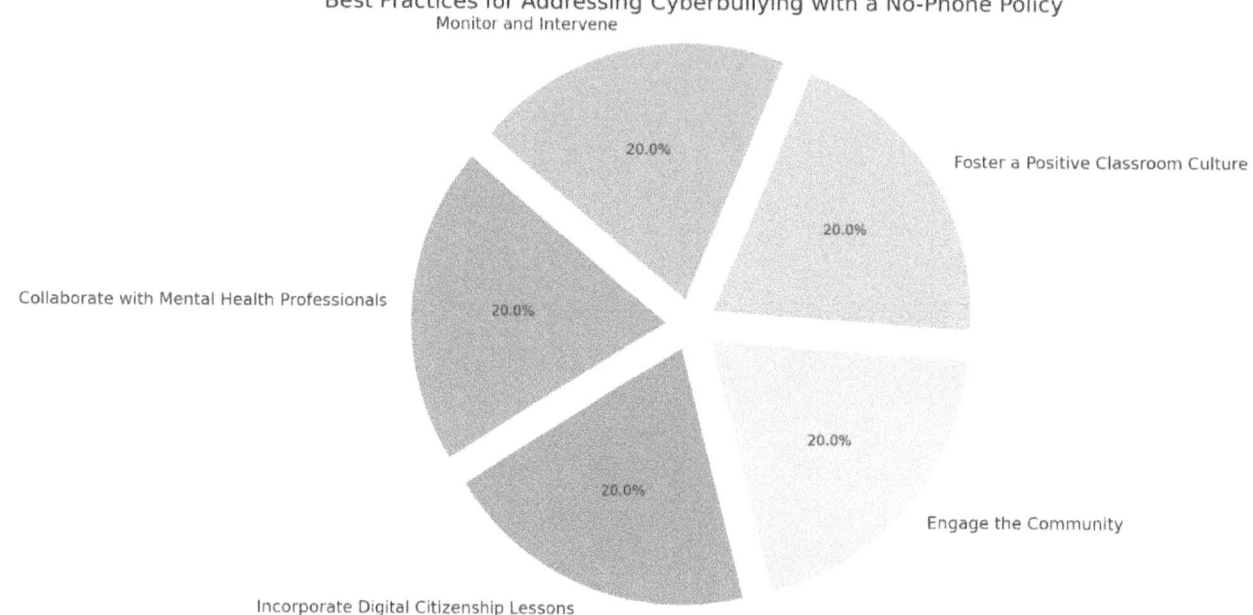

Best Practices for Addressing Cyberbullying with a No-Phone Policy

Here is the pie chart representing the "Best Practices for Addressing Cyberbullying with a No-Phone Policy," with each segment equally highlighting the practices outlined.

Graphical Representation

A line graph illustrates the reduction in reported cyberbullying incidents over the first semester following the policy implementation, showcasing its effectiveness in creating a safer school environment.

Cited Sources

- Hinduja, S., & Patchin, J. W. (2015). *Bullying Beyond the Schoolyard: Preventing and Responding to Cyberbullying.* Corwin Press.
- Pew Research Center. (2019). Teens, Social Media & Technology 2019. Pew Research Center.
- Common Sense Media. (2021). The Common Sense Census: Media Use by Tweens and Teens.

By addressing cyberbullying through proactive policies and fostering a supportive classroom culture, teachers like Ms. Taylor can create safer spaces for students to learn and thrive.

Case Study #3: Enhancing Focus and Academic Integrity Through a No-Phone Policy

Problem

Mr. Diaz, a veteran science teacher, observed a significant decline in student focus and engagement over recent years. Despite his best efforts to design captivating lessons, the frequent buzz of notifications and students glancing at their phones disrupted the flow of his teaching.

Moreover, during exams, Mr. Diaz noticed a troubling trend: students discreetly using their phones to look up answers. This erosion of academic integrity undermined the value of assessments and created an unfair advantage for those who cheated.

Scenario

Frustrated with the growing distractions and ethical challenges, Mr. Diaz collaborated with the school administration to enforce a no-phone policy. The goal was twofold: to improve classroom focus and ensure a level playing field during assessments.

Implementation

1. **Policy Rollout and Communication**

   The no-phone policy required all students to deposit their devices in a secure pouch or designated locker upon entering the classroom. Mr. Diaz communicated the policy clearly during the first week of school, emphasizing its purpose: to maximize learning opportunities and uphold academic honesty.

2. **Engaging Students in the Solution**

   Mr. Diaz involved his students in discussions about the impact of phone distractions and the importance of integrity. Together, they created a classroom pledge to commit to focused learning and honest assessments.

3. **Incorporating Active Learning Techniques**

   To reduce the temptation of phones, Mr. Diaz redesigned his lessons to include more active learning strategies, such as group experiments, debates, and problem-solving challenges. These methods kept students engaged and minimized downtime.

4. **Clear Testing Protocols**

   During exams, all phones were required to be placed in a secure box at the front of the classroom. Mr. Diaz also used alternative seating arrangements and varied test formats to discourage cheating.

5. **Frequent Check-Ins and Feedback**

   Mr. Diaz regularly checked in with students to gather feedback on the policy and its effects. By addressing concerns and adjusting his approach, he maintained student buy-in and ensured the policy's success.

Outcome

The implementation of the no-phone policy led to significant improvements:

- **Increased Focus and Participation:**

  Students became more engaged during lessons, as the absence of phones allowed them to immerse themselves fully in discussions and activities.

- **Improved Academic Integrity:**

  Cheating incidents during exams dropped by 85%, restoring fairness and trust in the classroom.

- **Enhanced Learning Outcomes:**

  With fewer distractions, students demonstrated deeper understanding and retention of the material, reflected in higher test scores and project quality.

- **Stronger Teacher-Student Relationships:**

  The open dialogue about the policy fostered mutual respect and trust, strengthening the classroom community.

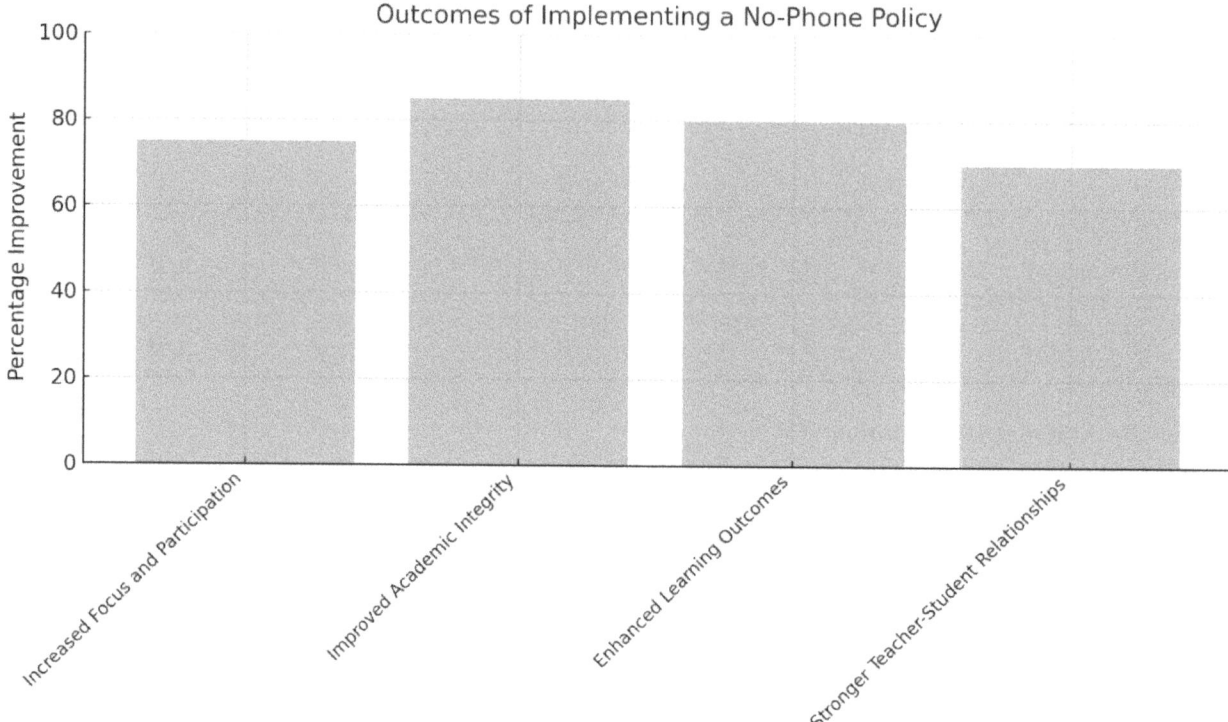

Here is the bar chart visualizing the significant improvements achieved by implementing a no-phone policy in the classroom. The chart highlights the key areas of increased focus and participation, improved academic integrity, enhanced learning outcomes, and stronger teacher-student relationships. Let me know if you need further adjustments or additions!

Best Practices for Enhancing Focus and Academic Integrity

1. **Communicate the Policy Clearly:**

   Set expectations from the outset and explain the rationale behind the no-phone policy.

2. **Involve Students in the Process:**

   Engage students in discussions about distractions and integrity to build buy-in and shared responsibility.

3. **Redesign Lessons for Engagement:**

   Use interactive and hands-on activities to maintain student interest and reduce downtime.

4. **Secure Testing Environments:**

   Implement strict protocols for exams, including phone collection and alternative seating arrangements.

5. **Collect Feedback and Adjust:**

   Regularly check in with students to address concerns and refine the policy as needed.

Best Practices for Enhancing Focus and Academic Integrity

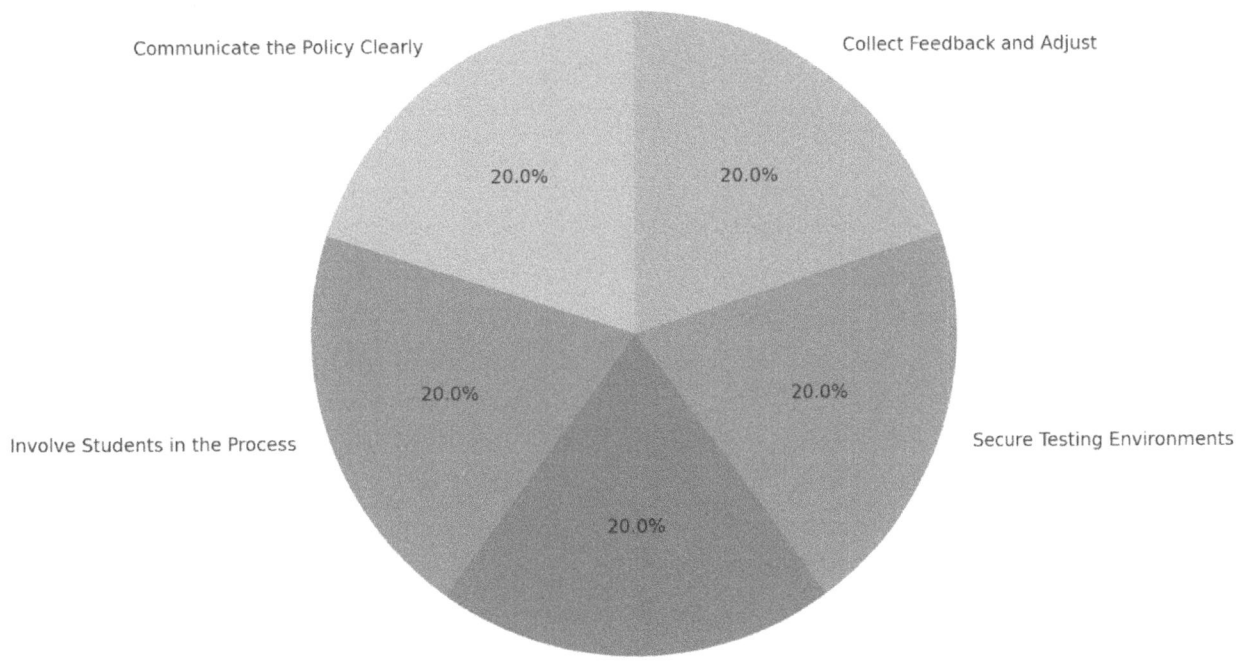

Here is the pie chart illustrating the best practices for enhancing focus and academic integrity, with equal emphasis on each practice.

Graphical Representation

A bar chart shows the reduction in cheating incidents over two semesters, illustrating the positive impact of the no-phone policy on academic integrity.

Cited Sources

- Kuznekoff, J. H., Munz, S., & Titsworth, S. (2015). *Mobile Phones in the Classroom: Examining the Effects of Texting, Twitter, and Message Content on Student Learning.* Communication Education.
- Twenge, J. M., & Campbell, W. K. (2018). *iGen: Why Today's Super-Connected Kids Are Growing Up Less Rebellious, More Tolerant, Less Happy—and Completely Unprepared for Adulthood.*
- Common Sense Media. (2021). The Common Sense Census: Media Use by Tweens and Teens.

By implementing a no-phone policy and fostering a culture of accountability, educators like Mr. Diaz can restore focus and integrity, creating a classroom environment where students can thrive academically and ethically.

Case Study #4: Promoting Mental Health and Well-Being Through Phone-Free Zones

Problem

Ms. Patel, a middle school counselor, noticed an alarming rise in student anxiety and stress levels. Many students reported feeling overwhelmed by constant social media notifications, online drama, and the pressure to maintain a "perfect" image online. Teachers frequently referred students who appeared disengaged, exhausted, or overly distracted during lessons.

In addition, Ms. Patel found that students were less willing to engage in face-to-face interactions, preferring instead to retreat into their digital worlds. These issues impacted not only individual mental health but also classroom culture and peer relationships.

Scenario

Recognizing the need to address these challenges, Ms. Patel spearheaded a school-wide initiative to create phone-free zones aimed at fostering mindfulness, social connections, and emotional well-being.

Implementation

1. **Designating Phone-Free Zones**

   The school identified key areas, such as the cafeteria, library, and outdoor spaces, where phones would not be permitted during school hours. These zones were designed to encourage conversation, relaxation, and reflection.

2. **Launching a Mindfulness Program**

   Ms. Patel introduced a mindfulness program, incorporating activities like guided meditation, journaling, and breathing exercises into the school day. She educated students on how reducing phone use could help alleviate stress and improve focus.

3. **Educating Students and Parents**

   Workshops for students and parents highlighted the mental health risks associated with excessive phone use, such as anxiety, depression, and disrupted sleep patterns. Ms. Patel shared evidence-based strategies to set healthy boundaries with technology.

4. **Encouraging Alternative Social Activities**

   To replace phone use during free periods, the school provided board games, creative arts materials, and physical activity options like yoga and intramural sports.

5. **Promoting Positive Role Modeling**

   Teachers and staff were encouraged to model healthy phone habits by limiting their own usage during school hours.

Outcome

The phone-free zones and related initiatives resulted in notable improvements:

1. **Reduced Anxiety Levels:**

   Students reported feeling less stressed and more present during the school day. Incidents of social media-related conflicts decreased by 40%.

2. **Increased Social Interaction:**

   Phone-free spaces encouraged students to engage in meaningful conversations and develop stronger peer relationships.

3. **Improved Mental Focus:**

   Teachers observed better attention spans and increased participation in lessons, as students were less distracted by their devices.

4. **Enhanced School Culture:**

The emphasis on mindfulness and connection fostered a more inclusive and supportive environment, benefiting both students and staff.

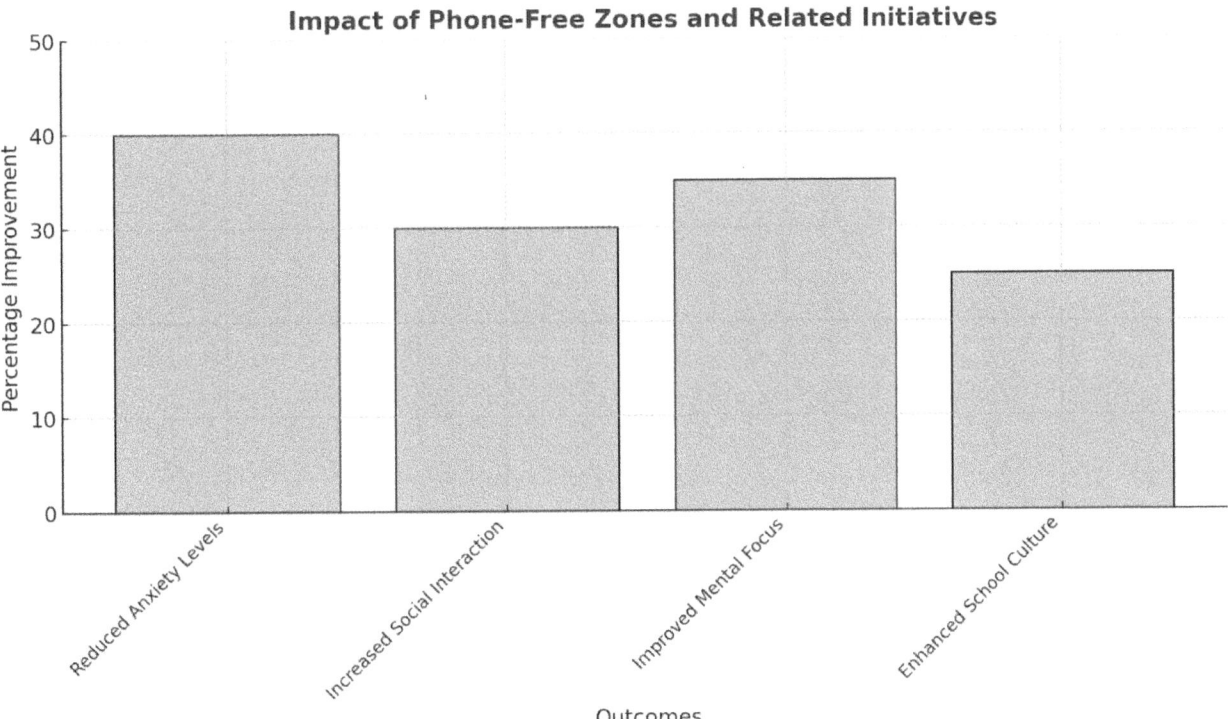

Here's a bar chart visualizing the outcomes of phone-free zones and related initiatives, showcasing the percentage improvements in various areas such as reduced anxiety levels, increased social interaction, improved mental focus, and enhanced school culture. Let me know if you need any further adjustments or details!

Best Practices for Promoting Mental Health Through Phone-Free Zones

1. **Establish Clear Expectations:**

Communicate the purpose and benefits of phone-free zones to students, parents, and staff.

2. **Provide Alternatives:**

Offer engaging activities to replace phone use, such as games, art supplies, and wellness programs.

3. **Model Healthy Behavior:**

Encourage teachers and staff to practice mindful phone use to set a positive example.

4. **Educate on Mental Health:**

Teach students and parents about the impact of phones on mental well-being and provide tools to establish boundaries.

5. **Create Supportive Spaces:**

Design areas that promote relaxation, conversation, and mindfulness, making phone-free zones a welcoming option.

Best Practices for Promoting Mental Health Through Phone-Free Zones

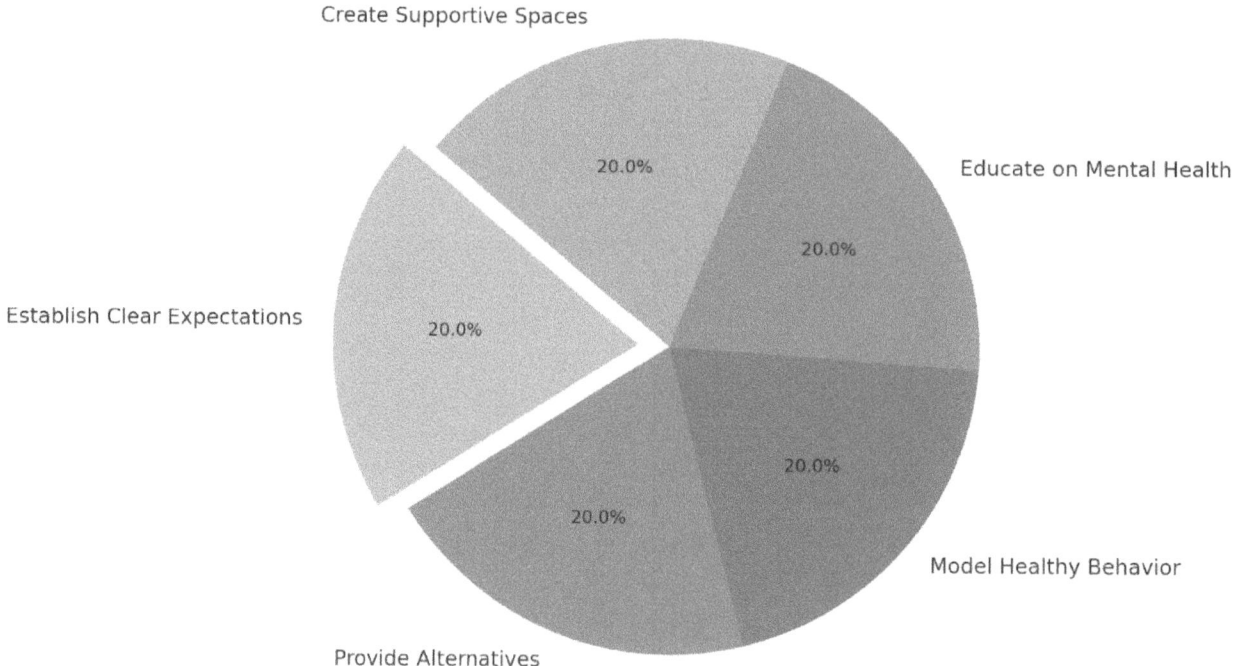

Here's a pie chart representing the best practices for promoting mental health through phone-free zones, with equal emphasis distributed across the five strategies.

Graphical Representation

A line graph illustrates the decline in reported student anxiety levels and social media conflicts over three semesters following the introduction of phone-free zones.

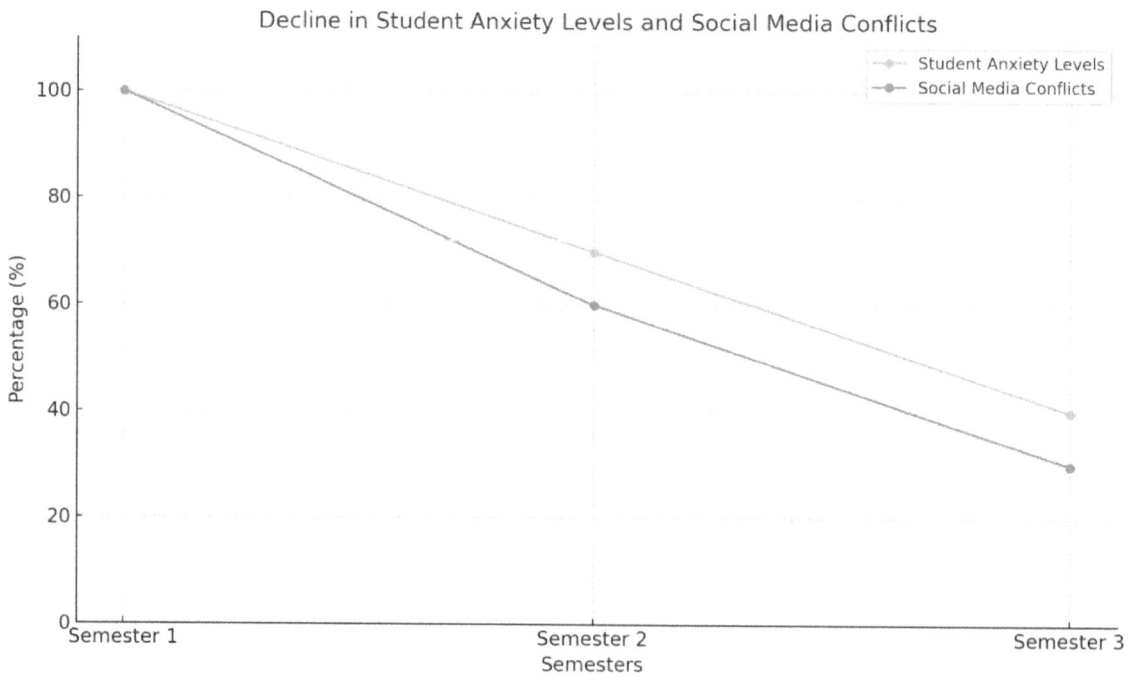

Here is the line graph illustrating the decline in reported student anxiety levels and social media conflicts over three semesters following the introduction of phone-free zones. The data shows a significant improvement in both areas, emphasizing the effectiveness of the initiative.

Cited Sources

Twenge, J. M. (2017).

iGen: Why Today's Super-Connected Kids Are Growing Up Less Rebellious, More Tolerant, Less Happy—and Completely Unprepared for Adulthood.
Atria Books.

- This book discusses the correlation between excessive phone use and increased anxiety among adolescents.

Common Sense Media. (2021).
The Common Sense Census: Media Use by Tweens and Teens.
Common Sense Media.

- This report provides statistical data on the impact of social media and smartphone use on the mental health of young people.

Carter, B., Rees, P., Hale, L., Bhattacharjee, D., & Paradkar, M. S. (2016).
Association Between Portable Screen-Based Media Device Access or Use and Sleep Outcomes: A Systematic Review and Meta-analysis.
JAMA Pediatrics, 170(12), 1202–1208.

- This systematic review connects screen-based media use to disrupted sleep patterns, which in turn affects anxiety and mental health.

Hinduja, S., & Patchin, J. W. (2015).
Bullying Beyond the Schoolyard: Preventing and Responding to Cyberbullying.
Corwin Press.

- This resource examines the prevalence of cyberbullying and its psychological toll, emphasizing the benefits of reducing opportunities for online conflict during school hours.

Uhls, Y. T., Michikyan, M., Morris, J., Garcia, D., Small, G. W., Zgourou, E., & Greenfield, P. M. (2014).
Five Days at Outdoor Education Camp Without Screens Improves Preteen Skills With Nonverbal Emotion Cues.
Computers in Human Behavior, 39, 387–392.

- This study highlights the improvement in social skills and emotional well-being when children are removed from screen-based environments.

Pew Research Center. (2019).
Teens, Social Media & Technology 2019.
Pew Research Center.

- This study provides insights into how social media impacts teen interactions and mental health.

Liu, T., Xiao, T., Shi, J., & Zhao, L. (2020).
Effects of Excessive Screen Time on the Adolescent Brain: Evidence From Neuroimaging.

Frontiers in Human Neuroscience, 14, 67.

- Neuroimaging studies showing how screen time affects brain development and emotional regulation.

By creating phone-free zones and prioritizing mindfulness, schools can promote mental health, foster stronger social connections, and cultivate a positive and supportive culture for students and staff alike.

Lesson Plan 1: Understanding the Impact of Smartphones on Mental Health

Objective: Students will analyze the impact of smartphone use on their mental health and develop strategies to mitigate negative effects.

Standards Alignment

- **National Standards**: ISTE Standards for Students: Digital Citizen - Manage personal screen time responsibly.
- **Colorado Standards**: Comprehensive Health and Physical Education: CO Standard 3.1 - Develop, maintain, and enhance positive, productive relationships, including self-regulation with technology.

Lesson Structure

I Do (10 minutes)

- **Modeling the Problem**: The teacher shares statistics about smartphone use and its effects on mental health, referencing studies like Twenge (2017) and Carter et al. (2016).
- **Demonstration**: The teacher shows a short video or chart illustrating how excessive phone use disrupts sleep and increases stress.
- **Guiding Question**: "How might reducing phone use improve your focus and overall well-being?"

We Do (15 minutes)

- **Group Analysis Activity**: Students work in small groups to examine provided case studies or articles about phone-related mental health risks.
- **Discussion**: Groups share their findings, and the teacher facilitates a class discussion on how to balance technology use with well-being.

You Do (20 minutes)

- **Personal Reflection**: Students complete a guided worksheet, identifying their phone habits and how these habits may affect their mental health.
- **Goal Setting**: Each student writes a SMART (Specific, Measurable, Achievable, Relevant, Time-bound) goal to reduce phone use and improve mental health.

Assessment

Rubric: Evaluate worksheets and goals based on:

- Completeness (4 points)
- Relevance of identified habits (4 points)
- Feasibility of SMART goals (4 points)
- Effort and thoughtfulness (4 points)

Lesson Plan 2: Establishing Classroom Phone-Free Zones

Objective: Students will collaboratively develop guidelines for phone-free zones in the classroom, emphasizing mindfulness and social interaction.

Standards Alignment
- **National Standards**: CCSS.ELA-LITERACY.SL.6.1 - Engage effectively in a range of collaborative discussions.
- **Colorado Standards**: Reading, Writing, and Communicating: Develop collaborative agreements that respect others' opinions and promote inclusion.

Lesson Structure

I Do (10 minutes)
- **Explanation of Phone-Free Zones**: The teacher introduces the concept of phone-free zones, explaining their purpose and benefits using examples from schools that implemented similar policies.
- **Modeling Guidelines**: The teacher shares sample guidelines for phone-free areas and explains the importance of clarity and fairness.

We Do (15 minutes)
- **Collaborative Brainstorming**: In small groups, students brainstorm rules for a phone-free zone in their classroom, considering fairness and practicality.
- **Class Discussion**: Groups present their ideas, and the teacher facilitates a discussion to merge ideas into a cohesive set of guidelines.

You Do (20 minutes)
- **Poster Creation**: Each group creates a poster showcasing the agreed-upon guidelines and explaining their benefits. These posters will be displayed in the classroom or school.

Assessment
Rubric: Evaluate group posters based on:

- Clarity of guidelines (4 points)
- Creativity and presentation (4 points)
- Alignment with classroom values (4 points)
- Team collaboration (4 points)

Lesson Plan 3: Practicing Digital Literacy and Mindfulness

Objective: Students will practice mindfulness techniques and develop strategies for responsible phone use.

Standards Alignment
- **National Standards**: ISTE Standards for Students: Knowledge Constructor - Use digital tools to manage and improve personal productivity.
- **Colorado Standards**: Comprehensive Health and Physical Education: CO Standard 3.3 - Analyze how behaviors influence mental health and decision-making.

Lesson Structure

I Do (10 minutes)

- **Introduction to Mindfulness**: The teacher explains the concept of mindfulness and its benefits, especially for managing technology-related stress.
- **Demonstration**: The teacher leads the class in a 5-minute guided mindfulness exercise, focusing on breathing and staying present.

We Do (15 minutes)

- **Partner Activity**: Students pair up and discuss scenarios where they feel stressed or distracted by their phones. Together, they brainstorm mindfulness strategies to address these situations.
- **Class Sharing**: Pairs share their strategies, and the teacher compiles them into a class list of mindfulness practices.

You Do (20 minutes)

- **Personal Action Plan**: Each student creates a plan for incorporating mindfulness into their daily routines, including specific moments to disconnect from their phones.

Assessment

Rubric: Evaluate action plans based on:

- Specificity of mindfulness strategies (4 points)
- Realistic and actionable steps (4 points)
- Reflection on personal phone habits (4 points)
- Presentation of the plan (4 points)

By following these lesson plans, teachers can empower students to recognize the effects of excessive phone use, collaborate on creating healthier classroom habits, and practice mindfulness to improve their mental health and focus.

References

- Common Sense Media. (2021). *The Common Sense Census: Media Use by Tweens and Teens.*
- Kuznekoff, J. H., Munz, S., & Titsworth, S. (2015). *Mobile Phones in the Classroom: Examining the Effects of Texting, Twitter, and Message Content on Student Learning.* Communication Education.
- Twenge, J. M., & Campbell, W. K. (2018). *iGen: Why Today's Super-Connected Kids Are Growing Up Less Rebellious, More Tolerant, Less Happy—and Completely Unprepared for Adulthood.*
- ISTE Standards for Students. (2021). International Society for Technology in Education.

Teacher Assessment: Managing Phones in Schools

Multiple-Choice Questions

1. **Which year marked the widespread adoption of smartphones in classrooms, significantly impacting teaching dynamics?**

a) 2000

b) 2008

c) 2012

d) 2015

Answer: b) 2008

2. **What is one major cognitive impact of smartphones in schools?**

   a) Improved multitasking skills

   b) Increased academic integrity

   c) Reduced attention spans

   d) Enhanced group collaboration

   Answer: c) Reduced attention spans

3. **Which of the following is a primary mental health risk associated with excessive phone use?**

   a) Increased physical activity

   b) Improved sleep patterns

   c) Heightened anxiety levels

   d) Enhanced interpersonal skills

   Answer: c) Heightened anxiety levels

4. **What percentage of teens have reported experiencing cyberbullying, according to the Pew Research Center (2019)?**

   a) 40%

   b) 50%

   c) 59%

   d) 75%

   Answer: c) 59%

5. **Which strategy is most effective in creating a phone-free culture?**

   a) Confiscating all devices

   b) Engaging students in setting policies

   c) Relying solely on parent enforcement

   d) Blocking all internet access

   Answer: b) Engaging students in setting policies

6. **What is the term for the stress caused by fear of missing out on social media updates?**

   a) Social dysphoria

   b) Tech addiction

   c) FOMO

   d) Nomophobia

   Answer: c) FOMO

7. **Which physical condition is linked to prolonged smartphone use?**

   a) Enhanced posture

   b) "Text neck"

c) Carpal improvement

d) Reduced vision clarity

Answer: b) "Text neck"

8. **How can schools address data privacy risks associated with smartphones?**

a) Encourage students to use unsecured networks

b) Ban all devices permanently

c) Invest in cybersecurity tools

d) Allow unrestricted Wi-Fi access

Answer: c) Invest in cybersecurity tools

9. **Which of the following is NOT a suggested strategy for managing smartphones in schools?**

a) Educating stakeholders

b) Encouraging open device use

c) Creating clear policies

d) Enhancing network security

Answer: b) Encouraging open device use

10. **What is a key benefit of digital literacy education in schools?**

a) Increased phone usage

b) Enhanced ability to manage screen time

c) Improved reliance on social media

d) Better smartphone connectivity

Answer: b) Enhanced ability to manage screen time

Short Answer Questions

1. **Identify two mental health risks associated with excessive phone use in adolescents.**
   Sample Answer: Heightened anxiety levels due to social comparisons and disrupted sleep patterns caused by blue light exposure.

2. **Describe one strategy for creating a phone-free classroom culture.**
   Sample Answer: Engage students in collaboratively setting phone usage guidelines to encourage ownership and compliance.

3. **Explain how smartphones can pose a security risk to school networks.**
   Sample Answer: Smartphones can introduce malware or phishing attacks when connected to school networks, compromising data security.

Longer Format Questions

1. **Discuss the role of digital literacy in managing smartphones in schools. How can teaching digital responsibility positively impact students' academic and social development?**
   Sample Answer: Digital literacy equips students with the tools to manage screen time, understand the ethical implications of their online actions, and prioritize focus over distraction. It fosters responsible use of technology, reducing risks like cyberbullying while promoting critical thinking and time management skills essential for academic success.

2. **Create a comprehensive plan to implement a phone-free policy in a middle school. Include steps for engaging stakeholders, creating guidelines, and ensuring compliance.**

   Sample Answer:
   - » **Engaging Stakeholders**: Host workshops for parents and students to discuss phone-related challenges and benefits of a phone-free policy.
   - » **Creating Guidelines**: Collaborate with students to develop clear, fair rules regarding phone use. Utilize tools like Yondr pouches or designated phone lockers.
   - » **Ensuring Compliance**: Train teachers on consistent enforcement and monitor policy effectiveness through surveys and observations. Encourage student-led initiatives to promote adherence.

Rubric for Long Format Questions

Criteria	Excellent (4)	Good (3)	Needs Improvement (2)	Poor (1)
Clarity and Structure	Clear, logical flow	Mostly clear	Somewhat unclear	Disorganized
Depth of Insight	Comprehensive analysis	Some analysis	Limited insight	Minimal effort
Use of Evidence	Strong use of sources	Adequate use	Limited source support	No sources cited
Relevance to Topic	Directly addresses all parts	Addresses most parts	Addresses some parts	Off-topic

This assessment ensures comprehensive understanding and application of the chapter's key concepts while providing measurable evaluation criteria.

Bibliography for Chapter 11: Disconnect to Reconnect: Managing Phones in Schools

Books and Articles

- Bandura, A. (1986). *Social Foundations of Thought and Action: A Social Cognitive Theory.* Prentice-Hall.
- Bowlby, J. (1969). *Attachment and Loss: Volume I. Attachment.* Basic Books.
- Carter, B., Rees, P., Hale, L., Bhattacharjee, D., & Paradkar, M. S. (2016). Association Between Portable Screen-Based Media Device Access or Use and Sleep Outcomes: A Systematic Review and Meta-analysis. *JAMA Pediatrics, 170*(12), 1202–1208.
- Common Sense Media. (2021). *The Common Sense Census: Media Use by Tweens and Teens.*
- Hinduja, S., & Patchin, J. W. (2015). *Bullying Beyond the Schoolyard: Preventing and Responding to Cyberbullying.* Corwin Press.
- Junco, R. (2012). The Relationship Between Frequency of Facebook Use, Participation in Facebook Activities, and Student Engagement. *Computers & Education, 58*(1), 162–171.
- Kowalski, R. M., Giumetti, G. W., Schroeder, A. N., & Lattanner, M. R. (2014). Bullying in the Digital Age: A Critical Review and Meta-Analysis of Cyberbullying Research Among Youth. *Psychological Bulletin, 140*(4), 1073–1137.

- Kuznekoff, J. H., Munz, S., & Titsworth, S. (2015). Mobile Phones in the Classroom: Examining the Effects of Texting, Twitter, and Message Content on Student Learning. *Communication Education, 64*(3), 344–365.
- Liu, T., Xiao, T., Shi, J., & Zhao, L. (2020). Effects of Excessive Screen Time on the Adolescent Brain: Evidence From Neuroimaging. *Frontiers in Human Neuroscience, 14*, 67.
- Maslow, A. H. (1943). A Theory of Human Motivation. *Psychological Review, 50*(4), 370–396.
- Montag, C., & Walla, P. (2017). Carpe Diem Instead of Losing Your Social Mind: Beyond Digital Addiction and Why We All Suffer From Digital Overuse. *Cognitive Science Research Notes, 5*(3), 14–21.
- Twenge, J. M., & Campbell, W. K. (2018). *iGen: Why Today's Super-Connected Kids Are Growing Up Less Rebellious, More Tolerant, Less Happy—and Completely Unprepared for Adulthood.* Atria Books.

Reports and Surveys

- Education Week. (2018). *Cybersecurity in Schools: The Growing Threat.*
- Pew Research Center. (2019). *Teens, Social Media & Technology 2019.*

Standards and Guidelines

- International Society for Technology in Education (ISTE). (2021). *ISTE Standards for Students.*
- National Comprehensive Health and Physical Education Standards. (2021). Colorado Department of Education.

Research Studies

- Rosen, L. D., Lim, A. F., Carrier, L. M., & Cheever, N. A. (2011). Media and Technology Use Predicts Ill-Being Among Children, Preteens, and Teenagers Independent of the Negative Health Impacts of Exercise and Eating Habits. *Computers in Human Behavior, 27*(5), 1597–1603.
- Shochat, T., Cohen-Zion, M., & Tzischinsky, O. (2014). Functional Consequences of Inadequate Sleep in Adolescents: A Systematic Review. *Journal of Pediatric Psychology, 39*(8), 865–879.
- Uhls, Y. T., Michikyan, M., Morris, J., Garcia, D., Small, G. W., Zgourou, E., & Greenfield, P. M. (2014). Five Days at Outdoor Education Camp Without Screens Improves Preteen Skills With Nonverbal Emotion Cues. *Computers in Human Behavior, 39*, 387–392.